From
COLD WAR
to NEW
MILLENNIUM

From
COLD WAR
to NEW
MILLENNIUM

The History of
The Royal Canadian
Regiment, 1953–2008

COLONEL BERND HORN

Foreword by Major-General (Retired) Tom de Faye

DUNDURN
TORONTO

Project Editor: Michael Carroll
Editor: Nigel Heseltine
Design: Jennifer Scott
Printer: Transcontinental

Library and Archives Canada Cataloguing in Publication

Horn, Bernd, 1959-
    From Cold War to New Millennium : the history of the Royal Canadian Regiment, 1953-2008 / Bernd Horn.

Companion vol. to Establishing a legacy.
Includes bibliographical references and index.
Issued also in electronic formats.
ISBN 978-1-55488-896-2 (bound).--ISBN 978-1-55488-895-5 (pbk.)

1. Canada. Canadian Army. Royal Canadian Regiment--History.   I. Title.

UA602.R55H673 2011   356'.10971   C2011-901159-X

1   2   3   4   5   15   14   13   12   11

We acknowledge the support of the **Canada Council for the Arts** and the **Ontario Arts Council** for our publishing program. We also acknowledge the financial support of the **Government of Canada** through the **Canada Book Fund** and **Livres Canada Books,** and the **Government of Ontario** through the **Ontario Book Publishing Tax Credit** and the **Ontario Media Development Corporation.**

Care has been taken to trace the ownership of copyright material used in this book. The author and the publisher welcome any information enabling them to rectify any references or credits in subsequent editions.

J. Kirk Howard, President

Printed and bound in Canada.
www.dundurn.com

Dundurn	Gazelle Book Services Limited	Dundurn
3 Church Street, Suite 500	White Cross Mills	2250 Military Road
Toronto, Ontario, Canada	High Town, Lancaster, England	Tonawanda, NY
M5E 1M2	LA1 4XS	U.S.A. 14150

This book is dedicated to the fallen and their loved ones.

CONTENTS

FOREWORD

T he Regiment. Those words carry a specific and very personal meaning for many of us who have been privileged to serve. This personal meaning is formed by our individual experiences and the friendships formed during our service. Collectively, the sum of these experiences represents the history of The Royal Canadian Regiment (The RCR). In this volume — the second part of a modernized history of the Regiment covering the period from 1953 to 2008 — Colonel Bernd Horn has the challenge of capturing and recording an extreme range of events in the life of The RCR from the decades of the Cold War to the violence of counterinsurgency operations in Afghanistan where the citizens of Canada, so well served by the Canadian Forces, have come to a new understanding and recognition of the value of military service and sacrifice to the nation.

From the early 1950s until 2008, well into its second century, The Royal Canadian Regiment's history parallels the complex post–Second World War era known as the Cold War, in which it participated in many United Nations and coalition operations that continue to this day. If a single theme can be identified, it is continual change and adaptation. The Regiment has during this period lived through the social development of our nation, many evolving world events, and the remarkable technological changes of the third millennium. All these realities have played and will continue to play a role in the remarkable evolution of The RCR.

This period of has been characterized by change unprecedented in all the previous decades of the Regiment's service. These events were geo-strategic, socio-economic, and technological. They shaped the evolution of our leadership, the attitudes of our soldiers, command relationships, regimental institutions, and, most important, the relationship between the Regiment and the citizens of Canada to whom we are accountable.

The Regiment played a major role in the Cold War with decades of service in Canada's formation within the North Atlantic Treaty Organisation (NATO). Units assigned to 4 Canadian Infantry Brigade Group (4 CIBG), and, subsequently, to 4 Canadian Mechanized Brigade Group (4 CMBG), enjoyed clearly defined operational taskings, which in turn provided higher levels of resources for training and equipping the Canadian brigade in Europe. This NATO commitment lasted some 40 years and the Canadian brigade became the army's cradle of profes-sionalism. Training facilities and resources were more abundant than in Canadian-based units, huge annual operational level exercises were conducted, and Canadian brigades were exercised and tasked by real, not notional, superior formation headquarters. We learned the mean-ing and importance of interoperability and, in terms of our taskings, made it work. Service in Europe, where the threat was clearly defined, shaped our equipment acquisition programs and the development of our army's doctrine and tactics.

Although the main effort during this period was the Cold War in Europe, Canadian sovereignty was not neglected. The RCR was often called out in aid of the civil power to help keep the peace as well as assist in natural disasters. Moreover, winter warfare skills and Arctic training exercises were a constant throughout the Cold War in Canada as part of the nation's vigilance in securing its northern frontier.

Likewise, The RCR played a pivotal role in military parachuting in Canada — the airborne service. From the early days of The RCR platoon in the Canadian Special Air Service Company, to the airborne battalion and company in the Mobile Striking Force and Defence of Canada Force, respectively, to the Canadian Airborne Regiment and 3 Mechanized Commando, to the parachuting entities created when those units were disbanded, and on to this day, the Regiment has always contributed more than its share of leaders and soldiers to the airborne organizations that were vital to Canadian sovereignty and international readiness forces. Quite simply, airborne service has been a pillar of service for Royals throughout these years.

The Regiment was also instrumental in building Canada's international reputation as a global citizen. Peacekeeping, in the Pearsonian tradition, formed the basis of a number of operational commitments and became a Canadian ideal that lingered long after the reality of the post–Cold War era of fragmentation rendered it unworkable. All the regular battalions participated in numerous deployments. The Regiment saw service in the Balkans after the disintegration of Yugoslavia, in Somalia as a commando of the Canadian Airborne Regiment, and in Ethiopia and other operational theatres. In addition, individual members of The RCR participated in many other challenging missions.

Technological developments played a major role in shaping the events and forcing change during this period of our history. Colonel Horn chronicles the many technological improvements over the decades, ranging from the evolution of the section vehicle, a Dodge 3/4-ton truck with a C2 Light Automatic Rifle (LAR) gunner leaning on the roof as a surrogate armoured personnel carrier (APC) in the 1950s and early 1960s, to the Light Armoured Vehicle (LAV) III of the mid-1990s equipped with the Bushmaster 25 mm stabilized night and day capable cannon.

But it is not just the tactical capability that technology affected. This factor was tremendously important in reconnecting Canadians with their army. The digital technological era of instant global communications gave the pervasive and persuasive media unprecedented access to military operations and, more important, the ability to report on these developments to Canadians and the world in real time. This technology is capable of rapidly shaping or changing attitudes. The result is a far greater level of understanding by Canadians of what their soldiers do in service to Canada, and, ultimately, the price that may have to be paid. The Highway of Heroes would likely not have become a national phenomenon before the digital era.

In the end, much has been written to describe the meaning and importance of the regimental structure. A regiment is larger than a family, but gives rise to similar feelings of empathy, affection, and attachment. Like families, there will from time to time be disputes that are resolved. Friendships are formed often in early days that endure for a lifetime. A defining element of these friendships is they are often formed in adversity or under arduous conditions. It is here that individuals rise above themselves, accepting great personal responsibility for their own actions, and sometimes depending on the actions of their comrades for their very lives.

Nor could the soldiers serve without the extraordinary support of their families — spouses, partners, children, parents, and friends. No words are adequate to acknowledge the burdens carried by the families during operational deployments where their loved ones are in harm's way. A regiment shares joy in accomplishment and grieves its losses, respecting and comforting its own. A regiment basks in the pride of honourable service and the respect of Canadians for whom we serve. It has been suggested by some that if you have never been a part of a regiment you will never be able to fully understand it. Read this remarkable history and decide for yourself.

Tom de Faye
Major-General (Retired)

ACKNOWLEDGEMENTS

Any work of this magnitude owes its completion to the assistance and efforts of many people. As such, I wish to thank all those who directly and indirectly, whether through the contribution of materials, time, a memory, or moral support, assisted me in the completion of this volume.

As always, however, there are some who assisted more than others, and whose efforts warrant special mention. In this vein I wish to thank Captain Tim Robinson, the former regimental adjutant, and Major Jim MacInnis, the regimental major, for their stalwart support of this project. They are the invisible hands behind the scene making regimental business happen. I would also like to make special mention of Chris Johnson who supplied the maps for this volume, and extend thanks to Lucie Ethier for her expertise and support in sourcing a great many photographs from the Canadian Forces Joint Imagery Library.

I must also convey a special thanks to Dr. Emily Spencer for her outstanding support in assisting me with research, interviews, and editorial advice. Similarly, I need to acknowledge the stellar support of Claus Breede, the curator of the RCR Museum, who always made sure I had the access to the documents and photographs necessary to complete the history. Their support was instrumental in completing this volume.

In addition, I would also like to make special mention of a number of individuals who assisted in various ways that made the volume much richer. As such, I wish to thank Colonel Roger Barrett, Sergeant Greg Collette, David DeClerq, H.R. Gardner, Dan Martel, Major Tom Mykytiuk, Silvia Pecota, Colonel Tim Riley, Pat Rossiter, Colonel Jim Simms, Master-Corporal V. Sellars, Brigadier-General Denis Thompson, Jerry Thompson, and Michel Wyczynski. Furthermore, I wish to acknowledge the support of the staff at the Directorate of History and Heritage (DHH), Library and Archives Canada (LAC), and the Royal Military College of Canada (RMCC).

Finally, but certainly not least, I wish to thank my wife Kim for her continuing patience and her tolerance of my many projects, pursuits, and idiosyncrasies. Without her support I would never accomplish the many initiatives I tend to take on.

INTRODUCTION

At the time of writing, Canada, its Army, and The Royal Canadian Regiment were engaged in a savage war in Afghanistan. To those in the Regiment, the war was all consuming as members mourned the loss of comrades, anguished over the struggles of the wounded and permanently scarred, and immersed themselves in preparation for tours in theatre. For the Regiment's youngest and newest members, Afghanistan is all they know. Even for others, the past, namely the Balkans and the stabilization campaigns of the 1990s, and, for the Regiment's old relics, the Cold War, are ancient history. In fact, few junior officers have probably experienced, much less seen, a combat team attack or the rigours of an Arctic exercise.

This reality underlines the fact that the memory of those serving in the line battalions of a regiment is very generational and fleeting. During the Cold War the fact that warfare and the operating environment stayed largely within a steady, predictable, and constant template for over 40 years helped mould and coalesce the military and regimental experience that a number of generations of soldiers and officers underwent. However, that changed in the post–Cold War period when rapidly evolving events made each decade vastly different in its impact on the military and those serving. Often those serving the Colours fail to understand what came before them; how and why certain traditions were developed and fostered, or their importance. All struggles seem new and insurmountable, when in fact they have, more often than not, been experienced before. Moreover, the hard won struggles that brought the Regiment to where it is today are often lost or forgotten.

It is for this reason that a regimental history is critically important. It connects the generations and reminds all of their roots and the efforts of those who came before. It also captures the reality of soldiering and the evolution of the Canadian Army and The Royal Canadian Regiment. Today mechanization is taken for granted, airborne service perceived as something disconnected from The RCR, and the Cold War almost contemptibly considered as peacetime soldiering of no consequence or value. This book, part two of the updated, modernized Regimental history (part one is *Establishing a Legacy: The History of the Royal Canadian Regiment 1883–1953*), will tell a different story. It will demonstrate the continuing evolution of The RCR and how each generation struggled through organizational, doctrinal, budgetary, and political challenges. It was through this constant adaptation and dedication to excellence in the profession of arms that the Regiment shaped its unique character and continued its legacy of service to the nation.

This brings me back to the introduction to *Establishing a Legacy*. As I stated then, in many ways a regimental history is one long war story, invariably of more interest to some than others. But it is more than just the actions and achievements of a small group of individuals that share membership in that particular group or regiment. Regimental history is testimony to the feats of courage and tenacity of Canadians tested in the furnace of combat, or during the sometimes tedious regimen of peace, as well as everything between those two extremes. Regimental history speaks to our collective Canadian military heritage and legacy. It is a window on our country and ourselves.

The RCR's last 55 years of service from 1953–2008 have definitely been challenging. In its service to country, the Regiment's history during this period has paralleled the growth and evolution of this great nation through dangerous and trying times. It has taken us from the Cold War that witnessed the world on the brink of nuclear Armageddon, through a free-fall of global destabilization, economic catastrophe, a resurgence of global terrorism, and the birth of transnational terror networks empowered through globalization and the proliferation of cheap technology to challenge states, including the world's only current superpower, the United States of America. Throughout this complex and dynamic period, The RCR has played a significant role. It contributed to the victory in Cold War, participated in the bitter stabilization campaigns of the 1990s, and fought and bled heavily in the reconstruction and counterinsurgency battle in Afghanistan. Its members, like those before them, continued to do the country proud.

At this juncture it is worth repeating what exactly this entity called a regiment means. In essence, a regiment is a body of troops with a formal organization and chain of command. The word *regiment* derives from the Latin term *regimentum,* meaning rule. Key to a regiment is the fact that it has relative administrative and tactical autonomy. Regiments began with the commencement of standing professional armies in the 16th century. They represented a dramatic change in military affairs. Armies became standardized and permanent. As such, the regiment became a regular, standardized formation of a defined size that included one or more battalions, each containing a set number of companies of a stated size. Significantly, throughout the organization command is exercised by an officially prescribed number of officers with standardized ranks and functions.[1] In essence, regiments have formed the basis for the combat organization of Western armies for the past 300 years.

The permanency of a regiment allowed for the creation of a regimental culture typified by regimental identity (e.g. distinctive uniforms, insignia, symbols, and traditions) and intense devotion. Not surprisingly then, it has been strongly argued that the regimental system is key to promoting cohesion, esprit de corps, and morale — all fundamental components of combat effectiveness. His Royal Highness, Prince Philip, colonel-in-chief of The RCR, observed, "the Regiment is an entity with a life of its own — a unit capable of the highest standards of combat, both in adversity as well as in victory; a brotherhood to which men are proud to belong and whose strength is greater than the sum of its individual members."[2] In this same vein, former Colonel of the Regiment

Lieutenant-General Jack Vance opined, "A Regiment is best understood if it is seen as a Family — a brotherhood of men, both serving and retired, Regular and Reserve who form up together under the same Colour, a shared tradition, common customs, a mutual respect for the same values, a collective willingness to honour the past and a united determination to serve to the same high standards in the future."[3]

Herein lie some fundamental attributes that underscore the importance of the regimental concept. "A Regiment is one of the institutions which form character, in particular the martial habits of discipline, courage, loyalty, pride and endurance," explained Captain J.A. Johnston, a former regimental officer.[4] Dan Loomis, then a lieutenant-colonel, wrote: "In our Canadian society the Regimental Family system is essential to uphold the ideals of the volunteer citizen-serviceman trained to professional standards." He added, "This is a system not of symbols and slogans, though they play a small part, but of deep human relationships, which have evolved in Western society from the days of ancient Greece."[5] Similarly, Arthur Bryant, another RCR, professed:

> The Regiment is something more than a vehicle for orders: it is a school of military virtue. Its value to our country is that it evokes men's love, pride and loyalty and by doing so, enables them on the battlefield to transcend their own natures. This sacred and undying brotherhood, drawn from all classes and standards of education but knit together in a common pride and code, has repeatedly given [an army] a fighting strength in excess of its numbers and equipment.[6]

Within the national context, the regimental system has long been a fundamental component of the Canadian military experience. It has shaped, and indeed continues to shape, the attitudes and values of our military personnel, as well as influence the decisions and policies affecting the Canadian Forces (i.e. organization, training, administration, force generation, and employment).

However, for the soldier, senior non-commissioned officer (NCO) and officer serving in the military, the Regiment takes on a meaning and significance far beyond a stiff definition. It is an emotive issue — a special bond that signifies the membership to something larger than oneself — to a family with a rich history, as well as a legacy of courage, valour, and accomplishment. This important emotional link assists, if not drives, individuals to strive to maintain and advance the Regiment's name.

Prince Philip captured the essence of the close personal interrelationship between a regiment and its members. "Generations of men have joined and served this Regiment," he stated. "Each individual," he explained, "has brought something to the Regiment — his concept of loyalty and comradeship, and his idea of justice and honesty. In return, each one has gained something from the Regiment — the strength of will and determination which comes with membership of an efficient and famous team, and a sense of protective service to fellow citizens and to the nation as a whole; the comradeship which is stronger than the pull of community, race, religion, or political affiliation; the sense of belonging to a system which demands the best and helps each member to give it — a system which embraces more than just working for a living and which continues to provide a focus of help and encouragement long after active service is ended."[7]

Similarly, Padre Captain J.F. Farmer said, "[In] an infantry regiment [one] can experience a fraternity of mind and outlook, even behaviour, which is often more meaningful to men than the bonds that unite them as members of their own family." He added, "It is a feeling of belonging, being part of something which is greater than they are." Farmer described:

> In many different ways the course of history of a Regiment is like the wanderings and uncertainties of a woodland stream. You can trace its source to some watershed of history, its uncertain beginnings, its tentative purpose. Then gradually it becomes evident that the stream is here to stay as it begins to grow in strength. Suddenly the geographical or historical necessity is placed in front of it and it becomes a raging torrent or

a sudden waterfall, for example, the 1st World War, and 2nd World War, or Korea. Yet always interspersed along the way are quiet pools where the current dies down and the water forms an eddy and its members become conscious of one another.[8]

"The record of the Regiment," asserted General Charles Foulkes, a former chairman of the chiefs of staff and an RCR regimental officer, "speaks for itself, and it is up to you to maintain and add to that record of achievement."[9] And so, to those who are members of a regiment, it is not a faceless organization, it is a vibrant living organism.

In his first book, *55 Axis,* Strome Galloway, another former regimental officer and colonel of the Regiment, quoted an unknown soldier-philosopher who stated: "Men die, wars end, but the Regiment lives on!" Although not an original observation, it is worth repeating that a regiment is a living thing. It is a reflection of the men and women that make up its substance. As such, the history of a regiment is really the story of its members — their trials, challenges, disappointments, and achievements. It is often a story of courage and tenacity; a tale of compassion, emotion, and comradeship. And so, to recount the history of a regiment, it is necessary to tell the story of its members.

This volume describes the trials, tribulations, and achievements of the members of The Royal Canadian Regiment from 1953 to their 125th anniversary in 2008. It recounts their commitment and service to country throughout the Cold War, the stabilization campaigns of the 1990s, and the beginning of the new millennium, as well as their operational tours in the savage counterinsurgency campaign in Afghanistan. In keeping with the legacy they proudly maintain, The RCR has continued to serve the country with honour and distinction.

This volume continues the mission of documenting the feats of courage and suffering experienced by soldiers of The RCR, as well as their duty in the pursuit of the national interest that began in *Establishing a Legacy.* Their story demonstrates that "Royals" have continued to build on the legacy of those who came before them and reinforce the great traditions of their Regiment, namely courage, duty, and professionalism.[10]

Nonetheless, to try and capture 125 years of dramatic and dynamic history is a challenging task. As such, not every detail can be captured to cover the exploits of a regiment and its members. This volume is intended to provide the major achievements, exploits, and events that shaped and forged The Royal Canadian Regiment in the period 1953–2008. A key event summary has been included that provides additional details for those who seek such information.

Of note, this volume is the second part of a two-part history of The RCR. It and part one, *Establishing a Legacy*, make up volume three of the overall RCR regimental history.[11] It is a modernized, populist history that captures the entirety of the RCR experience. Moreover, it is a project that was begun as part of the Regiment's 125th anniversary celebrations that transpired in 2008. But most importantly, it is intended to celebrate the Regiment's greatest strength — the men and women who made it the great institution that it is. In the end, however, the essence of The RCR's efforts has always been straightforward — *Pro Patria,* or simply "For Country."

1

Defending the Bastion of Freedom and Democracy: The Beginning of the Cold War – The 1950s

The Regiment closed off its first 70 years of service by establishing a legacy of service and sacrifice to the country. It had participated in five armed conflicts and in countless exercises and aid to the civil power operations in Canada. It had earned a reputation for professionalism and courage at home and abroad. Nowhere was this tradition better demonstrated than in Korea, where all three battalions of the Regiment rotated through successive combat tours. Once again, they had served their country well. [1]

With the Korean War over, the Canadian Army once again returned to its peacetime duties. However, the world had irrevocably changed. The ideological and political rivalry that erupted between the two superpowers, the United States of America and the Union of Soviet Socialist Republics (U.S.S.R.), or Soviet Union for short, at the end of the Second World War had split the globe into two opposing armed camps. The threat of Communism cast an ominous shadow over Europe and the world. Gordon Graydon, the parliamentary advisor to the Canadian delegation to the United Nations, speaking on the subject of Soviet intentions, warned of the "defiant and undisguised steps toward world domination."[2] Prime Minister Louis St. Laurent and his foreign affairs minister, Lester B. Pearson, both went on record as stating "the international situation was never more serious."[3] Other Parliamentarians' views were representative of the prevailing climate, viewing Communism as "a diabolical dynamic thing … aiming at the destruction of all the freedoms and the inherent hard-won rights of man" and describing it as "the darkest and direst shadow that has ever fallen upon this earth."[4]

Within this atmosphere of fear, it is not surprising that, similar to the U.S., for the first time in its history, Canada was maintaining a large peacetime standing army. In fact, from 1950–53, manning in the Canadian armed forces rose from 47,000 to 104,000 personnel.[5] The crises of the Communist coup in Czechoslovakia in February 1948 and the first Berlin blockade a few months later had caused many to accept that the Soviets were clearly no longer allies, strained though that relationship had always been. The Allies looked behind the newly titled "Iron Curtain" and saw an authoritative, militaristic superpower, the only former ally not to have demobilized its large wartime army.[6] The Soviet-sponsored Korean War a few years later further confirmed the fears that permeated European and North American political and military circles.[7]

By the 1950s, those fears were deeply rooted in North America where the vast North was still seen as a vulnerable open flank. Although the concept of an air-transportable, airborne Canadian Army, framed within the structure of the Mobile Striking Force (MSF) was still officially in place, reality said otherwise.[8] Initially, in 1948–49, the MSF concept was embraced by the military and supported by the politicians because it provided a viable means of convincing the Americans that Canada could deal with any "enemy" incursions in the North.[9]

For the military the MSF concept provided the rationale for attempting to get additional resources from a tight-fisted government. For the politicians it provided a politically expedient and inexpensive means of meeting their obligations under the American/Canadian Basic Security Plan (BSP). As a result, the Regiment had begun transforming itself into an airborne unit in May 1949 and continued training its personnel thereafter.

However, the MSF was a hollow concept that existed in all but name. Although the deputy chief of the general staff anticipated that the long-term objective of forming the nucleus of the Active Force Brigade, around

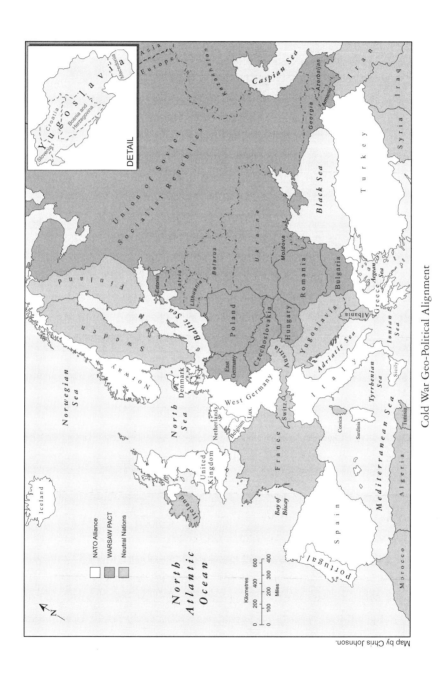

DETAIL

Cold War Geo-Political Alignment

Map by Chris Johnson.

NATO Alliance
WARSAW PACT
Neutral Nations

three infantry battalions, trained in airborne/air-transported operations, would be realized by April 1951, it never really happened.[10] With the eventual acceptance by the Americans, Canadians, and Europeans of the threat of the Soviet Union, and the onset of a Cold War, the creation of the North Atlantic Treaty Organization (NATO) in April 1949, provided the Canadian Army, and the entire Canadian Forces (CF) for that matter, with a new focus and viable rationale for existence.[11] The Canadian military, which had quit Europe in the summer of 1946 with the redeployment of the last of its occupation forces, was returning overseas.

In November 1951, Canada deployed approximately 10,000 troops to support NATO — 6,670 personnel as part of an Infantry Brigade Group and 12 fighter squadrons representing almost 300 aircraft. Amazingly, the defence budget accounted for 45 percent of the federal budget. This was the beginning of a commitment to what would become heavy mechanized forces serving as the tip of the spear to blunt any Soviet aggression. Not surprisingly it became the focus of the Army.

Despite the revelation, the MSF concept was still maintained as the foil to a Soviet incursion into the Canadian North. However, adequate resources simply did not exist. With the Korean War and then the budding NATO commitment demanding scarce resources, little was left for the MSF program. From its inception, the MSF was intended to be the "smallest self-contained force" capable of meeting peacetime requirements.[12] Added to this was the fact that no Canadian politician or senior military commander actually believed there was a credible threat to Canada's North other than the unilateral American initiatives to secure the northern gateway. The Minister of National Defence, Brooke Claxton declared, "the danger of direct attack upon Canadian territory was extremely remote … any attack on North America would be diversionary, designed to panic the people of this continent into putting a disproportionate amount of effort into passive local defence."[13]

The military assessment was similar. Army appreciations judged the chance of enemy airborne attacks as extremely slight because of the difficulties of resupply and re-embarkation of the attacking force.[14] An official NDHQ assessment regarding the direct defence of Canada in the early 1950s contained in the military's strategic operations plan,

Defence Scheme No. 3 — Major War, concluded that as a result of the extremely limited base facilities in Eastern Siberia, the Soviets were not capable of more than isolated airborne operations, none totalling more than a few hundred men.[15] Joint Intelligence Committee assessments from the early-fifties also clearly indicated that the data available "implies that the Soviet Union cannot land any airborne forces on Canadian territory."[16]

Nevertheless, prudence necessitated caution. More important, the Canadian government had to demonstrate that it could protect the Canadian North.[17] As a result, the Royals did their part to keep the Mobile Striking Force myth alive. The MSF mandate was limited to defeating the landing of small parties of approximately 30 to a maximum of 100 personnel, "by air or submarine, in the hinterland areas of Canada, with the intention of establishing a refuelling airstrip, a weather or electronic station or just to cause alarm and despondency."[18]

And so, despite all its warts, the Mobile Striking Force paratroopers were the guardians of the northern gateway. Within this context, the RCR continued its airborne training as best it could. In fact, it took its airborne role very seriously. A constant stream of parachute candidates, normally complete integral platoons, were sent to the Canadian Joint Air Training Centre (CJATC) in Rivers, Manitoba, for their basic parachutist course. In addition, the designated MSF RCR battalions conducted continuation parachute training and cold weather exercises in such locations as Churchill on a regular basis.[19] Private Ted Zuber recalled:

> We were MSF so we trained for the Arctic to repulse the Soviets. We trained as the first line of defense against the Soviets. We moved off the Arctic tundra to the sub-Arctic, to the tree line. Everything was based on stopping the Russians. We went into the back woods of Petawawa for three week exercises. We didn't have many jumps but we lived in the woods and snow-shoed [*sic*]. Every third day we lived out of doors without a tent.[20]

What has been lost to many is the importance of the airborne connection. Tim Riley recalled that when he joined 2 RCR in Canadian Forces Base Gagetown in the 1950s, it was a "a parachute battalion where all ranks wore British parachute helmets and jump smocks."[21] Lieutenant-General Jack Vance insisted, "Airborne operations played an important part in the development and capability of the RCR in the post war years." He explained, "I wasn't anyone until I had my maroon beret. Of our 1,000 man battalion we had the capability of fielding 800 parachutists." Vance asserted, "The airborne skill combined with our expertise in Arctic survival and warfare was a very challenging feature of, quite a big part of the RCR for quite a long period of time."[22]

But as already stated, by the early fifties, with the Korean hostilities still fresh in everyone's memory, the looming Communist threat in Europe gave the Army a new focal point. By the mid-1950s a government publication, *Canada's Defence Programme*, stated categorically that "almost everything Canada is now doing in the military field relates quite naturally to our participation in NATO."[23] The reality was simple. International tensions and growing public fear over perceived Soviet intentions provided support for large standing peacetime forces, even in Canada.[24]

So, as much as the Royals in Canada tried to focus their efforts on airborne operations, it was a losing battle. The difficulty in maintaining a sense of credibility with the MSF was pervasive.[25] In 1954, "X" Coy, The RCR conducted Exercise (Ex) Bulldog II in Baker Lake in the Northwest Territories. The exercise was designed to give the RCR parachute component practice in a defence of Canada role. Area Headquarters tasked the RCR paratroopers with recapturing the local radio station and destroying the hypothetical enemy lodgement. Unfortunately, equipment problems and poor weather held the rescue force at bay. The exercise was called off before the Royals were able to conduct their assault.[26]

The after action review of Ex Bulldog II revealed a major problem with the MSF concept.[27] One report complained that the exercise "indicated that paratroops cannot be relied on as an effective striking force in arctic regions and that many problems of mechanical maintenance have yet to be solved."[28] Another was blunter. It asserted that "many officers feel that the day of the paratrooper and the glider-borne soldier are

Courtesy Canadian Airborne Forces Museum (CAFM).

RCR paratroopers drop from a C-119 Boxcar for a winter exercise in the early 1950s.

Courtesy Library and Archives Canada (LAC) PA-204970.

No. 9 Platoon from The RCR practising advancing in extended line in the Arctic in the early 1950s.

finished … and it is felt that some new means of carrying this soldier to the attack area must be evolved."[29] Finally, Lieutenant-General Vance concluded, "The MSF was an unrealistic demand on the Canadian military at the time."[30]

It was not long before the changing dynamics of the defence mission consumed The RCR as well. In November 1953, the 2nd Battalion, The RCR (2 RCR) was deployed to Germany as part of Canada's continuing NATO commitment. They were part of the newly established 1 Canadian Infantry Brigade Group (1 CIBG), which was replacing 27 Canadian Infantry Brigade (CIB), Canada's initial overseas formation that was deployed to Hanover, Germany, in November 1951.[31] Fortuitously for the Royals, the second rotation of Canadians was leaving Hanover, which still bore the scars of heavy bombing during the Second World War, for the city of Soest. The Royals and the remainder of their brigade were being relocated to Fort York, a newly built garrison approximately six kilometres south of that city.

The advance party of 2 RCR left in early October 1953. The main party followed at the end of the month onboard the S.S. *Columbia*, and finally arrived at Fort York on 8 November 1953. Sergeant Bud Jones recalled, "It was quite a different experience. A lot of us were in Germany during the war and there was a difference between the old vet and the younger soldiers who just got in."[32] Despite the potential for animosity between the Canadian occupation troops and their German hosts — memories of the Second World War were still fresh — professionalism overrode any bad blood.

For the new soldiers the experience was exhilarating. Moreover, their new accommodations were first rate. The 2 RCR chronicler explained, "As this camp is more of a base than a training centre, the accent is on good living accommodation and recreational facilities rather than on training areas."[33] The name Fort York was chosen as a deliberate policy by the Department of National Defence (DND) to name its bases in Europe after historic forts in Canada. Fort York was by all accounts an impressive base. Members of 2 RCR described their new quarters with obvious pride. They reported:

Department of National Defence (DND) PC-7094.

RCR paratroopers loading for a jump.

Fort York is built in the new and modern military lines of low bungalow style·buildings. Stone blocks covered with stuccoed pumice were used in their construction. Cream painted exterior walls, with green roofs give these buildings a trim line, and give the visitor an impression of neatness and order. A wire fence surrounds the whole camp bordered on the north and east by woods, the road to the Mohne See on the west and open fields to the south.[34]

The rotation to Europe heralded another dramatic change for the Regiment. "For the first time ever," remarked Lieutenant-General Vance, "we had actual families with wives and kids moving with our soldiers over to and back from Europe." He explained, "the families experienced military life more closely and this new reality also changed military life. In the

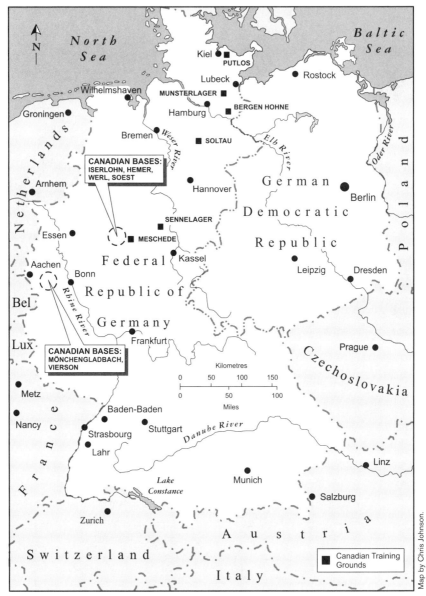

Canadian Bases in Germany: 1950 – 1969

process, wives won their right to be thought of as members of the broader Regimental family; not only through faithful support to their husbands but also in their contribution of family being stationed overseas."[35]

Moreover, the families added a reality to the Cold War that was not always felt in Canada. Vance explained, "It was like having your own personal piece of Canada with you to remind you to get up in the morning: 'You'd better stand to and stand tall in this job of warding off the Soviet hordes, because if you don't do it, your wife and kids are going to be directly involved' kind of thing." He added, "I think that the whole character of the Canadian military was altered through that marvellous experience — very expensive, but I would say priceless experience — that we had in having this little kind of Canada pop-up wherever we were stationing troops overseas."[36] Vance elaborated, "Soldiers came back as different people. The professional requirements of serving shoulder to shoulder with different regiments and nations — sharing the same challenges and undertaking competitions, provided a means of measuring

Courtesy Canadian Joint Imagery Library RE78-2949.

MSF paratrooper from 1 RCR fights off the DZ during an exercise at the Malton Airport near Toronto in the early 1950s.

ourselves and establishing a reputation." He continued, "It became a matter of great pride and led to better performance. It impacted our sense of professionalism — both individually and collectively."[37]

The new Cold War, however, brought more than just an exotic European posting. It represented more than just an ideological split between former allies. The Royals in Germany faced a formidable threat. From 1954–56, NATO planners viewed the Soviet troop dispositions opposite North Army Group (NORTHAG) to which the Royals belonged to as serious. The Soviet forces consisted of six "armies" organized into two operational echelons. The first included the 2nd Guards Mechanized Army, 3rd Shock Army, and 8th Guards Army. It was tasked with fixing NATO forces and creating gaps in the Allied defensive line. The second Soviet echelon, which included six tank divisions and five mechanized divisions was responsible for exploiting the success of the first echelon.

At the time, the main NATO defensive line was along the Rhine River. As such, 1 CIBG was expected, in coordination with other NATO forces to fight a covering force battle forward of the Rhine River and then conduct

Courtesy Sergeant Bud Jones.

RCR training exercise in the Soltau Training Area, West Germany, 1954.

a withdrawal to the river's west bank, thus delaying the Soviets so that other NATO formations could be mobilized and moved into theatre.

In the event of a surprise Soviet attack, 1 CIBG had little time to prepare. Therefore, they developed Ex Quick Train and the 70 percent rule. "Ex Quick Train" was the code word for a no-warning deployment exercise. These exercises could occur at any time. They could be initiated by NATO headquarters, I British Corps, British Army of the Rhine (BAOR), or brigade headquarters. On an Ex Quick Train, unit personnel would report to their respective camps after being notified by a wailing siren or by duty personnel banging on the door. In some cases, "Deuces" (2 1/2-ton trucks) would roll into villages and blare their horns, summoning the Canadians living there to load up and move to their base. Soldiers would then draw their weapons from quartermaster stores, load onto their vehicles, and rush out to their "Survival Areas," which were dispersed in the countryside around the bases. The 70 percent rule dictated that only 30 percent of a given unit's strength could be on leave or outside the Soest base area at any given point in time. More effective notification methodologies naturally evolved with time. These would later come together as the infamous "Snowball" or recall system that was used right through to the end of the Cold War, even in Canada.

The ability to notify the Canadian Brigade in a timely manner was critical as the Royals and their fellow Canadian combatants were an essential part of NATO. The Canadian brigade made up one-sixth of the strength of the BAOR to which it belonged. It was approximately half the strength of a British division and in terms of quality was equal to or better than anything the Allies could field. "The focus in Europe," explained former regimental officer Lieutenant-General Jack Vance, "gave us an indelible imprint and I don't mean just the RCR, but anybody in the Canadian Army who served in it. The chance to serve to a creditable standard, set of standards, defined by serious professional soldiers on the international level, and to be measured to those standards in what I think can properly be called the indicators of good soldiers — short of bullets flying and war happening — was constantly there."[38] In 1957, the commander of the BAOR pronounced that the Canadian brigade was "the best fighting formation in the world."[39]

2 RCR on a brigade parade at Fort York, West Germany, 1955.

Courtesy The RCR Museum and Archives.

Photographer Lee, LAC PA 131759.

Privates Roy Fraser and Jim Wingert, from 2 RCR, fire the 3.7-inch rocket launcher during a training exercise in Putlos, West Germany, 21 January 1954. Note the coveralls worn for exercises, since the Canadian Army had no "combat" environmental uniforms at the time.

Assault water landings are practised by 2 RCR soldiers at the "Mohnesee" in West Germany, 1955.

Training was key to the Canadian success. For the Royals training took on an annual sequence that would become almost ritualistic throughout the Cold War, both in Europe and in Canada. Training progressed from individual to sub-unit, unit, and combined arms training, culminating in formation level exercises. "The no-nonsense business of preparing for high-intensity war (i.e. equipment, tactics, level of training, leadership, logistical support)," said Vance, "provided a clear blueprint of what we had to do and how we had to do it."[40]

But the training focus was definitely different from what most had experienced. For the RCR veterans of Korea, who had returned to what they thought would be the venerable infantry war of patrols, trenches, and marching, they now found themselves on the cusp of a far more mobile age of warfare. Sergeant Jones recalled, "The training was more mobile than what we normally did. The tactics were meant to practice mechanized movement." He added, "Up until 1960 we used the 3/4-ton truck to simulate mechanized warfare. You really had to use your imagination."[41] However, the changes were far more dramatic than just mechanization. They now trained for what today seems completely unthinkable — fighting on an atomic battlefield.

Although the Soviets did not have tactical nuclear weapons until the 1960s, NATO had developed a plan to use tactical nuclear weaponry to close the gap in numerical inferiority in conventional forces on the battlefield. The updated *The Infantry Battalion in Battle (Motorized)* that superseded the 1952 the British pamphlet War Office 8716 *The Infantry Battalion in Battle* clearly captured the change in warfare. "Nuclear warfare has necessitated a reorganization and re-equipping of the battalion," it noted, "but the traditional role of the infantry remains unchanged." The manual went on to explain, "the tremendous increase in fire-power brought about by nuclear weapons, does not change the infantryman's basic method of fighting. He may fight as motorized infantry, or he may fight on foot; the vehicle merely serves to increase his flexibility of employment and his ability to move swiftly in and out of action." Amazingly, a major change to the role of the infantry battalion that was added was "to follow up and exploit nuclear fires."[42]

With what is known today, almost absurdly, the manual also exposed another revealing reality of the mindset of the era. It noted, "Though the bulk of this manual relates to nuclear warfare there may be occasions when the infantry battalion will be engaged in non-nuclear war, but with the nuclear threat ever present."[43]

To emphasize the new reality, on 21 August 1954, an Atomic Warfare Defence Demonstration took place at Castle Range in Sennelager, an area that appeared to replicate a miniature Vimy Ridge with bunkers and revetted trenches. Here the troops were exposed to an "atomic simulator" to practice their survival skills against the blast, heat, and immediate radiation.[44] The simulator was placed approximately 300 metres away from the trenches, supposedly the safe distance for the detonation of a 20 kiloton nuclear munition. The unit War Diary captured the event as just another training activity. The entry noted, "unit personnel dug bunkers and communications trenches 4–6 feet deep. Unit personnel were briefed 'on safety precautions to be taken in case of an atomic attack and the effects of an atomic attack.' A simulated atomic explosion was then activated."[45]

The idea of fighting on an atomic battlefield became the norm.[46] For example, 2 RCR participated in Exercise High Gear in the Soltau training area, where after several days of hard fighting, the battalion withdrew to new defensive positions from which it stopped the enemy advance. "The following day," reported the unit's chronicler, "The Battalion attacked across the river to follow up the effect of an 'atomic bomb' dropped by

Courtesy The RCR Museum and Archives.

RCR paratroopers conduct a "landing swings" practice at Wolseley Barracks, London, Ontario, 1956.

friendly forces."[47] The following year, in August 1956, during the brigade concentration, once again in the Soltau training area, 2 RCR concentrated on mining and wiring, battalion defence, and withdrawal exercises, as well as a battalion advance to contact in conditions of enemy atomic superiority. Even upon return home, the 2 RCR historical report noted the continuation of emphasis on the nuclear battlefield. It stated that divisional summer concentrations in Canada also emphasized "defensive positions as per nuclear concept" and the "Battalion advance to contact with support of nuclear weapons." In fact, four of the five major divisional exercises all emphasized operations with the support, or in support, of nuclear weapons. The exercise that did not have such a simulation had live field firing.[48]

The impact on soldiers was evident. Chief Warrant Officer John O'Quinn recalled as a young soldier, "The nuclear threat was always

Photographer Stephens, LAC PA-131763.

Sergeant Joe Kroskey and Private Joe Belben fire the 60 mm mortar during a training exercise in Putlos, West Germany, 19 March 1956.

Courtesy The RCR Museum and Archives.

2 RCR lines in Camp Gagetown, 1956.

in the back of our minds." He conceded, "The equipment and training we had, however, was primitive."[49] Colonel Tim Riley confirmed, "The emphasis on operations in Germany was placed on mobile defensive operations under a nuclear threat. We practiced moving from hide to hide at night."[50]

Undeniably, the era was a marked change from the past. The spectre of nuclear warfare and the wholesale acceptance of mechanization of all arms seemed to portend to dramatic changes. However, in the summer of 1958, the director of infantry reminded all of the infantry's ageless importance. He wrote: "the infantry's position on the battlefield, though threatened by some atomic theorists, was never more secure. We will continue to be the dominant arm on which all decision rests. Our tactical methods however must change, and this will involve major changes in organization and equipment. These changes are close at hand. The next few years will see APCs [armoured personnel carriers] provided, we will go through a series of organizations, new manuals will be issued, and the training system introduced particularly for the training of leaders."[51]

Key to the infantry's modernization was mobility. "Mobility," stressed the director of infantry, "will be the dominant factor in our new doctrine. Infantry will be mobile in organic amphibious APCs. All other corps will have an equivalent mobility."[52] This required a massive shift in thinking since, as he noted, "APCs classically have been associated with the armoured corps, and heavy mortars with the artillery." He added, "it is only in the last few months that it has become recognized that APCs are in fact an infantry vehicle."[53]

As a result of the increased emphasis of mobility and decentralization a new philosophy and technique of command was envisioned. Again, the director of infantry explained, "Responsibility, authority and initiative will be greatly decentralized. The brigade commander will formulate the tactical plan, the battalion commanders will execute it and will be given more freedom than in the past in their methods. All levels of command require a new approach to leadership."[54] The ground work was seemingly laid for what Royals in later decades would take for granted.

However, the changes also made clear that the new reality was an exponentially more lethal era of warfare. Colonel P.R. Bingham noted the requirement to balance the increased mobility with increased fire-power. He said this would be done by:

a. purchasing a nuclear weapon, the Lacrosse missile;
b. introducing the SS10 or SS11 or other type of anti-tank missile;
c. adding the heavy machine gun; and
d. adding the heavy mortar."[55]

Alarmingly, as already stated, commanders and leaders at all levels viewed atomic weapons as a normal part of the battle. During the Infantry Conference of 24–30 January 1958, the director of infantry spoke to the need for new doctrine and organization in the Army. He explained:

> We must realize that atomic weapons are a reality and that any consideration of non-nuclear, or so called conventional war, is futile. Any war whether it be all-out, major, limited, peripheral, or even police action, will be fought with atomic weapons or under the threat of their immediate employment. Our tactical concept and doctrine therefore must change. Our old concepts are unrealistic, and the doctrines of which our current organizations are based are not merely out-moded but are down-right suicidal.[56]

Inconceivably in today's context, he went on to stress that "movement and battle plans will be based on atomic fire." He reminded all that "HE [high explosives] merely supplements."[57] The director of infantry affirmed, "Nuclear weapons place in the hands of the commander unparalleled destructive power. The major problem, however, is securing timely and accurate target intelligence in order to make the best use of this power." He explained, "Atomic bombs are expensive and even in atomic plenty there will never be enough of them, therefore they must be carefully used. This means finding a worth-while target." He

Courtesy The RCR Museum and Archives.

Trooping of the Colours, 2 July 1959. All three battalions paraded at Wolseley Barracks, marking the first time in the history of the Regiment that three battalions paraded together in formal ceremony. The parade was conducted to allow the Colonel-in-Chief, HRH Prince Philip, to review the Regiment and present new Colours to the 1st and 3rd Battalions.

then clarified, "Obviously we don't take pot-shots at small parties with a weapon that can flatten a city. Without information then, the power of the atomic bomb is wasted. We will get little return from random shooting into the wide spaces of a modern deployment."[58]

By the late 1950s, however, it was no longer a one-sided nuclear contest. As Nikita Khrushchev proclaimed in November 1959, "We now have stockpiled so many rockets, so many atomic and hydrogen warheads, that if we were attacked, we could wipe from the face of the earth all our probable opponents."[59] For this reason and others, the director of infantry reminded the Infantry Corps:

> We must realize that we are faced with a modern up-to-
> the-minute enemy, equipped with new weapons all of
> which are equal to ours and some, principally tanks, are

superior. Their tactics are modern and intelligent and commend our study; they have a lot of good ideas. They are, however, adopting techniques to disperse their large armies, yet achieve concentration when it is necessary. The secret, of course, is mobility and they fully understand this; even their rifle divisions stress this characteristic and can in fact move faster over long distances than their mechanized and tank divisions. Their typical attack formation is tanks and mechanized divisions committed on a broad front. They recognize the need to hurdle water obstacles quickly and the bulk of their tactical vehicles, including some of their tanks, are amphibious.

His intention was "to ensure ... that we have erased from our minds the picture of a steam-roller attack by hordes of semi-trained peasants being driven forward by political commissars."[60]

In the end, the director of infantry summarized the new concept of war. First, he confirmed, "war will be atomic, or fought, under the threat of imminent use of atomics." Second, he underlined that "war may take various forms; it may be: an major all-out war, probably fought in Europe; a limited nuclear war; a limited non-nuclear war; or a peripheral or small-scale local war." He also pointed out, "we may be required to take part in police actions. This last requirement means that a portion of our force must have a strategic air-transport capability." Importantly, in laying out the Canadian Army position, he stated, "war will be relatively short, there will be no time to mobilize and train a large ground army. It will be fought with forces in being, that is the Regular Army as it is constituted and equipped at the time. Paper organizations are useless."[61]

The idea of a "come as you are war" became rooted in military thinking and planning. Major-General G. Walsh explained, "the original mobilization plan called for stock piling of equipment sufficient to meet one division's requirement. This policy has been reviewed recently and it has been decided that units will hold their basic scales of equipment. This means that if a unit goes to war, items of equipment now on issue is what they would have to fight with." Walsh emphasized, "our whole way of thinking would have to change in the light of this new policy to ensure that current equipment is maintained and ready for instant use."[62] This was a dramatic change from the nation's historic policy of a small regular force standing army that was viewed by politicians and society as the training cadre for the citizen army that would be raised and trained to actually fight the nation's wars.

The final doctrinal point was that the Canadian Army "will fight as part of a larger allied force." The director of infantry asserted, "Our basic organization will be the brigade group." He also pointed out that "this brigade group will have an organic atomic capability and will be 100% mobile, using tracked armored personnel carriers."[63] As inconceivable as it may be today, so was the perception of the next war. As such, the framework and culture of the military was shaped accordingly. Within this context the RCR marched deeper into the Cold War.

Back in Canada, the emphasis on the MSF airborne role had diminished by the end of the decade. The Soviets' successful testing of an Inter-Continental Ballistic Missile (ICBM) in 1957 radically transformed the nature of the menace to North America. The American fear of temporary Soviet bomber staging and refuelling bases established in Canada's North dissipated with the eclipse of the manned bomber threat emanating over the polar icecap.[64] Predictably, the importance of the Canadian Arctic died, as did the government and military requirement for the MSF. The resultant effect of this techno-strategic shift was immediate. The MSF parachute battalion concept was downsized to decentralized parachute companies. "It is considered now that the job can be done by a few company groups supported where necessary by an air-transported build-up," explained one senior officer, "this may be slow but this is accepted." He acknowledged, "Parachute units are now being run down to 250 parachutists each."[65]

This reorganization from "Airborne Battalions" to "Jump Companies" in 1958, represented the official demise of the MSF. Collectively, the respective parachute sub-units were now designated the Defence of Canada Force (DCF) to underline their "special" role. The parachute companies were established within designated battalions of The RCR, the Royal 22e Regiment (R22eR), and the Princess Patricia's Canadian

Light Infantry (PPCLI). The DCF now became the nation's guardians responsible for enforcing the existing joint security arrangements between Canada and the United States for the defence of North America.

And so the Regiment grappled with two competing, almost seemingly contradictory realities of the modern world. In Canada the focus was still seemingly the Arctic and air transportability.[66] In Europe, the emphasis was clearly nuclear firepower and mechanization. Yet, just as the Royals felt their way through the changing security environment, a third focus began to emerge. It was the concept of the "stand-by battalion" for engagement in peacekeeping type operations around the world.

By the late 1950s and turn of the decade, a new menace emerged elsewhere in the world. Tied irrevocably in many ways to the Cold War, the world witnessed an international explosion of nationalistic movements and political unrest. "Brush-fire" conflicts, insurgencies, and wars of national liberation flared-up around the globe. The concept of rapid deployable forces under United Nations (U.N.) auspices captured the imagination of the Canadian government which was still euphoric about its newly-won international role caused by its diplomatic and military success in the outcome of the 1956 Suez Crisis. Four years later, the emergency in the Belgian Congo reinforced the apparent need for international forces that could deploy quickly to avert the potential escalation of regional conflicts into superpower confrontations.

Unveiling The RCR Memorial, CFB London, 2 July 1959.

Courtesy The RCR Museum and Archives.

At the same time, as a result of the changing international security environment, the Americans embarked on a program to better address the "spectrum of conflict" ranging from low level insurgencies to high intensity nuclear war, with which they were now faced. The Americans realized that their existing force structure was not adequate to deal with "limited wars" in distant lands. Therefore, the Pentagon now stressed greater strategic mobility, the expansion of Special Forces to deal with the proliferation of guerrilla-type conflict, and the development of an airmobile capability.

As the decade drew to a close, Canada decided it would follow suit. Chief of the General Staff (CGS), Lieutenant-General H.D. Graham, observed, "units must be air-portable therefore a light scale must be devised." He asserted, "troops must become accustomed to travelling light and living hard."[67] Graham stressed the role of the new armoured personnel carrier, the air truck, and the use of helicopters and their effect on the Army's mobility. He said, "airlifting of troops would be the rule rather than the exception." The CGS also underlined that "the normal roles of the infantry remained unchanged."[68]

In the closing days of the decade this theme resonated with many Royals. Despite the emphasis on mechanization and atomic warfare, the importance of traditional skills and attributes was not lost on the Regiment's officers. "Our weapons, vehicles, and technical equipment need capable and intelligent young men to handle them," declared Brigadier T.G. Gibson, "our peacetime duties around the world require men of common sense and stability, and the possible conditions of modern war demand the highest qualities of initiative and physical endurance." Gibson reminded the Regimental leadership that "It is the Regiment's task to produce such men." He also unequivocally stated: "I am confident that it is doing so."[69]

And so, faced with many changes in an increasingly dangerous world, The Royal Canadian Regiment adapted and prepared its soldiers and leaders to continue its legacy of service to Canada and the world. Although the 1950s was marked by dramatic advances in technology and warfare, the next decade would prove to be equally challenging and a continuing test of the Regiment's ability to adapt.

2

An Era of Change: The 1960s

The 1950s ushered in an entirely new focus and mindset for the Army. NATO became its centre of gravity. Moreover, tactical mobility on the battlefield became the focal point of operations and mechanization, even if only simulated by the use of 3/4-ton trucks. But mobility and mechanization were only direct offshoots of the emphasis placed on the atomic battlefield. From the infantry officer's perspective, nuclear weapons were viewed in many ways as tactical tools to assist with manoeuvre. More worrisome were the technological advancements that made nuclear weapons strategic munitions that could target cities half a world away. Not surprisingly, a wider public concern began to take root.

And so, as the Regiment marched deeper into the Cold War, a public recognition of the looming nuclear Armageddon began to drive political agendas. But so too did the winds of change in the international security environment. The new decade ushered in a wide array of new equipment, organizations, ideas, as well as a series of new roles for the military. This era of change was soon felt by the Royals as they navigated through the 1960s.

The new decade began with the pall of nuclear war casting its shadow on all aspects of life. Rapid technological change produced missiles and munitions capable of unleashing devastation previously not even thought possible. The deepening of the Cold War only exacerbated the fear many people felt. By the summer of 1961, Berlin, Germany, became the centre of yet another tense stand-off between NATO and the Soviet Warsaw Pact.[1] With thousands of East Germans seeking asylum in West Berlin, the East German government and their Soviet masters felt obliged to shut the valve.[2] On 13 August, East German soldiers and workers began to tear up the streets running parallel to the border, thereby making them impassable to most vehicles. They also erected barbed wire entanglements and fences along the 156-kilometre border between the three western sectors and East Germany and the 43 kilometres of border within the city that actually divided West and East Berlin. Two days later, the first concrete blocks were put in place, which represented the commencement of the construction of the infamous Berlin Wall.

Subsequent Soviet actions heightened the tension of the Berlin crisis even more. A little over a week after cutting off access to West Berlin, the Soviets undertook an aggressive series of nuclear tests. They exploded warheads at a rate of five a week at ranges in the U.S.S.R. until October. The final detonation yielded 50 megatons, then the largest nuclear explosion ever.[3] The situation became so serious that Prime Minister John Diefenbaker addressed Parliament to announce that Canada would not only reinforce its Germany garrison to bring up the strength of 4 Canadian Infantry Brigade Group, or 4 CIBG, to a total of 1,106 all ranks, but also to inform Canadians that the Conservative government was increasing its military from 120,00 to 135,000 regular force personnel.[4]

At the same time, in Germany, 4 CIBG went on stand-by. Personnel were recalled from leave and all ranks were confined to the brigade area. At the height of the crisis the Canadian brigade group deployed to its survival areas fully mobilized with five days of combat supplies, including live ammunition in their vehicles. The Cold War seemed very real.

On 22 October 1962, President John F. Kennedy announced to the American nation and the world that he would confront the Soviet Union in their bid to establish missile bases in Cuba, which was less than 200 kilometres from the American mainland.[5] Americans, and Canadians, were soon embroiled in what would become known as the Cuban missile crisis. The U.S. president further revealed that until the Soviet bases were removed, Cuba would be blockaded. Immediately, the commander of North American Aerospace Defence Command (NORAD) ordered the alert status changed to DEFCON 3, the final stage before actual war. The stand-off brought the two superpowers to the brink of conflict. The Cold War appeared to be on the verge of going hot.

The implications for both the Royals in Germany, as well as those in Canada, not to mention the rest of the world in general, were significant. Tom de Faye, a young subaltern at the time, remembered, "The Cuban missile crisis was a very tense time." He noted, "that was the atmosphere we [1 RCR] deployed to Germany under." De Faye acknowledged, "Many of us thought we would be at war."[6] Phil Spencer, also a subaltern at the time, agreed. He recalled, "We moved to our survival areas and were ready to go to war."[7]

Nobody was under the illusion that if war began, the use of nuclear weapons could be averted. After all, the Soviet doctrine in the 1960s emphasized tactical nuclear warfighting. Moreover, it had little to no real emphasis on conventional operations other than to capitalize on nuclear fires to advance and occupy captured ground. If the Soviet Union and its Warsaw Pact allies initiated war against NATO, it was generally understood by the West that nuclear and chemical weapons would be used from the outset. In fact, the Soviets and their allies had created an entirely mechanized force that placed great importance on mobility and protection (against both conventional munitions and fallout from a nuclear battlefield).

In the end, war was averted. The Soviet Union recalled its ships carrying missiles to Cuba and dismantled its bases in that Caribbean country.[8] Nonetheless, while the standoff continued, everyone had braced for a potential nuclear holocaust. The confrontation just added to the fear of nuclear Armageddon and the reality that war with the Soviet Union, a seemingly aggressive, belligerent foe, was always a possibility.

NATO nations gathered to discuss the way forward after the crises they had just experienced. The resultant 1963 NATO Athens Guidelines, reached in the aftermath of the Cuban missile crisis, articulated that NATO would use nuclear weapons if the Soviets used nuclear weapons, but only on a scale proportional to that employed by the Soviets. However, it also allowed for the use of tactical nuclear weapons if the

Soviets attacked with overwhelming conventional forces, but again, only on a scale appropriate to the circumstances. In essence, the idea was that NATO forces would repel Soviet invading forces on conventional terms. If the Soviets broke through the initial screen, then NATO shield forces would be authorized the use of tactical nuclear weapons to stop them. NATO also agreed at this forum that their main defensive line would be pushed further eastward to the border between West and East Germany. This was done to avoid fighting a nuclear battle in the heart of West German territory.

The gravity of the situation led Canada, as well as all NATO countries, to place a large emphasis on preparedness of modern, mechanized, and well-trained forces capable of fighting on a nuclear battlefield. But this required a transformation in thinking and doctrine. It seemed technology had outstripped both. Colonel P.R. Bingham bemoaned the impact the era of change was having on collective training. "The one

DND, negative EF63-9559-9.

A Royal heavy machine gun section with the new .50 calibre HMG on exercise in West Germany, 1963.

DND, negative EF63-9559-8.

RCR exercise bivouac site in West Germany, 1963.

thing," the former RCR CO observed, "which was obvious [during the three brigade group concentrations] was the lack of uniformity in tactical doctrine and in concept generally." He lamented, "Every individual seemed to have his own idea of how a platoon, a company or a battalion should fight on a nuclear battlefield."[9]

The confusion was not lost on those serving in Germany at the time. Major-General de Faye vividly recalled his deployment from Camp Ipperwash to Germany in 1962. "We focused on defensive roles," he explained, "it was an interesting transitional period." He described the tour:

> We were equipped with Dodge 3/4-ton trucks. Each platoon had four vehicles. One for headquarters and one for each of the three sections. For firepower, we had a FNC2 light automatic rifle perched on the cab of the vehicle. More than one of those brave individuals fell over the cab and bounced down the hood of the vehicle. By the end of the tour in 1965 we had the new American M113 Armoured Personnel Carrier (APC). There was a bit of a doctrinal gap in the Army at the time. Going from truck borne infantry to mechanized infantry was a very large task. This forced us into a new level of capability.[10]

As utterly preposterous as it seems today, Royals prepared to fight on a nuclear battlefield. For example, during the 1960 infantry commanders' conference, the CO of 1 RCR led a discussion on the standardization of calling for, and warning troops of, friendly nuclear strikes since there existed a variety in methods.[11] The following year during the brigade controlled Exercise Chain Mail, from 16–18 July, the 1 RCR battle group practiced the elimination of a minor penetration, the containment of a major penetration, followed by the exploitation of a nuclear strike.[12] When the unit rotated to Germany in 1962, its emphasis, remained on mobile defensive operations under a Soviet nuclear threat.[13]

The context under which NATO would fight drove the approach to war. "Our theory," revealed Major-General George Kitching, "was that divisions and brigades must operate like fleets at sea; concentrations larger than a battalion were to be avoided; helicopters, amphibious tanks and armoured personnel carriers (APCs) would make concentrations at bridges a thing of the past. The whole battlefield would be fluid."[14]

One RCR officer explained, "on the modern battlefield, the dangers of nuclear weapons have made it necessary for fighting units to affect a mobility and dispersion to an extent never before practiced. Because of the difficulties of communicating over long distances co-operation is becoming more difficult to achieve."[15]

Pat Rossiter stated: "The nuclear battlefield was realistic. We knew we could never provide a target larger than a company group." He explained, "Therefore, being spread out was a way of life. We worried about the gaps but we worried more about the nucs. When we exercised we exercised around our nuclear arsenal." Rossiter noted, "We plotted downwind fall-out and we practiced strikes."[16]

To adapt to the new dispersed battlefield, 1 RCR designed a course to train the private soldier to lead a small group of men under adverse conditions in an emergency. Colonel Bingham explained the course was "patterned after a portion of the [U.S.] Ranger course and is of 10 days duration. Every man in the battalion must take this course during which he is subjected to: hard marching over many miles rough terrain at night, little or no food during patrols for two days duration, obstacles of all kinds to give realism and added hardship and many more things. During the training any member of the group may be called upon to be the leader at any time."[17]

Although just one course, it was representative of the impact of Germany to the RCR and the remainder of the Canadian Army. Frankly, the Germany experience drove the training agenda. Germany was, after all, the cradle of professionalism for the Army. "In Germany we had to deal with specific tasks and threats," explained de Faye, "It had a priority for personnel. It had an operational task that could be translated into a very clear focus and training goals. It had clear standards that had to be reached to attain the necessary goal, albeit it was not always properly equipped."[18] Lieutenant-General Jack Vance agreed. "The chance to serve to a credible set of standards," he professed, "defined by serious professional soldiers on the international level, and to be measured to those standards in what I think can properly be called the indicators of good soldiers — short of bullets flying and war happening — was constantly there."[19]

A Germany rotation also meant that units would be manned at full strength, approximately, 900–1,000 men — unheard of in later years. In addition, there were few changes in individuals during a tour; therefore, the unit and its personnel became well drilled and they developed tight bonds and camaraderie. But most of all, a tour in Germany meant realistic training to meet the needs of the mission. "The training year," described a former operations officer of 1 RCR, "is broken into a series of short sharp concentrations that tend to keep operational readiness at a high standard and maintain a continuing interest among all ranks. The training on the whole was very realistic and varied perhaps largely because of the training areas and the foreign environment."[20] The War Diary revealed, "The emphasis was on realism in all aspects of training. This was achieved by using disappearing balloon targets, real moving tank targets and authentic mock-ups."[21] A 2 RCR chronicler reported, "All ranks found the training in Sennelager to be unlike anything they had ever seen before. The infinite detail on the miniature range, the completeness of the Russian village, the mysteries of the Grimke patrol course — all these compounded to make it a most interesting training experience."[22]

The overall impact of Germany on The RCR and Canadian Army was incalculable. Vance believed:

> The impact on the Regiment of the service in Europe had to do very much with the no-nonsense business of actually training for war, of a describable finite war, of what was perceived to be the highest possible standard by way of demand, everything from equipment through tactics, to level of training, to leadership, administrative support, logistic support and the like. In every respect, there was a blueprint laid out — and, there was no part of the field army in Canada, or Canadian field army, that was not affected by this. If you were back home in Canada you were still emulating the level of training, the challenges of operational readiness, the type of equipment, the tactics and everything else that was being played out day by day on the central front. Even

if you were double-hatted, incidentally, to be ready to do CANUS [Canadian/United States] type operations or aid to the civil power or whatever else it happened to be, you still had as your principal focus that model that described what we were supposed to be like, what made a good outfit.[23]

Moreover, the 1960s was a period of dramatic change in many different ways. One way was the introduction of new equipment, such as APCs, helicopters, M-109 self-propelled artillery, the M26 grenade, the Carl Gustav anti-tank weapon, and the M72 disposable rocket launcher, to name a few. Germany became the proving ground for this new equipment, as well as for the doctrine, tactics, techniques, and procedures that accompanied the new weaponry.[24]

And so, Germany, with its "deep green rolling country dotted with red tiled roofed towns shading into the industrial giant of the Rhur Valley," became part of the very fabric of the Regiment.[25] The CO of 1 RCR on completion of his three year tour from 1962–65, stated, "The hours of work were longer, the duties heavier and the ever impending Roll Out practices kept the unit at a higher pitch of readiness than was normal in Canada. The training throughout the three years was so spaced that one never really had a chance to become complacent."[26]

The next group in, 2 RCR, quickly began to glean the same important lessons. Their operations officer commented after Exercise Test Tube, on 17 February 1966, "this was the first time during this tour that 2 RCR participated in a 'Bug-Out.'" He reminisced, "Who can forget the ominous ringing of doorbells in the wee hours, the tousled greetings of the alertmen, the subsequent throbbing of APC engines in the night? But one has only to remember our purpose in Germany to realize how important and real these early morning tests are."[27]

And, that was the essence of Germany — it was Canada's forward presence during the Cold War. Largely forgotten today is the fact that during the tumultuous early years of the 1960s, the world teetered on the brink of nuclear war on more than one occasion. For the Royals in Germany, it was a tense period. "We just accepted the nuclear battlefield as the reality of the day and got on with it," ruminated Carson Lambert, "At least by 1965, we had APCs instead of the 3/4-ton truck."[28]

And at times the Royals were brought to the brink of war. "In 1968, when the Soviets invaded Czechoslovakia," remembered Jay Gravelle, "we did a Corps border rush and deployed one kilometre from the border in a corps defensive position. It brought home there was a real enemy on the other side."[29] He explained, "To us it was real at the time." Gravelle recounted that the "East Germans practiced deception on the radio during exercises." He also noted, "There was also a very real threat from the population. The Warsaw Pact had a lot of people, spies, trying to get information on us."[30]

So no surprise then that Germany held a pivotal spot in the minds of many. After all, many Royals like Private Gerald Skibinsky manned the bastions of democracy. "I believed," stated Skibinsky, "we were the first line of defense in protecting Canada."[31]

Germany, however, was only one manifestation of the Cold War. Technological advancements made the safety of North America a thing of the past. For the first time in livable memory, North America could become a war zone. With the backdrop of increasing tensions between the two world superpowers, the Soviet Union continued to develop its nuclear arsenal and missile inventory. "The cow jumped over the moon, that's an old childish memory, which is almost coming true," opined a legendary Royal, Major-General D.C. Spry, at the time. He captured the mood when he explained, "Men are soon to land on the moon. Incredible, yes, but in an age of rapid technological change nursery rhymes can come true."[32] But reality was more menacing.

The global tensions and growing nuclear arsenals created a public hysteria. As a result, the government was required to act. As early as 28 October 1960, the minister of national defence (MND) stated: "If a nuclear attack took place, national survival would become the primary task of all our defence forces."[33] However, it was army that was the primary service responsible in National Defence with respect to all national survival matters. The Navy, Air Force, and Defence Research Board were strictly in supporting roles.

Unlike the questionable role of defending the Arctic against a Soviet incursion, the government and public considered the likelihood of a nuclear exchange to be a clear and present danger.[34] "If a nation is to survive nuclear attack, it is imperative that there be effective plans covering all aspects of national survival and that every man and woman in the nation play his or her part in this vitally important process," noted a government report. It stated:

> The survival of a nation, as opposed to the survival of individuals in the country, must involve many matters other than those having to do only with the immediate post-attack situation. There must for instance, be arrangements under which we may ensure the continued existence of government at all levels. There must, of course, be plans for the immediate relief of those in stricken areas, but there must also be plans to ensure the resuscitation and the recovery of the country as a whole: its people, its economy, and so on. There must also be the ability to reconstitute the armed forces because they will be needed for the continued prosecution of the war very shortly after the initial nuclear attack.[35]

What made the situation more worrisome was the military assessment that the nation could not rely on any strategic warning. At best, military planners considered that an advance warning of approximately a day could be expected. In the early part of the decade, the military estimate identified the primary threat to be that of attack by manned bombers armed with nuclear weapons. "Such attacks would probably allow us up to three hours tactical warning," acknowledged the military report.[36] It went on to clarify, "We believe further that the primary threat will change shortly to a missile attack, still with nuclear warheads." Alarmingly, it conceded, "The probable tactical warning that we may receive at that time will be reduced to some 15 minutes, or possibly less."[37] The weapons that were expected were five megaton air or surface burst munitions.

From a national survival planning point of view, defence planners assumed that 16 of the major cities had to be considered possible targets.

The nine most likely were: Edmonton, Halifax, Hamilton, Montreal, Ottawa, Toronto, Vancouver, Windsor, and Winnipeg. The remaining seven considered less likely were: Calgary, London, Niagara Falls, Quebec, Saint John in New Brunswick, St. John's in Newfoundland, and Victoria. In addition, there was an assumption that a number of random bombs would detonate over Canadian territory predominately in eastern Ontario and western Quebec. In the end, planners believed that up to one million people, or roughly five percent of Canada's 18.5 million population, would need to be rescued.[38]

The national survival task was not a popular one with either the regular or reserve components of the Canadian Armed Forces. Bob Mahar recalled, "It was a kind of dispiriting time with NST [National Survival Training] rescue party tasks looking for people in ruins, knocking on rubble 'can you hear me?'"[39] Oscar Lambert agreed. He acknowledged, "The troops didn't like it. They didn't feel it was military orientated. We accepted it and carried out the training."[40]

Despite the disdain felt by the soldiers, the importance of NST was recognized and all carried on as ordered. "We'll never again be able to spend a few years training for an emergency after it has taken place," voiced Brigadier K.H. McKibben, general officer commanding, or GOC, Western Ontario Area. He added, "I hope you'll never be called upon to do this task, but certainly with world conditions the way they are today, we must be prepared for it."[41]

And, the military did quickly begin to prepare for the mission. A six-week course in rescue designed for regular and militia personnel was implemented. In addition, national survival exercises were undertaken, which used local television and broadcasting resources to alert unit personnel. The Royals even solicited the assistance of the London City Police to aid troop and vehicle movement. For example, 1 RCR conducted Exercise Fire Ball, a three phase National Survival exercise that included: Stage one, mustering the battalion within camp, towns, villages, and farms; Stage two, loading of rescue stores and dispatch of two mobile columns; and Stage three, running through actual rescue operations at a disaster site. Major L.W.G. Hayes, the battalion operations officer, described the exercise, "very much like a village fire brigade going into action." He added, "the main difference being the size of the fire to be put out."[42]

To ensure the Royals were prepared to roll-out at a moment's notice, the units quickly received a large inventory of civil defence stores. One Royal commented, "Its like strolling through one of the larger hardware stores — you name it and he's [Quartermaster] got it."[43] Each of the battalions held two mobile support columns worth of stores — designed so four companies could load their rescue kits all at the same time.[44] Company load trials were also completed to establish the optimum load that could be carried in the cargo bay of the issue Dodge 3/4-ton truck. It was finally worked out so that each vehicle could carry seven men and rescue stores for an entire section.

For many commanders and soldiers, national survival, as critical a task in theory as it may have been, was an unwanted distraction. The focus on NATO and high-intensity warfighting remained the Army's primary focus. However, international tensions created additional turmoil, tasks, and changes for the military. In 1963, *The Connecting File*, The RCR's regimental journal, still noted that "the continuing roles for the Regiment are Defence of Canada, National Survival, and NATO."[45] Those tasks were neither in order of priority, nor were they fully in line with the government intent.[46]

As the Army leadership continued to insist that the NATO brigade in Europe (4 CIBG) "remains as a priority claim on our resources" the growing pull on forces for peacekeeping operations was in full play.[47] Already in 1958, 2 RCR was designated the stand-by battalion for international peacekeeping missions. At the time DND explained, "the government decided to maintain a stand-by battalion fully trained and prepared to be sent abroad in an emergency. The battalion designated is placed on constant stand-by alert and is prepared, if necessary, to leave this country at a moment's notice."[48]

As the decade progressed, there was an increasing concern with government leaders and military commanders for brush-fire wars, which was rooted in the fear of a superpower nuclear showdown. A special parliamentary report noted, "The nuclear stalemate, as well as the awesome potential of nuclear war has directed attention to the increasing need to deal effectively with local disturbances which hold the danger of escalating into major conflicts." It added, "The effectiveness of UN quasi-military operations to contain local brush-fire wars has won substantial support to the idea of an international force, a fact demonstrated to the extent of voluntary contributions to the UN forces in the Middle East and the Congo."[49]

The growing international acceptance of the idea of U.N. peacekeeping forces to provide stability in global hot-spots was readily endorsed by Canada. And, no where was the need for a U.N. force more compelling than in Cyprus. Tension and fighting existed in the British colony of Cyprus since the 1950s. An effort by Greece to unify isolated Mediterranean Greek communities during this period led to the creation of such independence groups as the National Organization of Cypriot Fighters (EOKA), who launched their terrorist campaign in March of 1955. By 1958, EOKA guerrilla warfare against the British forces and Turkish-Cypriot communities in Cyprus escalated to virtual anarchy with riots, shooting, bombings, and arson occurring daily. Under American

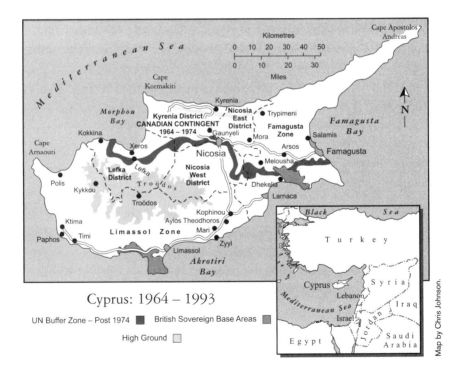

Cyprus: 1964 – 1993

UN Buffer Zone – Post 1974 ■   British Sovereign Base Areas ■

High Ground □

Map by Chris Johnson.

prodding, due to concerns that the situation could jeopardize the NATO southern flank if the pressure cooker that existed in Cyprus blew, the British finally took steps to address the question of independence.

In 1959, the governments of Britain, Greece, and Turkey reached an agreement that eventually led to the independence of the island.[50] The formula called for a Greek-Cypriot president and a Turkish-Cypriot vice-president. The constitution called for no ethnic partition, but rather equal rights and equality of both ethnic groups.

Cypriot independence actually occurred in August 1960, and Archbishop Makarios III became the president. The Legislative Assembly was 70 percent Greek Cypriot and the remaining 30 percent was Turkish Cypriot. However, the population breakdown was approximately 80 and 18 percent respectively. As a result, the Greek-Cypriot population resented the Turkish overrepresentation. Continuing ethnic and political tensions, fuelled by proposed constitutional amendments, finally bubbled to the surface and on 24 December 1963, the island erupted in violence once again. Enclaves became fortified, roadblocks were established, and a long stretch of "no-man's land," subsequently called the "Green Line," was established through central Nicosia.

British troops from the Sovereign Base Areas (SBAs) in Akrotiri and Dhekalia, quickly intervened. They uncovered evidence of massacres of both Greek and Turkish Cypriots. They were unable, however, to stop fighting altogether on the island. Tensions rose dramatically and both Greece and Turkey positioned troops to invade the island. A NATO peacekeeping force was rejected; however, all parties agreed to a U.N.-sponsored force. On 4 March 1964 the U.N. Security Council (UNSC) agreed in principle to the creation of the U.N. Force in Cyprus (UNFICYP). Its mandate was to: prevent a recurrence of fighting; contribute to keeping law and order; and assist in the return to normal conditions.[51]

But continuing violence against Turkish-Cypriot nationals and the intransigence and stalling by Makarios, which delayed the implementation of the peacekeeping agreement, finally pushed Turkey to launch their invasion fleet. At the same time, on 11 March 1964, Turkey issued an ultimatum that it would intervene in the defence of Turkish Cypriots unless a U.N. force was deployed immediately. The following

1 RCR Freedom of the City of Soest, 24 May 1964. Herr Walter Klemann, the Burgermeister of Soest, reviews the troops accompanied by the CO, Lieutenant-Colonel T.D. Lafferty.

2 RCR Battalion HQ during Ex Checkmate in West Germany, 1966.

day, fearing a war between NATO allies, American President Lyndon Johnson approached Canadian Prime Minister Lester Pearson and requested Canada send troops immediately, before the finalization of the actual details of the formal agreement, to help ease the tension. That day, 12 March, the MND approved the airlift and deployed Canadian forces to Cyprus on Operation Snow Goose. The deployment was for an initial three month commitment; however, it became a long-term operation that tied up 800–1,000 troops yearly until 1993.[52]

The Cyprus experience for The RCR commenced in 1966, with the deployment of 1 RCR. The CO at the time captured the historical significance. "As we proceed overseas to assume Canada's commitment in Cyprus with the United Nations," wrote Lieutenant-Colonel Phil Labelle, "it is to be remembered that this is the first time since Korea that the Royal Canadians have travelled abroad in the defence of peace and of the Realm. It is a responsibility which we do not accept lightly; but it is one which can mature us all and, at the same tie, reflect glory on our Regiment."[53]

The battalion commenced its training in May. "In order to become proficient in preventing arms smuggling, controlling infiltration and the other activities of peacekeeping," explained Labelle, "each of the rifle companies alternated to provide a controlled force to exercise a security force on four separate one week exercises at Meaford Area on Georgian Bay."[54]

The initial UNFICYP deployment witnessed military forces deployed generally in the areas of direct confrontation raised primarily by the population shift because of the previous fighting. The Finnish contingent was in Nicosia suburbs and enclave; the Swedes in Chatos/Trypemeni, Famagusta, Larnaca/Scala and Kophinu; the Danes in Nicosia Green Line and suburbs; the British held two sub-districts covering Limassol and Paphos/Ktima; the Irish Kokkina and Limnitis, as well as the Lefka area. The Canadians were deployed in the North in the Kyrenia district, which was approximately 44 kilometres long and 30 kilometres in depth. It included Cypriot government districts Kyrenia and Nicosia.

The initial fighting and continued conflict created a severe refugee problem. Many of the Turkish Cypriots living in mixed and outlying areas began moving into what were seen as Turkish enclaves. An RCR intelligence report noted, "There is only one officially recognized Turk

Cypriot enclave. This lies almost wholly within Kyrenia District on the Maesoria Plain from the Green Line in Nicosia to the Kyrenia Pass. There are three other large concentrations of Turkish Cypriot concentrations in Kokkina, Limnitis in Lefka District and Scala in Famagusta Zone"[55] The population in the officially recognized enclave doubled by the winter of 1964–65, from its original 3,600 a year earlier. By 1967, it was estimated at 10,000.[56] This led the 1 RCR intelligence officer to observe, "Many thousands of Turk Cypriots are homeless and have been forced to live in virtual ghettos."[57]

Despite the presence of the large U.N. contingent, the situation seemed grave. Even young Lieutenant J.V. Arbuckle was able to foresee the difficulties ahead. "There are very few places on the island where the lines are clearly drawn between the two factions," he noted. "The more definite the demarcation," he added, "the less the likelihood of sudden and unexpected violence." However, Arbuckle concluded, "The presence of large numbers of armed forces of both factions in confrontation areas makes a return to normal conditions an almost impossible task."[58] Tom de Faye agreed. "There was some real brutality in some segments," he concluded, "The resolution of those issues seems easy to outsiders, but it's difficult to resolve."[59]

But the Royals did what they could. Areas not under surveillance by static observation posts (OPs) were covered by mobile patrols. The RCR Standard Operating Procedures (SOPs) explained, "Patrol activity should be carried out unobtrusively and the frequency of visits is to be directly related to the current situation in the localities concerned." Furthermore, the SOPs stipulated, "The task of mobile patrols is reassurance of isolated Turkish-Cypriot communities by a show of UN presence in the area and reporting on activity in areas where no outposts exist."[60]

The SOPs were also clear in the desired effect the Royals were to have. "In carrying out the aim," explained the document, "UNFICYP is to avoid any action designed to influence the political situation in Cyprus, except through contributing to a restoration of quiet and thus creating an improved climate in which political solutions may be sought." The SOPs further articulated the "Principles of Peacekeeping" on which peacekeeping duties were to be based. These were as follows:

- negotiation is the primary means of solving problems;
- UNFICYP can only advise, suggest or condemn certain course of action; it has no authority under the Mandate to order either side to take a certain course of action;
- the use of armed force is permissible only in self defence or as a last resort in carrying out he Mandate given to the force;
- all members of UNFICYP must act with restraint and complete impartiality towards both the Greek and Turkish Cypriots; and
- The Government of Cyprus is the legal government of the island and under the Security Council resolution of 4 March 1964 has full responsibility for the restoration and maintenance of law and order.[61]

Although the patrols were intended to reassure the Turkish Cypriots in their sector, there were a number of incidents that demonstrated the operational tenor of the mission. Patrols were often physically "man-handled" by Turkish-Cypriot fighters and at times fired upon. In one instance, a line of stones was placed across a path and Turkish-Cypriot fighters warned the patrol that they would be fired upon if the patrol proceeded further. Sergeant Victor Balkam placed the patrol into arrowhead formation and proceeded to cross the "line of stones." A shot narrowly missed his head and another struck inches from the foot of another soldier. Balkam ignored the shots and calmly led the patrol to its destination. He was later awarded a commendation for his actions "in keeping with the highest principles of peacekeeping."[62]

Despite some confrontation, the initial Cyprus tours for The RCR were largely peaceful. Nonetheless, it provided an operational deployment aside from Germany and one that provided operational experience for soldiers, non-commissioned officers and officers in a "real," unpredictable environment. "The experience of Cyprus," opined one commanding officer, "has enriched the members of the Battalion in various ways: they saw a different way of life, new places and new faces but above all, this enrichment of new knowledge made each appreciate all the more the Canadian atmosphere of peace, order and elected government."[63]

Cyprus, however, was only representative of a growing concept both within the government and senior echelons of the military. Many in both camps believed the idea of strategic mobile forces would be beneficial to the NATO role, as well as to the seemingly expanding government intention to take on a larger international role in assisting with U.N. operations to stabilize a world that seemingly had gone mad.

In fact, regimental officer and former chief of the general staff General Charles Foulkes testified before the Special Committee on Defence that the Canadian defence effort should concentrate on the "operation of a mobile ready reserve available immediately for NATO or to meet an UN task anywhere in the world or maintain our sovereignty in the Arctic."[64] In a similar vein, the outspoken General Guy Simonds recommended the organization of the military along the lines of a "conventionally armed tri-service, highly mobile force adapted to deal with brush-fire wars in support of the United Nations or our allies."[65] The military position being espoused was identical to the new strategic doctrine being implemented by their American counterparts to the south, who were rapidly moving toward more operationally and strategically capable forces.[66]

Concomitant with the growing desire for strategic and tactical mobility, was new government direction led by the new Liberal MND, Paul Hellyer, a strong-willed and ambitious individual with dreams of becoming a future Liberal leader, if not Canadian prime minister. By 1963, the Conservative government of John Diefenbaker had been defeated by the Liberals, and Lester Pearson became the new prime minister. It was not lost on Pearson that Diefenbaker's demise was largely due of the handling of the Cuban Missile Crisis and the Canadian nuclear weapons debate. He blamed the military directly for Diefenbaker's political defeat. His assessment was that the defence establishment was only tenuously under government control. Instead, he perceived, arguably accurately, that the military was focused primarily on alliance duties and largely responsive to allied commanders. Pearson had no plans of suffering the same fate as the previous prime minister. As a result, he directed Hellyer to create a flexible military that was fully responsive to the demands of government, as well as integrating the command structure and unifying the entire armed forces. He also, albeit quietly, instructed his MND to streamline defence and make it more cost efficient.[67]

Besides the direction from the prime minister, Hellyer also derived much of his impetus for change from a 1964 government commission, headed by J. Grant Glassco, which examined government organization. Their findings were not confidence-inspiring. In DND, they found more than two hundred inter-service committees that smothered effective and efficient management and added to delays in projects and waste in general. They noted triplication of such core administrative functions as pay, recruitment public affairs, and intelligence services. Each of the three service chiefs had access to the minister, but there was no mechanism to actually assess the demands of each service. The Glassco Report simply reinforced the Government's perception for the need for change. Integration of the armed forces had been proposed as early as 1922; however, an internal bottom up solution was never achieved. As a result, a top down plan was now about to be imposed.

The first step for the MND was a defence review and the crafting of a new defence white paper. Hellyer took personal ownership of the document and wrote much of it himself. The consequences of his review would have serious consequences for The RCR and the military as a whole. Hellyer reiterated the perennial Canadian reality. Canadian defence was tied up in collective defence as exercised in the U.N. and NATO, as well as the North American partnership with the United States. Then of course there was the "national measures" for domestic defence. To meet all these requirements, Hellyer realized that Canada required a force structure that provided the maximum flexibility that allowed her armed forces to deal with assistance to the civil power; fight small brush-fire wars throughout the globe; participate in U.N. peacekeeping deployments; and fight a possible high-intensity war in Europe.

"The purpose of our forces in being," asserted the MND, was "to preserve peace by deterring war."[68] As such, he intended to restructure the military into a mobile and global force that could meet the widest range of potential requirements in the fastest possible time.[69] In this manner he believed the Canadian military could contain conflict and prevent it from escalating into a more dangerous and less manageable crisis. In the end, Hellyer's flexible, mobile, and global force was designed specifically to "answer the call of the UN or the Western alliance anywhere in the world."[70]

As a result, his plan called for a single unified defence force, which would link the Canadian Forces (CF) to a national strategy. In addition, his vision also included the integration of the three services (i.e. Navy, Army, and Air Force). Together, these steps, he believed, would solve the problems of responsiveness to government and the inefficiencies of the current structure. The reorganization also entailed the replacement of the three service chiefs and service councils with a single chief of the defence staff (CDS) and an integrated defence staff as part of a Canadian Forces headquarters.

Cabinet approved the new white paper, as well as Hellyer's integration proposal on 25 March 1964, thus setting the ball in motion. The second step was the reformation of the military's 11 operational commands. Hellyer trimmed them to six functional commands.[71] One of these commands, Force Mobile Command (FMC), was fundamental to the vision of Hellyer's new structure. As a result, in 1965, FMC became the new organization that was based on the entire Army, as well as elements of the Air Force, which were responsible for supporting and transporting ground troops. The MND proclaimed:

> Mobile Command is basic to the philosophy of Canada's new defence policy. The largest of the new functional commands, its task is to operationally train and maintain the land elements of the Canadian force and its tactical air support, and to keep this force in a state of combat readiness which will enable it to be deployed in units of the required size to meet Canadian commitments and undertakings anywhere in the world. The prime ingredients in the force are quick reaction-time, the ability to go where required with dispatch, and to perform its tasks with maximum effectiveness.[72]

The new changes were introduced aggressively, and not surprisingly resistance throughout the armed forces was present. In 1965, the climate of change had reached such a zenith that Major-General D.C. Spry felt compelled to reassure Royals everywhere. "In a period of rapid change such as we are experiencing now," he counselled, "it is more important than ever that we retain all those traditional aspects of the Regiment which give it its particular esprit, tone and style." Spry reminded all that "The Regiment has experienced many changes of organization, weapons, personnel, locations, assignments and so on, during its recent history." As such, he concluded, "The spirit with which changes are accepted and the loyalty with which they are executed are absolutely essential to successful and happy soldiering."[73]

One of the immediate changes that accompanied unification was felt at the depot. The commanding officer explained, "These changes leave us with the primary responsibility of training recruits of all corps in common to 'All Arms' training and RCR recruits up to infantryman Group 1." He added, "We are under command of Training Command in Winnipeg for all aspects of training. Needless to say our secondary responsibility is still Regimental administration which seems to keep some of us fairly involved a lot of the time."[74]

By 1966, other ramifications became apparent. The white paper represented the beginning of a steady decline of resources the government was willing to provide DND. Budgets were frozen, and from 1963–67, the regular force dropped from 120,781 to 110,000 personnel.[75] And this was just the beginning.

Ominously, that same year, as a result of the reorganization of the Army, the CDS directed a working group under the co-leadership of the regimental colonels from both The RCR and The Canadian Guards to work out a contingency plan to amalgamate the Regiment of Canadian Guards and The Royal Canadian Regiment. "Despite lengthy discussions, which were conducted with a spirit of cooperation and without acrimony, we were unable to make an acceptable plan," revealed the co-chairmen.[76] They explained that their problem was due to a number of unassailable issues. They revealed, "There is no administrative method of amalgamating The Regiment of Canadian Guards and The Royal

Canadian Regiment, because, 'since the Regiment of Canadian Guards stands in a special relationship to the Queen of Canada, no material change in establishment, uniforms or colours can be undertaken without Her Majesty's prior knowledge, or be given effect to without obtaining Her Majesty's prior formal approval through His Excellency The Governor General.'" The co-chairs went on, "Furthermore, 'if a line regiment amalgamates with a regiment of Guards, the resulting regiment, if it is to remain a Guards regiment, must retain the distinguishing marks, duties and responsibilities of a Guards regiment.'" The working group noted, "it is now clear that The Regiment of Canadian Guards, in whole or in part, cannot have its establishment changed nor can it be removed from the Order of Battle of the RCIC except with Her Majesty's prior consent." They also added, "It is also clear that The Royal Canadian Regiment finds itself unable to enter voluntarily into an amalgamation which would require it to surrender its identity and its long-standing characteristics as the senior regular infantry regiment of the line. The Royal Canadian Regiment believes that if it were absorbed in The Canadian Guards, this absorption would not be supported by a large section of the Canadian public."[77]

The exercise and its outcome reflect both the era and the military mindset that existed as a result of the various changes being imposed from above. The working group co-chaired by Major-General R. Rowley (colonel, The Canadian Guards) and Major-General D.C. Spry (colonel, The RCR) decided to reject the task they were given and instead use their mandate to challenge the direction and vision of the MND and CDS. Their misreading of both the intent and will of the very strong-minded MND and the CDS would eventually lead to unfortunate circumstances.[78]

By the mid-1960s, there were many moving parts for DND. There was the ongoing reorganization with its myriad of administrative and organizational consequences; the continuing focus on the NATO commitment; the introduction of large amounts of new equipment and weaponry, as well as doctrine; an increasingly turbulent world with brush-fire wars; and a growing emphasis on strategic mobility and U.N. peacekeeping operations. In the background remained, of course, defence of Canada operations (DCO).

However, domestic defence normally held a low priority because of the actual threat to the nation. The *1964 White Paper* reaffirmed, "It is, for the foreseeable future, impossible to conceive of any significant external threat to Canada which is not also a threat to North America as a whole…. The major threat to North America at this time is from the air."[79] In 1966, The MND reasserted a familiar theme, "forces for the direct protection of Canada remain necessary. While direct attack on Canadian territory is very low in the scale of probability, it is essential to provide appropriate surveillance of our territory and its sea approaches as well as to have the capability of dealing with lodgements of enemy forces in the unlikely event they should occur."[80]

Despite the rhetoric, in fact the government and senior military commanders rejected the need to defend the Arctic for all intents and purposes. Furthermore, the move to strategic mobility placed an even greater pressure on the DCF concept as well. Airborne soldiering, which had been a core component of training and identity to many Royals, had become by the mid-1960s a thing of the past. For example, the 1 RCR rear party in 1965 was required to create an airborne company group. It had been 10 years, 1955 in fact, since the battalion had had an airborne role. As a result, they were required to build the capability almost from scratch.

Nonetheless, by 1967, the DCF requirement had not gone away. The 1 RCR Airborne DCF SOPs clearly articulated the threat as it theoretically existed. "In future war," revealed the document, "there is a possibility that the enemy may launch small-scale Airborne/Airtransported/Amphibious commando-type raids up to company size on coastal areas and against vital points in Canada." Probable enemy missions were defined as:

1. to cause retention of more military forces in Canada than otherwise may be necessary for defence, particularly during mobilization;
2. to destroy facilities vital to the allied war effort and to our warning and air defence systems such as radio stations, radar sites, weather stations and retaliatory forces installations;
3. to establish navigation aids for enemy aircraft, submarines or missiles;

4. to impede the possible reinforcement of forces engaged in defence operations in other regions.[81]

As a result, 1 RCR, as the FMC DCF airborne unit responsible for immediate availability/response to meet the threat, was required to maintain a minimum manning of 60 percent of its authorized establishment. Its parachute element, totalling 250 all ranks, was required to be at full strength at all times.[82] However, reality was somewhat different. The government and senior military commanders continually opted to accept risk with the DCF task. As a result, units assigned the mission often found their DCF personnel and equipment stripped to meet other more pressing demands. In fact, the MND and the CDS conceded to the Special Committee on Defence that "to bring the balance of the [NATO] division up to effective strength and to provide the initial reinforcements for the brigade in Germany, today's emergency plan calls for the withdrawal of a number of troops from the defence of Canada brigade."[83]

The lack of support for the DCF became evident within the units as well. In short, the parachuting legacy of the Royals almost disappeared. By the late 1960s, The RCR paratroopers serving with the DCF complained that there were no special operational SOPs, no special training, and no special equipment. Furthermore, the parachute soldiers perceived that the application of airborne doctrine as disorganized, if it existed at all. The establishment and organization of parachute companies was identical to the other standard rifle companies within the respective battalions. Parachuting was seen strictly as another means to deploy to the battlefield and no effort was made to keep those on jump status current. Paratroopers on average jumped only two to three times a year. One RCR DCF paratrooper remembered that in 18 months he participated in only one parachute company exercise. He added that normally they operated as a normal rifle company, and although the "Jump Company" did in fact have an additional role, namely the defence of the North, it was never exercised. He described the DCF as "essentially a Jump [parachuting] Club."[84] Pat Rossiter agreed. "The jump company, 'B' Coy," he explained, "was a phantom company. When there was an exercise the jumpers in the battalion would be reorganized into 'B' Coy." He recalled, "You needed a couple of days to bring it all together. It was so unoperational. I never did a single tactical drop the whole time I was there [1 RCR]."[85]

Contrary to the importance regimental members derived from the MSF and their maroon berets in the previous decade, little status was pinned to the DCF. Few saw it as a viable airborne force. Most agreed that the jump companies had "no operational rationale or capability, but existed only to keep alive the parachuting capability."[86] Major-General Dan Loomis and Lieutenant-Colonel Swan both asserted that little status was attached to belonging to the Jump Companies because their existence was not much differentiated from the other companies within a battalion. The only distinction was the maroon beret and the jump allowance of $30.00 per month, which represented a substantial pay boost.[87]

The monetary benefit was also seen as a factor contributing to the continuing marginalization of a sound operational airborne capability. "The older guys wanted the money not the jumping," recalled John O'Quinn, "The young guys just wanted to jump." He noted, "To be fair the battalion started to rotate people through positions."[88]

Legendary RCR Chief Warrant Officer B.C. Robinson recalled that the parachute company was often used as a "compassionate posting" for those with financial difficulties.[89] The jump pay premium also created imbalances. "The monetary bonus," noted Swan, "resulted in a disproportionate number of officers and Senior NCOs [non-commissioned officers] filling the officially allocated jump billets." The net result was that motives other the optimal operational effectiveness were used to man the organization.

The final nail in the coffin of the DCF and jump positions within The RCR was the focus on strategic mobility and the creation of the Canadian Airborne Regiment (Cdn AB Regt). Already in 1966, Lieutenant-General Allard, the Commander of FMC, decided that the Canadian Army would develop a rapid reaction and Special Forces capability. Specifically, he aimed to have a completely "airportable" unit that could deploy, with all its equipment, into a designated operational theatre as quickly as 48 hours. As a result, on 12 May 1966, the MND announced, "FMC would include the establishment of an airborne regiment whose personnel and equipment could be rapidly sent to danger zones."[90]

DND, negative CF67-473-62.

An RCR soldier takes up a firing position during a winter "defence of Canada operation" exercise in 1967.

The Army commander believed that "this light unit is going to be very attractive to a fellow who likes to live dangerously, so all volunteers can go into it." His creation was to be open to all three services and manned exclusively by volunteers. "We intend," he asserted, "to look at the individual a little more rather than considering the unit as a large body of troops, some of whom might not be suited for the task."[91] The Cdn AB Regt was officially established on 8 April 1968.[92]

The Cdn AB Regt's mandate was impressive, if not overly optimistic. It was to be the Canadian Forces' "Fire Brigade," capable of performing a variety of tasks that included: the Defence of Canada; the U.N. "stand-by"

Corporal John Wycnch cleans his rifle during a pause in Exercise Praetorium Pacis, 20 February 1968.

role; peacekeeping operations; missions in connection with national disaster; "Special Air Service" (SAS) type missions; coup de main tasks in a general war setting; and responsibility for parachute training in the CF. The respective Canadian Forces Organizational Order (CFOO) stated, "the role of the Canadian Airborne Regiment is to provide a force capable of moving quickly to meet any unexpected enemy threat or other commitment of the Canadian Armed Forces."[93]

With the creation of the Cdn AB Regt, the parachute role within the line infantry regiments ceased to exist. Warrant Officer D.J. Lacroix correctly observed that the jump from a Buffalo aircraft on 25 September 1968, by a group of 1 RCR parachutists over CFB Borden marked an end of an "era in the life of The Regiment."[94] Lacroix poignantly wrote: "We remember the feeling of excitement and close comradeship that always accompanied each jump and the stories afterward." He concluded, "So, another significant chapter is written in the history of the Regiment and it is with a sense of achievement that all members can look back on our activities." He noted, "Many of our jumpers have gone to the Canadian Airborne Regiment and our thoughts will be with them on their jumps. We can only wish this fine new unit the best of luck and we are sure that they will continue, as we in The Regiment, to 'serve with pride.'"[95]

In essence, the parachute legacy of the Royals was carried on in the Cdn AB Regt, as many regimental personnel transferred to the new airborne unit when it formed, and others would continue to do so for years to come. Captain Bob Mahar, one of the first Royals to serve in the Cdn AB Regt recalled, "Royals, here from the beginning, have both benefitted and contributed to the active and varied training [of the new regiment]."[96] In fact, The RCR had from the beginning, and would continue to provide a significant physical component, as well as its special character, to the Cdn AB Regt.

For many there seemed to be no end to change in the 1960s. In 1968, as a result of continuing downsizing, infantry companies were reduced from four rifle companies to only three within a battalion. In Germany, this represented a loss of one quarter of the available Canadian infantry. And things would only get worse.

On 15 May 1968, the Liberal cabinet under Prime Minister Pierre Elliott Trudeau decided to conduct a "comprehensive review" of the current policy, structures, and cost of the Canadian Armed Forces. This included an examination of the Canadian role in NATO to determine whether the standing commitment was still appropriate considering the "current" situation in Europe. The official report argued for status quo,

Photographer Lorne Bamford, Courtesy The RCR Museum and Archives.

RCR recruits from San Leonardo Platoon, The RCR Depot, conduct drills on the 84 mm Carl Gustav anti-tank gun, 1968.

Courtesy Canadian Airborne Forces Museum (CAFM).

End of an era: one of the final DCF jumps made by Royals. As of 8 April 1968, Royals wishing to serve in the airborne role joined the Canadian Airborne Regiment.

but by autumn 1968, the government made a major change to its NATO role. Trudeau cut the commitment to send two brigades to Europe in the event of war. The commitment was reduced to a single brigade. Even this reduced commitment was completely cut by the end of the year. Moreover, Hellyer's reforms had already turned 4 CIBG, renamed 4 Canadian Mechanized Brigade Group, or 4 CMBG, in May 1968, into a lighter force, which made it difficult for the Brigade to fight alongside its more heavily armoured, mechanized, and nuclear-armed allies.

Canada's retrenchment was not well received by its NATO allies, particularly since it came mere weeks after the Soviets had rolled into Czechoslovakia and crushed the "Prague Spring."[97] However, to make up for its cancelled commitments, Canada pledged to contribute a Canadian Air/Sea Transportable (CAST) Combat Group to Norway or Denmark in the event of war.[98]

The government's apparent pull-out from Europe became more entrenched the following year. On 3 April 1969, Trudeau reversed Hellyer's defence focus. Instead, he issued a revised set of national defence priorities. These were:

1. surveillance of our territory and coastline — i.e. protection of Canadian sovereignty;
2. the defence of North America in co-operation with the United States forces;
3. the fulfillment of such NATO commitments as may be agreed upon; and
4. the performance of such international peacekeeping roles as we may from time to time assume.[99]

By the end of the decade, 4 CMBG was slashed from 6,000 to 2,800 personnel, based not on an operational rationale, but simply as an arbitrary cost saving exercise. As such, it was reduced to two infantry battalions of three infantry companies; an armoured regiment of two armoured squadrons and a reconnaissance (recce) squadron; an artillery regiment of M-109s; an engineer squadron; and a service battalion. The

Photographer Warrant Officer A.E. Scott, Courtesy The RCR Museum and Archives.

Private Eddie Leppars, 1 RCR, readies stoves so he can prepare warm meals during a winter exercise, 6 February 1969.

1 SSM Battery was disbanded, and with it, the Canadian Army's nuclear capability. No longer could 4 CMBG defend the right flank of 1 (BR) Corps in NORTHAG, a task for which it had trained since 1957.

Photographer Warrant Officer A.E. Scott, Courtesy The RCR Museum and Archives.

A 1 RCR patrol returns along the beach back to its bivouac as part of its jungle training during Exercise Nimrod Caper, 18 March 1969.

Major-General de Faye noted, "the reduction in the size of the force and the redeployment of focus to the Central region was undertaken without significant negotiation with NATO members." He asserted, "It created a defensive gap in the North and led to Canadian forces being placed on airfields." He also felt that this "led to a new period of searching for a meaningful role, as well as the requirement to rebuild our credibility with American, French and German forces."[100] As if there was not enough change already, it also meant 4 CMBG would move from Soest to Lahr and Baden.

But when it rains, it pours. Approximately three weeks later, the new MND, Léo Cadieux, announced to DND and Canadians that the CF would be cut by 20 percent to just above 80,000 personnel and that the reserves were to be slashed to 19,000. Moreover, The Canadian Guards, the Queen's Own Rifles, the Black Watch, and the Fort Garry Horse were all to disappear from the regular force order of battle. Third battalions, however, were added to The RCR and the PPCLI. Also, the Army created two new French language units (one artillery and one armoured). Finally, he announced

Courtesy The RCR Museum and Archives.

A M113 APC with a 106 mm recoilless rifle swims the Ottawa River, 1969.

that the defence budget was capped at $1.8 billion for the next three years.[101]

And so ended the 1960s, a decade marked by dramatic, if not turbulent change. The impacts would directly affect The RCR as it prepared to enter the 1970s. It would effect the make-up and character of the Regiment; how it was organized, as well as how it fought and where it fought. For many, the Regiment, particularly during such dynamic times, provided the necessary bedrock of stability. "It sometimes seems as if the whole world has gone through some sort of traumatic crisis," lamented Prince Philip in an address to members of all RCR battalions. "There are signs everywhere of unrest and confusion and it is just at times like these that sensible people need something solid and reliable to hold on to."[102]

The colonel-in-chief of the Regiment was not alone in his observations. Colonel P.R. Bingham also provided calming advice to Royals everywhere. "In the process of rebuilding," he asserted, "Many old and cherished customs will have to give way, sad as it well be. This is not a new experience for servicemen; in time, the new becomes old and cherished too." He explained, "Traditional symbols in one form or other will be retired in the time-honoured custom of the service; in time, these will be replaced by equally respected symbols like the new Canadian Armed Forces Ensign, impressive in design and colour, which took its place of honour to mark the formation of the single service." Bingham went on to add, "In the days ahead, it may be necessary to remember that The Regiment, since those far-off days of 1883, has seen organization and re-organization, naming and re-naming, increase and drastic decrease, hot wars and a cold war, yet through them all, the problems, large and small, were faced, overcome and are now part of the history of The Regiment."[103]

3

A Shift in Focus: Defence in the 1970s

The 1960s had proven to be a turbulent era of change for the Royal Canadians in a myriad of ways. Organizational, doctrinal, and philosophical transformation altered the landscape of the Army and the Canadian Forces in general. New equipment and operational doctrine changed the way Royals would fight. Politically directed policies and decisions fundamentally, as well as dramatically, altered many aspects of the Army and CF culture and make-up. It also began to drive a renewed emphasis on "Canada First" and a clear policy of downsizing budgets, manning, and the emphasis on Europe and NATO. In fact, it laid the groundwork for a new defence policy that would shift CF priorities.

For the Royal Canadians, the new decade ushered in was to be a fresh start. But, it seemed as if the turbulence of the last decade would not end. Change and adaptation would have to become the norm. And, the Regiment, as it had always done through its rich history, rose to the challenge. But then it had no choice, as 1970 began with a series of daunting challenges.

The first major challenge struck to the core of the Regiment. It pertained to the actual reorganization of the CF that was directed in the dying days of the 1960s. It entailed the closing down of some regiments, the creation of new regiments, and the amalgamation of yet others. The

RCR was not untouched, as it was ordered to absorb elements of the Canadian Guards and the Royal Highland Regiment of Canada (RHC), better known as the "Black Watch." For those who have served in proud, distinguished regiments, the implications of this directive is transparent. The execution of the order brings with it great sadness and a degree of resentment.

In addition, other constraints imposed by the department also created some challenges. For instance, fiscal economy was to be practiced, so therefore the conversion of 2 RHC in Gagetown to a RCR unit was timed to coincide with the move of 2 RCR from Northwest Europe back home to Canada. As a result, Lieutenant-Colonel G.S. Morrison found himself the CO of 2 RHC one day and then the CO of 2 RCR the next. Brigadier-General Jim Cox remembered, "We marched off the parade square as the Black Watch on 30 June 1970, and then the next day, Canada day, we marched in the gates of CFB Gagetown with our Colours as 2 RCR."[1]

Joe Aitcheson, then a young officer, recalled, "The announcement that the other regiments would be reduced was delivered to the unit when we were in the field on a major exercise. The Canadian Brigade 'stood down' from the exercise to permit all ranks to be informed of the Government decision." He described, "I was commanding 'B' Coy at the time and was called to the CO's caravan along with the other OCs (one of whom was Black Watch) where the CO informed us of the message that had been received and gave each of us a copy of the message that was to be read to the troops (and a shot of cognac as I recall)."

Aitcheson lamented:

> I'll never forget reading out the message. The Coy was in a woods and it was raining and generally miserable. It was the middle of the night. I stood on the ramp of my carrier along with my CSM — Dave Rennie — who was holding a Coleman lantern to provide me light to read. I read the message with tears rolling down my cheeks — all I could think of was how I would react if I were informed that my Regiment was to "disappear" — it was a bad day.[2]

Needless to say, such a rapid conversion comes with some trials and tribulations. "The Royal Canadian Regiment represents a new association, an abrupt change, and in many respects a totally new way of regimental life," explained Morrison. He added, "we are trying to learn the new traditions and embrace the deeper meaning of the Regiment but for a time some of the customs will be very strange to us and I hope we will all be forgiven if occasionally some obviously Highland traits are carried into our new Regiment by us."[3]

Others were not as diplomatic. Master Warrant Officer John MacNeil stated, "it was a total disaster for the battalion. We really didn't want to do it." He revealed, "It was a sad day for us. We only had about a week's notice." MacNeil noted, "For the first year our traditions were kept. The name changed but not much else." He explained, "However, as more RCR personnel were posted in we started to incorporate the changes."[4]

Another convert remembered the first days differently as well. He quipped, "Which way do you point these beavers on the tunic.... Your whistle cord is on backwards — what's a whistle cord? ... No you can't

Courtesy The RCR Museum and Archives.

Two Royals stand guard at a VIP residence during OP Ginger, Ottawa, October 1970.

Members of 2 RCR provide security for the airfield at St. Hubert during OP Essay, Montreal, October 1970.

wear your Red Hackle behind your cap badge ,... starched bush pants, polished combat boots, accoutrements sewn on the sweater — I know we're now in the RCR but this is ridiculous."[5]

For those who converted, the experience was clearly traumatic. But for the Royals coming into a unit that was formerly Black Watch and just recently converted with the bulk of the members still "Highlanders," it was similarly disconcerting. Eric McArthurs, then a subaltern, recalled when he arrived to 2 RCR in the early seventies, the unit was "essentially a Black Watch battalion with RCR trappings."[6]

The other RCR battalions did not escape unscathed from the turmoil of the reorganization in 1970. 1 RCR took a lot of members from the disbanded Guards Regiment. In addition, 3 RCR, the Regiment's militia component was forced to change its designation to 4 RCR to make way for the addition of a regular force third battalion based on the conversion of a Canadian Guards (Cdn Gds) battalion. There was an attempt by the commander, Force Mobile Command, based on the request of

Major-General D.C. Spry, that 3 RCR, the reserve battalion, retain its designation, and the rebadging of 2 Cdn Gds to an RCR battalion take the designation 4 RCR. The FMC commander, Lieutenant-General G.A. Turcot, stated: "To redesignate this Battalion [militia 3 RCR] as the 4th Battalion would have a very detrimental effect on the high spirits and morale of the unit and would cause a number of administrative problems concerning disposition of Colours, etc…. For this reason, I recommend that the personnel of the 2nd Battalion, The Canadian Guards be remustered to form the 4th Battalion, The Royal Canadian Regiment."[7] In the end, his request was not granted. All reserve battalions took on the designation 4th battalion, and 2 Cdn Gds became 3 RCR.[8]

The turmoil did not end there. For Royals in 2 RCR in Germany, most did not make the move back home. Instead they were posted to a new unit, 3 Mechanized Commando (3 Mech Cdo), which was a hybrid of members from The RCR and the PPCLI who were deployed in Germany. The Regimental journal captured the historic moment: "At 1010 hours on 28 June 1970 at Sennelager, when Lieutenant-Colonel C.B. Snider ordered the General Salute by 3 Mechanized Commando and engines roared in a mechanical accompaniment, all on parade realized that a new era for the Canadian Forces (Land) had commenced. 2 RCR and 2 PPCLI, two of the former infantry battalions of 4 CMBG had returned to Canada; yet they had left almost half their numbers behind. These officers and men now were on parade for the formation of their new unit which was to be part of the Canadian Airborne Regiment."[9] Because of the torrential rain that fell during the parade, the *Beaver* (the CF newspaper in Europe) ran the caption *Born in a Storm* when reporting on the event.[10]

The new unit was an anomaly. It was manned largely by Royals and Patricias, and was fully mechanized, but belonged to an airborne regiment.[11] Captain Bill Aikman recalled, "This combination of two different regimental backgrounds [RCR and PPCLI], plus the fact that three regular force infantry regiments were reduced to nil strength at approximately the same time, made for some interesting experiences when the unit began to organize at Fort York near Soest in April 1970. During the first few weeks, 3 Mechanized Commando looked more like a reincarnation of the Devil's

Brigade than anything else, as soldiers from different regiments marched about in a variety of caps, belts, boots and insignia."[12]

The new unit was clearly a hybrid and represented an expedient solution to a potentially acrimonious dispute. In fact it was an easy out for NDHQ to name it as a unit of the Cdn AB Regt, thus, avoiding the necessity of creating a new regiment to account for the composite nature of 3 Mech Cdo. After all, its creation was based on the FMC reorganization of 1969–70. The old structure had 11 infantry battalions (2nd Cdn Gds; 1, 2 RCR; 1, 2 PPCLI; 1, 2, and 3 R22eR; 1 and 2 RHC; and 1 QOR of C), as well as the Cdn AB Regt consisting of two commandos. The reorganization cut several regiments but established three battalions for each of the RCR, PPCLI, and R22eR. Therefore, the new structure now had nine infantry battalions and the Cdn AB Regt, consisting of two airborne commandos and a mechanized battalion, which allowed the 11 battalion structure to remain.[13] Regardless, 3 Mech Cdo's strong Royal constituency ensured that it was woven into the fabric of The RCR.[14]

It seemed like change just wouldn't stop. On top of the organizational alterations, those in Germany also had to deal with a move. Canadians were moving from Soest, where they had established firm roots and an exemplary relationship with their hosts, to the South to Baden-Soellingen and Lahr. "The move south to the area of the 'Black Forest' has been received with mixed feelings," acknowledged Lieutenant-Colonel J.A. Cowan, the CO of 2 RCR. "We in the Royal Canadian Regiment share with our colleagues in the Canadian Guards very fond memories of our past association with the City of Soest and surrounding area. The friendship that now exists with the local population is the result of tremendous efforts." He added, "It is not easy to say farewell to such a fine overseas home but like any professional soldier we accept the decision to re-locate without question."[15]

But as always, the realities of service quickly refocus attention on operational realities. For 1 RCR, a deployment to Cyprus in March 1970 quickly grabbed their attention. In late March 1970, 1 RCR took over duties in the Nicosia District during a period of high tension between the Greek and Turkish Cypriots. The island had a population of 600,000 Cypriots. Of these, 80 percent were of Greek and 18 percent of Turk origin. In 1964, the U.N. sent approximately 7,000 troops, of which about 1,000 were Canadian.[16] From 1964–70 the Canadians were responsible for a 880-kilometre-district from Nicosia north to the coast, including part of the Kyrenian mountain range. However, in March 1970, Canadians took over Nicosia and began to patrol the hot, dusty streets of the capital, as well as the countryside to the south. The responsibility for the 1,800-square-kilometre Nicosia district, which extended for 40 kilometres south of the city into the foothills of the Troodos Mountains, belonged to 1 RCR.

On 17 June, the 1 RCR UNFICYP contingent HQ moved into Wolseley Barracks in Nicosia, making it the first Canadian contingent to complete a tour in the new U.N. district that encompassed the central portion of the island and the whole of the capital city of Nicosia. In addition, they set up a joint operations centre with the Danish Civilian Police, which was another historical benchmark. It was the first time in U.N. history that a joint military and police headquarters was established. The operations centre entailed a duty room shared with Danish and Canadian duty officers, adjoining offices for the commanders and a daily briefing at 0800 hours, involving the commander and second-in-command of the Danish police, and the CO and operations officer of 1 RCR.

The operations centre was a needed addition to deal with the mission. A force structure review at the time noted that "The environment in which the Canadian Contingent finds itself in Nicosia is both complex and tense with a potential for becoming hostile at no notice in an unpredictable fashion."[17] But that is exactly why the Royals found themselves in the idyllic Mediterranean island. Their aim as part of UNFICYP was, after all, to: (a) to prevent a recurrence of fighting; (b) to contribute to the restoration and maintenance of law and order; and (c) to contribute to a return to normal conditions.[18] However, there were a number of constraints and restrictions. Standing Operating Procedures (SOPs) dictated:

> The principles on which peace-keeping duties are to be based are as follows: a. Negotiation is the primary means of solving problems; b. UNFICYP can only advise, suggest or condemn certain courses of action; it has no

authority under the Mandate to order either side to take a certain course of action; c. The use of armed force is permissible only in self-defence or as a last resort in carrying out the mandate given to the Force; d. All members of UNFICYP must act with restraint and complete impartiality towards both Greek and Turkish Cypriots; e. The Government of Cyprus is the legal government of the island and under the Security Council resolution of 4 March 1964, has full responsibility for the restoration and maintenance of law and order.[19]

For the peacetime, Cold War–centric Army, Cyprus provided an operational distraction. It was an opportunity to deploy a unit on a real mission, which allowed the unit to bond and test itself. Warrant Officer D.J. Lacroix noted, "Our young soldiers are doing very well. They look quite neat and soldierly on duty along the Green Line and we can be proud of them. This is certainly a great experience for them and I can see evidence already that they are maturing a lot with the various responsibilities they have here."[20]

But operations in Cyprus were not the only operational challenge of the new decade. Unbeknownst to many and unimaginable to most, Royals would soon deploy onto Canadian streets. As always, time has a way of washing away the sense of urgency and crisis. However, the call-out of troops at the time was dramatic and pressing. It was, however, not without warning. It was preceded by years of escalating violence. Québécois revolutionary ideologues formed a secret group called the Comité de libération nationale (CLN) in October 1962. This group called for the violent overthrow of the capitalist system and the establishment of an independent socialist Quebec state. Operating under the cover of, and within, a legitimate political party, namely the Rassemblement pour l'indépendance nationale (RIN), the CLN changed its name to Front de libération du Québec (FLQ) in February 1963 and began a serious bombing campaign.

They struck quickly. On 7 March 1963, the FLQ set a wooden Canadian National Railway (CNR) building in Montreal aflame with a gasoline bomb. The following month they graduated to dynamite as the weapon of choice. Nine buildings were quickly targeted. These included: military recruiting offices, an RCMP building, a radio/television tower, Canadian Legion offices, and an oil refinery. Overall the bombs did little damage, but on 20 April 1963, William O'Neil, the janitor at a recruiting office, was killed in one of the attacks. On 17 May, six more bombs exploded in Westmount mailboxes and a further five bombs were dismantled. That same day Master Warrant Officer Walter Leja, a Royal Canadian Engineer (RCE) demolition expert, was critically wounded during the process of try-ing to dismantle a bomb.[21]

The FLQ increased its pressure the following year. Four Montreal militia armouries were raided by the Armée de libération du Québec (ALQ), which was in effect several FLQ cells combined. They stole FNC1 and FNC2 assault rifles, Bren guns, sub-machine guns, pistols, and ammunition, as well as several mortars and rocket launchers. When the Canadian Forces placed armed guards from the regular force (R22eR) on armouries and released militia members with FLQ ties, the FLQ turned its attention to local gun stores. On 29 August 1964, two civilians were killed in an abortive raid on the International Firearms Limited store in Montreal. The FLQ also turned to armed bank robbery during this period to raise the necessary funds to finance its activities.[22]

By the summer of 1966, bombings and bank robberies were once again on the increase, with a resultant two additional civilian deaths.[23] The unrest grew by 1968, and the bombings continued. A major riot on 24 June 1968, during the St-Jean-Baptiste Day celebrations, resulted in 135 persons injured, 290 arrested, and 12 police cars burned. A firebomb was also hurled at Pierre Elliott Trudeau, later acknowledged by the FLQ as an attempt to kill the future Canadian prime minister. Later that fall, another 35 bombs were exploded in Montreal targeting government buildings, English-owned businesses, and defence contractors. By the end of the year, bombings in Montreal alone had reached 50 for the year. In addition, significantly, on 31 December 1968, the FLQ planted four bombs in front of government buildings in Ottawa.[24]

The insurrectionist activity continued in 1969. More dynamite and weapons were stolen. In February two militia armouries were bombed, as well as the Liberal Reform Club and the Queen's Printers office. On

13 February, the FLQ struck the Montreal and Canadian Stock Exchange, injuring 27 people. The following month, McGill University Marxist Professor S. Gray, an active supporter of the FLQ, organized a massive demonstration outside the university in an attempt to force the government to convert it into a French language university. A total of 9,000 demonstrators armed with gasoline bombs, rocks, batons, and chairs clashed with a security force of 1,700 police (municipal, QPP, RCMP) and 1,000 utility crews and firemen, with a battalion of 3 R22eR in reserve.

By late 1969, it became apparent that the FLQ movement was seriously undermining Quebec society. Bombings, robberies, and riots were actively undertaken. A police investigation focused on the Company of Young Canadians (CYC) concluded that the the organization had diverted funds and material to the FLQ, and up to 20 of its members were involved with terrorist activity on behalf of the FLQ. Documents captured revealed the FLQ had developed an elaborate plan that included:

- Enlisting working class support by legal and illegal acts to build up a broad base of support. To assist in this the FLQ organized various front organizations;
- Organizing violent street demonstrations to support strikes, intimidate juries, disrupt vital services, etc;
- Terrorism such as bombings, interference with elections and harassment of prominent officials; and
- Guerrilla warfare.[25]

By the end of 1969, the FLQ had implemented the first three categories and seemed to be in the process of planning and preparing for the fourth. They had stolen large quantities of weapons (estimated at up to 500 small arms), and members conducted training in Northern Quebec, as well as in Cuba and Jordan.[26]

Things only became worse in 1970. Politically motivated violence increased, as did the bombings. On 26 February, Pierre Marcil and Jacques Lanctôt were arrested for plotting to kidnap the Israeli consul general in Montreal.[27] On 24 April 1970, Block "B" of NDHQ was attacked. The explosion killed Jeanne D'Arc Saint-Germain, a 50-year-old female public servant. Shortly thereafter, a Hull armoury was attacked in a bid to steal more weapons. In June, bomb disposal experts defused the largest bomb yet seen when they successfully dismantled a 150-pound bomb contained in a vehicle in Montreal. That same month police raided a cottage in the Laurentians and captured weapons and explosives, as well as plans to kidnap the U.S. Consul-General in Montreal. In September and October, dynamite thefts in the period alone accounted for 9,110 sticks of dynamite, forcing the Quebec government to impose wartime controls on the possession and use of explosives. Clearly, the FLQ was gearing up its campaign.

Based on a leaked report, the RCMP believed that there were 22 active FLQ cells in the province, with a total membership of approximately 130 individuals. The RCMP also estimated that there were an additional 2,000 members not actively engaged in the work of the cells. Gérard Pelletier, the secretary of state for external affairs, "estimated that in October 1970 the FLQ appeared to consist of four elements: first, a nucleus of up to 100 extremists ready to plant bombs, carry out kidnappings, even to commit murders; second, a more limited group, or 'permanent cell,' holding itself apart from violent action, which constituted the editorial and propagandist element of the FLQ; third, a ring of 200 to 300 active sympathizers prepared to support the terrorists by financial aid, concealment, and to otherwise provide supportive infrastructure; and fourth, a periphery of some 2,000 to 3,000 more or less passive sympathizers who, without formally being members of the FLQ, desired its victory or approved its methods."[28]

There was also a Cuban connection. Radio Havana broadcast a half-hour program in French daily for FLQ activists, and Cuban newspapers carried stories of training camps in the Cuban mountains teaching subversion, terrorism, and guerrilla warfare.[29] Not surprisingly, the RCMP security service produced a threat report in July 1970 that reported the situation was "extremely confusing, complex and constantly changing." Moreover, it concluded, "the total of the activities carried out ... clearly represents a threat to the unity of the country."[30]

The government took action. Its immediate objective was to contain the situation and create confidence in the legitimate governments and non-confidence in the FLQ. Moreover, it attempted to pre-empt and dislocate the FLQ at every turn and isolate it from the mainstream of provincial political discourse at all levels in Quebec. It had some success and was able to arrest a number of FLQ members and prevent a number of high-profile kidnappings.

However, despite its achievements, on 5 October a four-man FLQ cell kidnapped British Trade Commissioner James Cross in Montreal. Five days later, Quebec Labour Minister Pierre Laporte was kidnapped by another FLQ cell. For their release the FLQ demanded $500,000 in gold, the release of 23 terrorists, the rehiring of the Lapalme workers, an end to police investigation of the FLQ, wide news media coverage of the FLQ Manifesto, and the disclosure of the name of an informant.[31]

The provincial Liberal premier, Robert Bourassa, was shaken by the kidnappings, as well as by the continuing rallies conducted by students, labour militants, and separatists. He believed that his government could be toppled. In Ottawa, Prime Minister Pierre Elliott Trudeau decided to intervene in a dramatic fashion to prevent public opinion from being influenced by the revolutionary rhetoric. On 12 October 1970, he ordered troops into the streets of Ottawa to guard public buildings and senior political figures. Operation Ginger (OP Ginger), the code name assigned to the mission, commenced with the movement of troops at 1315 hours, 12 October. Lieutenant J. Collinson recalled the surprise order had a dramatic effect. He stated: "Orders groups came fast and furious and everything had to be done NOW!"[32]

Trudeau decided that the CF would be used to supplement the RCMP on protective and security duties in Ottawa under the "assist civil authorities" statue, which means that one government department is assigned to assist another government agency (i.e. DND to assist RCMP). In Quebec, troops were used under the statutory provisions of the National Defence Act (NDA) dealing with the liability of the CF to be called out for service in "aid of the civil power," which requires the submission of a request by the attorney general of a province to the federal government.

On 12 October, 3 RCR deployed to Ottawa on OP Ginger. "I remember thinking to myself," wrote Lieutenant Collinson, "my god, here I am in my own country's capital wearing a loaded pistol! I'm sure the rest of my fellow Canadians were at least as shocked as I was."[33]

Three days later, Premier Bourassa requested aid to the civil power. Operation Essay, the CF code name for its mission in Quebec, began at 1245 hours, 15 October 1970, when the government of Quebec requisition for troops was signed by the Quebec justice minister. As a result, 3 RCR was quickly deployed to Montreal and came under command of 5 Combat Brigade Group (CBG). Vital Point (VP) protection tasks in OP Essay alone had soldiers deployed to 107 locations in Quebec from Val d'Or to Rimouski. One Royal assessed, "Looking back on the total situation, our troops in Westmount added to the effectiveness of the police patrols as well as acting as a deterrent for crime in the city. Of course, the presence of troops in station itself helped to prevent any attempts of sabotage. This area was the most heavily bombed part of Montreal since 1963."[34]

OP Essay now ensnared 2 RCR as well. On 15 October, when the CO of 2 RCR received his warning order for internal security duties in Quebec, his battalion was scattered in a 40-kilometre radius of Hibernia, which itself was 65 kilometres from their unit lines on the base. Nonetheless, within four hours the unit was ready to emplane, and by the next morning the battalion was on the ground at CFB Montreal's St. Hubert Air Base.[35] For example, "D" Coy, which was deployed in the field, received radio orders to muster in the drill hall, and so "began one of the wildest rides in the history of Gagetown. Ten hours after the order was given to muster at the Drill Hall, all of 'D' Company person-nel were in Montreal."[36] Most men were unable to call or go home before deploying to Quebec. The designation for 2 RCR was FMC reserve force. However, very quickly FMC HQ tasked them with VP and VIP security in Montreal: "2 RCR outposts sprung up on the island of Montreal and in suburbs, some of which were over a hundred miles from the city."[37]

But the deployment of troops throughout Quebec was only part of the unfolding drama. The following morning, at 0400 hours, 16 October, Trudeau invoked the War Measures Act to allow the authorities to deal with what he considered "a state of apprehended insurrection."[38] This was done in response to letters from the Quebec provincial government and Montreal municipal authorities. That morning, Prime Minister Trudeau appeared on television and addressed the nation. He stated:

> I am speaking to you at a moment of grave crisis, when violent and fanatical men are attempting to destroy the unity and freedom of Canada. If a democratic society is to continue to exist, it must be able to root out the cancer of an armed revolutionary movement that is bent on destroying the very basis of our freedom. For that reason the Government, following an analysis of the facts, including requests of the Government of Quebec and the City of Montreal for urgent action, decided to proclaim the War Measures Act. It did so at 4:00 a.m. this morning, in order to permit the full weight of the Government to be brought quickly to bear on all those persons advocating or practicing violence as a means of achieving political ends.[39]

Time has a means of mellowing all crisis and feelings. However, the lead-up to the kidnappings, as well as FLQ rhetoric created a sense of insurrection. After all, a week before the kidnappings, the FLQ announced, "The strategic objective is clear to all [Quebec revolutionaries]: the destruction of the Capitalist society and the construction of an egalitarian, just and free society founded on the practice of collective self-determination at all levels (economic, administrative, school and cultural)." The article went on to explain that "here in Quebec, the fight for the destruction of the capitalist system is inseparable from the struggle for national independence. One will not go far without the other."[40] Furthermore, it espoused, "Since 1963 and the explosions of the first FLQ bombs, we find ourselves in this first step of the revolutionary struggle and will progress as far as generalized agitation culminating in a social, economic and political crisis."[41]

In the end, Trudeau did not hesitate to act. That morning the police acted quickly and arrested 154 persons, including known FLQ members and high-profile sympathizers (e.g. intellectuals, entertainers, media figures). All were held without laying specific charges and none were granted bail.[42] But neither did the FLQ. The next day, 17 October 1970, they replied to the government decree. They murdered Pierre Laporte, the Quebec minister of labour, and dumped his body in the trunk of a green Chevrolet, which they parked outside the military base at St. Hubert.

The murder, however, had the opposite effect the FLQ had been hoping for. Public support rallied behind the established governments at all levels and denounced the savage act. On 25 October, Jean Drapeau was returned overwhelmingly as mayor of Montreal with a solid vote, and on 1 November, Robert Bourassa's Liberals were returned with a solid majority to the Quebec provincial legislature. Lieutenant-Colonel Dan Loomis wrote in his diary, "In the general context the revolutionaries, and in particular the FLQ, suffered a severe tactical reverse. This tactical reverse was confirmed at the polls in the Montreal civic elections on 25 Oct 70 and the subsequent Quebec provincial elections of 1 Nov 70."[43] Reflecting on his comments years later, he noted that it was a strategic reverse they had suffered, not a tactical one.

These events spurred the recall of 1 RCR. For them it was just back from Cyprus to deployed in Ottawa in less than a week. Most of the unit was on disembarkation leave when the word went out to recall everyone for operational duty. As one Royal noted, "there was a certain air of disbelief as we sought the FLQ in the misty early morning around the Low Dam and in the cold evenings on top of the Val Tetreau power Station. It seemed unreal that this could be happening in our country, especially, since most of us thought of the Cypriot socio-economic problems as being rather unfashionable or archaic for the latter part of the twentieth century."[44]

The recall and move for 1 RCR from London to Rockcliffe began at 1545 hours, 17 October and ended 19 October.[45] On 20 October 1970, BHQ and "A" Coy deployed to Area "E" in the Western Quebec region (encompassing Hull, Thurso, Montpellier, Low, Otter Lake, and Campbell's Lake, a total of 3,200 square miles). Tasks assigned under Aid to Civil Power were:

- secure bases;
- protect VIPs and VPs; and
- be prepared (on two hours notice to move) to conduct cordon and search operations; and be prepared support other units of the Combat Group.

1 RCR eventually totalled 665 in the field. Its mechanized company did not deploy with its armoured fighting vehicles (AFVs), but as a rifle company. BH HQ augmented its size with officers from the rifle companies because of the large liaison cell. In the first 24 hours the battalion stayed in Rockcliffe, and the troops received briefings and refresher training on:

a. QR & O chap 23 — Aid to the Civil Power;
b. The Public Order 1970;
c. Power of Arrest;
d. Orders for opening fire/minimum force; and
e. Duties of Sentries/Challenging procedure.[46]

"A" Coy (augmented with additional platoons from "B" and "C" Coys) was tasked with VIP/VP tasks. It was allocated 18 VIP and VP locations to protect in Hull and Area "E." This translated to 70 soldiers on duty at a time for 12 hour durations. VIP protection entailed the protection of the VIP, family, and property. Soldiers were detailed to guard the likely access areas to the home, deny entry of all personnel to the property and home until they were identified by the occupants, and to be alert for any suspicious cars or people near the residence. If the VIP moved from the house, a soldier would provide an escort and report the location to Coy HQ. The VIP could call for an escort at any time. Guards were armed with first line ammunition.[47]

The remainder of the battalion was given a myriad of tasks. "B" Coy remained in Rockcliffe attached to and under command 2 RCHA. "C" Coy also remained in Rockcliffe as the reserve company. Finally, "D" Coy was tasked with area reconnaissance and as a reserve. It conducted lots of three man patrols in 1/4-ton and 3/4-ton vehicles. Area "E" was divided into three sub-areas and assigned to platoons. The entire area was eventually, once all were familiar with it, split into 14 search zones. The patrols would visit major VP sites and drive the major road networks searching for suspicious and unusual activity. Also informal contact with the population was made, which by all reports was friendly and co-operative.

The biggest problem in all operations was the inadequate radio equipment that was not capable of long range communications for the widely dispersed elements. Also, there was a huge lack of French language capability within the unit, since only about 25 members in 1 RCR could speak French.

On 22 October 1970, the battalion undertook OP Underbrush, which was a cordon and search operation in Luskville. "B" Coy provided road blocks and "C" and "D" Coys provided search platoons. At 1400 hours, the companies were ordered to move. To ensure surprise, no prior reconnaissance was conducted. In essence, the operation was mounted off the line of march. The mission was completed by 1705 hours with no major results. One civilian was detained by police for having a disassembled .303 calibre rifle in his vehicle, and a reporter was detained for trying to photograph the operation. One opportunity, however, was lost. A car acting as an outpost starting blaring its horn as a platoon neared an objective. The platoon halted and spent 10 minutes searching the individual and vehicle before moving on to the compound of buildings nearby, allowing any individuals inside to escape.

By the beginning of November the crisis began to ease, and 1 RCR was withdrawn from Hull, returning to London on 5 November 1970. About a week later, on 13 November, 3 RCR returned to CFB Petawawa.[48] On 2 December a major break in the crisis occurred. Two people were arrested, and police now had good reason to believe they had found the house where James Cross was being held. At midnight that night, the authorities decided to conduct a raid. The CF cordoned off the area and provided explosive ordnance disposal (EOD). At 0830 hours, 3 December, the cordon and raid was conducted. The police had been correct. However, the raid led to a stand-off and negotiations. That evening the exchange was made. James Cross was released on St. Helene Island, and the kidnappers were flown by military helicopter to Dorval airport where they boarded a CF Yukon aircraft, special flight 602, and flew to Havana International Airport.[49]

In essence, this was the final chapter of the FLQ crisis. OP Ginger had already ended on 21 November, and OP Essay was officially terminated at 1200 hours, 4 January, a month after the release of British Trade

Commissioner James Cross. Throughout the crisis, the Regiment played an instrumental role, and it was not to be the last in an aid to the civil power capacity.

In fact, Royals were called on sooner than anticipated to assist their civilian colleagues. Late in the day, on 14 April 1971, approximately 500 prisoners at the maximum security Kingston Penitentiary seized six hostages and took over control of the main cell block. They then proceeded to smash the cell locking system. At 2355 hours that night, Warden Arthur Jarvis notified the base commander at CFB Kingston that he would require assistance. He requested the provision of "no less than 100 troops to aid the prison officers in maintaining security, external to the Main Cell Block which is being held forcibly by inmates."[50] By 0600 hours, 145 members from CFB Kingston were on site and 3 RCR was in the process of deploying. In fact, at 0400 hours on 15 April 1971, officer commanding (OC) "A" Coy was placed on 30 minutes notice to move as of 0830 hours. At 1000 hours, "A" Coy Recce Group had arrived at CFB Kingston and was briefed on the situation. By 1330 hours troops were formally committed to the penitentiary, and at 1830 hours that evening, members of 3 RCR marched through the gates onto the grounds of Kingston Penitentiary and immediately deployed to secure the perimeter. The presence of the troops made an immediate impression. "Prior to 'A' Coy marching in, the inmates had been chanting and beating metal objects inside. When the inmates saw the Company march in, a sudden silence descended and one observer had the impression that 'the spirit of the rebellion had been broken.'"[51]

The remainder of 3 RCR's committed troops ("A" and "B" Coys, as well as Armoured Defence and Mortar Platoons) arrived in Kingston that night by 2130 hours and were stationed in CFB Kingston. Within 48 hours of the crisis commencing, 3 RCR had in essence deployed three rifle companies and the CO, Lieutenant-Colonel G.R. Cheriton, had taken command of the military operation, which was code named OP Pelican. The task was somewhat surreal. "Kingston Penitentiary at first glance," observed one Royal, "looked exactly like an MGM movie production lot, but further experience proved that it was definitely of the realistic school."[52]

Courtesy The RCR Museum and Archives.

A hybrid born from necessity, mixing both soldiers from The RCR and the PPCLI. Shown is a 3 Mechanized Commando camp.

At 0530 hours, on 18 April, negotiators had finally broken the impasse. Soon groups of 60 prisoners began to voluntarily leave the main cell block. One by one the hostages were also released. By 1800 hours that night, all prisoners and hostages were accounted for. With the crisis over, 3 RCR was relieved of its duties at 2000 hours and the troops returned to Petawawa.[53]

Although the sudden emphasis on internal security operations and aid to the civil power was fundamentally opposed to the CF's primary focus on NATO operations and conventional high-intensity war to counter Soviet and Warsaw Pact forces, they did seem in perfect consonance with the government's new "Canada first" policy. In fact, the new defence white paper had laid out a whole new direction for national defence.

On 24 August 1971, the MND, Donald MacDonald, released the new document *Defence in the 70s: White Paper on Defence*. It gave internal security a high priority. In addition, it gave the Department of National Defence an important role in national development including assistance in natural disasters, as well as in research, communications and protection of the environment, which were new responsibilities. The white paper stated defence of North America was the second priority (mainly an air force task) and committed to no more reductions with regard to Canadian contributions to NATO than those already imposed at the end of the 1960s. It also clearly stated that peacekeeping was the last priority for the CF. In fact, the white paper tasks were clearly delineated as:

a. the surveillance of our own territory and coastlines, i.e. the protection of our sovereignty;
b. the defence of North America in co-operation with United States forces;
c. the fulfillment of such NATO commitments as may be agreed upon; and
d. the performance of such international peacekeeping roles as we may, from time to time, assume.[54]

Not surprisingly, the white paper clearly stated: "the threat to society posed by violent revolutionaries and the implications of the recent crisis … merited close consideration in projecting Canadian defence activities in the 1970s."[55] This was juxtaposed against other threats Canada faced, which were seen as minimal. "A catastrophic war between the super powers constitutes the only major military threat to Canada," revealed the policy document, "It is highly unlikely Canada would be attacked by a foreign power other than as a result of a strategic nuclear strike directed at the U.S. Our involvement would be largely a consequence of geography; Canada would not be singled out for separate attack."[56] The white paper also noted that "Canada's military role in international peacekeeping helps to prevent the outbreak or spread of hostilities in other areas of tension, so that underlying political problems can be settled through negotiation or a process of accommodation, and so that the possibility of great power involvement is minimized."[57] Nonetheless, it reinforced the idea that peacekeeping was a low priority for defence.

What was surprising to many was the new roles and responsibilities the Trudeau government assigned to DND. It was clear that DND was

Courtesy The RCR Museum and Archives.

Soldiers from 3 RCR march through the main gate of Kingston Penitentiary in support of the civil power, April 1971.

Photographer Warrant Officer A.E. Scott, Courtesy The RCR Museum and Archives.

Soldiers from 3 RCR stand perimeter guard inside the walls of Kingston Penitentiary, April 1971.

seen as a nation building tool and as a vehicle to introduce and push social change and policies. The white paper stated: "Although maintained primarily for purposes of sovereignty and security, the Department of National Defence provides an important reservoir of skills and capabilities which in the past has been drawn upon, and which in the future can be increasingly drawn upon, to contribute to the social and economic development of Canada."[58] It went on to note that "the Armed Forces make an important contribution to Canada's unit and identity." It also said that "the Forces will make a major contribution to the preservation of an unspoiled environment and an improved quality of life by supporting the civil agencies in exercising pollution control in the North and off Canada's coasts."[59]

It was clear that the white paper rationale was focused on sovereignty protection. "Other national aims," the document revealed, "fostering economic growth and safeguarding sovereignty and independence — dictated increased emphasis on the protection of Canadian interests at home."[60] Also at play was the reality of continuing financial constraints. For Royals and others in the CF it meant in many ways a return to the 1950s and an emphasis on the North. Arctic warfare would once again become important to those stationed in Canada.

Immediate evidence was the creation of the "New Viking" exercise series of training activities in the North. These involved company-sized deployments in the High Arctic for so-called sovereignty exercises, as well as Arctic warfare training. Royals from across the regiment spent time learning the ropes of Arctic survival. For example, "A" Coy, 3 RCR stated of their experience in July 1971, "Our two-week excursion in the high Arctic wastes would confirm in all our minds that the land of the midnight sun should remain in the fine hands of the Eskimos and polar bears."[61]

Despite the tongue-in-cheek comment, most agreed that "The New Viking Exercise was a fine test of a rifle company's ability to remain in a relatively harsh environment and move from place to place under all climatic conditions,"[62] since after all the New Viking series was meant to familiarize personnel with living, moving, and fighting in the Canadian North. This renewed government focus on the Arctic had an immediate impact. For instance, 1 RCR spent 50 of 365 days in 1972 living in arctic tents. The experience was not lost on the soldiers. "The extremely cold weather and the deep snow encountered, tested the resolve of each man to do his job," insisted Private D. Lamb. "For the newer members of the Company," he added, "it was a good introduction to cold weather training, as it became readily apparent that long days of training are essential for survival in an Arctic environment."[63]

Although the far North apparently became important to the government, so too did further focus on budget reductions and internal economy, which was a key underpinning to changes in defence that led to some other major initiatives that would impact on the CF during this era. One such monster was the Management Review Group that studied the department's organization to ensure effective planning and control. The CDS and deputy minister (DM) at the time convinced the MND that the best solution was a DM and CDS equal in status with a combined staff serving both. In essence the DM would be responsible for management and the CDS for operations. This became the model for what has since been called the civilianization of defence. Dr. Jack Granatstein, renowned Canadian military historian, remarked, "In the integrated Canadian Forces Headquarters, however, civilian officers could outrank military officers, and managers, civilian or military, could outrank commanders. The resulting civilianization of the department — the dominance of managers over the military, and of military bureaucrats over operational commanders — had major long-term implications for the arm and the other environments."[64] This reality would play itself out over the next two decades, leading to monumental crisis for the CF in the 1990s. That, however, was still far off in the future.

Despite the new white paper and its focus on sovereignty and "Canada First," in reality for the military, the focus was still on NATO and West Germany. After all, to their uniformed colleagues and allies, there was only one real focus — being able to defeat the Soviets and the Warsaw Pact. And although the politicians "may not get it" — for Canada's senior military commanders, being a modern, connected military meant being recognized as a player in NATO.

And this was not easy considering the cuts imposed by the Trudeau government or their clearly ambivalent attitude toward NATO. As already noted, Trudeau's cuts were dramatic and had an incredible impact on 4 CMBG. The brigade group lost an entire infantry battalion, a tank squadron, and an artillery battery, as well as many support troops. The brigade's 1969 war establishment (WE) had numbered 6,606, of which 5,517 were deployed in Germany. By the end of 1970, the brigade had only 3,220 soldiers deployed with no augmentation plan.[65] In addition, Canada clearly stated that it would not send a reinforcement brigade to Germany by sea in the event of war. Instead, the Canadian government offered up a brigade-strength formation, the Canadian Air Sea Transportable (CAST) combat group, which would be available for deployment to either Norway or Denmark. The CAST group included the air-transportable battalion earmarked for the AMF(L) in the north of Europe. The other Canadian AMF(L) commitment to the south was terminated.

The explanation for the redirection of Canadian resources to the CAST combat group at the expense of cutting troops assigned to, and stationed in, Germany, aside from the obvious saving of money, was rationalized because of the perceived increased threat to Norway, which was a direct result of the large increase in the size of the Soviet fleet operating from ports on the Kola peninsula next to Norway and in the Baltic Sea opposite Denmark. The reasoning was, if NATO was to stop these forces from threatening North American-European sea lines of communications in the Atlantic, Norway, and Denmark had to be retained as a base from which to launch attacks against Soviet naval forces.[66]

The CAST combat group would be Canada's contribution to this effort. It consisted of a headquarters and signal squadron; three infantry battalions; a light artillery regiment; a tracked reconnaissance squadron; an engineer field squadron; a tactical air element with medium transport helicopters (i.e. Chinook helicopters), light observation helicopters (i.e. Kiowa helicopters), and utility helicopters (i.e. Huey helicopters); a service battalion; and a field ambulance.[67] The actual commitment of these forces entailed deployment to North Norway, specifically the Troms area; Denmark, namely the Zealand group of islands; and potentially Germany — the Schleswig-Holstein area including the contiguous areas of Denmark on the Jutland Peninsula.

The CAST Combat Group was given specific tasks in each of the deployment areas that consisted of acting as a quick reaction force (common to all deployment areas) to specific tasks such as reinforcement of allied forces, manning specific blocking positions, defence of vital points, and key terrain and offensive operations to clear enemy penetration.[68] The challenge was daunting, as NATO intelligence assessments put the Soviet advantage in ground forces at 5 to 1; with a 15 to 1 superiority in tanks. In addition, the assessments also put the Soviet advantage in air support at 5 to 1.[69]

Although the threat to NATO's northern flank was real, many suspected the government's posturing to take the CAST role was just a sop to placate NATO allies, since it had gutted its forces in Europe and scaled back its overall commitment. The CAST role was largely one that would not actually have to be provided until actual war was imminent. In the interim, the government could double task units so that on paper, it was meeting its obligations to NATO, but in reality was banking on peace. Nonetheless, the commitment required Canada to deploy the AMF(L) battalion group within a period of seven days after warning. That meant the designated AMF(L) battalion had a week to prepare itself and then a further six days to move to its deployment area. The CAST combat group had 30 days to move itself after warning.

How this was to be accomplished was anyone's guess. The new commitment, as the FMC commander stated, was "a national effort."[70] The complexity of trying to deploy large amounts of personnel, equipment, and materiel to such a distant location was not lost on those who would have to do it. Early planning exercises did not placate concerns. One Royal observed after one such activity, "It must be admitted that there was some degree of uncertainty as to how this force, called CAST Combat Group, was to be deployed and exercised."[71]

Even two years later, in 1973, the magnitude of the problem was clearly realized by military planners. In a secret document, planners stated unequivocally, "the CAST Cbt Gp [combat group] was manned and equipped only with unacceptable degradation to our other missions. Even then, our present national capability to deploy and support the force was questionable." The planners went on to point out, "Mobile Command does not have sufficient forces-in-being to undertake its assigned tasks." They explained, "The impact of the implementation of either of the two major tasks (CAST Cbt Gp and ALCANUS [Alaska/Canada/U.S.]) is so significant as to demand mobilization." Somewhat shockingly, the planners also noted that "Mobile Command is not adequately organized or equipped to fight a war."[72] It is not surprising then that the CAST brigade group would not actually be exercised in its in-theatre role until 1986.

But there were additional NATO woes. With the close-out of CFB Soest, 4 CMBG dropped all operational commitments in NORHTAG (Northern Army Group) on 1 June 1970 and deployed unit advance parties to Lahr in July. Canada now maintained a brigade commitment in the central region (CENTAG [Central Army Group]) and a brigade plus a battalion (AMF[L]) to the Northern Flank. However, American and NATO allies were not exceedingly happy with what they saw as Canada's diminution of commitment. Moreover, they were not overly sympathetic to 4 CMBG's efforts at getting a realistic role in its new area of operation. In July 1971, SACEUR finally assigned 4 CMBG a role, though vague, captured in CENTAG's General Defence Plan as a brigade in Corps reserve for either V (US) Corps or II (GE) Corps.

The draw down in Europe was clearly a political decision taken by the Canadian government for economic and political reasons. The impact of the decisions taken by Trudeau was somewhat mitigated by the easing of tensions between the superpowers. The early 1970s have been described by historians as a period of detente between the West and the Soviet Union and its Warsaw Pact allies. The actual definition of détente, however, is unclear. To some it was a permanent relaxation of tension between the two adversaries, which boded well for future peaceful relations. To others it was seen as a conscious strategy by the Soviets to buy themselves some time so that they could better prepare for a future conflict.

During this period NATO's conventional forces were weak compared to those of the Soviets, and the West still relied heavily on its tactical nuclear weapons to augment its ground forces and conventional firepower. Nonetheless, MC 14/3 or "Flexible Response" remained NATO's dominant strategic concept. And ironically, despite the continued reliance on tactical nuclear weapons to make up for the gap in conventional forces between NATO and the Warsaw Pact, the idea of fighting with them as a normal method of operation became less and less dominant in Canadian thinking. Exercises that explicitly included scenarios of following up nuclear strikes became fewer and fewer.

But the reality of the Soviet peril was in no way dismissed. The threat Canadians and their allies faced in CENTAG was from the Group of Soviet Forces Germany (GSFG) and the East German Army, as well as from the Soviet Central Group of Forces (CFG), the Soviet Southern Group of Forces (SGF), and the Czechoslovakian People's Army (CPA). Forces from the GSFG alone included 8 Guard Army (consisting of one tank and three motor rifle divisions) with 2 Guards Tank Army (consisting of two tank and two motor rifle divisions) in the second operational echelon. Soviet CFG in Czechoslovakia amounted to another two tank and three motor rifle divisions and an independent artillery brigade, while the CPA represented another five tank and five motor rifle divisions, as well as an artillery division. In addition, there were a number of other forces, such as airborne divisions and second strategic echelon forces available for commitment. All in all, the Warsaw Pact forces arrayed against CENTAG were formidable.[73]

For the Royals, the threat was real. The CENTAG operational area was a hilly and heavily forested belt of land, 10 to 30 kilometres wide, flush along the border with East Germany and Czechoslovakia, and finishing at the Austrian border. The overall NATO concept had not changed. NATO forces-in-being were required to delay the Soviets until reinforcements could arrive from North America and until European nations could mobilize their reserve forces. As such, the whole effort in CENTAG focused on stalling the enemy as far forward as possible until help arrived. This was the reason for the genesis of the REFORGER (Return of Forces to Germany) exercises every fall. The operating concept also led to the expansion of pre-positioning of equipment in Germany for U.S. reinforcement divisions in the 1970s.

To ensure maximum readiness, the Canadians introduced the "Snowball," which replaced "Quick Train" as the code word for a "bug-out." The lack of a widespread accessible phone system led, initially, to the use of air raid sirens to alert the troops. However, activating this system in the early morning hours, and following it up with the noise of vehicles clattering along the cobblestones of Lahr and Baden for the next several hours, proved extremely disruptive for the local population. As a result, sound trucks with loudspeakers were implemented. Approximately 10 or more "Snowballs" a year were conducted. The "Snowball" was representative of how training in Germany actually drove training practices in Canada. Clearly the need to rapidly mobilize and deploy was evident in Germany, because of the proximity of the fortified border. The same urgency was not normally the case in Canada, yet "Snowballs" became part of unit life in the RCR garrisons across Canada, and Royals could count on a least one fan-out, initiated at 0430 hours, each month.

Without a doubt, service in Germany retained its allure. Tom de Faye recounts, "It was a very exciting time for us. The thing that consumed us I think and inspired us and directed most of our efforts were the fall exercises. No doubt about it. The Fallex's had to be the real highlight, and I think that tested us, tested our abilities — one certainly went through them and assessed oneself quite stringently against what happened. "[74] And the results, were a boost for Canadians overall. Foreign military observers routinely assessed 4 CMBG as "An elite, well-disciplined, well-trained professional fighting unit," after watching it in action during the fall exercises.[75]

The NATO exercise and readiness cycle remained the focal point of service in Germany for the Regiment. It created the opportunity to operate within the context of large mechanized formations and practice high-intensity warfare within the context of what was reasonably perceived to be the next battlefield. Captain Dave Nolan remarked, "Baden-Soellingen is one of the few places where the soldier has the opportunity to work with large mechanized formations, deploying over terrain that is usually outside the normal confines of training areas." He added, "[The soldier] is intimately involved in helping to maintain the expertise in mechanized tactics. He serves as a valuable asset to his comrades when he returns to his parent unit for he is well versed in the art of mechanized warfare."[76]

But there was a high degree of stress that went along with operating in Germany. "We got all our vehicles across and commenced our advance," explained David DeClerq, "By this time my radio communications were horrible — either outside jamming or one of my own call signs on permanent send (it was the latter)." He recalled, "I personally spent the rest of my day chasing down wayward platoon commanders, issuing verbal orders and generally wearing myself to a frazzle as things became twice as difficult without radio. I eventually tracked the culprit APC down and rectified the comm[unication]s problem several hours later." DeClerq opined, "I always believed that if real war ever started in that theater that our communications would be fragile and out most of the time. Even on these exercises there was frequency overlap and interference. Imagine when all NATO and Warsaw Pact radios were functioning at the same time with real jamming in effect!"[77]

But even these experiences were preparation for the friction of war. The other major benefit Germany provided was a singular focus for a unit. Units were up-to-strength and there were no taskings to strip away personnel.[78] Units and sub-units could build solid, cohesive teams, and focus on the business of soldiering. The singular operational focus, however, did result in a training cycle that became routine. In fact, many described the training regimen by the acronym "SALY" — "same as last year." Captain Bill Aikman recalled, "the annual training program settled into a definite routine — weapons concentration at Grafenwoehr in midwinter; sub-unit training and unit courses in the spring utilizing nearby training areas such as Heuberg, Munsingen, and Hagenau, to mention only a few (or that almost limitless training area — the Black Forest itself); summer rotation; and then build-up for the large unit concentration at Hohenfels in the autumn."[79]

Clearly, Germany continued to provide a professionally rewarding experience. To this end, the AMF(L) and CAST NATO commitments provided an opportunity for those stationed in Canada to also share in the NATO experience. A yearly series of exercises allowed troops to deploy overseas to North Norway. Canadian participation was normally in four distinct phases. Phase I began with the warning order that triggered a multitude of preparation to ready the designated contingent for overseas deployment. Phase II consisted of the airlift of the battalion group to North Norway. Phase III was the actual combat phase that normally started with a period of deterrent patrolling to show the flag/NATO solidarity and then transformed into a field exercise revolving around

Courtesy The RCR Museum and Archives.

HRH Prince Philip presented 3 RCR with their Colours on Parliament Hill in Ottawa, 2 August 1973.

combat to repel the invading enemy forces. The final phase was the redeployment of the battle group to Canada. The exercises represented major NATO effort. Ex Strong Express, in 1973 for example, involved a total force of 64,000 of all elements, with close to 15,000 troops committed in the land manoeuvres."[80]

Royals seemed ideally suited for North Norway. Their winter and Arctic warfare skills gave them a definite advantage in the cold, snowy Norwegian landscape. However, that did not mean there was nothing to complain about! "Up early in the darkness of midwinter day and off on our first exercises — patrols, snowshoeing, platoon and company tactics, and always the gut-wrenching slugging of loaded toboggans up mountains which were never meant to be traversed by toboggans," extolled Major K. Reeves.[81]

The mountainous terrain created a number of challenges. Another Royal recalled, "we have been operating 335 miles inside the Arctic

Courtesy The RCR Museum and Archives.

3 RCR on a ski exercise in northern Norway, December 1973.

Circle in temperatures as low as 35 degrees [Fahrenheit] below zero." He explained, "The troops are using skis and snowshoes, while over-snow vehicles transport them to bivouac sites high in the timber line of the mountainous countryside." Amazingly, he pointed out that "most of the transport duties are being carried out by small pack-horses loaned to the Canadian by the Norwegian army. With miniature snowshoes strapped to their hooves, the hardy animals can carry 200 pounds of ammunition and supplies through the snow-covered mountain passes."[82] However, "the going was tough, even for the horses."[83]

The AMF(L) and CAST commitments also had an effect on training in Canada. In fact, Ex Running Jump was a perfect example of how NATO commitments and European requirements translated to emphasis of training in Canada. This exercise was designed to exercise Canadian commitments to AMF(L). Since budgetary constraints limited the ability to actually go to Norway or Denmark, the staffing, planning, and actual execution of a large scale move was done from CFB London and CFB Petawawa to CFB Gagetown. In total, more than 5,000 personnel with their personal equipment and approximately 5,000 tracked and wheeled vehicles were deployed, using CF C-130 Hercules aircraft, trains, naval ships, and a commercial carrier from Canada Steamships.

Although training was predominately focused on winter warfare in Canada's far north and preparation for the high intensity NATO battlefield in Europe, the continuing conflict in Vietnam, along with many other wars of national liberation and insurgency around the globe, fuelled some interest in jungle warfare. Training undertaken included tropical hygiene, jungle navigation, obstacle crossing including mountaineering and watermanship, basic jungle tactics, ambush and counter ambush drills, daily routine in the jungle, and night operations. As such, Royals conducted a series of yearly exercises in Jamaica to practice the craft. This was both a novelty and a great learning experience. John Robertson remembered the briefing of the medical sergeant on arrival in Jamaica. He perfunctorily told the troops, "Welcome to Jamaica. Don't eat the food, don't drink the water, stay out of the sun, and don't go out with the girls. Don't sit under a coconut tree and watch out for the scorpions and centipedes. And don't swim in the ocean — sharks and barracudas are also trained killers."[84]

Ex Nimrod Caper was the actual vehicle used to provide the jungle familiarization. It consisted of a six-day jungle training school in the hot and humid jungle setting near Ken Jones airstrip in the Blue Mountain ranges of the North shore of Jamaica. "Troops learned," explained Captain Bill Whitehead, "to live off the land, to navigate in the dense foliage and to survive in the jungle." He described the situation: "Operating individually, the long-range patrols trekked over the rugged country, each man travelling with little more than a machete to cut the tangled underbrush, a poncho, a weapon, a little food and a clean pair of socks."[85] Lieutenant-Colonel Scotty Morrison, the CO of 2 RCR during one such iteration assessed, "The training enhanced our military skills under conditions which permitted us to look at each man's ability and capability in detail."[86]

However, training in the jungle was not the only test of mettle for Royals. In April 1974, 1 Commando of the Canadian Airborne Regiment relieved 2 RCR and assumed a normal peacekeeping rotation to Cyprus, as part of the Canadian commitment to UNFICYP. A coup staged by the Greek-Cypriot National Guard in mid-July triggered a Turkish invasion of the island. The resultant conflict necessitated the deployment of the remainder of the Cdn AB Regt as reinforcements for the Canadian contingent that found itself stuck between two warring parties.

Photographer W.H. Cole, CFPU CNL, Neg. CYPC-74-156.

Royals, as members of the Cdn AB Regt, participated in peacekeeping efforts during the Turkish invasion of Cyprus in 1974.

As such, the paratroopers, who included many Royals, quickly distinguished themselves during fighting and its aftermath. The airborne soldiers continually displayed a steely courage and exhibited a firm, disciplined, and resolute stand. By late-August a demarcation line was finally established, and the Canadian paratroopers aggressively enforced it.[87] In the brief period they were engaged in the conflict, the paratroopers suffered 30 casualties, including two dead.[88]

As a result of the conflict, Secretary-General Kurt Waldheim reported to the Security Council on U.N. operations in Cyprus and "described the July coup and Turkish intervention as the gravest crisis in Cyprus since UNFICYP was formed in 1964." He recommended the current mandate be extended for an additional 56 months "in order to help maintain the ceasefire and also to facilitate the search for a peaceful solution." As a result, the U.N. Security Council approved the extension of the mandate on 13 December 1974 and at the same time "endorsed a General Assembly resolution calling for continuing talks between representatives of the two communities."[89]

Meanwhile, Archbishop Makarios had returned to Cyprus on 7 December 1974. Massive celebrations were held in Nicosia, and people were bussed in from throughout the government-controlled area. Estimates varied of between 100,000–200,000 people. Makarios stressed the reassertion of the recognized constitutional government and the need for unity and for discussions at all levels. He announced an amnesty for all who took part in the July coup and opposed any partition of the island. He refused to accept this as a fait accompli. The Turkish-Cypriot representative asserted that the return of Makarios could only harm negotiations already underway. He believed the Archbishop, as a religious figurehead of one community, could not be accepted as head of state in Cyprus.[90]

Concurrently the local U.N. forces put forward the inner wall city proposal. The essence of the idea was the establishment of a Buffer Zone in the inner walled city of Nicosia, where combatants were extremely close. The plan called for each side to pull back slightly and for most of the buildings between them (some key buildings would remain) to be destroyed. The Turkish forces agreed, but the Greek-Cypriot government

Courtesy The RCR Museum and Archives.

The Green Line, Turkish defences in the Nicosia City sector, 1970s.

did not. They did not want to set a precedent for partitioning the island before a political settlement.[91]

And so, with continuing tension and conflict bubbling below the surface, 1 RCR relieved the Cdn AB Regt in Cyprus during the period 4–13 December 1974. The battalion was now organized on an establishment of 790 all ranks. It included two rifle companies, a support company, a headquarters company, a logistics company, a reconnaissance platoon, a reconnaissance troop, and an engineer troop.[92] The battalion was kept extremely busy providing escorts for, and coordinating, repairs of public utilities and telecommunications (including the transfer and exchange of major stock items needed to complete repairs; and negotiating for the return of private property (e.g. automobiles, farm machinery, construction equipment). Escorts for farm workers needing access into their fields in the buffer zone halted in mid-December, and there were no incidents as they cultivated their fields.[93]

Irrespective of the progress being made, trouble was always just under the surface. The British decision to allow Turkish-Cypriot refugees in the Episkopi Sovereign Base Area (SBA) to be evacuated to Turkey led to violent demonstrations in Nicosia and elsewhere. Protests started 16

January 1975 in Nicosia and Limassol and escalated the next day after a youth was killed by a U.N. armoured car that had knocked him to the ground near the Akrotiri SBA. In retaliation, British and American facilities were attacked in Nicosia on 18 and 20 January. Violence continued until the personal intervention of Archbishop Makarios.

As a result of anti-British demonstrations, a detachment from Reconnaissance Platoon and a rifle section from "D" Coy deployed to Limassol to assist in joint patrolling with British forces, to demonstrate U.N. solidarity. In addition, Lynx and APCs deployed to the U.S. Embassy during demonstrations in Nicosia on 18 January to assist in the evacuation of civilian staff. Because of the violence, U.N. forces were placed on increased vigilance and "R&R" (rest and recuperation) was restricted in Nicosia and Limassol for a one week period. [94]

An unofficial duty log captured the pulse of the period:

17 Jan 75- Denktash/Cleredies, (presidents of the Turk and Greek sides of the Island) meet today. Crowds gather at Metaxas square today to demonstrate against the Brits allowing the Turk refugees to go to Turkey. It's getting hot. Standby platoon from D company put on alert.

18 Jan 75- Another exciting day. Crowds are wrecking Brit buildings in Nicosia.

A report from UN HQ that Gk National Guard stole, at gunpoint, cows, sheep and goats from a Tk Cyp. OC 6 Pl investigated and found that the story was that a Turk Cyp sold three cows to a Gk Cyp for 255 pounds. Another great FU from higher HQ. Too bad I didn't tape this, it would have sold a million copies. One platoon from D company with three APC's and three Lynx were tasked to evacuate the American Embassy. It was something to behold. The battalion net sounded like a HAM radio network. The Americans let go with gas and that got things even more confused. The platoon commander from D company sounded, on the radio, very excited.[95]

The remainder of the tour for 1 RCR remained tense as all parties settled into their positions. Shots often escalated to full firefights as the Royals attempted to broker the uneasy peace. On average there were at least three shooting incidents a day.[96] Phil Spencer recalled, "There were lots of ceasefire violations. People were very leery and nervous." He elaborated, "We reminded our guys to be solid, cool and calm and we tried to solve incidents at the corporal level."[97]

Similarly, Bob Mahar described, "There were frequent bursts of gunfire and lots of infiltrating into houses in the UN area." He asserted, "We had to go out every day/night and clear the houses." Mahar explained, "Tempers were still hot between the antagonists and we were able to establish a professional presence between them and thwart their frequent attempts to move their lines or advance their positions."[98] Nonetheless, with time tensions began to ease somewhat. As a result, by May 1975, the Canadian contingent was scaled back down to 515 personnel.

Photographer Corporal F.F. Smith, Courtesy The RCR Museum and Archives.

A 3 RCR patrol deploys on the outskirts of Nicosia, Cyprus, February 1977.

Although Cyprus proved to be a distraction for some, by the mid-1970s, back in Canada, budgetary pressures forced DND to undertake another series of dramatic cuts. In December 1974, the Cabinet authorized the initiation of a Defence Structure Review (DSR). The review was conducted by a committee that consisted of the deputy minister of DND, the under-secretary of state for external affairs, the secretary of the treasury board, and General Jacques Dextraze, the chief of the defence staff. Phase one of the DSR consisted of reviewing and reaffirming the military tasks as laid out in the white paper. Phase two examined the optional force structures to meet the military tasks as assigned (and options were based on combat capability rather than sovereignty or peacekeeping tasks). Phase three examined the specific weapon systems and funds required to meet the assigned tasks. Dextraze clearly announced that "hard operational needs would determine the basic structuring of the forces."[99]

Almost a year later, in November 1975, one of the first impacts of the DSR became public. James Richardson, the new MND, addressed a gathering of militia "Honorary Colonels." At this forum, he stressed the government's recommitment to NATO and Europe. Richardson, in a clear reversal of the 1971 white paper, asked the rhetorical question, "Where is the threat?" He went on to answer, "The threat is largely in Europe, on the Central Front. The threat is not as we see it, in North America."[100] This was the government's signal that NATO was once again the de facto top defence priority.

This set the stage for the CDS to lay the groundwork a few months later for his new force structure plan. In January 1976, Dextraze addressed the Conference of Defence Associates (CDA) at the Château Laurier in Ottawa. For years this group of mostly reserve force representatives and retired regulars had been used by ministers and their generals as a platform to announce new programs and test reactions. They usually supported conventional ideas for the good of the Canadian Forces as a whole. To this group the CDS confided:

> My two major problems with the current army posture are that it could be better balanced geographically, and that I do not have enough people to fill the sharp end

vacancies which exist. I could correct these problems
in a number of ways. Something along the following
lines could work well: The Airborne Regiment could be
relocated and form part of the order of battle of another
formation; we would then have three, rather than four,
major army formations in Canada, each with integral
supporting arms and services.[101]

General Dextraze also revealed his plan to the assembled audience.
He informed them that he visualized the formation of a highly mobile,
rapid reaction formation, in the centre of Canada, with its headquarters in Petawawa. He outlined that the organization would consist of an
air-landed battalion and a major airborne unit formed from the current
Canadian Airborne Regiment, in which there would be RCR, PPCLI, and
R22eR commandos. He also postulated that 3 Mechanized Commando
would be disbanded, thus freeing up almost 1,000 established positions
that could be used to bring up other units to full peacetime strength.[102]

Not surprisingly then, the CDS directed Formation Mobile
Command Headquarters to study and prepare a plan for the reorganization and relocation of the Army in Canada. In the end, Dextraze
did not believe that the posture of the Army field formations in Canada
was in balance with the military requirement. Almost a year to the day
after his initial musing to the CDA, Dextraze briefed the gathering once
again on his final design. He revealed that a "military appreciation" had
led him to believe that "on mobilization day the minimum Field Force
requirement is for four brigades and an Airborne Regiment manned to
War Establishment."[103] Once again, he laid out a detailed rationale for the
CDA delegates:

> I decided to go in peacetime with a standard brigade
> group in the West, a standard brigade group in the East
> and a force of Regimental size in the centre, which I have
> tentatively called "The Special Service Force." ... The
> Special Service Force in the Centre is slightly different.

It must be capable of executing the peacetime missions assigned to it with its "Peace Establishment" but be capable, using reservists, of expanding to a full Airborne Regiment plus a brigade in time of emergency/mobilization. This will allow us to maintain a relatively light — "Airborne — Airportable" Quick Reaction Force in the demographic centre of the country in peacetime which can be moved quickly to augment either of the flanking brigades for internal security tasks, to the Arctic, or to UN-type operations.[104]

By late summer 1976, General Dextraze created his Special Service Force (SSF).[105] The official DND explanation was that the SSF was "Canada's immediate response force for any National or International commitment." It further stated, "to fill this role, the Special Service Force is trained, organized and equipped to deploy rapidly and conduct operations in any environment." It explained that to ensure rapid deployment, all the SSF weapons and equipment were air-droppable or capable of being air landed by C-130 Hercules aircraft. Key to the messaging was the fact that "the Canadian Airborne Regiment, capable of deploying by parachute, and the First Battalion Royal Canadian Regiment, form the infantry spearhead of the Force."[106]

But as always, for the troops in the battalions the larger scheme of reorganization was lost in the focus on operations. In the summer of 1976, the twenty-first Olympiad became the largest CF operation since the Korean War, involving 16,000 personnel.[107] The CF provided security assistance to the Ministry of the Solicitor-General through the RCMP.[108] The attention to security was easy to understand. After all, in the aftermath of the tragedy that occurred on 5 September 1972, at the Munich Olympics, when a combination of terrorist action and a bungled German rescue attempt resulted in the death of Israeli athletes. It was not lost on senior Canadian political and military decision makers that the 1972 Olympics had irrevocably changed the landscape of the event. Those hosting such events now had to protect against political terrorism. As such, necessary precautions were the order of the day.

To fulfill the security task, the CF effort took the form of four task forces, which were based on small brigades.[109] Task Forces 1 and 2 were given the responsibility for security of Montreal and its environs. Task Force 1, based on 5 CBG, was assigned responsibility for many aspects of athlete security, the protection of the Olympic Stadium and Village, as well as many other competition and training sites in that area. Task Force 2, based mainly on 2 Combat Group from CFB Petawawa, was predominately responsible for security at some of the training sites and competition sites, VIP hotel and baggage security, and airport security. Task Force 3 consisting of 2 Airborne Commando was the strategic reserve stationed at CFB St. Jean, 40 kilometres south of Montreal. Finally, Task Force 4, also based on 2 Combat Group, was assigned the responsibility for DND security operations at Kingston, Toronto, and Ottawa. In reserve was 2 RCR, available for special tasks such as security of the Queen during her visit and the security of CFB Montreal.

A key aspect of security plan was the security corridor. This was a system by which all the athletes and dignitaries were assured of constant protection from the moment of their arrival in Canada until the moment of their departure. The corridor joined the Canadian points of entry to the Olympic Village and to the competition sites and training sites (of which there were 28 and 27, respectively) spread from Bromont in the east, through Montreal and Kingston, to Toronto and Ottawa. As long as an athlete stayed inside the corridor, they were protected.

Task Force 2 included 1 RCR. In early April, in preparation for the Olympics, the unit reorganized by forming two large companies, numbering approximately 400, to conduct airport security duties. A small battalion headquarters and a large administration company made up the remainder of the force. Battalion personnel attended courses such as general security, VIP security, airport security, counter-vehicle kidnap, and VIP baggage security before the operation.

"Our task during OP Gamescan," explained the CO, Lieutenant-Colonel Bill Pettipas, "was to assist the RCMP security detachment at both Dorval and Mirabel airport from 15 June to 6 August 1976." He elaborated, "Our taskings ranged from gate and vital installation guards, vehicle and foot patrols, to special reserve elements entitled 'Quick

Reaction Forces."[110] Specifically, 1 RCR guarded airport installations such as the main gates to the airfields, the control towers, the cargo areas, the heating plants, and the radar sites.[111] This enabled the RCMP to concentrate its force inside the terminal buildings.

Meanwhile, 2 RCR deployed half its strength in Montreal on Olympic related security duties, and maintained one rifle company back in CFB Gagetown on "stand-by." The reserve company was also responsible for assisting the Combat Training Centre with summer courses being run at the same time. In support of the RCMP, 2 RCR employed its Reconnaissance Platoon along the New Brunswick–Maine border on surveillance duty. Specific to OP Gamescan, "H" Coy, 2 RCR, reinforced with a platoon from "G" Coy, maintained the security of the village compound, which had a perimeter of more than three kilometres, as well as military VPs on Montreal Island, Longue Point Supply Depot, Chabanel Ration Depot, and Major-General Reid's chief Olympic headquarters.

"G" Coy maintained seven guard posts at St. Hubert that controlled access on and off the base, as well as into FMC HQ. They also manned a vehicle patrol covering the south side of the St. Hubert. In addition, "G" Coy provided security for the voyage of Her Majesty's Yacht *Britannia* as it made its way through the St. Lawrence Seaway and locks to Kingston. The sub-unit created a security bubble at each of the locks as the yacht made its way up the Seaway.

In Kingston, a 1,300 man security force, of which 800 were military, secured the Olympic Games in this venue. The security force made up a tenth of the CF's total security commitment to the Olympic Games.[112] Here, 3 RCR, as part of Task Force 4, worked in support of the RCMP, Ontario Provincial Police (OPP), and Kingston City Police. It provided round-the-clock perimeter foot patrols and roof top surveillance at the Queen's University residence-turned-Olympic Village, at hydro and public utility installations, and at various border points. The unit also carried out other VIP security duties. For the troops on the ground that translated to each sentry walking 24 to 32 kilometres during an eight-hour shift.[113]

In the end, the Olympics finished without any significant incidents. The Royals, as part of the larger CF effort, contributed significantly to the success. "It was," in the words of one Royal Canadian, "hectic, boring, educational, uneventful, spectacular, dull — but nearly everyone who lived it agreed it was fun!"[114]

The following year, on 5 October 1977, The RCR were part of another major event in the history of Canada's participation in UNFICYP. Having just assumed command of Sector 4 from 12e RBC, 2 RCR was settling in when UNFICYP headquarters informed the battalion that the Finnish contingent responsible for Sector 3 (Nicosia Airport) was leaving UNFICYP in late October, and 2 RCR was to take over their sector. This meant a shuffling of the battalion's sub-units and their responsibilities. "H" redeployed into the airport area and was responsible for the airport and several observation posts to the immediate west up to the Old Kyrenia Road. "J" Coy, based in the Ledra Palace complex, took over responsibility for certain OPs and patrol routes on the west edge of Nicosia and for the Green Line running through the centre of the city east to the New Famagusta Road. Reconnaissance Platoon was reduced somewhat in strength to provide reinforcements to the rifle companies and was given responsibility for patrolling along the line and in the area between "J" Coy OPs and SWEDCON, including several unmanned OPs. HQ Coy (including the Pipes and Drums and the Regimental Police section) was responsible for manning checkpoints at the battalion HQ complex, and 2 RCR took control and responsibility for the new sector on 19 October.[115]

Each rifle company operated six OPs, with two soldiers at all times, as well as several temporary ones that were occupied at random intervals, usually by the Reconnaissance Platoon during their patrols. In addition, there were OPs that would be used only when the situation required. The mortars and 106 mm recoilless rifles anti-tank weapons were held with "H" Coy at the airport. There was no dedicated manning for these weapons. Rather the crews were employed as riflemen unless a crisis required the manning of the heavy weapons.

The Joint Operations Centre was operated 24/7 by the senior duty officer and three subalterns, who worked in shifts. The battalion was also supported by a section of Australian Civil Police (AUSCIVPOL) who worked closely with the operations staff and provided valuable local knowledge and capabilities in dealing with Cypriot civilians of both factions.

Aside from the changes to the sector, which would lay the template for following Canadian UNFICYP contingents, the tour was generally quiet.[116] Most incidents involved one of the belligerents attempting to make incremental improvements to their defensive positions. These actions were always quickly dealt with at the company level. However, the Turks did not delegate significant authority to negotiate to their company or unit commanders. As a result, minor issues tended to require discussion with their regimental commanders. In the "H" Coy area there remained an ongoing thorn. Greek-Cypriot civilians continually attempted to cross a U.N. fence to inspect their abandoned houses that faced Turkish-Cypriot positions in the buffer zone. Eventually a program of visits under U.N. escort was arranged that helped to reduce tension. One problem that remained, however, was boredom. As such, frequent line checks were carried out by officers and senior NCOs. And so by the late-1970s the template for Cyprus was largely set.

The end of the decade also witnessed the results of the Defence Structure Review. Much like the preceeding decade, the 1970s proved to be a period of continual and dramatic change. The announcements were both positive and negative. In 1976, the government announced another cut to its NATO commitments. The option of sending the CAST Combat Group to Denmark was dropped and planning centred only on a deployment to Norway. This decision also drove an agreement with the Norwegian government to pre-position vehicles and equipment. Two years later, the MND also announced that the CAST Combat Group would be based on the SSF.

A positive development emerged on 18 February 1977, when Barney Danson, the MND, announced that the government, in an effort to address equipment deficiencies, had purchased 350 armoured vehicles general purpose (AVGPs) (i.e. the "Grizzly," "Cougar," "Husky"). Fielding to regular force units was to begin October 1978 and be completed by early 1981. Defence officials said the need for the new vehicles was based on the fact that the "tactical integrity of the army's all-arms combat team had deteriorated since 1969, when tanks were withdrawn from most army units based in Canada. Since then the CF relied on an incompatible mix of trucks, jeeps and personnel

Photographer Sergeant Rodger, Courtesy The RCR Museum and Archives.

Two German soldiers stand guard at the approaches to a floating pontoon bridge as 3 RCR APCs cross during a NATO exercise.

carriers, pending a decision on a replacement for a direct fire-support vehicle. Combat elements equipped with this incompatible mix could not keep pace with each other in cross-country operations, assaulting water obstacles or in training at the formation level."[117] The new vehicle could reach speeds of up to 100 kilometres per hour, had a normal driving range of 600 kilometres, and was armoured against small-arms and artillery shell fragments.

But the DSR also called for additional dramatic restructuring beyond the move of the Cdn AB Regt and the creation of the SSF. Effective 15 July 1977, 3 Mechanized Commando was disbanded. Its disbandment allowed for the creation of 3 Airborne Commando (3 AB Cdo) within the Canadian Airborne Regiment. However, the positions were not yet allocated to the new airborne commando. Rather the positions accruing from the disbandment were reallocated within existing FMC units.[118]

Additional changes included the reallocation of 2 RCR from CTC to 5 Combat Brigade Group and the deployment of 3 RCR to Europe as a unit allocated to 4 CMBG (this was largely accomplished by posting members from 3 Mech Cdo on disbandment). Finally, on 29 June 1979, 3 Airborne Commando was officially added to the order of battle of the Cdn AB Regt. There were now three equal-sized rifle commandos comprised of four platoons (one of which was a support weapons platoon) made up of 154 all ranks.

And so ended yet another decade of service for country. The Regiment once again set a high standard of duty both in Canada and internationally, whether in Germany, Norway, or Cyprus. Royals stayed focused on their operational readiness and weathered another barrage of dramatic organizational changes with stoic perseverance. After all, the focus was still the Cold War and the nation's commitment to NATO and defence of the West.

4

The Last Hurrah: The End of the Cold War – 1980s

Very rarely is one able to predict at the start of a decade that it will be a truly defining period. Rather, these assessments are made looking into the rear view mirror with the assistance of hindsight. The start of the 1980s was no different. As Royals entered the new decade, they had in excess of 30 years of Cold War experience behind them. They had become accustomed to the threat and routine of the conflict. Service and requirements in Europe remained the template for force preparation and training. Cyprus provided a not too onerous operational distraction. During the early years of the decade, the Cold War took on a renewed intensity that almost rivalled the tensions of the 1960s. Few if any would have predicted that the 1980s would be the last hurrah for an era; that the Cold War would come to a sudden and dramatic end.

The 1980s began as just another cycle in the training year. The Cold War, which one can argue began in 1948, was in its fourth decade. Despite tumultuous changes throughout that period, there was a calming pre-dictability and stability throughout the Cold War to date. The "SALY" or "same as last year" principle became well-rooted. Not surprising then that it shaped the culture of the Army, as well as The RCR.

One major driver of the Army culture was its myopic inward focus; almost a complete disassociation from the society it served, which was

Royals from 3 RCR undergo a battle inoculation course in West Germany, May 1980.

reinforced by a virtual self-seclusion within the confines of its many bases. This distance was reinforced by a society that was quite satisfied with totally abrogating to its military the business of national security. After all, throughout the preceding decades one idea was always prevalent, namely, that the Cold War was just a breath away from becoming a hot war, one laden with consequence if the superpowers turned to their nuclear arsenals. Or at least one was led to believe it was.

And so, the world from 1948 on was seemingly on the brink of disaster. To most Canadians the Cold War and the threat it represented seemed frighteningly real. Pictures of huge missiles pointed toward North America, impressive May Day parades in Moscow that revealed a large and very lethal military arsenal, the continued occupation of territory liberated from Germany in the Second World War, and the brutal suppression of nationalist movements therein, reinforced the need for large Western forces in a constant state of readiness. And in the event this was not enough, every year (coincidently around budget appropriation time) the U.S. Department of Defense published its glossy *The Soviet Menace,* which showcased the Soviet Union's bulging military arsenal. In sum, governments and the public at large could easily recognize the threat. Accordingly, Western militaries were largely left alone to secure the Western way of life in the prosperous booming post war era.

For the military, this was significant. They had a clear mission — counter the Soviet threat. And its implementation was left largely to the professionals. National security dictated secrecy and the Soviets' active espionage campaigns, which often were made quite public once compromised, reinforced the need for a heavy cloak of secrecy on all things military. As a result, the military could easily, and it did, hide behind this veil to avoid explaining those things it rather not discuss. Not surprisingly, at times this list was large. However, the threat mitigated disclosure and the public was content not to interfere, trusting its politicians and military professionals were acting in the best interest of the state. Therefore, a very closed mindset, one that avoided public disclosure, if not almost totally contemptuous of it, developed. Simply put, the military knew best — and those who did not serve could not possibly understand the context of national security. Therefore, the military was largely allowed to work on its own (within the context of its national institution and NATO framework) with little interaction with the outside world.

The Cold War Army culture of the period was also shaped by an operating security environment that was straightforward and easy to understand. The world was largely divided into two spheres (i.e. NATO and the Warsaw Pact), and each was careful not to interfere dramatically in the other's interests. The actions and non-actions of such events as the Hungarian Revolution in 1956, the Cuban Missile Crisis in 1962, and the Czechoslovakian Revolution in 1968 (Prague Spring) provide clear examples of the unwritten understanding that existed. Efforts to support insurgents or proxy wars in theatres around the world (e.g. Vietnam, Middle East, Angola, Afghanistan) were always carefully managed. Rarely would the superpowers allow themselves to come into direct confrontation. Both camps understood and largely abided by the unwritten rules. Equally important, both camps propped up their surrogate, proxy and/or

Courtesy The RCR Museum and Archives.

Mortar Platoon, 3 RCR on the move during a NATO exercise in West Germany, 1982.

supported allies and ensured they maintained the global status quo. All together, this provided a great deal of stability during the Cold War.

Even peacekeeping during this period fell into the clearly understood model under Chapter VI of the U.N. Charter. Peacekeepers were only employed when both antagonists agreed to their presence. Their role was to monitor a ceasefire or peace agreement once the fighting had stopped. Their employment, therefore, was always within a prescribed boundary — in the buffer zone between the two former warring parties.[1] Their operating environment was very clear. Each side had its fortified line. Each side was clearly delineated by its front line, and all participants were in clearly identifiable national uniforms. Moreover, the entire operational area was quarantined. There were rarely civilians or media to deal

Photographer Wall, Courtesy The RCR Museum and Archives.

2 RCR Trooping the Colours in Fredericton, New Brunswick, 18 June 1983.

with. When there was, it was under carefully controlled and escorted circumstances. Once again, the military was allowed to operate in almost complete isolation.

The relative simplicity of the operating security environment bled into the fabric of the institution and shaped its behaviour. The Cold War bred a techno-centric culture. What became important was one's capability as a proficient technical warfighter. After all, the enemy was almost perfectly symmetrical — almost a carbon copy of its antagonist. Inventories and tactics were designed to fight a conventional (and possibly nuclear) war against forces of a similar type. Everything was templated. Soldiers, NCOs, and officers were taught Soviet order of battle and tactics. Exercises revolved around set initiators (e.g. the arrival of the combat reconnaissance patrol of a mechanized motor rifle division), which would indicate exactly what the enemy consisted of and where he was located. Based on the distances from friendly front lines, it could now be determined what tactics he would adopt.

In essence, the key to training was learning the enemy's order of battle. As such, training institutions provided lessons, handbooks, and exams on the Soviet enemy. Students would memorize the organizational composition (including numbers of personnel, specific weapons and their ranges, vehicles, and tactics) from section level to motor rifle division and higher depending on the respective rank level.

Furthermore, staff tables, NATO reports and returns, and common doctrinal publications simplified operating procedures and tactics. NATO policy, dictated largely by the "Big Boys" of the organization relieved Canada of much of the burden of strategic, as well as operational, decision making. Canada's tactical role whether on the Central Front in Germany or its Allied Command Europe (ACE) AMF(L) (ACE Mobile Force [land]) role in Northern Norway reinforced the simplicity of the Cold War for the CF. It knew its role, its routes to the front, its actual fighting positions, and the exact enemy it would face. As such, much of the training revolved around rehearsals for the possible show down between NATO and the Warsaw Pact on the actual ground and exact fighting positions where this would happen. This was, of course, the catalyst for the "SALY" concept and emphasis on filling specific roles that allowed an individual to get the requisite experience and training to meet the known requirements should conflict erupt.

This templated Cold War paradigm shaped how the Army and The RCR evolved. Technical expertise and actual experience (particularly in Europe) within the conventional NATO warfighting framework became the key drivers for success. It nurtured a system that relied on the traditional military concept that leadership is a top-down hierarchical action that depends on unit command and staff appointments, specifically experience, as the mechanism to prepare individuals for higher command at the strategic level. Within this model, higher education was not deemed important. The system and culture stressed training.[2] What was important within the military hierarchy was individuals who understood the system — the operating environment; the Soviet enemy; NATO doctrine and SOPs; and Canadian equipment, tactics, and staff work.

In essence, the Cold War created techno-centric, experienced-based officer and senior NCO corps that were largely isolated from outside thought or criticism. Their intellectual development was severely limited and depended largely on experience and training, which focused on the

A Royal puts the finishing touches on his tent group during Ex Avalanche Express, Bardufoss, Norway, March 1984.

application of NATO warfighting doctrine to prepare itself for the Third World War on the North European plain and adjunct theatres.

"While it was good to have a predictable training and deployment cycle, so predictable that we coined a phrase for it — SALY meaning 'same as last year' — the implications were not good for the mindset of the Canadian Forces," explained General Rick Hillier, a former CDS. He asserted, "Nobody really had to think, particularly at the strategic level, and consequently our leaders were not trained, selected or experienced enough to think beyond the stalemate in Europe." Hillier assessed, "That 'sameness' each year led inevitably to a focus on picayune detail and measurable process."[3]

Not surprisingly then, throughout the Cold War the system prospered for the most part. Commanders cloned themselves, thereby assuming they had ensured the well-being of the institution. Through the years, the myopic viewpoint and isolation created an officer and senior NCO

Author photograph.

A 1 RCR Grizzly cammed-up for battle during RV 85. One Sr NCO conceded: "When we received the AVGP [in the 1980s] we were uncertain how to employ it."

corps that were intolerant of criticism, self-scrutiny, or wider intellectual stimulation. They focused on process and spawned a culture where experienced Cold War technicians, who did not rock the boat and supported the status quo tended to do well. It was an era, explained Chief Warrant Officer "Kit" Charlebois "in which you did as you were told — without question. It was blind obedience and if you challenged the leadership you didn't last long in the Unit."[4]

The Cold War "SALY" mentality and reliance on training also fostered an officer and senior NCO corps that were arguably aloof from the day to day soldiering and training of the enlisted ranks. There existed for the most part a hierarchical system that relied on an industrial age understanding of leadership, specifically a directive, authoritarian approach. Day to day supervision of soldiers was left largely to junior NCOs, and garrison routine often devolved to boredom and routine maintenance.

Recollections of the era capture this aspect of soldiering. Master Warrant Officer Jay Gravelle quipped, "We really didn't see much of warrant officers and above. To see an officer was a treat, unless you were in trouble and had to go to HQ."[5] Master Warrant Officer Rob Douglas recalled joining the RCR as a private in the 1980s. "I was really proud to be a Royal but I was also a bit disheartened." He explained, "The RCR was really anal on some issues. We had chicken shit morning inspections and parades. We would then be told to be back at 1000 hours and then told to be back at 1300 hours. We wanted to soldier but instead did maintenance or just wasted time."[6] Dave Preeper recalled:

> the highest rank we would see was a master-corporal. We would do morning PT, shower then have a parade and then play cards until lunch. Then we would have a parade at 1300 hours and more cards, clean-up, sweep the floors and dismissal. I never saw my platoon commander. We would normally only get two days warning before an exercise — pack your kit, we're going to Norway."[7]

Then a subaltern, Brigadier-General Denis Thompson recalled, "You tended to get along better with the junior NCOs than the Sr NCOs. Those were the dart throwing years. The Sr NCOs maintained discipline but their heart wasn't with the soldiers — it was more about the Mess and drinking beer."[8]

The prevailing leadership model also created an environment that was not nurturing of administration. Documentation of accidents, injuries, and other minutia of peacetime soldiering was not encouraged, fostered, or diligently actioned. It was very much an Army that viewed field soldiering (and competitions) as the only really important activities that required focus. On the whole, NCOs could not be bothered with tiresome paperwork, and the officers had greater concerns than the tedious, onerous task of mundane personnel administration.

The Cold War also spawned, as alluded to earlier, a culture that held sports and military skills competitions as almost sacrosanct. In a peacetime garrison existence these activities became the measure of individuals and units. It was a gladiator mentality that promoted competitiveness and fitness. It allowed for tangible results on a "field of battle" of sorts.

Some commanding officers, units, and even regiments would go to almost ridiculous extremes to win. "Professional" athletes who devoted their entire time to training for sports was not uncommon. Postings to facilitate hockey teams in Europe were well known. Predictably then, the largest sections from the battalions submissions for the RCR journals *Pro Patria* and *The Connecting File* normally consisted of recounting individual and collective victories and successes in sports or military skill competitions.

The emphasis on sports, however, had its purpose. Lieutenant-Colonel Bill Bentley explained, "It was not just fun competitiveness but a belief that the infantry should have a fierce aggressive competitiveness that sports engendered."[9] Jim Cox agreed. "Sports," he asserted, "was important because it fostered a spirit of competition." He elaborated, "We saw a link to the battlefield — to operate in adversity. It also promoted physical fitness."[10] Chief Warrant Officer John O'Quinn added, "When you compete," he insisted, "you learn more about the others and we all got to know each other. It also gives you bragging rights and you felt good about it."[11] Colonel Don Denne captured the overall essence:

> First, soldiering is hard physical work and demands general fitness and coordination. Sports likewise demand their participants to be physically fit; there is an automatic commonality between the two — and in my experience a good sportsman is probably going to be a decent soldier. Second, team sports that involve semi or full contact are wonderful tools to develop aggressive spirit, trust, comradeship and esprit de corps. Soldiers tend to thrive on adversity if they know others around them are experiencing the same adversity in quest of a common goal. Training hard for sports, then competing (even if not winning) as a "band of brothers" is a hugely beneficial bonding mechanism. Third, "bragging rights."[12]

Bill Peters concluded, "Sports was one of the principal basis for cohesion in the unit, that and the Mess."[13]

Fiscal pressures in the 1980s. A shortage of spare parts required mechanics to cannibalize parts from broken vehicles to keep others running.

One aspect of the culture that still existed to the end of the 1980s, which was also related to sports as well, was the idea of toughness. The almost exclusive focus on field exercises led to a "train hard" attitude. There was a common understanding by those who served in the Regiment that soldiering was hard, that an individual would need to endure pain, discomfort, and hardship without whining about it. Toughness became a hallmark of soldiering. Pain and injuries were accepted as natural occurrences of the profession, and they were accepted stoically.

In fact, it became a point of individual pride. "The culture of soldiering in the 1980s was different [than today in the new millennium]," assessed Master Warrant Officer Rick Duncan, "there was an understanding that soldiers had to be hard, endure pain and discomfort."[14] Chief Warrant Officer Charlebois agreed. He remarked, "soldiering was physically tough. You soldiered with peers that came from backgrounds where most had previously worked in physically demanding or blue collar jobs."[15]

But there was a flip side to the hard soldiering. The adage "train hard, play hard" was rooted in actual practice. Heavy drinking and brawling was a fact of life. Drinking in the Mess or in bars in the nearby areas was a common pastime in the off hours. "Smokers" in the field after an exercise were alcohol-only events where soft drinks were unheard of. The tedious nature of peacetime soldiering and a lack of activity at times, compounded by a dearth of adequate leadership, and the acceptance of heavy alcohol consumption led to not unsurprising results. By the mid-1980s, then Brigadier-General R.I. Stewart, the commander of the SSF stated:

> The problem in a nutshell is that we have far too many cases of ill disciplined behaviour, assault, disobedience, disrespectful behaviour; theft of private and public property by soldiers; impaired driving offenses; vehicle accidents; inadequate control of stores; ammunition/ pyrotechnics, weapons and equipment that result in loss or theft; and a general laxness in properly controlling soldiers, all which contribute to an erosion of disciplined/soldierly behaviour. We have in many cases lost our regimented pattern of behaviour and our standards of performance are seriously in jeopardy. The danger of allowing standards to slip is self-evident. Once started on the decline, the process picks up momentum and reaches a point when we have no junior leaders who comprehend the standard and it is then impossible to reverse the process.[16]

Stewart's observations were not unfounded or restricted to the SSF. It was an Army-wide, problem at the time, including the Regiment. Chief Warrant Gravelle conceded, "Drinking was more acceptable. Stuff we did than, I'd be on C & P [counselling and probation] now."[17] Similarly, Major-General Denis Tabbernor acknowledged, "it was a drinking army — there were lots of alcohol problems."[18] In essence, it was in part of the tough soldiering mentality.

A final aspect of the Cold War culture was battalion life. The garrison routine, tough training regimen, and the closed, inwardly focused military, as well as the authoritative hierarchy model actually created a close, cohesive environment for members of the Regiment. Mandatory coffee breaks and Happy Hours, along with, at a minimum, monthly mandatory Mess events, fostered an active battalion life and regimental esprit de corps. "It was old school," explained Lieutenant-Colonel Rusty Bassarab, "You had to go to coffee breaks; you had to go to the Mess after work; you didn't leave happy hour until excused by the CO; and you didn't leave a Mess Dinner until excused by the CO. It began to slip a bit in the 1980s, but it didn't fully change until the 1990s."[19] Doug Maclean agreed, "Mess life was very good. Officers would convene in the Mess everyday at 1600 hrs and they would go to coffee break a minimum of once or twice a week. There was an active social program as well, with at least one mess function every month."[20]

Similarly, Denis Thompson asserted, "There was a sense of family among the junior officers Although many felt they had little choice but to participate, it did generate bonds of friendship and family. Individuals knew they belonged to something bigger than themselves, steeped in tradition, camaraderie and purpose."[21] And it was no different in the senior NCO Mess. Master Warrant Officer Tom France commented, "There was lots of Mess life. You'd get to network on the 'old boys network.'"[22]

In the end, Brigadier-General Thompson summarized, "Soldiering in the 1980s had a routine and rhythm to it. Everything that happened in garrison made sense from duty shifts, to PT [physical training] with the soldiers to coffee break."[23]

The fact that the Cold War shaped the culture of the Army and The RCR is not an amazing revelation. And nothing was more influential in forming that culture than the continued service of the Regiment in Europe. It was the zenith of regimental service. One RCR commanding officer who was preparing to take his battalion overseas remarked, "We were living the best of circumstances of the time. In preparation for the rotation to Germany I [my battalion] was the brigade main effort. Therefore, I received no taskings. My only role was to prepare to join 4 CMBG." Thompson insisted, "Going to Germany took seriousness up a notch. In Germany you had equipment and troops."[24]

But the threat was also there. Tom de Faye clearly articulated, "There was an absolute belief of the Soviet threat. We knew there was absolutely no ability to trade space for time. We would not give up a metre of ground."[25] And, as the RCR transitioned into the 1980s, the Soviet threat was once again at a high level reminiscent of the early 1960s during the Cuban Missile Crisis. Arguably the Cold War was at its zenith. The Soviet invasion of Afghanistan at the end of 1979 reinforced the perception of the Soviet Union as a hostile imperialist state. Under the newly elected President Ronald Reagan, the U.S. put great pressure on its nemesis as they sought to take the initiative away from the Soviets in the realm of weapons development, armed forces modernization, and arms control negotiations.[26] This aggressive stance put great pressure on the Soviet Union, which was already struggling because of its economic inefficiency and aggressive foreign policy. Its decaying economic system was hard pressed to keep up with the more robust capitalist economies of its enemies, and its leadership was also aging. The reinvigoration of defence programs in the U.S. and Britain in conjunction with their aggressive foreign policies, further pressed the Soviet system and its leadership.

Moreover, the NATO decision in 1979 to modernize its theatre nuclear forces allowed it to restore the balance of power. This also strengthened deterrence. In addition, the technological superiority of NATO's conventional forces also gave the West a significant edge conventionally. This realization became a catalyst for developing new NATO defence strategy for the Central Region. NATO now focused on "deep battle" and "follow on force attack" (FOLA).

The Canadian government underlined the continuing threat. It asserted, "It is a fact, not a matter of interpretation, that the West is faced with an ideological, political and economic adversary whose explicit long-term aim is to mould the world in its own image. That adversary has at its disposal massive military forces and a proven willingness to use force, both at home and abroad, to achieve political purposes."[27] It also noted that the principal direct threat to Canada "continues to be a nuclear attack on North America by the Soviet Union." It explained that our geographic proximity forced Soviet strategic planners to "regard Canada and the United States as a single set of military targets no matter what political posture we might assume."[28] While discounting an attack in Canada, the government noted, "Although Canada is unlikely to be invaded in a conflict, limited incursions, principally to neutralize installations, or for diversionary purposes, are conceivable."[29] It also acknowledged that Canada's defence effort was required in Europe since that "is where the conventional threat is concentrated and, in war, where the decisive conventional battle would be fought."[30]

Indisputably, the Soviet threat in Europe still loomed large. The Warsaw Pact had a standing force of approximately six million personnel, of which about four million faced off against NATO in Europe.[31] In addition, there were more than 800,000 personnel with some military training enrolled in the national security forces.[32] Warsaw Pact forces that faced ACE, the Allied Command Europe force, which stretched from the northern tip of Norway to the eastern borders of Turkey consisted of about 167 active and mobilizable divisions, plus the equivalent of nine airborne, air assault, and airmobile formations that could be used in a number of different countries. Furthermore, there were 115 divisions positioned well forward considered ready to fight on short notice, as well as 16 additional divisions from the strategic reserve based in the central military districts.

Arrayed against the Soviet juggernaut, NATO had standing forces that totalled 4.5 million personnel of which nearly 2.6 million were stationed in Europe.[33] NATO land forces positioned in or rapidly deployable to Europe to oppose the Warsaw Pact numbered approximately 88 active and mobilizable divisions.[34] With respect to the Canadian sector, DND assessed, "opposite the NATO area where Canadian forces are currently committed, the northern and central regions, the Warsaw Pact can readily deploy some 64 divisions, against 26 for NATO."[35]

Although the threat was as real as ever and Soviet forces were always increasing, for Royals, 4 CMBG from 1979 to the mid-1980s changed little. It was still based on two mechanized infantry battalions (with three rifle companies), an armoured regiment (with three tank squadrons (only two actually manned), and a reconnaissance squadron), and an artillery regiment (with three M-109 batteries). However, when one added up all the deficiencies that existed, particularly in combat service

Courtesy The RCR Museum and Archives.

1 RCR sovereignty exercise in Rankin Inlet, 1984.

Author photograph.

The Green Line in downtown Nicosia, 1984. Nothing had changed from the invasion in 1974.

support, the brigade could only muster about 58 percent of the equipment and personnel it needed to fight as a full-strength brigade group.[36]

Its mission, despite its shortcomings, or perhaps because of them, was to act as a blocking force to prevent enemy penetration and force the enemy to deploy. NATO commanders hoped that using the Brigade in a static dug in defensive position and utilizing its Tube Launched, Optically Tracked, Wire Guided (TOW) anti-tank guided missiles (ATGM) and leopard tanks it would be able to attrite the Soviet forces and fix their lead elements until NATO counterattack forces could complete the destruction of the enemy.[37]

Nonetheless, although deficiencies still remained and although training cannot have changed much from the 1970s, nothing replaced Germany for realism. It provided exactly the conditions that the Royals would have to fight in should the "balloon go up." The Fighting in Built Up Area (FIBUA) site developed by the Americans was for all intents and purposes a small village. It boasted a town hall, *gasthaus*, post office, school, church, and a gas station. It even had a sewer complex. Nothing even close existed in Canada at the time. "The training covered everything," professed Major Bob Near. He insisted, "the FIBUA training we conducted at Hammelburg was really superb, probably the best training the battalion did in Germany."[38]

This was but one aspect. Training also spilt beyond the training areas for realism. For instance, in the late 1980s, 3 RCR moved from the training area in Hohenfels, to the Requisitioned Manoeuvre Area (RMA) north of Frankfurt. As the 3 RCR chronicler noted, "this is not a training area as we think of in Canada, this is a populated area of Germany designated as a manoeuvre area for this one exercise."[39] During one FALLEX as part of an Exercise Reforger conducted by U.S. Army (VII Corps) he described, "With two full corps at each other's throats, thousands of armoured vehicles and fighter aircraft, 3 RCR saw the most realistic interpretation of Soviet tactics as we're likely to see."[40]

In the essence the theme had changed little from decades earlier. As far as the Army was concerned, Germany was the centre of the universe. Denis Thompson lauded, "When you were in Germany you had all the resources. It was the pinnacle of our profession." He assessed, "It made us a world class army. When we went into Yugoslavia years later we could stand on our own two feet and we could give as good as we got." Thompson believed, "Germany gave us an NCO corps that was extremely experienced. You could lean on them heavily and not worry. All this magic stuff happened behind you. You didn't always have that in Canada."[41]

Importantly, Germany continued to set the barometer how the Army would train and what threats it would focus on. In the 1980s one threat that was increasingly emphasized during exercises in Europe and at home was the Soviet chemical weapons capability. The confirmed Soviet usage of nerve and blister agents in Afghanistan showed their willingness to use such weapons. It also underlined the lack of preparedness of the CF and other NATO countries in this regard. NATO's own chemical weapons inventory, which had provided a retaliatory deterrent, had large deteriorated during the 1970s.[42] Therefore, emphasis on defensive measures was important. The limited stock of NBCD (Nuclear, Biological, Chemical Defence) suits available were shipped to Europe. As a result, those in Canada donned their rain suits and gas masks to simulate operating under NBC conditions. The theory was that once conflict began all the necessary equipment would magically appear.

This lack of seemingly essential equipment was testimony to the continuing budgetary shortfalls and pressures that DND endured into the 1980s. The NBCD suits were just one small symptom of a larger commitment capability gap. The CAST Brigade Group and AMF(L) commitments that were longstanding tasks for the various RCR battalions represented larger issues. Many continued to wonder how Canada would deploy and sustain the necessary forces once crisis erupted. Nonetheless, the mission provided an important operational focus and opportunity to train overseas.

It was this NATO focus, whether in the rest of Europe or in Norway, that was key for the military. For those not fortunate enough to be posted to Germany, the CAST and AMF(L) tasks were the next best option. Denis Tabbernor insisted, "The value of the AMF(L) was that it gave you an operational focus, it allowed you to concentrate on skills. Everything my company did was focused on our AMF(L) role so when we got to Norway we knew what we were doing at all levels."[43] Similarly, "Norway," argued Rick Duncan, "was a real role. It was worthwhile as training since it was in a foreign location." In what was a common longstanding senti-ment, he asserted, "It also allowed us to practice our deployment proce-dures and in the end it provided us the opportunity to train in the terrain we would be fighting in."[44] For example, 1 RCR assumed the AMF(L) role in July 1977 and surrendered it in 1989. In the 12-year period, the battalion deployed to Norway seven times and to Denmark three times.

The exercises remained, however, very scripted.[45] Once the Royals deployed to Norway, the "Key Company" would immediately begin the deterrent patrolling phase. "Deterrence patrolling," commented Major Sam McInnis, "[is where] the Canadians are meant to be seen and to effect liaison with the local community."[46] McInnis explained that "The Key Company concept is designed to show that an attack on Norway is an attack against all of NATO." He reinforced, "It demonstrates NATO solidarity and unity of purpose."[47]

The deterrence phase of each of the exercises was obviously important. "Even though the primary purpose of the AMF is deterrence, it is a force fully equipped, trained and manned to fight alongside the local forces in

Author photograph.

A 1 RCR platoon 2IC briefs a section foot patrol preparing to depart their platoon house.

Photographer Corporal J. Baars, Courtesy The RCR Museum and Archives.

3 RCR APCs wait in reserve during WAINCON 88.

defence of the areas concerned, if deterrence fails," insisted Major-General Andrew Christie, a former Canadian AMF(L) commander. "This force is the conventional option, which is a plus," he added, "It is the physical manifestation of [NATO's] Article Five declaration that an attack against one is an attack against all." He concluded, " AMF is a military/political force that illustrates the Alliance's resolve. Our primary mission is deterrence, but if deterrence fails then the AMF(L) is prepared to fight and would acquit itself well."[48]

To ensure it did, each exercise rolled into a combat phase. This, once again, provided Royals with an opportunity to measure themselves against their allies, since the exercises were impressive events. For example, Exercise Anorak Express, in 1980, was a joint AMF field training exercise designed to test rapid deployment of both allied and Norwegian forces to northern Norway, as well as to test the multinational force under winter conditions. The exercise allowed the Canadians to participate with

24,000 other military personnel from Germany, Italy, the Netherlands, Norway, the U.K., and the U.S.[49]

Several years later Exercise Avalanche Express provided another opportunity that involved more than 150 ships and 300 aircraft from nine countries, as well as 40,000 personnel in what was the largest military exercise ever held in Norway.[50] As Master Warrant Officer Duncan noted, "To be a Canadian was always a good thing stacked up against the others. Our soldier skills and leadership were certainly never second to anyone."[51]

The emphasis placed on the AMF(L) task and the standing forces in Europe underscored once again the importance of NATO to the Army. The primary focus even in Canada was on fighting in Europe. Battalions regularly practiced "Snowballs" normally on a monthly to quarterly basis to test their response time. The fact that most, if not all, were initiated at 0400 hours on a normal working day when most individuals would be conveniently in their beds, seemed to matter little. Moreover, the logic of the necessity of Snowballs in Canada was seemingly never questioned. It was a fact of life in Germany, so it became a part of soldiering in Canada as well.

The emphasis of training for Europe was such that an entire series of exercises, called the Rendezvous or RV series were designed, starting in 1981, to better prepare forces in Canada to meet the Soviet threat in Europe. Specifically, the RV series was designed to allow FMC to exercise troops at all levels of command from the section to the division. Leaders welcomed the exercises because it allowed them almost two months of solid field time in which to conduct training, with minimum distractions. The soldiers largely enjoyed the exercises because it broke the normal tedium of garrison routine and offered a new training area, nominally more resources than they were normally allocated and exciting training. Master Warrant Officer Duncan believed that the RVs were "really important for the young soldiers. They actually gained an appreciation of the vastness of the resources of the CF and they had an opportunity to work with the other units, tanks and aircraft."[52] Thompson felt a unit had the greatest level of confidence during RVs. He insisted, "It felt like home, a cohesive battalion."[53]

Planning for the first exercise began almost two years before the actual event. RV 81, conducted at CFB Gagetown, New Brunswick, boasted 10,300 service personnel, including 500 reservists. It was the largest Canadian military exercise since Ex Eastern Star in 1957. FMC formed a division headquarters for the occasion. In what would become the template for the series, the exercise allowed for a two week shakeout at the unit level to provide refresher training on basic drills. It then rolled into combined arms training, including live fire and then a series of formation exercises.[54]

Lieutenant-Colonel W.T.J. Kaulbach, the CO of 2 RCR stated: "RV 81 was a long overdue army concentration." He added, "the fact that the armies of the west and the east shared the same training area allowed the soldiers to make comparisons in standards and adjust if necessary. Above all, however, it proved to all that were there that double-hatting combat units with base tasks does not work. Without the critical third line capability, you cannot sustain field units for long."[55]

The first RV proved to be a success, and a sequel (i.e. RV 83) was conducted two years later in CFB Wainwright, Alberta. For this iteration, more than 7,700 service personnel (including 220 reservists), 2,500 vehicles, and 52 helicopters were deployed. In keeping with the Army's NATO/Europe focus, the exercise was designed primarily to test the capabilities of the CAST Brigade Group since it had never been completely assembled prior to this large exercise.[56]

Once again commanders hailed RV 83 a great success since the FMC division and CAST brigade group were transported across Canada by air, road, and rail with "surprisingly few mishaps." Moreover, the FMC commander noted that at Wainwright the CAST brigade group "assembled, trained and fought together as a formation for the first time, in an exhausting series of exercises designed to test it in all phases of war."[57] The soldiers agreed. As one individual noted, "even though RV 83 was long, most of the troops were too active to notice it, too tired to resent it and too interested to be bored."[58]

The RV series climaxed in 1985 with the largest concentration yet. More than 10,000 troops (including approximately 900 militiamen), 4,000 vehicles, and 90 helicopters were deployed once again to CFB Wainwright. In addition, over 40,000 tons of supplies and equipment were moved by rail and by CC-137 freighter and CC-130 Hercules aircraft. The concentration focused on all phases of war (advance, attack, defence, and withdrawal) up to and including the divisional level. Specifically, RV 85 was conducted in three phases. In the first phase units and formations trained up to brigade level, specifically combined training for infantry and armour units. In the second phase, Ex Proud Warrior, attack and defence techniques were practiced at the divisional level. The final phase, Ex Antelope, was a live-fire for battle groups that entailed a 25 kilometre advance across CFB Suffield.[59]

Lieutenant-Colonel Larry Bowen, the CO of 1 RCR, recalled:

> The exercise started with sub-unit training concentrating primarily on individual fieldcraft, patrolling and mounted operations. The concentration included a battalion exercise practicing armoured/infantry cooperation. A Brigade exercise, emphasizing obstacle crossings was conducted, followed by the battalion. Rendezvous 85 also provided an excellent opportunity for members of the unit to participate in realistic live fire exercises. The live training progressed from section level attacks and culminated with Exercise Antelope, an all arms battle group advance held at CFB Suffield.[60]

The Army continued with its RV series conducting serials in 1987 and 1989, but by the end of the decade financial pressures and the beginning of the implosion of the Soviet Union diminished the importance, emphasis, and resources that were allocated compared to the earlier concentrations. A renewed political focus on sovereignty at the time also cast a shadow. After all, as one officer observed, "the general war scenarios for manoeuvres such as the Rendezvous series are excellent training tools, but do not address key problems faced in protecting our own vast land."[61]

The observation was valid. Although geared to potential combat in Europe, it didn't address domestic security. And the relevance of heavy mechanized battle in the North America context was minimal to nonexistent. After all, few actually believed in a Soviet land threat to North America. The Canadian concern for a Soviet incursion into the Arctic had always been suspect. Any efforts or rhetoric to throw resources at this threat had always been largely to appease the Americans, who had an almost paranoia about the "open flank" to the North.[62] However, by 1979, a joint Canadian/U.S. intelligence estimate reported the unlikelihood of the Soviet use of general purpose conventional forces to initiate hostilities against installations in the Canada/U.S. (CANUS) area. The document stated categorically that Soviet "airborne attacks, unlikely as they are, would consist of no more than small highly specialized teams."[63]

Subsequent appreciations began to identify, or more accurately transform, the potential land threat to North America. Analysts consistently stated the risk, at best, as the insertion of small groups of airborne forces, or the more likely the commitment of Soviet Special Purpose Forces (Spetsnaz) teams operating against the continental periphery including the North. The intelligence reports assessed the most probable threat to CANUS, in the event of general war, as "a series of simultaneous small party raids in isolated communities, in conjunction with sabotage/terrorist operations in any of the major Canadian cities."[64] However, even this level of menace was hotly debated.

In early 1988, Admiral R.H. Falls, a former CDS and chairperson of the NATO Military Committee, testified before a Special Senate Committee on Defence that "I just cannot imagine a scenario where Canada is under attack by land forces."[65] His doubt was shared by Dr. Cynthia Cannizzo of the University of Calgary. Her study of possible threats to the Canadian Arctic led her to believe that "the possibility of a land invasion over some five thousand kilometres of arctic terrain is minuscule."[66]

Even the newly identified Soviet Spetsnaz threat emerging in the eighties was widely questioned. Intelligence experts clearly delineated targets for the Soviet "Special Forces," in priority, as nuclear delivery systems; command and control systems; key installations; key transportation or communications links; and key personnel.[67] Although the possibility was always acknowledged, the likelihood of attack was considered almost negligible. Most analysts concluded that Spetsnaz units would be concentrated on the target rich and logistically supportable European theatre. As Admiral Falls remarked, "it would be suicidal on their part [to operate against North America]."[68]

Nonetheless, the Spetsnaz threat model drove much of the Army training Royals were involved with in Canada. The SSF developed an entire series of exercises called "Lightning Strike," which were first simulated through war games and command post exercises and then actually conducted as a series of field training exercises (FTX). Captain Richard Moore wrote in *Sentinel,* the CF's official magazine, "Lightning Strike demonstrated that Canadian Forces personnel and equipment — both on the land and in the air — can and do operate well anywhere in Canada. And that can't help but reinforce our ability to deter aggression before it starts!"[69] For example, Exercise Lightning Strike 88 was advertised specifically to practice the territorial defence of Canada. It was conducted in the dead of Canadian winter and across a distance of more than 6,400 kilometres. It included a joint task force of more than 3,000 soldiers and airmen from the SSF, 10 Tactical Air Group, Air Transport Group, Fighter Group, and Communications Command. It was the largest defence of Canada operation to date.[70]

Although it focused on the Spetsnaz threat, which placated Army commanders focused on NATO, for Canadian politicians, the important aspect was presence in the nation's northern regions. For them it was about sovereignty, specifically reinforcing Canadian claims to Arctic regions. The government professed:

> After the defence of the country itself, there is no issue more important to any nation then the protection of its sovereignty. The ability to exercise effective national sovereignty is the very essence of nationhood. The Canadian Forces have a particularly important, though not exclusive, role to play in this regard. The protection and control of our territory are fundamental manifestations of sovereignty. Our determination to participate fully in all collective security arrangements affecting our territory or the air or sea approaches to our country and to contribute significantly to those arrangements is an important affirmation of Canadian sovereignty … The government will not allow Canadian sovereignty to be

diminished n any way. Instead, it is committed to ensuring that the Canadian Forces can operate anywhere within Canadian jurisdictional limits. Our Forces will assist civil authorities in upholding the laws and maintaining the sovereignty of Canada.[71]

By the mid-1980s the government was once again consumed with its sovereignty.[72] In 1985, without any warning or request, the American government announced the impending voyage through the Northwest Passage of the U.S. Coast Guard cutter *Polar Sea*. This unilateral act incited yet another shrill cry for protection of Canadian sovereignty.[73] And once again the military was mobilized to meet the non-military threat to its North. As a direct result, many Royals found themselves conducting "SOVOPs" (sovereignty operations) in remote northern communities to show the flag.

The "SOVOPs" and focus on winter/Arctic warfare further defined the Army and Royals in the 1980s. It was another component that made the Canadian soldier who he was — hard, tough, and capable. "Winter training was an important skill set," affirmed Master Warrant Officer Duncan. He maintained, "It taught soldiers self-preservation; the ability to survive in a hostile environment. It was also important for team building and enhancing cohesiveness." Duncan avowed, "It also hardened individuals, something that is often lacking in the CF."[74] John O'Quinn agreed completely. "The hardest training I ever did in the military," he avowed, "was the winter training in the North, functioning with weapons in extreme conditions."[75]

The renewed focus on SOVOPs spawned another entire exercise series called Sovereign Viking. Major Dave Brigden explained, "Sovereign Viking is a unique experience. It's an opportunity to evaluate the physical and mental endurance of troops under extremely cold conditions." He emphasized, "But before learning how to fight in the Arctic, soldiers must be taught how to survive."[76] And Royals quickly learned that engines had to be run 24 hours a day. One experienced participant stressed, "We can't stop the motors because after a few hours they would be completely frozen." Furthermore, he noted, "We also have to move the wheels several metres every three hours, to keep the vehicles from freezing on the spot."[77]

Despite the challenge and excitement of Arctic operations, and notwithstanding the government's emphasis on sovereignty operations, from the Regiment's perspective, the NATO focus on its heavy mechanized forces and European-centric battle space, whether stationed in Germany or deployed under the CAST Brigade Group or AMF(L) commitments, remained its primary focus. Sovereignty operations were an easy day and actually played into skill sets required to meet NATO missions, namely the ability to operate in harsh winter environments.

In addition, when considering The RCR's priorities, close behind NATO operations was the occasional Cyprus tour. This was always welcomed. After all, it was a real operation, was not an onerous tasking, and it allowed Royals to earn a campaign ribbon. In the 1980s, individuals considered three ribbons to be impressive. Most had only one, the Canadian Decoration for long-time service. Those lucky enough to get a Cyprus tour also sported the UNFICYP medal. few had the opportunity to earn additional campaign medals or awards. Therefore, a tour in Cyprus was keenly sought for both the experience and the ribbon.

Although popular, by the 1980s, operationally, Cyprus was no big event. It had changed little from the 1970s.[78] By the 1980s, Cyprus much like the Cold War, had become a routine. The Canadian contingent was responsible for Sector 4, which comprised the divided city of Nicosia. The sector itself was further divided into two lines, Line East and Line West, each manned by a rifle company. Battalion HQ was located at Ledra Palace, while administration support company was located at Blue Beret Camp (BBC) next to the abandoned Nicosia International Airport. Each line company maintained two platoons on the line, housed in platoon or section houses, while the third platoon was held in reserve at Ledra Palace. A typical shift entailed soldiers working 12 hours on duty either in the CP or OP, then 12 hours off shift, and finally 12 hours of standby general duties. The platoon rotation worked on a schedule of four weeks on the line, followed by one week of general duties at Ledra Palace, a week of field training, and then a return to the line.

Undeniably, the Canadian sector, because of the close proximity of the belligerents, was the most sensitive. The Canadian UNFICYP chief of staff, Canadian Brigadier-General Bill Hewson, acknowledged, "If trouble is going to happen, it will happen there [Canadian sector in Nicosia]."[79] As a result, there was always some definite value in participating in UNFICYP. In many ways, it was the only show in town. Moreover, "the soldier becomes a better Canadian for serving outside the country," insisted Hewson, "Regardless of where he comes from, he leaves here with a greater understanding of just how divisive religious, linguistic and ethnic difference can be."[80]

This would prove useful in the coming decades. However, overall, except for minor, petty, if not often laughable incidents between belligerents or politically motivated low level demonstrations by the population, there were few operational challenges in Cyprus in the 1980s. Denis Thompson assessed, "Cyprus was the classic peacekeeping operation." He conceded, "Frankly, the last three months [of my tour in 1986] all I did was train for the military skills competition." He proudly recalled, "The RCR platoons in 1986 actually finished 1st, 2nd and 6th place. It really increased our confidence. We beat the British 3 Parachute Regiment (four years after the Falklands)."[81] But he categorically affirmed, "The tour itself was of marginal value — there were no real incidents."[82]

Others had similar views but saw intrinsic value in the deployment nonetheless. "Cyprus," believed Kit Charlebois, "was the highlight of the soldiers' time in the 1970s and early 1980s and it gave the soldiers something to train for and look forward to as opposed to the repetitive all phases of war training that was conducted on an annual basis."[83] John O'Quinn felt, "It was different and any time you go someplace different or do something different it's exciting."[84] In the end, insisted Colin Magee, "Cyprus was *the* operational tour. You had live ammo and a chance to do your stuff."[85] Tom France concurred. He explained, "Cyprus was the only thing we had. It was a chance to get out of the country and do stuff."[86]

Aside from the occasional Cyprus tour, the RCR battalions were also required to support the Canadian Airborne Regiment, which in effect sustained the RCR airborne legacy. For those in 3 Airborne Commando, there was also an effort to maintain the RCR link. As Major Bruce Archibald, a former CO of 3 AB Cdo captured in writing, "Your Royals within the AB Regt are very busy and upholding the tradition and spirit of the RCR."[87] But there were issues sustaining the Royal affiliation, as there were for the other regular infantry regiments. By the 1980s, the chronic shortage of those willing to serve in the Cdn AB Regt was sorely felt.

Major-General Bob Stewart, a SSF commander during the 1980s revealed, "there was not a large reservoir of soldiers in the remainder of the army that wanted to experience the challenge and hardship of airborne service, particularly [vital leaders and trainers like] Warrant Officers and Senior NCOs."[88] In May 1985, the manning issue became so sensitive that the director of infantry requested the FMC Commander to consider modifying the voluntary aspect of service in the Cdn AB Regt "because of the long-standing difficulties in obtaining sufficient numbers of volunteers, especially to fill Senior NCO positions."[89] The Army commander at the time, Lieutenant-General Charles Belzile, refused the request. He insisted that the regimental identification of the three infantry commandos for manning purposes was working well. Furthermore, Belzile believed that voluntarism was the core of the airborne spirit.[90]

General Belzile's faith in the regimental affiliation of commandos was actually the brainchild of General Jacques Dextraze in the late-seventies. In June 1979, with the CDS authority to man 3 AB Cdo, the concept was actually implemented and The RCR received its "own" commando. The Dextraze initiative to link the commandos to their parent regiments was designed to actually assist the Cdn AB Regt. The Army's senior leadership believed it was possible to solve the Airborne Regiment's chronic personnel shortage by ensuring that each of the rifle commandos was independently manned by the three regular force infantry regiments (i.e. RCR, R22eR, PPCLI). They felt that this system would ease the problem of replacements. Each parent infantry regiment had a quota to fill to meet the requirements of its respective commando. Any shortfalls could be easily attributed to the source. The senior Army commanders further postulated that affiliated commandos would create, within the parent infantry regiments, a distinct pride. Therefore, they argued, feeder regiments would send only their best officers and soldiers. The success of the initiative has been debated ever since.[91] However, the designation of a RCR commando was instrumental in maintaining the linkage to the Royal's airborne legacy.

Manning issues, however, soon became a moot point. By 1985, the domestic political and the international geo-political environments were shifting, ironically, in opposite directions. Financial pressures and the government's apparent apathy toward its military and international commitments had a negative effect on the CF. In September 1980, all infantry COs were called to FMC HQ for a manning conference where the Army commander briefed them on the situation. Lieutenant-Colonel Kaulbach, CO 2 RCR, commented, "There is light at the end of the tunnel. What now must be determined is, is that light an oncoming Freight Train?!"[92] Those serving during the 1980s were only too familiar with the shortfalls. One officer conceded, "There were constraints, particularly a lack of people. Platoons numbered only about 20 personnel."[93] Lieutenant-Colonel A.D. McQuarrie, a CO during the period, lamented, "Like many of our activities these days of restraint, the exercise has to be shortened due to lack of funds."[94]

The effect was the same even in Germany. "The constant refusal in the Canadian government to honour its commitments was nothing short of an embarrassment to those of us that were trying to work in the NATO staff to carry our fair share of collective defence," acknowledged one officer. "There was nothing you could do about it. The politicians would be given good military advice but they would ignore it. The decisions they made were made for political purposes."[95]

For a while, the election of a new Conservative government in the fall of 1984 held promise for the CF. Perrin Beatty, a MND in the new regime, later affirmed, "I think there is a broad consensus in Canada that our capabilities had been allowed to deteriorate."[96] In its annual review, DND openly commented that "1985 was a momentous year for defence policy.[97] After a period of 15 years without any major re-assessment, a comprehensive examination of Canada's national defence policy, including a renewed evaluation of the strategic situation in the world and this country's place in it, was initiated by the government."[98] On 5 June 1987, Beatty tabled *Challenge and Commitment: A Defence Policy for Canada,* the new defence white paper in the House of Commons. The bold white paper was welcomed with open arms by the military. The policy stated, "Since coming to office, the Government has reviewed Canada's military commitments in relation to the current capabilities of the Canadian Forces and those they can be expected to possess in the future. This review has confirmed that we are not able to meet those commitments fully and effectively. After decades of neglect, there is indeed a significant 'commitment-capability gap.'"[99]

Aside from the acknowledgement of "rust-out" within the CF, the white paper also represented a reinforcement of the Cold War mentality — large conventional forces such as heavy mechanized forces in Germany and nuclear submarines. It also symbolized a halt to the continual downward spiral of defence spending that started in 1964, with the Liberal white paper, and remained unabated ever since.[100] However, the influence of the Conservative white paper, much like their government, was fleeting. Elsewhere, the Cold War was beginning to thaw.

By 1985, Mikhail Gorbachev began a transformation first of the Soviet Union and then its Warsaw Pact satellites. The new Soviet leader pushed the concepts of *glasnost* (enlightenment) and *perestroika* (restructuring) in an effort to invigorate the Soviet Union, which was on the verge of paralysis. The reform effort, however, actually began to derail the Soviet system and produced political upheaval, economic chaos, and ethnic tensions.

At roughly the same time in Canada, in March 1985, the Conservative government increased Canada's military strength and level of preparedness by deploying an additional 1,220 military personnel in central Europe. It addition, it designated an infantry battalion to the AMF(L), separating it from the CAST Brigade Group.[101] It was also looking to realign its commitment to NATO.

From 12 August to 25 September 1986, 2 RCR as part of the CAST BG participated in Exercise Brave Lion, which was the largest movement of Canadian troops to Europe since the Second World War.[102] More than 5,500 troops and 15,000 tonnes of equipment and supplies were air and sea lifted to Norway. The exercise consisted of brigade and division level exercises designed to:

1. demonstrate NATO solidarity;
2. test plans for the deployment, reception, and employment of the force; and
3. test Canadian and Norwegian plans for supporting the force while in Norway.[103]

Photographer Sergeant M.J. Reid, Courtesy The RCR Museum and Archives.

A RCR platoon deploying for battle during Exercise Arrowhead Express, Norway, March 1988.

The MND, Perrin Beatty, revealed, "We exercised the CAST commitment for the first time in September of 1986 and we were able to see the results of the exercise and the difficulties we would have in properly fulfilling that commitment in time of war." He conceded, "we should not have commitments that are not honest."[104] The government concluded, "There are particularly severe problems associated with the deployment of the CAST Brigade to northern Norway. The force requires some weeks to reach Norway, making timely deployment questionable, and it cannot make an opposed landing." It further acknowledged "once deployed, it would be extremely difficult to reinforce and resupply, particularly after

Photographer Sergeant M.J. Reid, Courtesy The RCR Museum and Archives.

A BV-206 drives past an ice wall in northern Norway during Exercise Arrowhead Express, Norway, March 1988.

the start of hostilities. The result is that, even if successfully deployed, the brigade could rapidly find itself in an untenable position." As such, the government decided that "consolidation in southern Germany is the best way to achieve a more credible, effective and sustainable contribution to the common defence in Europe. Consolidation will reduce, although not eliminate, the critical logistic and medical support problems posed by our current commitments. It will ensure that in time of need there will be an identifiable, operational and sustainable Canadian force in Europe."[105]

Therefore, the government shifted the task of the Canada-based CAST BG from northern Norway to the central front. This, in theory, enabled the Canadian army to field a division-sized force in crisis. The government believed, "the resulting combat power will be enhanced and made more effective than what could have been achieved by two separately deployed brigades. Consolidation will thus be of significant value to NATO's Central Army Group, as the size of its operational reserve will be doubled."[106] Despite the shift of emphasis, Canada still maintained the existing battalion group commitment to the AMF(L) for service on the northern flank.[107]

But it mattered little. With the beginning of the withdrawal of Soviet troops from Afghanistan in the spring of 1988, returning disillusioned soldiers just added to the turmoil that was already apparent within the Union of Soviet Socialist Republics (U.S.S.R.). Although the Soviets had been able to hide the internal fissures, by the end of the decade the country began to implode, and soon after, it and its Warsaw Pact alliance collapsed. On 9 November 1989, East Germany announced that its border with West Germany was open. The wall had had come down; the Cold War was over.

By the end of the month, on 30 November 1989, Canada ceased its CAST BG commitment and consolidated its forces in central Europe in the form of the 1st Canadian Division. Bill McKnight, the MND at the time, wrote: "Like all Canadians, we hope that the easing of international tensions and the genuine progress achieved in arms control herald a new era of peace and cooperation."[108] Like the MND, the public at large now looked for a huge peace dividend. After all, with the Soviet threat gone — what need was there for large military forces?

The dramatic effect of events was not fully or immediately felt. To many it seemed surreal. The primary purpose and framework, in practice, of virtually the entire CF was seemingly wiped out overnight. NATO scrambled to find continued purpose and to redefine itself. The CF leadership was left stupefied. The world they knew and were rooted in was disappearing. First, the Soviet threat; then the role and existence of NATO; and, moreover, a stirring in German society. In Germany, the late eighties revealed a civilian population that was no longer accepting of careless manoeuvre damage by NATO forces, and exercises were curtailed.[109] With the fall of the wall, units quickly found themselves confined to bases and manoeuvre areas.

In Canada, winds of change had begun to blow as well. The Canadian public began to show signs of defiance. They were no longer willing to defer to authority or blindly accept the actions or practices of government, corporations, professionals, or the military. Canadians wanted transparency, openness, and accountability.

But scant attention was paid to the changing tides. At the moment all that was important was that the war was over and we had won. The decades of preparation and training had paid off. NATO had prevailed, and Royals shared in that victory. "One of the great hallmarks of the Cold War era," reinforced Lieutenant-General Jack Vance, "was the fact that we actually did win it."[110] The Cold War was over and what the future would bring was for tomorrow. At the time no one even imagined the storm that was waiting to be unleashed.

5

The New World Order: Entering the 1990s

Much like the previous decade, not a soul could have predicted that the 1990s would severely test the Canadian Forces and forever change its nature and character. The West had just won a stunning victory over the menacing Soviet empire. The Cold War was over and publics around the world naively looked to a period of peace and tranquility. All expected a peace dividend. For the Canadian government the end of the Cold War was welcomed in part because it now battled a record deficit that detrimentally impacted Canada's financial well-being and international standing.

For the military, the end of the Cold War did create some angst. NATO and the Soviet threat had been its rationale for relatively large allocations of the federal budget every year. Its training, sense of purpose, and professional framework were all tied to the Cold War paradigm. Alas, the question of what next required immediate attention. Not surprisingly, the Cold War routine carried on, and all continued to do what they had always done. However, for Royals and all other members of the CF, the 1990s ushered in a dramatic change in the world order that would have a dramatic impact on The RCR.

For Royals the decade began with a bang. Both 1 and 2 RCR quickly found themselves deployed operationally as they were called out in aid

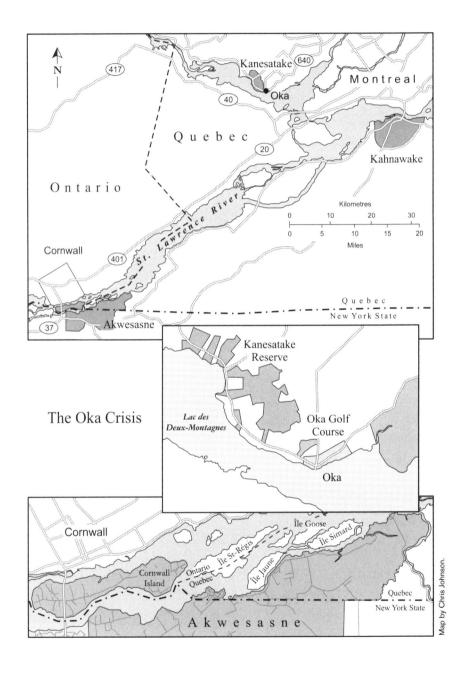

The Oka Crisis

Map by Chris Johnson.

of the civil power in Quebec and Ontario. On 8 March 1990, Mohawks of the Kanesatake community set up a blockade on a road leading to the Oka municipal golf course as a local protest in an attempt to stop the Quebec town from expanding the course on land the Natives claimed belonged to them.[1] This launched a chain of events that would end 78 days later. However, before it ended, there was much violence.

Up until this point, the quiet little 3,000 person community of Oka, located 65 kilometres to the northwest of Montreal, and situated at the confluence of the Ottawa and St. Lawrence Rivers, had existed in relative solitude. However, all that was to change. The conflict at Kanesatake centred on an area known locally as "the Pines." The Oka town council had decided to expand the local golf course by adding nine holes. They also intended to build 50–60 luxury homes along the fairways of the proposed course. However, this plan clashed with existing land claims that the Natives claimed dated back to the seventeenth and eighteenth centuries.

However, the crisis also revealed that other agendas were at play. Mohawk Nation sovereignty and self-determination became principal points of demand that actually overshadowed the effort to save the white pine forest.[2] Moreover, under the guise of Native rights, elements of the Mohawk Nation's Warrior Society attempted to protect and advance interests and activities in illegal gambling and smuggling (i.e. cigarettes, alcohol, weapons, and human trafficking).[3]

Not surprisingly, the brewing situation in Oka had quickly attracted national attention. Prime Minister Brian Mulroney was so concerned about the escalating situation in Oka that already on 28 April 1990 he had secretly directed Bill McKnight, the MND, to prepare contingency plans to support law enforcement operations. His apprehension was not hard to appreciate. Government intelligence revealed that the number of Warriors and sympathizers ranged between 300–500. Moreover, many were identified as former members of the U.S. or Canadian military, as well as individuals with Vietnam War experience.

More worrisome was their confirmed arsenal. The Warriors were known to have in their possession grenades, semi-automatic rifles (e.g. AR-15, M-16, and shotguns with 30-round magazines), automatic rifles (e.g. AK-47, .223 Ruger Mini 14, and 9 mm Uzi), as well as hand guns.

They were also believed to have more than 25,000 rounds of various calibres of ammunition. Finally, and of great significance, the Warriors were also in possession of, or could acquire on short notice, two .50 calibre heavy machine guns, as well as a number of M-72 light anti-tank weapons (LAW). In addition, the Warriors also possessed a sophisticated communications network capable of monitoring police frequencies, maintaining excellent command and control between themselves, and conducting effective jamming operations with white noise, music, and verbal threats.[4]

By the end of April, the federal government was forced to act. Over a period of two days, a nine-hour gun battle set the Mohawk Akwesasne Reserve ablaze. Approximately 3,000–4,000 rounds of ammunition were expended. Two natives were killed and many houses were burned to the ground. Between 1–3 May 1990, approximately 500 police officers from six different law enforcement agencies converged on Akwesasne from both borders and sealed off all access to the reserve.

As a result of the violence, at 2045 hours, 1 May 1990, the solicitor-general of Canada, Pierre Cadieux, requested the MND to provide military assistance to the Royal Canadian Mounted Police (RCMP) in and around

Courtesy Major Rusty Bassarab.

Major Rusty Bassarab, DCO 2 RCR, listens to Chief Joe Norton during the Oka Crisis.

Courtesy 2 RCR.

One of the many confrontations during OP Salon that witnessed Native protestors assaulting Royal Canadians.

Akwesasne. This request initiated Operation Feather. By the morning of 2 May, the CF was largely poised to conduct its mission, which was "to provide armed assistance to RCMP to restore law and order on Canadian portion of St. Regis Akwesasne Indian Reserve."[5] However, the MND clearly stipulated that the "CF assistance [was] to be confined to provision of armoured vehicles for transport and protection of police personnel, mobile VHF/FM secure communications for LEA [Law Enforcement Agencies] use and any non lethal operational support requested to ensure success and safety of personnel involved."[6] Although the initial commitment was only for seven days, the duration of the operation was left open-ended. In addition, the MND ordered contingency planning to take place to allow for any increase in scope of operations.[7]

The immediate task fell to 1 RCR. The CO, Lieutenant-Colonel Norris Pettis, became the tactical commander in charge of 248 personnel, 81 vehicles, various boats and rafts, and two CH-145 helicopters all deployed from the SSF in CFB Petawawa. "I can't imagine a more complicated problem," asserted Norris, "We're dealing with three police forces [Sûreté du Québec (SQ), Ontario Provincial Police (OPP) and RCMP], two provinces and two national governments."[8]

The soldiers wore body armour and helmets, and carried weapons and live ammunition. However, rules of engagement (RoEs) specified that magazines could only be loaded on weapons when ordered by a superior officer or in self-defence. The armed military posture was predictable. After all, besides the arsenal of weapons already in possession of the Warriors, LEA had determined that the Natives had purchased additional heavy machine-guns and rocket-propelled grenade (RPG) launchers. On the night of 2 May, two boatloads of weapons were identified being transported from Cornwall Island to St. Regis Island.

Despite the build-up of weaponry, the police presence surrounding the reserve seemingly quieted the violence. On 16 May, Operation Feather was renamed Operation Akwesasne, but within two weeks the CF support was no longer required, and on 7 June the 1 RCR element was redeployed to CFB Petawawa. By 25 June, the CF commitment was limited to only 12 personnel, mainly intelligence operators.

However, things quickly heated up. On 29 June 1990, the Quebec Superior Court granted the Municipality of Oka another injunction calling for the dismantlement of the Native barricades. The injunction was served to Grand Chief George Martin in the Band Council office; however, he conceded that he was powerless to enforce it, as not all those involved in the civil disobedience recognized his authority. As he predicted, his subsequent direction was promptly ignored by the Native protestors.

Events began to take on an ominous turn. On 5 July, Sam Elkas, the Quebec Minister of Public Security, pronounced that the injunction would be enforced. He warned the Mohawks to remove the barricades by 9 July, which was the expiry date of the injunction, or face the possibility of police intervention. Five days later, on 10 July, The Oka Municipal Council requested the assistance of the SQ to deal with the continuing problem.[9]

In preparation for the intervention, the SQ requisitioned equipment from the CF and received 18 armoured vehicles, night vision goggles (NVG), flak jackets, and C-7 assault rifles. The request was prudent, as the Mohawks had transformed "the Pines" into a fortified redoubt. There were heavy barricades under constant surveillance that severely restricted vehicle approach. In addition, trenches and low walls were constructed using sand bags and logs. Moreover, on the night of 10 July, barbed wire was added to the perimeter of the barricades.

The next morning, on 11 July, SQ special weapons and tactics (SWAT) teams from the SQ emergency service unit, as well as other SQ officers assembled at the edge of "the Pines" in preparation to forcibly dismantle the barrier. Tear gas was fired to disperse the crowd. Subsequently, at around 0853 hours, the Quebec provincial police rushed the barricades. There was an exchange of gunfire that lasted less than half a minute but resulted in the death of SQ Corporal Marcel Lemay.[10]

The SQ were completely unprepared for the violence they encountered. They quickly retreated down Highway 344 to the village of Oka itself. The Mohawks promptly seized three SQ patrol cars, as well as the SQ front-end loader that had been brought up to dismantle the barricades. Ironically and humiliatingly, it was now put to use to construct yet another barrier out of the abandoned SQ cruisers, as well as logs and stones to further block access to "the Pines." In all two more barricades were hastily constructed with the result that all three paved roads leading into Kanesatake were now under armed control of the Warriors and their supporters. The SQ rallied and began to erect barricades opposite to those of the Mohawks.

The defiant Mohawk action at "the Pines" also elicited Native support from the Kahnawake Reserve. Already at 0545 hours, on 11 July 1990, before the police assault, Mohawk sympathizers blocked the Mercier Bridge, which was a key conduit connecting the suburbs of the south shore to Montreal.[11] They then erected additional barricades at Highway 138 directly opposite the town of Chateauguay and another at the southern entrance to the reserve on Highway 344.[12]

The following day the crisis rapidly escalated. Canadian and international media arrived and made it headline news. In addition, the CF provided additional personnel and materiel support to LEA. This included: 151 personnel, 37 vehicles, 113 C-7 assault rifles with 22,000 rounds of 5.56 mm ammunition, NVGs, armoured vests, and helmets. CF intelligence and electronic warfare personnel were also busy secretly taking pictures of Mohawk defensive positions on all three reserves and building an intelligence picture of the Warriors.

The failed SQ raid had been a significant error. It had strengthened Mohawk resolve to forcefully resist any attempt to remove them from "the Pines." Moreover, events had given the Natives the excuse to turn "the Pines," as well as the Kanesatake and Kahnawake Reserves, into fortified camps. In addition, the confrontation and death of a SQ officer had exacerbated long-standing animosity between the Mohawk population and the SQ. This dynamic, compounded by the fact that LEA did not possess the firepower or training to seize the barricades by force, made direct CF involvement inevitable.

As a result, on 6 August, Sam Elkas, acting as the Quebec attorney general, invoked Part 11 of the *National Defence Act*. He issued a requisition for the assistance of the CF in *Aid to the Civil Power* to, "repress the troubles which subsist at this moment in Oka and Kahnawake to secure the protection of works, public and private, which are essential to the general welfare and to the security of the population of Quebec."[13] Two days later, the Army commander, Lieutenant-General Kent Foster, met with Quebec Premier Robert Bourassa to discuss limitations and options with regard to CF intervention.

By 9 August, 2 RCR, as part of 5 CMBG, was recalled from leave to begin preparations for Operation Salon. The Royals, similar to their sister units in the brigade, began intelligence briefings and preparatory training that included full scale rehearsals. The unit chronicler noted, "Training, in anticipation of deployment, became long and hard, and focused primarily on a worst case scenario: a barricade assault."[14] Under the provincial request for assistance the CF was specifically requested to:

1. Remove all barricades in the affected areas;
2. Restore freedom of movement on all roads and bridges;
3. Remove all strong points; and
4. Restore normal conditions of public order and security.[15]

The intelligence picture assembled by CF personnel on site was fed into the unit to assist with preparations. As always, training was conducted to prepare for the worst case scenario — a direct assault on the barricades. Lieutenant-Colonel Colin Magee, then the 2 RCR operations officer, remembered, "We had full information on the barricades and how they were manned, their construction as well as how they were booby-trapped." He explained, "We set up mock barricades to those specifications, including booby-traps, and then we proceeded to conduct live fire including the use of Leopard Main Battle tanks and 105 mm artillery in a direct fire role." Magee revealed, "We practiced mounted, dismounted, combined arms assaults on the barricades by day, by night, noisy approach, as well as stealthy assault to get our skills and drills honed."[16]

At the time, two significant issues were downplayed, or overlooked, depending how one wishes to describe it, that would have tremendous effect on the soldiers. The first was the absence of any crowd control training or equipment. In the mid-1980s the CF had cut crowd control from its responsibilities, determining that it was a task that was best left with LEA. As a result, the CF no longer had doctrine, training, or equipment to address the matter. The second issue was the lack of understanding of clear easily understood RoEs for Operation Salon. The operation was guided by two principles that seemed easy enough in theory, but proved difficult in the acid test of real operations. The first principle was the use of minimum force. The second was the oft-publicized declaration that the CF would under no circumstances fire the first shot.

The lack of clear RoEs created real problems for CF personnel. With a clear declaration that the CF would not fire the first shot, the onus on escalating the crisis was shifted to the Warriors. However, this removed from the Natives any fear of the unknown, i.e. how would the CF react if pushed? As such, arguably, the courage, bravado, and will to resist of the Natives was exponentially increased. Moreover, without clear RoEs the soldiers were unsure of exactly what actions they were permitted to take when they were physically assaulted, or pelted with rocks and other dangerous objects. To many the definition of minimum force was not fully understood. A senior CF officer elucidated on the dilemma. He stated:

> It was really quite an experience. We did not want to hurt anybody and we didn't want our guys to get hurt. But we were told that we have to take casualties before we can shoot back which is a pretty grim thing to say and have to do. We are supposed to have the inalienable right to self-defence. There we did not. That is a hell of a thing to ask soldiers to do, but they did it.[17]

So, as 2 RCR prepared for possible deployment, intelligence operations were well underway.[18] Updated CF intelligence now placed Warrior strength at approximately 150–250 at Kanesatake and about 300–500 at Kahnawake. Intelligence assessments confirmed that the more radical members were prepared to violently oppose any military action taken by the government.[19] They had also taken great pains in preparing their positions. The Warriors had placed booby-traps (e.g. fish hooks hanging from trees, planks of wood with nails protruding, holes and spikes in the ground) throughout their positions and surrounding areas.

The Warriors had also continued to build on their arsenal of weapons. They now were known to hold: approximately 164 AK-47 (7.62 mm) variants, 82 Mini-14 Ruger Assault Rifles (5.56 mm), six Uzi Ingram M9-M10-M11 submachine guns (9 mm), five 82A1 Barett .50 calibre long-range sniping rifles, and one .50 calibre HMG (heavy machine gun (HMG), many AR 15/M-16s, RPK light machine guns (7.62 mm), Ruger Mini-30s (7.62 mm), and FN Browning 125S, as well as 87 hunting rifles, 109 shotguns, and 203 handguns of various makes and models. In addition, during this time they legally purchased over 50,000 rounds of various calibre ammunition and 400 magazines. Adding to this impressive inventory, the Warriors also possessed over 400 grenades, dynamite, homemade Molotov cocktails, and pipe bombs. Other equipment included night-vision devices and police scanners. Unconfirmed weapons included mines, Claymore mines, M-60 7.62 mm general purpose machine guns (GPMG), M-72 LAWs, RPG 7/8s, and mortars.

Making the weapons and defensive positions more dangerous was the fact that the Warriors had established an excellent command and control framework. The reserves were broken into sectors and specific areas of operations (AOs). Within each AO they had structured small groupings of 12–20 personnel under a tactical commander. They had shift schedules and rotated through the barricades to maintain a constant alert presence. In addition they monitored police frequencies and had their own reconnaissance personnel outside the barricades to report on LEA and military activity.

The Warriors maintained constant communication through a network that consisted of cellular phones, band radios, very high frequency marine band radios, and a secure fax link. They maintained discipline on their nets and used code names and code words for locations and activities. Furthermore, the Warriors also possessed commercial encryption devices that allowed them to use low level code in their conversations. They also had a communications intercept receiver at the Warrior command post (CP) at Kanesatake, which allowed them to intercept unsecure military communications.

The stand-off between Mohawks and the SQ dragged on for over a month, when, on 17 August 1990, the CDS announced that the CF would replace the SQ at the barriers. As a result, at 0800 hours on 20 August, CF personnel relieved the SQ at their 12 main barricades at both Kanesatake (taken over by 2 R22eR) and Kahnawake (taken over by 3 R22eR). Immediately, the barricades were turned into military positions. Vehicles were tactically deployed to maximize observation and cover, trenches were dug, and defensive wire was strung along the perimeter. All this was completed by 2000 hours without any violence.

The handover from SQ to the CF was inevitable. First, overtime for the SQ personnel manning the barricades was costing the province a lot of money. Second, the task was now beyond police. "The Sûreté du Québec was not capable of facing the kind of weaponry in the Warriors' arsenal," explained the Army commander. He added, "My view was that the army would eventually have to confront the natives. No police force in the country could be expected to deal with the circumstances that confronted the Sûreté du Québec."[20]

While the CF manned the barriers, negotiations between the government and the Mohawks continued. On 21 August 1990, the Natives tabled a three-point proposal. The first item called for the acquisition of the disputed lands at Kanesatake. The second point required both the federal government and the province of Quebec to recognize a unified Mohawk Nation consisting of six Mohawk territories in Quebec, Ontario, and New York State. The final point was a demand that the SQ and other Quebec authorities not interfere with gambling operations at the gambling facility at Kahnawake.[21]

The following day, detailed aerial reconnaissance reports and photographs revealed the Warriors had made substantial improvements to their trench system and anti-tank ditch. In addition, they had added other obstacles that would require infantry to dismount and fight through the objective. These revelations, compounded by the incredible demands issued the previous day, prompted the government to order the CF to commence operations in Kanesatake and Kahnawake.

As a result, at 0800 hours on the morning of 23 August, elements of "C" Coy, 2 R22eR, advanced 1,500 metres until they reached a vacated Warrior barricade, which was soon dismantled. According to Colonel Tremblay "The massed arrival of the 14 Grizzly [AVGPs] each armed with two machine guns was the best deterrent. While uttering their death threats, the Warriors nevertheless realized that they would never come out on top in an exchange."[22] The CF manned its new advanced positions and settled in while negotiations continued.

However, little progress was made. The Mohawk negotiation team insisted that the Warriors be given criminal amnesty and that they would not lay down their weapons or remove the barricades until the CF and police completely withdrew. Frustrated with the ridiculous and ever-changing demands, on 27 August, Premier Bourassa ordered all negotiations to be terminated. The CDS, General John de Chastelain, then publicly announced that the premier of Quebec had directed the CF to carry out the four tasks, which amounted to the removal of all barricades and the return of law and order.

After the announcement, the following day, in preparation for military operations, 2 RCR moved from its holding area in Farnham to an assembly area east of Kahnawake in Delson. Three Leopard main battle tanks (MBT) equipped with dozer blades were also moved forward should a direct assault be required on any of the barricades. Concurrently, the Army commander pleaded with the Warriors. He beseeched them "not to force my soldiers to resort to the use of force as the Army moves to carry out its orders." Foster reiterated, "We will not fire the first shot."[23] In addition, DND also released videotape that revealed graphic details of the Warrior positions, fortifications, and weapon systems to justify to the Canadian public the military's impending operations.[24]

Later that night, on 28 August, following up the CF briefings and the public disclosure of the Warriors' arsenal and defensive positions, Prime Minister Brian Mulroney held a national press conference on the CBC to further underscore the government's decision to take military action. Mulroney announced, "They [Mohawks] have put on the table a series of totally unacceptable claims, including immunity from criminal law." He assessed the Warriors "sought to give themselves the status of an independent nation within the boundaries of Canada." Finally, Mulroney concluded, "Obviously there will be no pleasure in this task but the Canadian Forces will do their duty and the barricades will come down."[25]

Behind the scenes, the local tactical commanders had already been discussing the dismantlement of the barricades. Lieutenant-Colonel Robin Gagnon, the CO of 3 R22eR revealed:

> It took nine days, from the 20th to the 29th ... to convince them to co-operate in lifting the barricades. We gave, in return, our word that we would: first respect the Mohawk people; and, secondly, that we would not use the press or make statements to place them in a situation where they would lose face. They gave credibility to our engagement and, on the afternoon of the 29th,

we lifted the first row of barricades. By 1 September, the
Mercier Bridge was in our hands.[26]

It was on 29 August 1990 that 2 RCR was moved forward to take
over a number of R22eR positions on the eastern portion of the perimeter around Kahnawake. By 1900 hours, that night the blockades on
Highways 132 and 138 were peacefully removed in a joint CF/Mohawk
effort.[27] By the morning of 31 August, all barricades had been removed or
were in the process of being dismantled. The following day the Mercier
Bridge was also turned over to the CF.

Despite the success at Kahnawake, the situation at Oka remained the
same. But not for long. At 1300 hours on 1 September 2, R22eR began
to collapse the Mohawk positions. They advanced rapidly and used the
element of surprise to maximize confusion within the Warriors ranks.
Van Doo APCs pushed through "the Pines" along back roads and, despite
Native threats and warning shots, swept through a number of barricades
and continued to pressure the Warriors.[28] By 2030 hours, 2 R22eR was in
control of all barricades except the barrier at the top of the hill on Highway
344 facing down toward the village of Oka. The French Canadian soldiers
then established a temporary perimeter around the last Warrior position.

The following morning, just as the first light of dawn began to
seep into the horizon, 2 R22eR APCs slowly advanced toward the
last barricade and began to systematically seal it off using razor wire.
Approximately, 20–30 Warriors were defending the position and began
to yell and shout. However, they subsequently withdrew and retreated to
the Rehabilitation Treatment Centre on the reserve. By 1800 hours, the
final barricade at Kanesatake was dismantled. At the same time, a tight
perimeter was placed around the treatment centre.[29]

Although the barricades were removed, the crisis was not yet over.
There still remained the tasks of restoring freedom of movement on all
roads and bridges, as well as removing all strong points and restoring normal conditions of public order and security. The situation re-ignited on 3
September when Mohawks and Warriors attempted to retake the Mercier
Bridge. A prompt CF response quickly quelled the attempt. However, it
became the catalyst to enter the reserve. Brigadier-General Armand

Roy, the 5 CMBG commander, ordered 2 RCR and 3 R22eR to enter the Kahnawake Reserve to increase patrols and control the main access points.

The failed attempt to re-occupy the bridge also had another consequence. CF surveillance assets tracked the armed Warriors who had participated in the attempt to retake the bridge back to a longhouse on Highway 207. This location was known to be their communications centre, but now it was also suspected of being a major weapons cache as one Warrior was seen with what was believed to be a .50 calibre heavy machine gun. Brigadier-General Roy quickly ordered 2 RCR to investigate.

Subsequently, Major Lawrence O'Neill, OC "G" Coy, 2 RCR, advanced toward the longhouse. He fully expected resistance from armed Warriors. Instead, he was met by a group of 30 women who blocked the progress of the APCs. As it was impossible to bypass, the woods were thick and the ditches deep, the lead platoon dismounted and pushed forward to their objective on foot. "The women immediately offered violence to the soldiers," captured the War Diary. "The troops resisted passively as possible [but] in many instances three to four women would attack a single soldier."[30] One officer was forced to the ground and his pistol was taken. Males could be seen in the background talking on cell phones. Very quickly another 50–60 Mohawk women materialized, making progress even more difficult. At 1750 hours, the Royal Canadians finally struggled their way to the longhouse, where they were met by a hostile crowd of approximately 100 Mohawks, again mainly women.

"G" Coy, now supported by "K" Coy, set up a cordon around their objective. Although it was extremely difficult to hold back the throngs of Native protestors, by 1900 hours the Royal Canadians were able to provide a cordon so that a search of the longhouse could be executed. Five minutes later, six SQ personnel and a rifle section acting as a protection force charged toward the longhouse. When a number of Native males who had been watching the violence noticed the movement toward the longhouse, they immediately moved to prevent entry.[31] The War Diary noted, "A great deal of violence broke out as the SQ and soldiers forced their way into the Longhouse."[32]

The pushing and shoving on the perimeter eventually began to slowly dissipate once the CF personnel began to uncover hidden weapons and ammunition. "Inside a vast array of weapons, uniforms and ammunition was found."[33] In total, 2 RCR seized 20 weapons, particularly assault rifles, including a number of AK-47s, a Ruger Mini-14, a FNCI, an M-16, and a .50 Calibre 82A1 Barrett sniper rifle, as well as over $500,000 worth of illegal cigarettes, which was one of the largest contraband cigarette seizures in Canadian history."[34] By 2230 hours the operation was finally over.

The next five weeks were spent providing security along the main eastern and southern commuter routes on the reserve. The routine consisted of 24-hour traffic monitoring at selected checkpoints, vehicle searches, mounted and dismounted, covert and overt patrols, area searches, and intelligence gathering.[35] However, another raid would soon make the operation at the longhouse pale in comparison. On 18 September, 2 RCR conducted the largest raid of the Oka Crisis. The objective was a large suspected weapons cache on Tekakwitha Island, which is adjoined to the northern part of the Kahnawake Reserve by a single bridge.

A reliable source had reported to the SQ the existence of a large arms cache, and they in turn passed on the information to 2 RCR at 0900 hours. Brigade headquarters authorized the raid, and 2 RCR immediately began to plan. Surprise would be difficult, as there were only three approaches to Tekakwitha Island: by land through the reserve (which would be difficult to transit); by sea (but they lacked the necessary vessels to transport all the personnel and equipment) or by air.[36]

The plan quickly took shape. One platoon would be inserted at the bridge in a single CH-147 Chinook helicopter lift. Another platoon would be similarly dropped at the western end of the island in the vicinity of a reported defensive position that supposedly had a number of bunkers. Once these east-west blocks were secure, two platoons would then be inserted to conduct the actual sweep. In addition, an SQ SWAT team would be inserted by SQ boats to seize the marina buildings at the southwestern tip of the island. The boats would also remain in the vicinity to block any attempted escape by watercraft. Finally, two CF sniper teams were inserted on another tiny island approximately 1,000 metres west of Tekakwitha Island.

H-Hour commenced at 1430 hours. However, 10 minutes prior, in keeping with the intent of providing the Natives with prior notice of any movement or operation on the reserve, Lieutenant-Colonel Gagnon informed Band Council spokesman Jack Leclair of the impending operation. Similarly, Brigadier-General Roy contacted Elvin Delisle five minutes later. As a result, the Mohawks had a 10 minute warning of what was about to transpire.

The first detailed elements of 2 RCR landed at 1433 hours after having conducted a single pass over the island to situation themselves with regard to the objectives. They had barely situated themselves and strung out concertina wire when they were met by a large and violent onslaught. The reaction of the Natives was extremely rapid. A mob of approximately 300 Mohawks moved on the wire barrier. A truck easily ploughed through the wire at the end of the bridge, and the angry mob exploded through the gap, pelting The RCR soldiers manning the barriers with rocks and golf balls. A number of soldiers were knocked down and beaten by groups of Natives. The soldiers, without crowd control equipment or training, responded by shoving the crowd and using rifle butts to fend off their attackers. Six CS gas (i.e. tear gas) grenades were quickly detonated. This temporarily stunned the crowd and provided a momentary pause. However, the Natives quickly regrouped and surged forward again. Private Pellecchia then fired a single warning shot, which once again momentarily halted the violence, but the situation quickly worsened. Soldiers donning SQ helmets and riot gear were mistaken for actual SQ personnel, which further enraged the Mohawks. In addition, the 2 RCR reconnaissance platoon commander had captured a Mohawk Warrior Flag, tied it to his APC antennae and commenced to drive up a strip of beach sporting it as a trophy. This latest act simply added to the emotionally charged atmosphere and fuelled more violence.[37]

The mayhem at the bridge quickly threatened to overpower the small force in place. As a result, the CO ordered the adjutant, Captain Pat McAdam, to round up personnel in the rear area and deploy to reinforce the bridge. "I got a phone call telling me to prepare everybody I had and that we were needed on the Island immediately," remembered McAdam, "So I grabbed all of the cooks, clerks, truck drivers and everyone lying around and the Regimental Sergeant- Major (RSM) jumped in to be my Platoon Warrant." McAdam explained:

We flew into the island and tried to give as much help to keep that bridge route shut. I started talking to Chief Joe Norton and tried to get him and the Peacekeepers to control the crowd. By then the weapons on the island had been confirmed. One of the Natives caught me looking the other way and hit me on the head with a large rock, the size of a basketball and I went unconscious. I actually have pictures of it. I went down and Captain Shayne McArthur, a platoon commander ordered another round of gas. John Fife who was south of me came up with some soldiers in a reinforcement role same as me. He was the one shown on television being dragged by his binoculars and being beaten. I then got Medivaced [medical evacuation]. I ended up with 15 stitches.[38]

Lieutenant John Fife also rushed his platoon forward to assist with the chaos at the bridge and help facilitate the medical evacuation of the injured adjutant. He and his soldiers quickly came face to face with the crowd, who spat at and punched the soldiers. Fife was at the forefront of his platoon and was quickly pulled into the crowd and beaten. As he fell to the ground Private M.L. Tilley released a short burst from his C9 light machine gun (LMG) and Private M.P. Robertson fired five rounds into the air. This provided enough hesitation in the mob to allow The RCR soldiers to drag their platoon commander back into friendly lines and pull back to create a larger space between antagonists.

During the fighting two C-7 assault rifles were taken from troops who had been dragged into the crowd and beaten. The individuals who stole the weapons were extremely fortunate. The nearby sniper teams tracked these individuals with the weapons. They were given authority to engage the targets if the C-7 rifles were turned toward friendly forces.

The violence eventually subsided. Mohawk leaders and the Native Peacekeepers were finally able to calm the mob and restore order. By 2100 hours, the withdrawal of troops commenced by aviation lift, including Chinooks as well as CH-15 Twin-Hueys. In total, approximately 244 soldiers and 78 SQ personnel participated in the raid. In the end, 22 soldiers were injured, nine of whom required serious medical attention. The Mohawks had approximately 75 individuals treated for minor injuries, broken bones, and gas inhalation.[39]

The actual raid netted a total of 48 weapons from five different caches, as well as 6,000 rounds of ammunition, a crossbow, knives, communications equipment, and other military clothing and equipment. Only three weapons were actually illegal, the most significant of which was a six shot Striker Automatic Grenade Launcher. In addition, a small amount of alcohol and tobacco products was confiscated.[40]

In the aftermath, the battalion was somewhat stunned by events. "We were shocked and surprised at what happened," conceded the CO, Lieutenant-Colonel Greg Mitchell. He revealed, "We had conducted five previous searches without any major confrontation, and we figured that about 30 men would be enough to block access to the bridge leading to the island." The CO stated: "By the end, we needed 140 men."[41] Mitchell acknowledged, "Our troops were not prepared for riot control." He added, "In addition, the principle of minimal use of force played against my troops. They were getting hit, thinking they were not allowed to hit back. What they should have been doing was hitting back to avoid being hit again."[42]

The raid also bred some hard feelings. First, the agreement between the CF and the SQ was that the CF would provide the cordon and the SQ would execute the warrant and conduct the search. However, on Tekakwitha Island the SQ refused to co-operate and fulfill their duties, forcing 2 RCR to do both.[43] The second issue concerned the warning of impending military operations. It became quickly apparent and was later confirmed by a Mohawk informant that the Band Council, the Mohawk Nation Council, and the Warrior Society co-operated and coordinated fully with one another. As a result, when the chain of command informed Leclair and Delisle of the impending operation, this information was quickly shared. Moreover, the Kahnawake community had a number of redundant systems (e.g. an air raid/tornado siren, the fire hall bell, a telephone fan-out roster, mobile patrols, handheld radios, and the Kahnawake radio station [103.5FM]) in place to quickly alert and mobilize Natives on the reserve. This hard-learned reality prompted

Lieutenant-General Foster to warn that future operations would not necessarily be announced in advance.

The latest battle did not help with the resolution of the crisis. On 20 September, Lieutenant-General Foster publicly stated that he would entertain no other negotiation points from the Warriors other than total disengagement. Foster went on to provide courses of action to end the crisis. The most dramatic were: a final assault; and dramatically increasing pressure (i.e. cutting off supplies of food, water, clothing, electricity, and heating oil) to those still in the TC. Already in play were restrictions on communications. As of 14 September, the CF through its Electronic Warfare (EW) capacity deactivated known cell phones of Warriors or journalists operating in the Oka area and created conditions that would make cell phone use in the area difficult. Two days later the CF stopped the flow of all text, tapes, and films to, or from journalists who were co-located with the Warriors in the treatment centre.

Finally, on 26 September 1990, the Warriors and their supporters in the detoxification centre decided to unilaterally end the resistance. Before leaving the centre, they destroyed weapons and equipment to deny the government any evidence by either burning them or throwing them into the cesspool. Consistent with their behaviour throughout the crisis, they also failed to adhere to the agreed upon course of action. At 1855 hours, as the CF waited for their arrival at the discussed exit point, the Natives approached the main exit gate where the soldiers and buses were waiting, and when at the mid-way point, they suddenly broke off and headed to the northeast corner of the perimeter where the media was assembled. The Natives quickly threw stretcher boards over the wire and began to make their escape. The Warriors pushed the women and children over first and pushed hard from behind to break through. Once again, chaos erupted.

In the end, the majority of Mohawks were captured. However, in the words of one officer, "It was quite nasty, because there were no weapons so we got into hand to hand trying to control and restrain people." By 1955 hours, it was all over. A total of 26 men, 16 women, 10 journalists, and six children arrived at Farnham in military custody at 2215 hours.

Amazingly, the conflict was not yet over. That same night at 1924 hours, a Warrior communication was intercepted calling all Warriors and supporters to the Legion Hall. Then, 10 minutes later, the Kahnawake fire station alarm was rung. Approximately, 45 minutes later a mob of 200 Mohawks armed with bats and axe handles attacked an EW installation and set its tent on fire. As military reinforcements rushed to the site, the mob quickly withdrew to strike at other CF targets.

At roughly the same time, another group of approximately 100 Mohawks attacked the 2 RCR barricade at Highway 138. By 2030 hours, the Mohawk group had grown to 300 in strength and now managed to overrun the battalion's forward position. The Natives continued to advance, pelting the soldiers with rocks and bottles. Many of the Natives were armed with bats, batons, shields, and gas masks. One soldier was struck down with a rock and then beaten. A section of troops surged forward and after hand-to-hand combat managed to retrieve the injured soldier and withdraw.

The mob was relentless and continued to aggressively push forward. The order to stop was completely ignored by the Natives. Finally, the platoon commander, Lieutenant Dave Selhany, ordered his troops to load their weapons, fix bayonets, and form a defensive line. The Natives continued to advance. CS gas was fired into the crowd with little effect. Next, warning shots fired at the ground with similarly negligible results One of the section commanders recalled, "He [Salhany] then calmly walked along our line giving each soldier a ringleader and told them to shoot on his order." The section commander noted, "He gave these orders very loudly so the crowd could hear and they started to fall back."[44] Only then did the crowd stop.[45]

At the same time a reinforcement platoon arrived and a disengagement was negotiated. In the aftermath of the melee, one soldier suffered a fractured skull and required 45 stitches after being beaten over the head with a lead pipe. The incident became known as the "Riot at K3B." At the height of the riot, 28 soldiers had held off 400 Natives.

This, however, was the end of the long drama, as 2 RCR was redeployed to CFB Gagetown on 10 October 1990. In sum, 4,500 soldiers were deployed throughout the crisis. The government of Quebec officially terminated its request for military assistance on 30 May 1991, ending the 10 month long Operation Salon.[46]

When it was over, the Army commander pronounced, "This was an operation of life-threatening circumstance." Lieutenant-General Foster explained, "Once the orders are issued down the chain-of-command, the operation is in the hands of the company commanders, the platoon commanders and the soldiers." He noted, "If you train your people, well, they will know their business and be professional. It is this training and professionalism that results in success."[47]

And, once again the Royal Canadians demonstrated their strengths. The 2 RCR operations officer, Major Magee noted, "Oka was quite interesting trying to balance all of the political sensibilities and the military task."[48] Despite trying circumstances, the Royals rose above the challenges and through courage, self-discipline, and professionalism prevailed in circumstances that should have bred failure.[49] The 2 RCR CO concluded, "We reflected positively on the way Canada will go into the next decade. If we had blown it — if people had been killed or if we had lost control of the situation — we would have spent the next 10 years crisscrossing the country putting out fires. I hope this can now be avoided."[50]

As some Royals were engaged in conflict at home, others were deployed to assist with international crisis. On 2 August 1990, Iraq overran and occupied Kuwait, its smaller, oil-rich neighbour to the south, to resolve a number of unresolved political issues related to territory, debt, and oil pricing. This action threatened the delicate balance of power in the Middle East and posed a significant menace to Western economic interests, including those of Canada. One omnipresent fear was the possibility of Iraq continuing its expansionist designs and attacking Saudi Arabia or other Gulf States, which would then threaten the flow of Middle East oil, potentially triggering a global economic crisis.

Moreover, the unprovoked brutal nature of the invasion of Kuwait, compounded by horror stories of wanton violence and atrocities committed by the occupying troops, provoked a massive outcry. Adding to the outrage in general was the fact that Saddam Hussein's armies seized Western embassies and citizens, including Canadians. Not surprisingly, the invasion was quickly condemned by the U.N. and economic sanctions were imposed within days, followed by a naval blockade to enforce the sanctions.[51]

On 10 August 1990, Canada announced the deployment of a naval task group to the Persian Gulf under the code name Operation Friction.[52] By 25 August, the U.N. passed Resolution 665, which authorized the use of military force to back up the economic sanctions against Iraq. A little less than three weeks later, on 14 September, the Canadian government announced the deployment of a squadron of CF-18 fighter jets to fly combat air patrol (CAP) over the embargo area. As part of the latest addition, the CF announced that an airfield protection party from 4 CMBG in Germany would also be deployed as part of Operation Scimitar. Although it eventually became clear that for practical and political purposes Canada would not be sending combat ground forces to join the war effort, the Royal Canadians would nonetheless see service in the Gulf.[53]

The task of defending the airfield fell to 3 RCR in Germany. The CO quickly directed Major Mike Blanchette, OC "M" Coy, to provide a 100 man force to provide airfield security for Operation Scimitar. The company conducted weapons refresher on all support weapons, grouping and zeroing of all personal weapons, challenging procedures, search techniques, a myriad of intelligence briefings, environment lectures, and desert hygiene briefings. It deployed on 5 October from Baden to Qatar, in time to secure the first of the CF-18 fighters as they arrived on the

Courtesy Canadian Forces Imagery Library, regative IWC90-370-13a.

Members of "M" Coy, 3 RCR, responsible for airfield security in Qatar as part of OP Scimitar, site a GPMG.

following day. The battalion also later provided 12 Platoon, "P" Coy, as a defence and security platoon for the Canadian Joint Headquarters Middle East that was stood-up on 27 October 1990 in Bahrain to coordinate support for CF units in the Gulf.

The mission for "M" Coy, in Qatar was straightforward — defend Canadian personnel, aircraft, and combat supplies from ground attack.[54] This was deemed necessary because Saddam Hussein publicly announced that terrorist groups sympathetic to Iraq would strike with vengeance against any nation arrayed against it. As such the Coalition rated the threat in theatre as high.

The potential target was also appealing. The actual airfield which the Canadian Air Task Group Middle East (CATGME) selected had a runway that stretched 15,000 feet and was reportedly the second longest airstrip in the world. The airfield itself was divided into two sectors. The first held the busy international terminal and the home of the Qatari Emirate Air Force. The second sector contained the deployed Canadian elements in two separate camps designated Canada Dry 1 (CD1) and Canada Dry 2 (CD2). There were also two other designated Canadian areas, namely the military aircraft ramp and the Quick Reaction area. The four distinct Canadian areas were allocated as three separate platoon tasks.

Within the Canadian sector, CD1 was approximately 3.5 kilometres from the main airfield. It became the home of the Canadian Support Unit Qatar (CSU[Q]) and the responsibility of 2 Platoon. CD2 became the airfield accommodation site. It was a 100-metre by 300-metre Canadian-constructed compound surrounded by a Type 2 concertina fence and guarded by 1 Platoon. The remaining two Canadian sites became the responsibility of 3 Platoon.

Although simple in theory, the actual task of creating the defensive positions was extremely challenging in practice. First, it was impossible to dig in. Underneath six inches of powdery sand, the ground was solid as concrete. Moreover, the Qatar government refused permission to even attempt to dig any positions. Therefore, bunkers and observation posts were all constructed above ground. In fact, each individual position had to be personally approved by the Qatari Base Commander. In all 100,000 sandbags, 1,000 feet of 4 x 4 lumber, and 600 pieces of CG1 galvanized sheet metal were used to construct a total of 14 positions, which took 10 weeks of hard labour.[55] Once the positions were constructed, "M" Coy was replaced by "C" Coy, 1 R22eR between 19–23 December 1990. During their deployment the Royals had to endure the threat posed by no fewer than 17 SCUD missile launches and warnings.[56]

Meanwhile, the stand-off continued in Kuwait. On 29 November 1990 the U.N. passed U.N. Security Council Resolution (UNSCR) 678, which ordered Iraq to withdraw from Kuwait no later than 15 January 1991. It also empowered the U.S.-led, 34-country coalition to use "all necessary means" to force Iraq out of Kuwait after the deadline. Hussein failed to heed the warning, so, on 16 January 1991, the Coalition commenced an air campaign to prepare the ground for offensive action. The Coalition flew over 100,000 sorties, dropping approximately 88,500 tons of bombs targeting key military infrastructure, troop concentrations, and command and control facilities. On 23 February, the Coalition began its ground offensive and in an amazing 100 hours had completely routed the Iraqi forces. By 28 February the Persian Gulf War was over.[57]

However, in anticipation of the ground offensive and the expected number of casualties, Canada deployed a full surgical Field Hospital to theatre. Again, The RCR were involved. From 19 February to 20 March 1991 Charles Coy, 1 RCR deployed to Al Jabail, Saudi Arabia, as the security force for 1 Canadian Field Hospital during Operation Scalpel. The hospital was located 30 kilometres from the Saudi/Kuwaiti border. Tasks for the Royals included security of the hospital and stretcher bearing for allied and enemy casualties.

However, The RCR were also used for handling and processing of prisoners of war at a British PoW camp a few kilometres from the hospital. The facility held over 6,000 PoWs and was guarded by only three overworked and very tired British platoons. The Iraqis, most undernourished and dehydrated, arrived in groups of 60 by helicopter and were then herded into a holding pen before being searched, examined by a medical team, and documented.[58] As such, the members of Charles Coy provided badly needed reinforcements to assist with the PoW processing.

The Persian Gulf War also had knock-on effects in Europe necessitating an indirect role for 3 RCR back in Germany. The conflict in the

From Cold War to New Millennium

Courtesy Canadian Forces Imagery Library, negative ISC91-6102.

Members of "Charles" Coy, 1 RCR, assist British allies with the processing of in excess of 2,000 Iraqi prisoners of war (PoW) in a three-day period at a British PoW camp near the Saudi/Kuwaiti border.

Courtesy Canadian Forces Imagery Library, negative ISC91-6103-2.

A Royal Canadian from "Charles" Coy covers an Iraqi prisoner during the initial search on arrival to the PoW camp.

Middle East spurred increased terrorist activity. Bomb threats against schools and bases in Baden prompted increased vigilance. As such, 3 RCR became responsible for increasing security at the base, the private military quarters (PMQs) as well as the schools and the bus routes to and from. Peter Devlin, then a major, acknowledged, "It was a demanding task to look after the base." He explained, "We had a number of observation posts, we had people that reinforced the gates, we had people in their vehicles ready to go. We also had rovers that roamed around at night, and we had a platoon quick-reaction force that was also available."[59]

As busy as 3 RCR became, it was also to be their swan song of sorts. Their continued presence in Germany was not to last. The collapse of the Soviet Union and Warsaw Pact, which heralded the end of the Cold War, provided the government with a timely opportunity. Undisputedly, the global situation had changed. By 1992 the Soviet military presence in East Germany had shrunk to 10 divisions. This was reduced even further, to six by the start of 1993, and these were in the process of packing up and returning to the Soviet Union. Predictably, NATO nations throughout the Central Region were reducing their commitments. Not surprising then that the Canadian government quickly examined its options as well.

In fact, the decision to look at Canada's commitment to Europe had begun already in the fall of 1990. German reunification on 3 October 1990 just reinforced the apparent irrelevance of stationing troops in Germany. This change in circumstances combined with the huge government deficit made the decision to withdraw Canadian forces from Europe so much easier. The Department of Foreign Affairs and International Trade's (DFAIT's) concern that Canada would lose its "seat at the table" and influence within NATO if CFE was closed down was placated by the continuation of a symbolic presence. NATO's evolution to the concept of an ACE Rapid Reaction Corps (ARRC), which was based on a concept similar to the AMF(L), meaning that in a period of crisis, contributing NATO nations would deploy their earmarked forces to the ARCC, provided one such option. Fiscal reality removed any doubt. The mini-budget of 26 February 1992 actually accelerated the close-out of CFE. It directed that the CF would be out of Germany by 1994. In addition, it clearly stipulated that 4 CMBG would not be

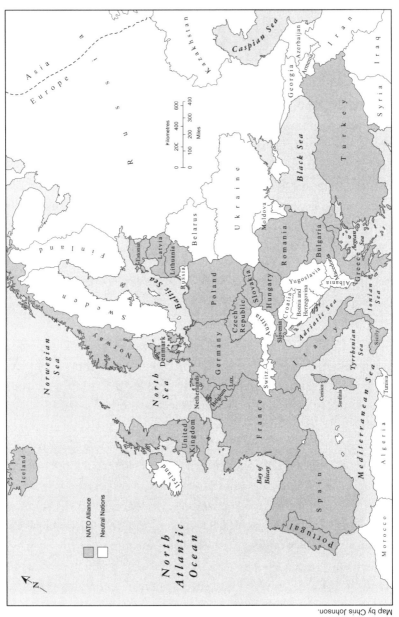

Post Cold War Geo-Political Realignment

Map by Chris Johnson.

reconstituted. The two infantry battalions, the artillery regiment, and the armoured regiment were to become "Total Force" reserve units. The remaining units within 4 CMBG were to be disbanded.[60]

With this direction in hand, 3 RCR began to close down and prepare for its return to Canada. However, the tumultuous world situation required the Royals to deploy troops one more time before leaving Germany. The latest crisis occurred in Yugoslavia. Patched together at the end of the First World War, it was at best an ethnically fragmented state. The Second World War unleashed the pent-up ethnic hatred that dated back centuries. However, at the end of hostilities, infamous Yugoslav partisan leader Josef Broz Tito became communist dictator of Yugoslavia. He quickly suppressed the ethnic tensions throughout the country through imposed order by means of military force if required, as well as complex power sharing agreements. However, his death in 1980 was the beginning of the end for Yugoslavia.

The problems were legion. First, Tito had failed to groom a successor and had kept power mainly to himself. Moreover, in 1974 he created a

Courtesy 1 RCR.

Soldiers of 1 RCR conduct their farewell to Wolseley Barracks and Sunset Ceremony, 17 June 1992, to mark the move of the Battalion from CFB London to CFB Petawawa.

The Former Yugoslavia

new constitution that accelerated the devolution of power to six republics that were defined as nation-states endowed with sovereignty but united to Yugoslavia in a confederation.[61] Therefore, by the time of his death, Communist Yugoslavia was faced with a power vacuum; an economy that was encumbered with a heavy foreign debt, hyperinflation (at one point hitting a rate of 1,000 percent), high unemployment, and a significant decline in the standard of living. These problems quickly translated into social and political tensions, which were exploited by nationalist extremists.

Adding to the turmoil was the collapse of the Soviet Union in 1989. Suddenly, the strategic importance of Yugoslavia in the eyes of NATO vanished. One scholar observed, "What counted for the West was denying Yugoslavia to the Soviet Union … once the Berlin Wall fell and the communist regimes in Central and Eastern Europe had collapsed, the purpose was gone. As communism dissolved and East-West cooperation developed, Yugoslavia ceased to be strategically significant."[62] As a result, NATO was no longer ready to provide "easy aid" to Belgrade as it had earlier when in competition with the Soviet Union.

The actual disintegration of Yugoslavia began in June-July 1991 when Slovenia declared independence and its irregular forces battled the Yugoslav People's Army (JNA) in an effort to enforce their break away from the federation. However, Slobodan Milosevic, the president of the Republic of Serbia, terminated the use of military force against the Slovenes, as he believed there were too few Serbs in Slovenia to warrant a major military operation.[63] He signed the Brioni Agreement on 7 July 1991, which formally ended the fighting in Slovenia. The JNA was completely withdrawn from Slovenia by 19 July.

Milosevic made a huge mistake. The Slovenian success quickly spurred on the Croats. Franjo Tudjman now pushed his vision of creating an independent Croatia. However, 15 percent of Croatia's population

Courtesy The RCR Museum and Archives.

"N" Coy, 3 RCR keeps surveillance on the Sarajevo airport.

Courtesy Rick Hatton.

Corporal D.L.A. Ott observes the Muslim village of Butmir from the tarmac of the Sarajevo airport.

was Serb, living in two large Serbian enclaves, the *Krajina* and Eastern Slavonia. For them an independent Croatia meant potentially becoming second class citizens. Moreover, many remembered and all knew of the stories of the Second World War, when Croatia sided with the Germans and was involved in conducting brutal operations against Serb-dominated and Communist-supported resistance movements. The struggle was vicious and bloody, with reprisals conducted by all sides. Not surprisingly, with the spectre of Croatian independence, the Serb minorities quickly mobilized and declared autonomy for the *Krajina* and Eastern Slavonia.

This dynamic also influenced Milosevic and the senior command of the Yugoslav Army, who were both determined to fight in support of the Serbs living in the *Krajina* and Slavonia. The stage was now set for a bitter conflict. The Croatian Serbs wanted to maintain their enclaves, as well as establish corridors to Serbia proper to ensure their safety. Conversely, the Croatians wanted to cleanse their newly declared republic of Serbs to safeguard their territory. The disintegration of Yugoslavia impacted its army as well, as Croatian members grabbed their equipment and deserted, joining in the defence of their newly declared independent state.

Between July and December 1991, heavy fighting resulted in high casualties as a savage struggle ensued between antagonists that included ethnic cleansing in an attempt to create homogeneous areas. During this period over 10,000 people were killed and 30,000 wounded.[64]

Although the European Community (EC) quickly created a EC Monitoring Mission, Yugoslavia (ECMMY), the 150 monitors, tasked with trying to disengage belligerent forces and establish ceasefire lines, were simply too few and did not have the communications or support to have any effect.[65] The international community realized that the mission required U.N. intervention. In November 1991, The U.N. secretary general's special mediator for the crisis, Cyrus Vance, achieved an apparent breakthrough. He had achieved agreement that under the "Vance Plan" there would be three U.N. Protected Areas (UNPAs) divided into four sectors: (Krajina) North, (Krajina) South, (Slavonia) East and (Slavonia) West. Each would be occupied by a United Nations Protection Force (UNPROFOR), whose mandate was to protect the civilian populations, while the JNA withdrew. In addition, inhabitants within the UNPAs were to be disarmed and their irregular defence forces disbanded. Once this was achieved, U.N. humanitarian assistance would begin.

The UNPAs were officially established on 21 February 1992, after the U.N. passed UNSCR 743.[66] Subsequently, on 10 March 1992, the MND announced Operation Harmony, the code name for the Yugoslavian mission, to Canadians. The mission was staged from Germany and the 4 CMBG commander selected 1 R22eR to be the lead unit because of its location in Lahr, which was closer to the planning staff and the Canadian logistical base that would be responsible for dispatching the force.[67] However, 3 RCR was tasked with augmenting the Van Doo unit with a fourth rifle company.[68]

The Royal Canadians quickly "de-mothballed" their APCs, which had been prepared for the return to Canada and painted them white with large black U.N. insignia. The almost 300 soldiers from "N" Coy, Recce Platoon, and pioneer section from 3 RCR deployed by rail from Lahr to Zagreb. Destroyed rail lines made the trip from Zagreb to the end point in Daruvar in UNPA Sector West tedious. Each train chalk (i.e. load of soldiers designated for a specific train serial) took approximately 40 hours to cover the distance. The last elements arrived 13 April 1992.

Their arrival was unforgettable. The War Diary noted, The troops "arrived in theatre to be greeted by ten rounds from a 120 mm mortar battery just as they had settled into their bivouac area."[69] Corporal Tony Carew remembered, "As the rounds hit, we all scrambled … to our APCs." He added, "all hell was breaking loose."[70] Without prompting, after the barrage, the troops began to dig in. In all, four soldiers were wounded.

Within Sector West, the ethnic composition was a 40/60 percent mix between Serb and Croats. Of the four battalions allocated to Sector West, the Canadians held the central area. However, as the first battalion on the ground, they had to control the entire UNPA until the others arrived.

For the next few months the Canadians patrolled several additional sectors including their area of responsibility to show the U.N. flag while awaiting the arrival of other U.N. contingents. Unfortunately, as always, the theory of the "Vance Plan" and the realities on the ground were two completely different worlds. The JNA was reluctant to leave the UNPAs as they lacked the confidence in the U.N. to protect the Serb population in the *Krajinas* from Croat attack. Conversely, the Croats rightly assumed the JNA would never leave or that the Serb irregular forces would disarm. In the end, this created great problems for UNPROFOR. Moreover, the belligerents were still conducting operations in the vicinity of the AO, often through the UNPA. Notwithstanding the ongoing conflict, the greatest threat to the Canadians was from mines and unexploded ordnance. In addition, the Canadian peacekeepers routinely were stopped at impromptu roadblocks and came under fire from mortars and machine guns. Nonetheless, "N" Coy, as part of the 1 R22eR BG, had great success. By spring/summer 1992, the UNPA was demilitarized, and life for the people in the sector had returned to a more normal state.

The Royals were kept busy trying to establish accommodation in bombed out buildings. However, just as life was about to become routine, Canada agreed to a United Nations request to provide security for relief flights into Sarajevo."[71] Elsewhere things had not improved. Despite the success in the North, by April 1992, conflict had spilled from Croatia into

Bosnia. Alija Izetbegovic had gained control of the Muslim-dominated Party of Democratic Action. In December 1991, as president of the Bosnian government, he requested the EC to grant recognition to Bosnia as an independent state. As a result, Radovan Karadzic, the leader of the Serbian Democratic Party (SDS), quickly tried to out-manoeuvre him by declaring the creation of the Serbian Republic or *Republika Srpska* on 9 January 1992. Izetbegovic ignored Karadzic's actions and held a referendum on the issue of independence. Only 66.4 percent of eligible voters, mainly Muslims and Croats, cast their votes. However, the message was clear. An impressive 99.7 percent of the voters favoured independence.[72] As a result, on 5 April 1992, Izetbegovic declared the independence of Bosnia. That same day fighting broke out once again in Sarajevo, which was now the capital of Bosnia-Herzegovina.

The following day, the EC recognized Bosnia as an independent state.[73] This prompted the JNA to occupy the Sarajevo airport. The conflict now erupted into yet another brutal and bloody phase. A state of chaos and anarchy quickly prevailed. The Bosnian Serbs formed irregular forces and squared off against the newly established Bosnian Territorial Defence Force (BTDF). By 20 April 1992, the BTDF had blockaded the JNA, which retaliated by bombarding Sarajevo. Sensing an opportunity, Croatia invaded Bosnia-Herzegovina from the North and Southwest.

The EC tried to end the conflict by demanding that the JNA withdraw immediately from Bosnia. Milosevic complied by pulling out approximately 20,000 troops in the first two weeks in May. However, 80,000 soldiers, mainly Bosnian Serbs, remained behind under the command of General Ratko Mladic, who now formed the Army of *Republika Srpska*. In addition, a number of Serbian paramilitary organizations supported Karadzic, the self-proclaimed president of the republic, to assist him in his pursuit of creating a strong *Republika Srpska* that could become part of the "greater Serbia," which was the intent of Milosevic.

Then on 5 June, surprisingly, the Bosnian Presidency and the Bosnian Serbs agreed to re-open the Sarajevo airport for humanitarian reasons. Both parties stated that anti-aircraft weapons were to be removed and other heavy ordnance such as tanks, artillery, and other heavy weapons, would be withdrawn to areas subject to observation and verification by

U.N. forces. The following day, plans were made to send the Canadians to the airport.[74]

The mission was twofold. First, secure the airport for humanitarian flights so that aid could be brought into the besieged population. Second, the Canadians had the task of opening corridors between the airport and the city proper to allow the distribution of food and relief supplies. However, before any of this could occur, on 30 June, "N" Coy, 3 RCR, as part of the larger BG had to negotiate 400 kilometres of difficult terrain, inundated with roadblocks, as well as drunken soldiers and warlords.

On arrival to the airport on 2 July, everyone immediately dug in. The airport was located to the southwest of the city and was key terrain as an approach to the capital. It was also surrounded by all factions of the conflict. And, despite earlier arrangements, it was clear none had fully complied with the agreements to disarm in the region. Heavy fighting in Dobrinja and in Ilidza resulted in artillery, mortar, and tank rounds flying over, and landing in, the airport. Often fire was targeted directly at Canadians and U.N. workers. On several occasions contingency plans were made to evacuate the airport, since it seemed imminent that one side or another would overrun it.

Peter Devlin, then the OC of "N" Coy, quickly identified a major challenge that they continued to face. "One challenge that appeared quickly," he noted, "was the fact that the Army still had a U.N. peacekeeping culture, yet we were occupying OPs between warring factions." Devlin explained, "As we occupied our turf and built relationships it came clear very quickly that it was not the role of the UN to put themselves between warring parties." Finding a bright side, he acknowledged, "Nonetheless, we were facilitating understanding between both sides of the line."[75]

The War Diary captured the essence of service in Sarajevo. "Our peacekeepers spent the month of July in the cauldron of Sarajevo," it recorded. It explained, "Even though several personnel had been injured in Croatia, Sarajevo was completely different. Bombardment and sniper fire were just another part of the soldiers' 15 to 18 hour work day. A number of soldiers were hit and on one occasion one of the sections resorted to returning fire."[76] Finally, at the end of the month the Canadians were relieved by French, Egyptian, and Ukrainian troops. They left Sarajevo on 3 August 1992 and returned to Sector West.

On return to Croatia, the Royals picked up where they left off. "Our peacekeepers spent the first six weeks of their return to Croatia securing new accommodation and adjusting their boundaries due to a requirement to put more peacekeepers on the Serbian side of the cease fire line," the War Diary recorded. The War Diary also noted, "The company spent a lot of time conducting vehicle patrols around PAKRAC to confiscate illegal weapons and some military vehicles. Seven platoon also rescued some Nepalese soldiers who got caught in a mortar bombardment."[77] The Royals eventually passed the sector over to 3 PPCLI.

"N" Coy's service in the Former Yugoslavia was exemplary. In fact, they were awarded a sub-unit commendation for their service. Former Chief of the Defence Staff Rick Hillier noted, "November Company had gone into the region as part of the first Canadian battle group and pushed through Croatia and Bosnia, confronting rogues, criminals and mass murderers time and time again, to open up Sarajevo, which was under siege by the Bosnian Serbs."[78]

In the interim, while "N" Coy dodged munitions in the Former Yugoslavia the rest of 3 RCR continued to close out its lines in Baden in preparation for the move back to Canada. The battalion held its farewell parade on 3 December 1992. Needless to say, many mourned the close-out. "The soldiering there [Germany] surpassed anything in Canada," was a common sentiment. The overwhelming belief was that "The training facilities were better and we participated in huge division and Corp exercises with our NATO allies, not in the confines of training areas, but in a German countryside dotted with villages and town."[79]

The fate of 3 RCR itself was also a contentious issue — it was to be struck from the regular force order of battle. A small cadre of 3 RCR personnel was deployed to CFB Borden to establish the nucleus of a "newly recreated" 3 RCR. As of 1 August 1992, 3 RCR transformed into a 10/90 battalion, which translated to 10 percent regular force and 90 percent reserve force personnel. The rifle companies and combat support platoons were drawn from units in the Toronto and Hamilton Militia Districts. Meanwhile, 4 RCR received an operational tasking to provide a full 103 person light infantry company for the unit. In total, the new total force 3 RCR 10/90 battalion was allocated 877 all ranks, 84 regular and 40 full time Class B/As.[80] Its mission was to put a fully equipped, ready to fight, company in the field in 90 days, and the battalion complete in just 10 days.

The CO, Lieutenant-Colonel Mike Sweeney, explained, "We were like a training cadre." He also conceded, "We were also a fly by night outfit. We had to scrape money together to do activities."[81] But also quickly noted, "We were good at it." He went to describe that the 10/90 battalion "was an experimental unit." Sweeney posed the rhetorical question, "could it work?" He then reported, "It was very effective in the training role as it was an extremely good training vehicle. We did stuff that reservists couldn't or wouldn't normally do. Our cadre were all skilled subject matter experts in a varied number of areas of expertise."[82]

The unit was focused 100 percent on light infantry skills. But it did not last. Sweeney lamented, "We were never fully allowed to finish.

Members of 3 RCR participate in one of their last exercises in "Bonnland," Germany, in 1992, prior to the close-out of CFE.

People were just posted away because of a higher decision to re-establish 3 RCR/light infantry battalions once the Cdn AB Regt was disbanded."[83]

However, not all agreed with the change. Colonel R.M. Dillon, The RCR colonel of the regiment lamented, "The 3rd Battalion is going through a traumatic transformation. Having lost its place in the Regular Force Order of Battle, it is learning by experience just what the meaning of 10/90 really is. Who knows?"[84]

But Dillon's observation did not matter. Change, for good or for bad, was clearly in the air. The closing of CFE and the re-roling of 3 RCR were just two of the latest manifestation of the governing Liberal Party's axe that was cutting into DND. For example, on 1 July 1993, the last Canadian contingent was withdrawn from Cyprus, ending that operational commitment.[85] As the decade wore on, things would only get worse.

6

Into the 1990s: The Decade of Darkness

The initial years of the 1990s had been tumultuous. The disintegration of the Soviet Union and the Warsaw Pact had completely
transformed the international security environment and arguably created a new world order. Where many had expected a peace dividend
to be reaped — since the showdown between global superpowers was
over, which suggested less money would need to be spent on military
forces, equipment, and readiness — the world instead seemed to explode.
Lacking the constraints and support of superpower sponsors, many
failed or failing states spiralled into anarchy and chaos. This necessitated
an operational tempo not seen since Korea.

However, in the background, other pressures were building. A huge
national deficit forced the Canadian government to take draconian fiscal measures that would impact severely on the CF at a time when its
operational tempo was never higher. Concurrently, Canadian society
was gripped by societal, economic, and political changes that had been
brewing since the mid-1980s. Together, all these factors, combined with a
scandal of epic proportions, would produce the perfect storm that would
plunge The RCR, as part of the larger CF, into the decade of darkness.

No one saw the end of the Cold War coming. The CF had failed to
anticipate this event and arguably failed to adequately adapt and/or change

to the events around it until forced to do so. Although a scathing criticism, one can understand the issue to a degree. First, the CF was required to react to a large spike in its operational tempo because of events at home and abroad. Second, the magnitude of the fiscal crisis and the cuts delivered to the CF left it reeling. Third, when one is responsible for national security, one must institute change carefully so as not to accept too much risk too quickly, since so much is at stake. Nonetheless, the 1990s also demonstrated a shortfall in the Cold War mentality of the CF.

The defeat of the Conservative government and the return of the Liberals under Prime Minister Jean Chrétien in 1993 did not bode well for the CF. The Liberals' focus on the burgeoning national deficit meant deep cuts across all government departments. But none was more heavily hit than DND. The government announced plans to reduce CF strength from 75,000 to 66,000 personnel by 1998, with a reduction of $7 billion over the same period. In fact, defence spending was slashed 23 percent during this timeframe.[1] In short, the new Liberal government, perched on a crumbling fiscal precipice, looked to the military and saw a "peace dividend" to solve part of its problem.

The magnitude of cuts, particularly at a time when operational tempo was higher than at any point since the Korean War, created great stress within DND and the CF. Moreover, the changing security environment further exacerbated tensions. Entire generations of officers and senior NCOs were trained, inculcated, and progressed through the post–Second World War Western military model. But now, the safe, templated, and well-known Cold War paradigm disappeared almost overnight. The new security environment was marked by complexity, ambiguity, and ever-present media, as well as nefarious enemies and threats embedded in the context of failed and failing states. In many ways this overloaded a traditional, conservative, and intellectually inflexible officer corps that saw the world in terms of absolutes.

This is not surprising; after all, it was not until the post–Cold War era that the sanctity and security of the old conventional wisdom that held true for almost half a century was shattered. Overnight, the carefully prepared plans for the defence of Germany became irrelevant. Gone was the familiar and carefully templated Soviet enemy. Senior officers and senior

NCOs, whose entire careers were rooted in, and defined by, the comfortable predictability of the Cold War, were faced by a brave new world.[2] Conflict had become exponentially more complex and unpredictable.[3]

As a result of the chaos and turmoil in the new international landscape, many Western nations, including Canada, embarked on peace support operations that no longer resembled the classic peacekeeping model of simply juxtaposing a force between two belligerents who had agreed to a third party presence to monitor a mutually agreed ceasefire. In a clear rejection of the concept of sovereignty embedded in the West since the Treaty of Westphalia in 1648, the West now selectively embarked on peace enforcement operations. Moreover, the tempo of operations increased dramatically. During the nineties, the CF underwent a threefold increase in missions compared to the previous four decades.[4]

Quite simply, military leaders raised and bred in the Cold War environment were unprepared for what the new era brought. General Rick Hillier, a former CDS, observed, "While it was good to have a predictable training and deployment cycle, so predictable that we coined a phrase for it — SALY meaning 'same as last year' — the implications were not good for the mindset of the Canadian Forces. Nobody really had to think, particularly at the strategic level, and consequently our leaders were not trained, selected or experienced enough to think beyond the stalemate in Europe. We paid a high price for that mindset later, because it led directly to some of the challenges that we faced in the 1990s and early 2000s. That 'sameness' each year led inevitably to a focus on picayune detail and measurable process."[5]

The full implications of this mindset soon hit home as the requirement for CF deployments to assist with the stability campaigns of the 1990s continued unabated. By September 1992 the situation in Bosnia-Herzegovina (BiH) had worsened. The *Republika Srpska* aggressively deployed its forces and now controlled 70 percent of Bosnia, forcing an exodus of approximately 375,000–400,000 refugees. The Serb success in northeastern Bosnia prompted the Croats and the Muslims to respond in kind. To add to the misery, ethnic cleansing was practiced on a large scale by all three warring parties.[6]

The resultant escalation of violence forced the U.N., on 14 September, to authorize UNPROFOR to provide security in support of the distribution

Courtesy The Canadian Airborne Forces Museum.

Members of 3 Cdo deliver humanitarian supplies to an outlying village in their area of operations in Somalia.

of humanitarian aid in BiH, which was subsequently divided into five zones, each of which was designated to one of the UNPROFOR international battalions.[7] UNPROFOR's tasks now included ensuring the safe arrival of aid flights into Sarajevo, monitoring the pullback of heavy weapons from around the Sarajevo, as well as preserving the freedom of movement for international humanitarian aid convoys.

For Canadians, UNPROFOR's expanded mandate to allow for the provision of international humanitarian aid to the distressed populace of BiH meant injection of additional resources. This new mission was initially codenamed Operation Dagger, but was quickly changed to Operation Cavalier. As part of the expansion, a second Canadian battalion (CANBAT 2) was required. The first Canadian battalion deployed to the Former Yugoslavia under Operation Harmony (CANBAT 1), was the PPCLI battle group that replaced "N" Coy and its parent 1 R22eR Battle Group in Sector West.

The new task went to 2 RCR. Although just returned from Cyprus eight months previous, NDHQ tasked the battalion with the mission,

Courtesy 2 RCR.

A 2 RCR APC provides a mobile observation post beside a gutted church near Bijela, Sector West, November 1992.

Author photograph.

A "B" Coy, 2 RCR convoy passes through the mountains ringing Sarajevo, March 1993.

since it was already at a high level of operational readiness and it was equipped with M-113 APCs. As such, the unit was a logical fit for a rapid deployment. "B" Coy, 1 RCR was placed under command to the Battle Group (BG) as the third rifle company.

The 2 RCR BG deployed in October 1992 to Lipik/Pacrac/Sirac and Bijela in Sector West to stage before moving to its intended operating base in Banja Luka in the *Republika Srpska*. Although it was intended to be a short stay, the BG became extremely frustrated as its attempts at moving to its objective area were repeatedly thwarted by the Bosnian Serbs. With no apparent movement in sight, sub-units conducted training, assisted with presence patrols in Sector West, and established a refugee camp in Sector South, while negotiations continued at the highest levels.

What struck everyone was the sheer level of devastation throughout the theatre. Warrant Officer Grant Gervais captured the sad scene. He wrote: "War torn, homes destroyed, villages levelled. Families homeless, starving, dying. Children living inhumanely, eating food at dump sites, living in cardboard huts waiting for the next load of garbage so they can have their next meal."[8] Another Royal described the carnage in a similar way. He related, "The land tells a story of merciless struggle waged to destroy the military, economic and social fabric of opposing ethnic factions. Orchards deliberately and systematically destroyed, churches, schools and hospitals pounded to rubble and indiscriminate destruction of residential areas strain the belief of the existence of humanity in this otherwise beautiful land."[9] Master-Corporal Jordie Yoe described, "[you] arrive in this village where everything was burned out. No roofs on the houses, people lying in the streets, and there was this incredible smell — a smell that you can't really describe because it's a mixture of burning flesh, rotting flesh, human feces, urine, decaying bodies, smoke and fire and gas, diesel, you name it. It was a stench that was unbelievable and it just hung there in the valley."[10] The magnitude of the tragedy was inescapable and burned itself into everyone's minds.

Despite the tragedy that surrounded the BG, the Royals attempted to help wherever they could. A diversion for some members of the BG occurred when the U.N. passed UNSCR 795 on 11 December 1992, which authorized an additional UNPROFOR mission in Macedonia. The U.N. labelled it as a U.N. preventive deployment force. As such, "H" Coy set out on 6 January 1993, where for the next two months it operated five observation posts (OPs) and conducted patrols along the borders of Macedonia, Serbia, and Kosovo, in preparation for the arrival of a Nordic battalion that took over responsibility for the sector in February 1993.

Meanwhile, the BG did what it could while awaiting its authority to move. At one point, an advance party actually deployed to Banja Luka and established a temporary camp from 1–24 December. The camp, however, was abandoned when Serb intransigence to international demands to halt the fighting and ethnic cleansing led to Western threats of air strikes and a pull-out of all U.N. personnel in Bosnia. This, coupled with the Bosnian Serb refusal to provide authorization for the 2 RCR BG to deploy into the *Republika Srpska* effectively spelled the end of the 2 RCR BG's original mission.

Notwithstanding the latest events, not all was lost. Contingency planning was already in effect for an alternate employment of the BG west of

Sarajevo to conduct convoy escorts into eastern Bosnia. Then, finally on 16 February 1993, the BG was given approval to move into BiH.

The news was well received. The CO captured the mood. "At long last we deployed to Bosnia-Hercegovina," he wrote: "An arduous and difficult exercise using every mode of transport less mule train."[11] The BG quickly established two camps in Visoko and Kiseljak, both approximately 25 kilometres west of Sarajevo. The main task for the BG was to support the U.N. High Commission for Refugees (UNHCR) deliver aid to the needy populace. This entailed convoy escort missions into cities under siege such as Gorazde, Srebrenica, Breza, and Zepa, as well as running convoys, normally with 100 metric tons of supplies, from the Sarajevo airport to UNHCR warehouses in the city itself. In addition, escorts were provided to protect infrastructure repair teams in the city itself, and platoon-size groupings were dispatched to conduct traffic control over critical mountain main supply routes such as the Tarcin-Kresevo road.

Throughout the conduct of these duties the soldiers faced constant danger as they continually had to run gauntlets of belligerent and drunk host nation soldiers at check points, as well as harassing sniper and indirect fire. Furthermore, there was a constant mine threat as thousands of mines had been laid, many, if not most, without proper identification or recording. It was bad enough that the tasks had to be conducted in a context of conflict, because the warring factions had not yet agreed to peace and still fought, often catching the Royals in the middle. However, more disturbing was the fact that all sides often targeted the U.N. and the BG to either attempt to blame their enemies for the offence; or because they felt, without cause, that the U.N. was siding with their enemies; or simply because the soldiers were ill-disciplined and/or drunk.

The state of affairs frustrated the troops. They were always outnumbered and outgunned. They had neither the weaponry, the necessary numbers, nor the RoEs to actually force compliance of U.N. resolutions on belligerents or enforce their freedom of movement. "The escort group commander," captured a 2 RCR BG report, "must not return fire unless absolutely necessary — if he is not very careful, he will bite off more than he can chew."[12] Sergeant Jim Davis agreed. He explained, "We knew we couldn't finish any fight, so why start one? We just had to duck down and soldier on because that's all we had. At that time we had nothing. So the commonsense soldier says 'Don't start a fight you can't finish.'"[13]

In addition, there was another reality that was ever present. The drivers of the trucks that hauled the aid supplies, both civilian and military, from contributing nations, made it clear that they would not proceed if there was any conflict, or even the threat of violence. As a result, attempting to force a road block became a moot point — why risk casualties if only the armed escort would follow through? In spite of the constraints and the frustration of constantly being targeted without recourse to respond, the BG executed its mission with a characteristic Canadian professionalism.

Of the many convoy escorts that the 2 RCR BG conducted into Sarajevo, Zepa, and Gorazde, none stands out as much as the mission to Srebrenica. On 9 March 1993, the BG received a warning order to escort a UNHCR convoy to the isolated mining town in southeastern Bosnia. The besieged Muslim enclave held approximately 30,000 refugees and had been cut off because of fighting for over eight months. The UNPROFOR commander, French Major-General Phillip Morillon, often described as an erratic and indifferent, decided to take action and launched the mission. It would later become evident that it was an ad hoc and poorly thought out plan.[14]

Nonetheless, in the early hours of 10 March 1993, elements of "B" Coy, 2 RCR BG, under command of Major Bernd Horn, made their way to a rendezvous point at Zvornik, in Serbia. Although the Bosnian Serbs would not allow the large convoy to pass, they did permit Morillon and one APC acting as a personnel escort, to proceed to Srebrenica. Once in the enclave, the section, led by Sergeant Gordon Morrison, and the UNPROFOR commander, quickly became hostages of the Muslim populace of Srebrenica, who demanded U.N. action and a halt to the Bosnian Serb offensive in return for the U.N. soldiers. Very quickly what UNPROFOR headquarters had described as a three day task turned out to be a 22-day ordeal that was fraught with confusion, a lack of clear direction, and intent, as well as daily tense confrontations with Serbian forces. Moreover, it became clear that there had been no authority to proceed — Morillon had simply decided to grandstand.

Eventually, the small U.N. force won over the Muslim population in Srebrenica, and on 19 March, Morillon was allowed to leave the pocket and attempt to negotiate with the Bosnian Serbs for the passage of the humanitarian aid convoy into the city. Once again, the convoy was blocked and another tense confrontation at a checkpoint ensued, which devolved into a violent melee that spiralled out of control with shots being fired. Finally, the Bosnian Serbs allowed the trucks with humanitarian supplies, less the armed escort, to proceed into the encircled enclave. The process of sending unescorted humanitarian trucks continued over the next several weeks. The UNHCR cargo trucks would enter the city and unload the desperately needed supplies and then fill the empty trucks with people. In the end, 2,400 refugees escaped to Tuzla in this manner.

Throughout the ordeal, the Royals (a small group of "B" Coy personnel) kept a presence in Srebrenica. It started with a section under Sergeant Morrison who had entered the pocket with Major-General Morillon on 11 March. Despite their small size they quickly had an effect. Morillon wrote: "The crew of 42B performed an outstanding job reducing tension in Srebrenica and reassuring the population with their

Muslim civilians scramble to board trucks taking them from the doomed city of Srebrenica to Tuzla, spring 1993.

constant good humour, patrols around the town and non-stop entertainment of the crowd who were ever present in front of the PTT building."[15] However, the war still waged around them, and the sporadic shelling eventually caught up with them. On 24 March, Master-Corporal Donald Paris and Private Tim Parrell were seriously wounded when they were caught in a mortar barrage.

Morrison's crew was finally extracted over two weeks after their insertion and replaced by Captain Tom Mykytiuk, the 8 Platoon commander, and his headquarters crew. The CO decided that he needed a junior officer in the enclave to try and establish a more substantial presence in Srebrenica. After all, the situation was grim. "Each assessment from the UNMOs [UN military observers] and the local Muslim commanders," wrote Mykytiuk, "indicated that the noose around the Srebrenica Pocket was tightening and we waited for the final coup de grace that would deliver the enclave into Serb hands." He added, "As the Muslims lost ground, refugees from the surrounding countryside flooded into Srebrenica looking for safety, adding to the humanitarian crisis developing in the city." On entering the war ravaged zone, Mykytiuk described, "travelling down a streetscape littered with burned out vehicles, and obscured by wood smoke and an atmosphere of despair."[16] He reflected, "Throughout my time in Srebrenica I witnessed acts of compassion and generosity among the residents and refugees, as well as ugly self-interest and desperation as part of the struggle to survive in a city under siege." For the next three weeks Mykytiuk and his soldiers endured almost daily shelling and the prospect of being overrun by a Serb offensive.

But this was not to be the case in the short term. The leading elements of 2 RCR BG had created the embryo of a new U.N. "safe area." On 16 April 1993, the U.N. passed UNSCR 819, which established zones "free from armed attacks and from any other hostile acts that would endanger the well-being and the safety of their inhabitants and where the unimpeded delivery of humanitarian assistance to the civilian population." The resolution went so far as to call on UNPROFOR "to deter attacks against the areas, to monitor the cease-fire, to promote the withdrawal of military or paramilitary units other than those of the Bosnian

Government and to occupy some key points on the ground, in addition to participating in the delivery of humanitarian relief."[17] The following day, UNPROFOR became responsible for demilitarizing the newly proclaimed "safe area" around the beleaguered town of Srebrenica. On 18 April a ceasefire was agreed upon by the warring factions, which allowed the U.N. the opportunity to force their hand.[18]

Not surprisingly, the task fell to 2 RCR. Their mission was "to deploy a company group or combat team to Srebrenica to reinforce the current UN presence there with a view towards demilitarizing the pocket."[19] Their tasks included the establishment of an OP line to monitor the ceasefire, corralling of weapons, establishment of holding areas for non-combatants, security for non-combatants, security for landing zones (LZs) for medical evacuation (MEDEVAC) operations, and assisting UNHCR in their evacuation of Srebrenica.[20]

But the task was not initially apparent. "At first I had no mission," revealed Perry Poirier the "G" Coy OC designated to deploy to the doomed city. He stated: "I was just told 'get there.'"[21] Poirier's company actually entered Srebrenica on 18 April 1993. Mykytiuk, who was still in the pocket, wrote: "In a scene reminiscent of the liberation of Holland, 'G' Company entered Srebrenica under a shower of yellow flowers thrown by the grateful inhabitants lining the main road into the town."[22] Poirier had a similar impression. He remembered, "I thought I was General Clark liberating Rome [in the Second World War]. As we drove in people were lining the streets throwing confetti. When General Morillon visited us it was like de Gaulle entering Paris."[23]

First they evacuated the wounded. Then Poirier had to figure out how to demilitarize Srebrenica. He established his TOW overwatch positions on the outskirts of the town and then had to press the Muslim forces from digging section positions around the armoured vehicles. Poirier also brought in Serb officers to show them what was being done to ensure transparency and neutrality. Three days later, Srebrenica was declared a militarized zone.[24]

For those in the pocket, Srebrenica proved to be surreal. Sergeant Peter Vallee described the situation:

We knew we were cut off. Golf Company was there, and one platoon of Hotel Company. And that's basically it. For a month. We established our patrols and observation posts and weapons caches as best we could. We washed when we could. We were on rations the whole time. Bottled water, of course, no services whatsoever. We were absolutely outnumbered by the Serbs, but our UN presence helped, I guess, to get them [belligerents] to a standoff. You had Muslims living in Srebrenica and up and around Srebrenica. Some of them were living in shacks, little shacks close to the mountains, in the mountains. It was a strange sight.[25]

Once the situation was in hand, "G" Coy fell into a routine of framework patrolling. They maintained their presence in Srebrenica until 6–8 May 1993, when they conducted a relief in place with "C" Coy, 2 Re22R. Then the eight-month tour finally came to an end. Despite the war that continued to rage around The RCR peacekeepers, one that often consumed them in its intensity, and often witnessed them being deliberately targeted and denied freedom of movement, the 2 RCR BG provided yeoman service and wrote another proud page of Regimental history.

Nonetheless, many felt incredibly frustrated by the inability to do all that was needed. Lieutenant-Colonel Rob Walker noted, "In 1992/1993, the war was on and there was fighting and ethnic cleansing go on. We tried to create safe havens. However, the RoEs and UN strategy constrained the contingent with regards to interventionism. We lacked the necessary combat power to do what was required. It seemed as if we were sitting on our hands."[26] Master-Corporal Yoe lamented, "That was the part that was difficult to accept. The Government of Canada has sent us here, the United Nations has sent us here, yet we're powerless."[27]

Despite the frustrations, Royals would continue to serve in the Balkans. The 2 RCR BG was soon followed into the former Yugoslavia by 1 RCR, who conducted Rotation (Roto) 4 of Operation Harmony in October 1994. Located in southwestern Croatia, their primary mission was to dominate the zone of separation and implement the ceasefire agreement of 29 March 1994. In addition, they were responsible for monitoring the crossing of military personnel, equipment, supplies, and weapons over specified international borders, facilitating humanitarian assistance to BiH through the territory of Croatia and monitoring the demilitarization of the Prevlaka peninsula. In sum, 1 RCR was responsible for establishing a safe and secure environment, creating demilitarized zones, and monitoring the zone of separation.

Despite the gap in time, the experience was not much different. Corporal Kurt Grant described:

> What I saw on patrol today saddened me. We drove through entire communities where there wasn't a soul. One town had a school where a number of the students and teachers were simply lined up against the wall and shot. I'm told they were Muslims. You could still see the bullet holes and bloodstains on the wall. The houses all had their roofs blown off and were in various states of disrepair. From piles of rubble to almost fully intact…. Another place we drove through had a hospital — or what was left of it. Everywhere you looked there was evidence of fighting. Hull down positions, trenches and bunkers were in abundance. Along one wall that had holes from rocket grenades and hundreds of bullets, there was a bunch of graffiti. Nothing special, it's all over the place. But in the middle of all the Croatian lettering were words "welcome to hell" in English. An interesting concept in light of the surroundings![28]

The level of frustration with the restricted U.N. mandate and inadequate RoEs had not changed either. "The biggest problem," wrote Grant, "is that most of us wonder what it is we're doing here." He noted, "The UN, as far as I can see, serves no useful purpose here. For example, in the two villages where we're stationed, we've been given no clear mandate. We are told to protect local Croats, but we haven't been given enough people to do it, or allowed to do it properly." Grant lamented, "We just sit in our camp, and every couple of hours or so wander the streets. Some protection."[29]

In the end the soldiering tasks were not complicated. "Patrolling is pretty straightforward stuff," acknowledged Grant, "We have two of the three patrol routes given to us first thing in the morning. There are

Courtesy The RCR Museum and Archives.

3 RCR receiving its new Queen's Colour on 1 July 1997 at CFB Petawawa.

221

Courtesy The RCR Museum and Archives.

A 2 RCR AVGP, as part of SFOR, on patrol in the former Yugoslavia.

bunkers and troop positions we're supposed to check, and we're always on the lookout for extra activity or vehicle/equipment movement." He noted, "Essentially you're looking to see if anything has changed from the last time. After you get to know an area, you can tell at a glance if anything's up."[30]

Much like sister battalion, the 1 RCR BG had a successful tour and accomplished its mission. If nothing else, it was valuable experience. Master Warrant Officer Tom France believed, "The tour got the guys operational (e.g. being observant; carrying loaded weapons; being conscious of a real threat). It gave them a focus."[31] Sadly, they too, suffered a number of casualties as a result of accidents, direct and indirect fire.

However, by the spring of 1995, the level of frustration was mounting. Canadian troops were being killed and wounded in a theatre that was still in the grips of war. General Hillier explained, "We were doing things in the former Yugoslavia that no one had been prepared for, and even though it was dawning on some of our military and civilian leaders that UN peacekeeping operations were a thing of the past, there was no way that we could get past the mantra of 'peacekeeper, peacekeeper, peacekeeper." He noted, "The vast majority of people in the Canadian

Forces, at every level, realized the futility, frustration and danger of what was occurring, and yet there was no way that we could break out of that peacekeeping bubble." He conceded, "As a result, we put soldiers and sailors and airmen and airwomen, who served on the ground, in positions where they saw brutal acts that they were powerless to stop. That was a scar that a lot of our people brought back from the Balkans, and a scar that the entire Canadian Forces, particularly the army, brought back as an institution." Finally, Hillier concluded:

> So we put Canadian soldiers, as part of the UN mission, on the ground in the former Republic of Yugoslavia without a clear mandate, without a clear plan as to how we were going to accomplish anything, and constrained them to be peacekeepers in a region that had no peace for them to keep. Once we got there and realized what we had gotten ourselves into, nobody seemed to be able to do anything about it. We had soldiers on the ground getting shot at, and sometimes killed, in Bosnia, Croatia and all the other parts of the former Republic of Yugoslavia. The concept of peacekeeping was meaningless in practice. In fact, it was worse than meaningless: it was farcical, and far too many of our young men lost their lives there for no discernible effect.[32]

Hillier had a point. Despite UNPROFOR's size, which by 30 November 1994, reached 38,810 military personnel, 727 policemen, and 1,870 U.N. staff, making it the largest peacekeeping mission in U.N. history, the mission was stalled. From the outbreak of the war in Bosnia to the end of 1994, no fewer than 13 ceasefires had been agreed upon and subsequently broken.[33] The greatest issue was the fact that UNPROFOR lacked the ability to use military force in support of international objectives. It could not enforce a peace that did not, in fact, exist, nor could it enforce compliance of U.N. resolutions. Major-General Lewis MacKenzie observed, "It's not peacekeeping anymore anyway: there's rarely a peace to keep."[34] As such, the Bosnian conflict dragged on for three and a half years until December 1995, when the first important step in resolving it was finally taken.

Nevertheless, what could not be disputed was the fact that the operations in the Balkans did have a positive effect. For one, the tour provided an excellent method of assessing personnel. Major Tony Balasevicius noted, "Some individuals froze when fired at on operations and then wouldn't go back out. We had been brought up with a peacetime army where individuals were promoted up the entire rank structure without knowing whether they could actually do the job." He observed, "We found out that some individuals who are great in garrison are not necessarily great on operations and others who may be quiet and not showing a lot in garrison, actually rise to the challenge on operations."[35] In addition, Denis Thompson, who returned to battalion duty in 2 RCR in 1995, three years into UNPROFOR, explained, "There was a greater sense of urgency to make sure we had it right." He noted, "We weren't digging holes because someone wanted holes but we were doing things now because of necessity. The reality of Yugoslavia was fully absorbed. People were taking the business much more seriously. Things were not enforced or done just because it was an order." Thompson also remarked, "Later in the 1990s the routine garrison things we were use to in the previous decades were phased out. The 'nice to dos' such as annual technical inspections (ATIs) and brigade sports competitions slid off the schedule."[36] The fact of the matter was that real operations, real casualties, and palpable threat began to focus the Army.

Regardless of the realities of operations in the Former Yugoslavia, the Balkans were not the CF's only focus at this time. On Labour Day, 1992, 1 RCR conducted a fan-out to sign over its AVGPs to the Canadian Airborne Regiment (Cdn AB Regt) in preparation for a deployment to Somalia. In addition, the 1 RCR mortar platoon was also readied to accompany the paratroopers, that included the Royals of 3 Commando (3 Cdo). The failure to deploy 1 RCR, recently moved to CFB Petawawa, stung the battalion that had so quickly impressed its sister units in the SSF with its skill and professionalism.

Nonetheless, throughout the fall the Cdn AB Regt prepared for its mission, and after an agonizing series of delays was finally deployed on

Members of 3 Cdo control a crowd outside the wire in Belet Huen.

7 December 1992. The mission was originally designated as Operation Cordon, a classical U.N. peacekeeping operation mandated under Chapter VI of the U.N. Charter.[37] The Canadians as part of the U.N. Operation in Somalia (UNOSOM) were to be deployed to Bossasso, in northern Somalia, to provide security for the distribution of humanitarian relief, as well as participate in limited local humanitarian projects. However, on 3 December 1992, UNSCR 794 created an American-led enforcement operation entitled the Unified Task Force (UNITAF). UNITAF was authorized to use all means necessary to "establish as soon as possible a secure environment for humanitarian relief operations in Somalia."[38] Two days later, NDHQ formally cancelled Operation Cordon, and then on 5 December issued a new Warning Order to the SSF. The Canadian involvement in the UNITAF mission to Somalia was subsequently designated OP Deliverance. The Royals of 3 Cdo, as part of the Cdn AB Regt, were now part of the newly evolved U.N. peace-making mission.[39]

The CDS, General John de Chastelain, announced that the new mission was a "peace enforcement action to ease the suffering of the Somalian people." Furthermore, he added, "the contingent was authorized terms of engagement to take all steps to ensure that the job gets done."[40] The specific mission assigned to the Cdn AB Regt BG was to provide a secure environment for the distribution of humanitarian relief supplies in the Canadian Humanitarian Relief Sector (HRS), an area covering approximately 30,000 square kilometres. Their specific tasks included the security of airports; the protection of food convoys; the protection of food distribution centres; the rebuilding of infrastructure, which included roads, bridges, and schools; the re-establishment of a local police force in Belet Huen; and many other humanitarian projects.[41]

The overall performance in-theatre, particularly 3 Cdo, was laudable. The paratroopers landed in Somalia during the hottest time of the year into conditions that were later acknowledged "as extreme as Canadian troops have ever encountered."[42] Aside from the temperature, the soldiers were faced with the threat of diseases such as malaria, cholera, hepatitis, typhoid, tuberculosis, and more. Venomous insects and snakes were widespread and tenacious parasites were virtually unavoidable. In addition, all local water, even when boiled, was undrinkable.[43]

The climatic and environmental conditions were accentuated by further difficulties unique to the Canadian area of responsibility. Specifically, the Canadian zone encompassed an area that housed major militia formations of the three most powerful faction leaders in Somalia. Furthermore, the Canadian sector was also in close proximity to the turbulent Ethiopian border.[44]

Despite these challenges, the Cdn AB Regt BG actively proceeded to fulfil the mandate. Success was achieved through a combination of dialogue and firm military operations. Joint committees with local authorities and clan chiefs were reinforced by dismounted and vehicle patrols throughout the sector. This unremitting physical presence soon created an atmosphere of control, dominance, and security.[45] The aggressive patrolling and confiscation of weapons quickly stabilized the entire region. Village sweeps and road blocks were highly productive. The paratroopers projected such control and dominance over the area that the local militia commanders acquiesced to placing their heavy weapons in compounds, thus taking them out of circulation. As a result, UNITAF

Headquarters declared the Belet Huen HRS "secure" less than three months after the arrival of the Canadian paratroopers.[46]

As remarkable as the pacification program was, the humanitarian effort was even more praiseworthy. Hugh Tremblay, the director of Humanitarian Relief and Rehabilitation in Somalia, used the paratroopers as a model for others. His simple advice revolved around the theme, "If you want to know and to see what you should do while you are here in Somalia, go to Belet Huen, talk to the Canadians and do what they have done, emulate the Canadians and you will have success in your humanitarian relief sector."[47] Robert Press, a writer for the *Christian Science Monitor*, wrote: "Belet Huen appears to be a model in Somalia for restoring peace and effectively using foreign troops during this country's transition from anarchy to a national government."[48]

The chaos that existed in Somalia had originally prevented the humanitarian relief agencies from distributing the required aid, particularly into the outlying villages in the more remote areas. The arrival of the Cdn AB Regt BG radically changed this state of affairs. U.N. organizations and non-governmental organizations (NGOs) were now capable of expanding their operations not only in the settled areas, but also into the hinterland.

The Somalis themselves heaped lavish praise on the Canadians. General Mohammed Ahmed Hubero, a United Somali Congress Official from Belet Huen, stated, "the Canadians have done more for this region in five months than the two previous regimes did in thirty years."[49] The Somalia clan chieftains were also "effusive in their praise" of the paratroopers during the visit of the Land Force Central Area Commander, Major-General Brian Vernon.[50] Comparably, Major-General Lewis MacKenzie, Vernon's predecessor, also publicly acknowledged that during two visits to Belet Huen, he was repeatedly told by the elders and local police chief that they all wanted the Canadian paratroopers back. The Somalis asserted that the Regiment had done far more for Belet Huen than the Italian, German, and Malaysian troops that came after them.[51]

In total, the Cdn AB Regt BG's achievements included: the formation of five local committees to restore local government; the conduct of approximately 60 humanitarian convoys that provided aid to 96 villages;

the construction of four schools attended by 5,400 students at end tour; the instruction and training of 272 school teachers; the supervision and training of local doctors and nurses; the training of 150 policeman in Belet Huen, 20 in Matabaan, and 15 in St. Emily; the provision of potable water to local refugees; the repair of approximately 20 wells; the repair of village generators; the repair of the Belet Huen and Matabaan hospitals; the construction of a bridge; and the repair of over 200 kilometres of road.[52]

Robert Oakley, the U.N. Special Envoy to Somalia, wrote that "in six months, with only 1,200 soldiers operating in a nightmare of violence, heat, disease and conflict, the Canadians have secured and supported all relief operations, organized local schools and medical clinics, and negotiated cease-fires among warring factions. The tragedy has been suspended and a real foothold of peace has been established in the region as a result of Canadian efforts."[53] He extended his admiration with the comments that "there is no question but that their discipline, operational readiness, immediate responsiveness to assigned tasks, care and use of equipment, and ability to operate effectively in difficult climatic conditions were considered to be at the very top of all Unified Task Force units."[54]

Despite the great accomplishments, the tour was marred by a number of tragic and unforgivable events that increasingly defined the overall mission by the media as a complete failure. Moreover, the events would prove to be the catalyst that created a storm that engulfed DND and the CF and brought them to their lowest ebb in their existence. Sadly, through the course of the mission, Canadians killed four Somali nationals and wounded many others. Some of the deaths were unquestionably avoidable. One such killing occurred on 4 March 1993. Increased security at the Engineer Compound and neighbouring helipad, undertaken by the reconnaissance platoon, resulted in gunfire as two would-be thieves attempted to escape. Initially, the shooting was termed justifiable within the RoEs by a unit-controlled investigation. However, continuing allegations by one of the contingent's medical officers, who professed that the death of one of the interlopers was the result of a deliberate execution-style killing, eventually raised some disturbing questions.[55] Although these allegations have never been conclusively proven or refuted, the shootings themselves have been declared unjustifiable. The carefully planned ambush operation obviously was "designed to send a strong message to would-be infiltrators that any attempt to penetrate the perimeter of Canadian installations would be met with gunfire."[56]

As disturbing as these allegations are, they are not the only ones. Mixed messages reverberated through the Canadian compounds in Somalia. Not only was a questionable shooting very quickly dismissed and the participants praised, but there existed a perception that abusive behaviour was ignored and not punished. This outlook became prevalent in some elements of the Cdn AB Regt BG. This was due in part to the fact that mistreatment of prisoners was condoned by some officers and NCOs within the Canadian contingent. In sum this laid the groundwork for the defining moment of the Somalia mission.

On the night of 16 March 1993, an apprehended looter, Shidane Arone, was systematically beaten to death while in the custody of 2 Commando. What made this tragedy even harder to understand is the fact that throughout the beating, many soldiers, Senior NCOs, and officers either heard the cries or actually dropped by the bunker and witnessed the beating in progress; yet no one stopped it until it was too late.[57] The tragic killing changed the manner in which the mission was ultimately assessed.

The incidents soon became national news, and the Canadian public was shocked. The media now put DND and the CF under a microscope, and the result was shattering. A better movie script could not have been written. A brutal killing, an evident breakdown of military leadership, a cover-up, and a minister of defence who was the acknowledged frontrunner in the Progressive Conservative leadership race. Somalia had finally dragged DND and the CF, as well as its officer corps, into the post–Cold War era. And, as the CDS, General Maurice Baril, conceded — "part of it was broken."[58]

The close scrutiny now only added fuel to the fire. It quickly became evident that other Canadian military units deployed overseas also had a plethora of problems. For example, many of the Canadian contingents that deployed to the former Yugoslavia experienced disciplinary difficulties, particularly in relation to drunkenness. Examples abound: 2 Service Battalion had their commanding officer, regimental sergeant major, and numerous soldiers sent home during their tour in Yugoslavia for proven malfeasance or alleged misconduct; and soldiers in the Royal Canadian Dragoons (RCD) gave their unit the nickname "ChargeBat" because of the large number of charges that had been laid against its soldiers for disciplinary infractions.

Elsewhere, serious questions were raised about lost equipment and vehicles during tours; and another national scandal erupted in 1994 as the result of the questionable behaviour of 60 Canadian peacekeepers at the Bosnian Bakovici mental hospital. Cambodia and Haiti were equally fraught with incidents of scandalous and unprofessional behaviour that included black market activity, corruption, drunkenness, and prostitution.[59]

The operational scandals overseas were matched at home by allegations of unethical behaviour, particularly the misuse of public funds, as well as opulent spending practices by senior military officers at a time when the country faced a financial crisis as a result of its burgeoning national debt.[60] This was compounded by an officer corps whose efforts at responding to questions in regards to Somalia were "characterized by inconsistency, improbability, implausibility, evasiveness, selective recollection, half-truths, and plain lies." In fact, they were accused of letting undue loyalty to their regiments or military institutions, as well as "naked self-interest," take precedence over "honesty and integrity."[61]

The criticism was relentless and went so far as to suggest that "Somalia is seen as a sign or symbol of a crisis in command, as the result of a weakened, corrupted military ethos." Many went on to say that "senior commanders are held to have been corrupted and distanced from their soldiers ... preoccupied by careers and perks, they are seen as having abandoned traditional values, ideals, and loyalties."[62] Not surprisingly, the Canadian public came to perceive that misconduct and leadership failing were widespread, if not endemic. Moreover, CF personnel felt betrayed and abandoned by their senior leadership who said nothing and withdrew behind a cloak of silence.[63] The CF appeared to have sunk into a deep hole. "The confidence of Canadians in the Forces," conceded Doug Young, the MND, "has been shaken."[64]

Despite the trauma at home, operations abroad still required attention. At least, at long last, it appeared as if the situation in the former

Yugoslavia would turn for the better. But first, it had to bottom out. The circumstances began to shift when the international community finally tired of the massive scale of killing. On 11 July 1995, the Bosnian Serbs seized Srebrenica, completely ignoring the Dutch battalion that was at that time responsible for protecting the U.N. safe haven. The Serbs proceeded to expel 23,000 Muslim women and children and executed thousands of Muslim men.[65] Then on 28 August 1995, mortar rounds exploded in the Sarajevo marketplace, killing 38 civilians and wounding at least 85 more.[66] This flagrant disregard for yet another U.N. safe area and a NATO-designated heavy weapons exclusion zone triggered U.S. President Bill Clinton to finally take action as Washington took this to be a deliberate attack on its emerging policy with regard to BiH. As a result, Clinton ordered retaliatory action to demonstrate U.S. resolve.

NATO launched Operation Deliberate Force on 30 August 1995. The campaign lasted until 20 September. It began with an initial strike of 13 Tomahawk cruise missiles against the Bosnian Serb army's command centre in Banja Luka and ended after NATO flew 3,515 sorties that hammered vital Serb military targets.[67] At the same time, both Bosnian and Croat forces launched land offensives of their own and captured large swaths of territory.

The sudden turn of events brought Karadzic and Milosevic to the bargaining table. Karadzic was willing to settle on a deal that gave the Bosnian Serbs half of Bosnia. Milosevic was willing to pressure the Bosnian Serbs into a settlement in order to end the U.N. embargo on Yugoslavia. As a result, the Clinton administration brought the warring parties to Dayton, Ohio for negotiations in November. A month later, on 14 December 1995, the belligerents signed the General Framework Agreement for Peace (GFAP) in Paris, France.

The following day the U.N. passed UNSCR 1031, which authorized NATO to carry out its military mission under Chapter VII of the U.N. Charter for peace enforcement. The mandate for the NATO Implementation Force (IFOR) commenced on 20 December 1995. IFOR, unlike UNPROFOR that it replaced, in accordance with the Dayton GFAP, was not constrained by narrowly written RoEs that would not effectively allow it to enforce U.N. resolutions. IFOR was fully empowered to apply force in response to any act of noncompliance. More important, it had both the personnel and equipment to do so. IFOR increased UNPROFOR's troop strength from 38,000 to 60,000.[68]

IFOR's mission was to implement the military components of the Dayton Accords and patrol the 1,400 kilometre Inter-Entity Boundary Line (IEBL) or more commonly known as the zone of separation. The U.N. gave IFOR a one year mandate to accomplish its mission. To ensure IFOR met its mandate, all three Bosnian armies were given only 120 days from the signing of the agreement to deploy to their barracks and place their heavy equipment in cantonment sites. The Supreme Allied Commander Europe (SACEUR) later revised the deadline for the cantonment of heavy weapons to 180 days.

Once the military tasks were achieved, IFOR became responsible for ensuring the cessation of hostilities and creating a peaceful and secure environment to allow for reconstruction and development. IFOR also became involved with the holding of free and fair elections, the continuation of humanitarian missions, the protection of refugee returnees, and the supervision of the clearing of minefields, and obstacles.

The RCR were not involved with IFOR, except for "G" Coy, 2 RCR, deployed in December 1995 as part of the Queen's Royal Hussars Battle Group, in the area of Klujc, southwest of Banja Luka. Their task was to provide security for 2 CMBG headquarters and to assist with the enforcement of the terms of the implementation of the Dayton Accords within their sector.

Denis Thompson, then a major, was the OC of the independent company group. "It was great — one of my best experiences!" he recalled. "The cavalry were not big on details. I met the operations officer as he was fly fishing in a stream and the instructions were basically 'Here's your patch [AO] carry on.'"[69]

But, clearly circumstances had changed in Bosnia. Thompson noted, "Every time we went to challenge the Croats or Serbs, they would back down. There was no push back. They recognized that the balance of power had changed. For instance, we would be cut a troop of Challenger main battle tanks when we went on operations."[70] He assessed it as an "interesting tour." Thompson explained, "We arrived in January to a Bosnian winter. It was post-apocalyptic. There were few military, no electricity, no humans and all the houses were burnt down. When we left in the summer they [local population] were planting gardens, roofs were going up. You could see changes on the ground and we all felt good about it."[71]

Thompson's assessment was largely supported. IFOR had actually enjoyed great success in implementing the military component of the GFAP. Within the year IFOR established, as a minimum, minimal security and order, improved freedom of movement, establishment and clearing of a zone of separation, enforcement of the cantonment of heavy weapons, inspections, support for elections, maintenance of a visible presence across the country, and arbitration of disputes among the former warring factions.[72]

Despite the relative success, the international community, as well as Bosnians, feared that the pull-out of NATO, when the mandate expired on 20 December 1996, would mean a return to violence. As a result, the U.N. passed UNSCR 1088 on 12 December 1996, which created the Stabilization Force (SFOR) to provide a continued international presence in BiH. Its mission was to stabilize the peace implemented under IFOR and to contribute to the safe and secure environment necessary for the consolidation of peace. However, the security situation had greatly changed, and the force structure was reduced to only 35,000 troops.

The RCR actively contributed to SFOR. Troops were provided by 1 RCR to Roto 1 (July 1997) and the BG for Roto 2 (January-June 1998); 2 RCR provided the BG for Roto 4 (January-June 1999); and 3 RCR provided the BG for Roto 3 (July-December 1998) and Roto 8 (April-October 2001). Training for the missions had advanced dramatically since the earlier tours. Battle groups preparing to deploy were given test exercises that were run within communities and townships across Ontario. Sub-units rehearsed foot and vehicle patrols, checkpoints, vehicle and building searches, de-mining and cantonment site inspections. They also reacted to events such as illegal checkpoints, mine strikes, vehicle accidents, and violations to freedom of movement for Canadians in local communities. "The exercises proved to be the closest thing to actually being in Bosnia."[73]

Although the training was more realistic and focused, the actual threat levels in theatre had spiralled. The massive NATO infusion of troops and firepower, and the willingness to use it, had achieved the necessary effect. Matthew Sprague asserted, "There was a big difference with SFOR. In the early days [1992–93] we were making it up as we went along. With SFOR it was a 'do it our way or we will crush you.'"[74] As such, Balkan tours were much more subdued, and the major danger now was leftover land mines that had not yet been cleared. The main task of all Canadians serving in SFOR was "framework patrolling." The patrols would demonstrate presence and ensure security. Master Warrant Officer Rick Duncan affirmed, "Our task was basically to provide a secure and stable environment while the host nation was rebuilding. Key was providing the basic necessity of security for the population. Presence patrolling reassured the population so that people can move about freely. The net effect was an increase in commerce and schooling."[75]

The Royals also conducted meetings with lower-level community leaders, school teachers, police chiefs, mayors, and village leaders. Royals also provided security for "Key Leader Engagements" whenever the leadership of the former warring factions would meet. They also carried out special tasks as assigned. For instance, they provided security cordons for special operations forces to arrest war criminals, as well as for the International Police Task Force to seize weapons banned by the Dayton Accord. Royals also conducted unannounced inspections of weapon cantonment sites, random vehicle searches for weapons, and cordon and search operations for illicit weapons hidden in towns and homes. Moreover, Royals also assisted UNHCR with the repatriation of displaced persons, refugees, and evacuees (DPRE), as well as community reconstruction work.

Lieutenant-Colonel Rob Walker noted that "By 1998/1999, the fighting was over and the Dayton Accords were in place. We established cantonment sites and we were buying time for the civilian leadership to create the necessary economic and political reforms, as well as for the Bosnian police and military to form. It was very much different."[76] Chief Warrant Officer Jay Gravelle agreed. "We did framework patrolling," he explained, "Established a platoon house and patrolled. Like Cyprus in the early years we were keeping an eye on the former warring parties. We'd check their TDMS, inspect their equipment and storage sites."[77]

But for most it had become a routine tour, in many ways such as Cyprus. Gravelle noted, "It was a comfortable tour. It was nowhere near Yugoslavia in 1992–1993 or the Afghan theatre of operations. Our biggest threat was mines so you'd have to stay on marked routes."[78] Jim Davis saw it as simply, "Framework patrolling and outreach to villages." He noted, "We wrote off IMPs [individual meal pack] by the thousands."[79] Captain Piers Pappin, like most, simply shrugged and remarked, "My tour in 1999, not much to talk about."[80]

However, there were still key moments that tested the courage and professionalism of The RCR. One such moment was the Drvar Riots of 24/25 April 1998. The city and region of Drvar in western Herzegovina fell under the Multinational Division — Southwest (MND-SW). It was a Serb enclave with 97 percent of its 17,000 population of Serb extraction. However, in August 1995, the Bosnian Croat Home Defence (HVO) force seized Drvar in conjunction with Operation Storm. The Serb population, fearing ethnic cleansing, fled the city and region. In place of the Serbs, approximately 6,000 displaced Croats arrived and occupied the vacated homes and apartments in the town. A HVO brigade and their families also took over abandoned apartments. As a result, Drvar was converted virtually overnight into a Croat locality.

But the U.N. declared 1998 the year of the return of refugees, and accordingly Drvar was to become a showcase. As such, the international community began to force the issue of repatriation. In May 1997, a small number of Serbs began to trickle back in small numbers to the outlying region. Initially, local Croats intimidated the first returnees from staying in the area by torching their homes.

However, as the MND-SW commander assigned the Drvar area to the 1 RCR BG, aggressive Canadian patrolling provided a sense of security, and a steady flow of Serbs returned to the region. What also added to the complexity of the situation was the fact that under the Dayton Accords elections were to serve as a major instrument for reversing the results of ethnic cleansing. In fact, the agreement allowed displaced persons and refugees to vote in their prewar municipality, even though they now resided elsewhere. As a result, displaced Drvar Serbs voted in the local election of 13–14 September 1997 and elected a Serb mayor in what was a virtually homogeneous Croatian city. Although Serbs now dominated the town's executive council and began to fill positions in its the civil administration, the local police force was Croat. Not surprisingly, the local Croats, all recent settlers, began to fear losing their newly gained home.

The international community's approach did not assist matters. The SFOR commander urged the 1 RCR BG to "adopt a hammer approach" whenever necessary. Moreover, the UNHCR pushed hard for the return of refugees and displaced persons to Dvrar. In fact, on 23 February 1998, Lieutenant-General Sir Hew Pike, deputy commander of operations at SFOR headquarters in Sarajevo, affirmed, "the International Community will not tolerate anything less than a Serb led Canton, with Drvar a Serb town."[81] By April 1998, approximately 1,600 Serbs and 6,000 Croats co-existed tenuously in Drvar.

The 1 RCR BG CO, Lieutenant-Colonel Peter Devlin assigned Major Howard Coombs, OC Charles Coy, to protect the Dvrar area. Occasionally, Devlin would provide a second rifle company to patrol the countryside to allow Coombs to concentrate his troops in the city itself. Nevertheless, with forces thin on the ground, the Canadians expressed constant concern to their SFOR chain of command that the rate of returnees was moving too fast for them with their small force to provide the necessary security. Their warnings were continually ignored.

Local Croats began to increase their resistance. Canadian troops were harassed during patrols and vehicles would be aggressively used to target foot patrols in town. On 16 April, unknown assailants murdered a Serb couple and set fire to their home. This latest event incensed the international community. Deputy High Representative Jacques Klein, a retired U.S. Air Force general, arrived in Drvar by helicopter and perfunctorily fired the deputy mayor and demanded the removal of the chief of police and the cantonal interior minister, all of whom were Croats.[82] To the Canadians, this knee-jerk reaction played into the hands of the Croat radicals.[83]

Then on 24 April 1998, the tinderbox erupted. One of Coombs' patrols notified him at approximately 1130 hours that there was a small crowd of 30 to 40 persons gathering in the centre of town. Ten minutes later the crowd had grown to 70 strong, and the mob started to hurl rocks at the municipal building, breaking windows. Then the crowd suddenly burst inside the city hall and sacked it. Without warning they rushed across the street and inflicted significant damage to the local offices of a number of international organizations (i.e. the High Representative, UNHCR, and the Organization for Security and Co-operation in Europe).

Realizing the danger, Coombs ordered the evacuation of all international personnel to Camp Drvar. Some U.N. officials were already making their escape on foot and/or in vehicles toward the Canadian compound. Fire trucks racing to put out the fires were forced back as they were pelted by rocks, bricks, and stones. Canadian soldiers were required to intervene to help the firefighters escape the chaos.

Major Coombs made his way to the scene of the riot. Foremost in his mind was the need to extract international workers back to Camp Drvar and to protect the Serb population. By this time the mob had exploded to about 500, including women and children. They had beaten the Serb mayor almost to death, and he was evacuated to the Canadian camp. By 1245 hours, the riot scene was one of complete anarchy. Vehicles and buildings were ablaze. Seventeen Canadian soldiers under the command of Captain Brian Bedard had just managed to evacuate approximately 150 Serb returnees from an apartment complex and transported them to a nearby school. There 51 Royals were confronted by a crowd of up to 500 angry Croats who were armed with knives, baseball bats, rocks, and a myriad of other weapons. Bedard had already been forced to fire a warning shot to keep the rioters at a distance.

Coombs made his way to the school, where the confrontation was reaching a crescendo. He brought with him 20 reinforcements. Coombs deployed his meagre force to establish a perimeter around the school. He also stationed 20 soldiers inside the school building, specifically to man the windows to prevent anyone from tossing in firebombs. Rioters had already attempted to set the school's generator on fire with gasoline, but they were frightened off by two warning shots. Significantly, his lack of personnel prevented Coombs from forming a wall. Rather, he had a very porous perimeter with soldiers standing approximately 10 feet apart.

Based on the actions of the mob thus far, Coombs feared for the lives of the Serbs in the school. Luckily, a SFOR light observation helicopter was on scene and provided excellent information on the crowd's movement behind the front line. The helicopter also informed Coombs that some of the rioters were armed with AK-47 assault rifles. Then suddenly, the helicopter notified Coombs that the mass of the crowd was rushing for a narrow passage way between the school and a neighbouring warehouse building. The OC quickly shifted his forces to meet the rush. As the crowd rapidly closed in on his position, Coombs realized he would have to act quickly. "I drew, cocked my pistol and took aim towards the lead person in the crowd," recalled Coombs, "They [the Croatian rioters] advanced to within six to seven meters of me. I then fired a warning shot into the soft ground at the leader's feet ... They stopped prior to the point of impact, drew slightly back, screamed and taunted me and then promptly sacked and set fire to the ITI warehouse next to the school."[84]

The worst of the storm had seemed to pass. At 1400 hours, 1 RCR BG reinforcements in the form of "D" Coy and a reconnaissance unit, arrived on the scene. Within the following hour, the mob had largely dissipated, although small groups of 20–30 people continued to roam the streets until evening.

In the aftermath of the riot, of the approximately 160 Serbs who had moved into the apartment complex near the school, only about 20 remained in town; the others decided to leave. Master Warrant Officer Duncan lamented, "People who my platoon made friends with — seeing them loaded back up and leaving with less than they came with was a huge sense of disappointment both as a soldier and human being."[85]

Despite the destruction of property and departure of some of the Serbs, the Royals had protected and saved the lives of the international workers, as well as the Serbs in Dvrar. In addition, they had shown great restraint and had not killed any of the Croat rioters. The deputy chief of the defence staff (DCDS), Lieutenant-General Ray Hennault, would later award 1 RCR a unit commendation in recognition of steadfast and professional action in the face of large scale civil unrest in the town of Drvar, Bosnia-Herzegovina, on 24 April 1998. The citation read, "Soldiers of the 1 RCR Battle Group acted quickly and with great composure to place themselves between a violent crowd and unarmed refugees, preventing almost certain injury and loss of life. Having acted with courage and restraint in resisting the temptation to shoot hostile belligerents, the Battle Group preserved the foundation for a restoration of peaceful relation between ethnic communities, bringing credit to themselves and to the Canadian Forces."[86]

In the end, although tours in the Balkans had become somewhat routine, with the odd exceptions, they still provided Royals with an operational challenge and an important training and learning experience. Colonel Davis concluded, "Bosnia became the Cyprus of the 1980s, but it was the only show in town." He insisted, "Everyone wanted to be there. Soldiers honestly believed they were making a difference in the everyday life of Bosnians."[87] Master Warrant Officer Rick Duncan commented: "We came away from the tour [1998] with a sense of accomplishment."[88] Most agreed. Gravelle asserted, "It was still very valuable. Soldiers returned to Canada well trained and highly motivated. It made individuals innovative, very fit, good leaders with a can do attitude who would go the extra mile."[89] Even Captain Pappin, who found his tour almost boring, agreed. "There was definitely value in the Bosnian tours for the junior ranks," he explained, "They learned to plan and operate on their own, to be independent since most of the tasks were section level operations. The tour fostered a decentralized command environment."[90]

But, as the Balkans were winding down, things had simply gotten worse in Canada. Continuing public criticism simply drove the wedge between DND/CF and the Canadian government and people even deeper. Continuing scrutiny of the Cdn AB Regt's performance in Somalia, as well as a number of new scandals finally forced the government to act. They had lost trust in the unit. As a result, it was disbanded on 5 March 1995.[91]

However, the end did not come as quickly for 3 Cdo. In the ensuing turmoil and confusion of closing down the Cdn AB Regt, just a scant few days before the actual disbandment ceremonies on 4–5 March, that Petawawa received a signal from Land Forces Command Headquarters (LFCHQ), which said that "there are some outstanding operational tasks for which an element of the Regiment must be prepared to execute. For these reasons, Commander LFC has directed that the CO Canadian Airborne Holding Unit[92] develop a company size group (based primarily on RCR members) with appropriate command and control and elements of Airborne Service Commando not to exceed 300 members to provide contingency troops in the event of short notice operations."[93] A more detailed directive 10 days later, on 13 March 1995, emphasized the need for a parachute force. It simply concluded, "Canadians will not accept the contention that we cannot put troops on the ground anywhere in this country at anytime."[94]

As such, the former 3 Cdo, now redesignated 3 Cdo Group (Gp), was brought back to life and authorized a strength of 187 personnel.[95] Individual and sub-unit equipment which had been cleaned and packed away was now re-issued. In addition, a training plan was quickly resurrected. The establishment of 3 Cdo Gp, which represented Canada's interim airborne capability, officially took effect 6 March 1995.[96] Six months later, on 1 September 1995, 3 Cdo Gp was finally shut down as the last vestige of the Cdo AB Regt. The sub-unit was officially redesignated the RCR Parachute Company (Para Coy) on that date.

If any positive could be seen as coming from the disbandment of the Cdn AB Regt, it was the fact that 3 RCR would be reborn as a regular force battalion. In the aftermath of the disbandment, the Army decided to transition to a model of Light Infantry Battalions (LIB), each with an integral parachute company, in each of the regular force infantry regiments. In effect, the Army had returned to the DCF model. As such, 3 RCR was reactivated as a regular force battalion allocated to 2 CMBG in accordance with the Light Infantry Battalion Implementation Order, dated 8 December 1995. It was reformed from the nucleus of the Airborne Holding Unit and the regular force component of the 10/90 3 RCR battalion.[97] The headquarters of 3 RCR moved from CFB Borden to CFB Petawawa during the summer. By January 1997, 3 RCR as a LIB, had an authorized strength of 518 personnel. Of these, 162 positions were designated full-time parachute positions. Para Coy was authorized only 102 of these. However, much like the MSF/DCF era, parachuting was increasingly marginalized and would become almost non-existent once the Army became totally committed to the war in Afghanistan after 2006.

The government's lack of trust, however, extended beyond the Cdn AB Regt. By the spring of 1995, the continuing scandals, what appeared to be an intractable officer corps, and apparent failure of DND and the

CF to provide clear and complete answers to lingering questions related to the Somalia Affair and some other incidents or practices seemingly left the government with no choice but to appoint a separate independent commission to determine the truth. Sadly, for DND, the reality was that politicians and many other people no longer trusted the military to investigate itself. As a result, the government established the "Commission of Inquiry into the Deployment of Canadian Forces to Somalia," known commonly as the Somalia Commission, in an attempt to finally bring resolution and transparency to the issue.[98]

The Somalia Commission in turn, frustrated by a seemingly obdurate, if not at times dishonest, officer corps produced a scathing report in 1997. Of the 160 recommendations contained in the Somalia Commission Report, 112 were leadership and management-related. In sum, the Somalia Commissioners found that "a failure of military values lies at the heart of the Somalia experience."[99] Of the 160 recommendations contained in the Somalia Commission Report, 132 were accepted for implementation by the MND. Including a number of other reports, such as the *Report of the Special Advisory Group on Military Justice and Military Police Investigative Services;* the *Report on the Quasi-Judicial Role of the Minister of National Defence;* and the *Report of the Special Commission on the Restructuring of the Reserves,* the MND endorsed some 250 recommendations for change.

The accepted recommendations covered most aspects of the functioning of DND.[100] To add insult to injury, and just in case the nuance was lost on the CF officer corps, the government also established a "Minister's Monitoring Committee on Change [MMC] in the Department of National Defence and the Canadian Forces" to "monitor progress with respect to the implementation of change."[101] Quite simply, the government did not trust the military to make the necessary changes without being monitored and held to account.[102]

For the Canadian officer corps, this was a low point in its history. It had been unable to foresee, adapt, or even realize that the world no longer fit its archaic Cold War paradigm despite the substantial and significant geo-political and societal changes that occurred around it. It was unwilling, or perhaps unable, to realize this. Moreover, as is incumbent on all professions, it was also unwilling, or unable, to maintain its professionalism (i.e. responsibility — special duty to Canada; expertise, identity, and vocational ethic). This last failing, specifically its inability to maintain a healthy military ethos (i.e. the values, beliefs, and expectations that reflect core Canadian values and the imperatives of military professionalism) was catastrophic.[103]

The post-Somalia crisis climate did not help. In fact, scandal seemed to feed a frenzy of further criticism of DND and the CF. Books detailing opulent spending practices and the squandering of resources by senior officers, sensational articles in *Maclean's* alleging widespread rapes and cover-ups, the continuing reporting of the Somalia courts martial and the alleged continuing cover-up, as well as the perceived indifference to injured soldiers returning from the stabilization campaigns in the former Yugoslavia all fed the claims of abuse of authority, lack of support for, if not indifference to, the welfare of subordinates, as well as claims of rampant harassment at all rank levels rocked the institution.[104] However, the pressure on the institution, particularly senior officers and those in positions of supervision, prompted many to run for cover. Many abrogated their responsibility and rather than do the right thing chose to do nothing. Rather than risk being accused of harassment or being labelled a supporter, they simply failed in their moral responsibility of ensuring fair treatment for everyone. During this era, as one RCR general openly acknowledged, an "allegation was all that it took to ruin a career."[105] Jim Davis recalled, "It was an unhealthy time, a reign of terror."[106] So for most, taking cover was seen as the safest thing to do.

Not surprisingly, amid all the criticism, the government and people of Canada lost faith in the officer corps. Moreover, the soldiers no longer trusted the officer corps to protect, or ensure the best interests of, their subordinates. General Hillier conceded, "The perception across the junior ranks was that we, the leaders, had broken faith with those we led, and if there is one thing I learned over the years, it is that perception is reality. Our soldiers did not trust us."[107]

Further adding to the complexity of the problem was the fact that the government was directing DND to undertake an enormous amount of new social initiatives and programs. The inclusion of the Canadian Charter of Rights and Freedoms in the Canadian constitution in 1982, made it incumbent on DND and particularly the CF, to become more inclusive in employment (specifically in relation to women) and transparent in its processes and practices. This was met with great resistance. DND attempted to fight the direction but was unsuccessful.[108] The CF was also under pressure, because of the federal Employment Equity Act, to increase its quota of visible minorities from under two percent to nine percent, which was the approximate percentage of visible minorities in the labour force. In addition, the CF had been directed to abolish its restrictions on homosexuality in 1992. In light of ongoing criticisms of DND/the CF, and allegations that the institution was systemically biased against women and minorities, the MND ordered all ranks to undertake sensitivity training under the Standard for Harassment and Racism Prevention (SHARP) program in 1998.

Finally, another significant factor that added to the crisis in trust and stewardship of the profession was the continuing impact of significant and debilitating budget cuts that DND and the CF was forced to absorb. Training was cut, programs were curtailed, equipment life was extended, capital projects were postponed or cancelled, and personnel was reduced, all at the same time as operational tempo was higher than it had been since the Korean War. "There were real resource constraints," remembered Major Jay Feyko, "There was no ammo and we didn't have blanks. We honed skills that did not involve going to the firing range. We did rucksack marches and Ironman training. We did what we could with the limited resources we had."[109] Captain David Gavin recalled, "Soldiering in the 1990s was lean. On a brigade exercise you'd be given a box of rounds that were to last you the entire week."[110] Similarly, Tom France lamented, "In the mid-1990s we were constrained by everything. We had no money, no equipment and we couldn't do anything. Not a lot of people were happy."[111]

Lieutenant-General Andrew Leslie agreed. He publicly stated that the budget cuts in the 1990s meant that "we had to fight to train."[112] The Army's own assessment noted the deterioration of its training regimen. "Over the course of the 1990s the training focus of Canada's Army has narrowed steadily toward current operations," noted a DND report, "Skills at brigade and combined arms battle group level have eroded, and collective training as a whole has centred around pre-deployment training events."[113] But then, there was no money for anything but the absolute necessities.

The change in the reality of soldiering was quickly captured by a number of the RCR colonels of the Regiment during the decade. "Change is the watchword. Today, as perhaps never before, the Army is being enjoined to place greater responsibility and accountability on junior leaders and to seek innovative ways and efficient procedures to do the job better, and to accomplish more with less," asserted Colonel R.M. Dillon.[114] He observed, "With the end of the Cold War, public support and understanding for the armed forces appears to be diminishing and fiscal restraint has sharply reduced military expenditures."[115] Lieutenant-General Jack Vance wrote, "The conditions under which the Regiment serves today are noteworthy: financial constraint remains a constant backdrop for soldiering today; the intense pace of operations both at home or abroad maintains unabated; and, our armed forces in Canada are experiencing inevitable shifts in purpose and character as we move into the 21st Century."[116]

So as the decade came to a close, it was abundantly clear that the Cold War era was over. Furthermore, peace support operations and soldiering had dramatically changed. Adding to the complexity of change was continuing criticism and reform of DND and the CF, all placed against a backdrop of unprecedented budget cuts. Throughout the seeming chaos, the rank and file members of The RCR continued to soldier on, doing the Regiment and country proud at home and abroad. In fact, by the end of the 1990s they once again proved their professionalism. In the spring of 1997, 1 RCR on minimal notice deployed to Southern Manitoba to assist with the flood control operations to stem the Red River. Assigned an area of responsibility in North Winnipeg, the Royals assisted in reinforcing existing dykes, building new dykes, and manning traffic control points around washed-out bridges and roads.

Less than a year later, in January 1998, the Regiment participated on OP Recuperation, an Aid to the Civil Power deployment, which was the result of an ice storm that ravaged parts of Ontario and Quebec, leaving millions without power. The mix of freezing rain, ice pellets, and gale force winds prompted the largest mobilization of CF personnel since

Korean War. The 1 RCR rear party deployed to Eastern Ontario; 2 RCR deployed by road to the regional municipality of Rouville in Quebec under the operational command of 1 CMBG; 3 RCR deployed in the Outaouais region and later in the Glengarry region; and 4 RCR soldiers assisted in the town of St. Andrews West. In sum, the objective of all Royals was to assure the preservation of life and property, while providing stabilization and support and assistance to Quebec Hydro and Bell Canada crews, as many areas were without hydro for 72 hours, and some would not get full service for months.

And finally, in December 1999, 1 RCR deployed to Kosovo. It appeared the Balkans had once again erupted in conflict. This time the catalyst was the continuing conflict between Serbian forces and the Kosovo Liberation Army in the former semi-autonomous province of Kosovo. This conflict prompted Slobodan Milosevic to launch a program of ethnic cleansing of Albanian Kosovars in an attempt to keep the province in the Serbian orbit. As a result, NATO began Operation Allied Force, an air campaign that ran from 24 March until 11 June 1999, which was directed against Serbian forces and military infrastructure in an attempt to halt all Serbian military activity and all ethnic violence in Kosovo. It was also the precursor to the NATO sponsored Kosovo Force (KFOR), established under UNSCR 1244, which had the mission to establish and maintain a secure environment in Kosovo, including public safety and order, as well as monitor, verify, and when necessary enforce compliance with the conditions of the Military Technical Agreement (MTA) for the demilitarization of Kosovo.

The task for Operation Kinetic, Roto 1, commencing in December 1999, was assigned to the 1 RCR BG. Their mission was to create a safe environment that would permit the return of Kosovar refugees and the re-establishment of a functional economy, and if necessary enforce the MTA. In addition to the patrolling and observation duties that are integral to peace support operations, the Royals also carried out humanitarian aid operations such as reconstructing schools and medical buildings, as well as roofing buildings and installing bridges. The Battalion returned in May 2000, closing down the Canadian main force contribution to KFOR.

Kosovo

Map by Chris Johnson.

Courtesy Canadian Forces Imagery Library, negative ISC99-074.

Royals observe the departure of Serb forces from Kosovo during OP Kinetic.

And so ended, the 1990s, much like it began, on operations. However, the decade had been a turbulent one, which rocked the very foundation of DND and the CF. The RCR, as always, persevered and adapted and changed as required to meet its remit to Canada and the Canadian people. However, the Regiment, like all others in the CF, was affected by the turmoil — whether budgetary cuts, crisis in leadership, changing dynamics in the geo-political security environment, or the myriad of changing social policies and reforms. For those who endured the 1990s, the "decade of darkness" held special meaning.

7

The New Millennium: A World on Fire

The 1990s had been a traumatic period. Despite many successes operationally at home and abroad, the underlying perception held by the government and people of Canada with regard to its military was one of mistrust and derision. General Rick Hillier publicly acknowledged, "We have come out of a decade of darkness. We have been disowned, abandoned, divorced by the population of Canada."[1] He explained, "Budgets [were] cut by more than 25 percent, our training slashed to an almost non-existent state, bases closed and the numbers of uniformed men and women reduced drastically. In a perfect storm, then, our confidence in who we were and our pride in being soldiers, in the most generic sense, was shattered. Several scandals, including those in Somalia and Bosnia, compounded our stress, while frozen, insufficient wages spoke eloquently as to our value in the eyes of our government and Canadians."[2] As such, he conceded, "Morale was at an all-time low; we had not recovered from the challenges of the 1990s, when it had bottomed out."[3]

There were many factors that led to the "decade of darkness," some external to DND and the CF, but others internal systemic flaws that required correction. Although this reality was resisted for far too long, it finally sank in. "The Canadian Forces and the Department of National Defence," wrote General Maurice Baril, "like many other Canadian institutions, have not always been quick to anticipate and react to these new transitions." He conceded that "some of our slowness to change was because of prevailing institutional attitudes and cultures."[4] But the government had intervened and forced evolution on the military. "The Army was forced to change," conceded Lieutenant-General Mike Jeffrey, "I mean *forced*." He added, "The challenge is not to forget those institutional failures took place. We had significant failures."[5]

And so the transformation of DND and the CF began with the new millennium. The tragedy in Somalia and disappointing aftermath sparked a virtual reformation of the CF officer corps and the institution itself. Fundamental reform was accepted and the 250 recommendations for change were consciously undertaken. Changes included: a new appraisal system and succession planning processes that diluted the influence and power of unofficial "Regimental councils"; a degreed officer corps; a public affairs policy based on transparency and accuracy with an attendant obligation to adhere to the access to information legislation; a multitude of change initiatives that addressed issues from employment equity, soldier, and family quality of life, to more fiscally responsible management practices; and greater emphasis on professional development that would foster a culture of adaptation, change, and proactive vision.[6]

In the end, the change initiatives that were forced on the CF took it out of its Cold War practices, processes, and mentality, and a much stronger and more vibrant organization emerged. The evolution was timely, as the new millennium thrust The RCR into a world seemingly on fire. As such, the Royals would be required to draw on their experience from both the Cold War and the period of stabilization campaigns of the 1990s to meet new and far greater challenges.

As the new millennium began, the operational tempo had not decreased in the slightest. At home and abroad, Royals were kept exceptionally busy. In fact, Major R.J. Martin captured the change in tempo over time in a tongue-in-cheek, yet arguably accurate, snapshot of the times: "1980s drunk; 1990s — deployed; 2000s — overworked."[7] Colonel Jim Davis asserted, "The tempo of work began to spiral out of control. We had draconian cuts in resources and manpower. Each year tempo

Courtesy Silvia Pecota.

A member of 1 RCR takes up a supporting firing position during Ex Thor's Hammer, a fighting in built-up areas exercise in Sudbury, Ontario.

became bigger and bigger and we lost the balance of life." Brigadier-General Cox agreed. "People higher up," he insisted, "wouldn't accept we couldn't do everything and stop things. It was the start of the phrase 'do more with less.'"[8] Davis added, "Sr NCOs became sick and tired of the phrase 'do more with less.'" He noted, "We were jumping from one activity to the next without learning the lessons of what we had just done. They were just tired of doing things half-assed."[9]

The aspect of being overworked was no exaggeration, as operations and commitments at home pressed the available Royals into continuous service. For instance, a new generation of armoured personnel carriers, the Light Armoured Vehicle III (LAV III), was entering service, and Army headquarters designated 2 RCR as one of the lead agencies in testing tactics, techniques, and procedures for the new APC.[10] As such, on 31 March 2000, 2 RCR began the transition to a LAV battalion. It was also responsible for the LAV Mobile Automated Information Systems (MAIS) trials that provided the Army with an array of important lessons on fighting the LAV, particularly at night, that would later prove vital in

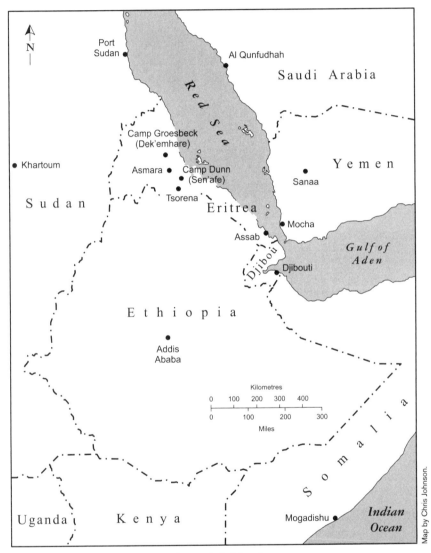

Eritrea / Ethiopia

combat operations. Conversion of 1 RCR into a LAV battalion began the following year.

The new millennium also maintained the crushing operational tempo. 1 RCR was still on duty in Kosovo as part of KFOR, and in November 2000, NDHQ tagged 2 RCR to provide the Canadian contingent for the U.N. Mission in Ethiopia and Eritrea (UNMEE). The U.N. peacekeeping operation was code-named Eclipse.[11] It was also the first deployment of the U.N. Stand-By High Readiness Brigade (SHIRBRIG).

The mission entailed monitoring the cessation of hostilities and assisting in ensuring the observance of the agreed ceasefire protocols. In May 1998, Ethiopia and Eritrea went to war over a border dispute. The short but bloody two-year war, fought roughly along the lines of First World War with trench systems facing each other, killed approximately 70,000 soldiers and wounded thousands of others. Both sides having depleted their military strength and having destroyed their already weak economies, and with no clear resolution achievable by either side, agreed to a U.N.-brokered peace. As such, the Canadian Task Force East Africa (TFEA), which was commanded by the 2 RCR CO, acting Colonel Jim Simms, consisted of 450 personnel largely from 2 RCR. It was responsible for monitoring the cessation of hostilities and establishing the 25-kilometre Temporary Security Zone (TSZ). Upon completion of this first phase, TFEA then focused on the successful return of the internally displaced persons to the area and the successful re-establishment of community life.[12]

In addition, 3 RCR, with augmentees from its sister battalions, also deployed on Operation Palladium, Roto 8, to continue Canada's commitment to the former Yugoslavia under SFOR. Of note during the mission, which was largely a continuation of the framework patrolling done on earlier tours, was a bank raid conducted by Para Coy. Operation Athena was a simultaneous theatre-wide operation to seize documents from offices of the Hercegovaka Banka throughout Bosnia. NATO headquarters believed the bank was supporting hard-line extremists within the country and decided to act. Para Coy's mission was to conduct a dawn raid on the local branch in Tomislavgrad, which was carried out without any major problems. In fact, Para Coy was in and out so fast that the inner and outer cordons were collapsed, the necessary documents seized and on their way to Sarajevo and the Royals on their way back to camp before the town knew what had occurred. This was in comparison to other NATO operations, where at least two seizures went sour and resulted in the upwards of 20 injured NATO soldiers.

Besides the "bank heist," continuing ethnic tensions in the country also necessitated the 3 RCR BG taking over the control of a number of major weapon storage sites to ensure peace and stability. In the end, the tour was successful and was the last contribution of a full RCR BG to Operation Palladium.

Notwithstanding the success of operations, the continuing pressure on the Army to do more with less began to take its toll. The Army commander consistently, and publicly, informed DND and the government that "we have too little Army to sustain our tasks and too much Army for our budget."[13] Therefore, the Army's dilemma required drastic solutions. With no relief from the government or higher headquarters, the Army took on solving its problem itself. One immediate fix was a reduction

A 2 RCR LAV in Eritrea. This was the vehicle's first operational deployment.

in manning levels. Another was putting the Army on a rotational cycle of readiness that included three distinct categories: reconstitution, high readiness, and deployment. The theory behind the plan was that a unit just returning from a overseas deployment would go into reconstitution, where it would be given minimal resources to train, instead sending its personnel on career courses or directing them to fill the various "taskings" that came up, such as instructor requirements at the Army and national schools. Once a unit completed its reconstitution phase, it would go into high-readiness training and receive less taskings so that its personnel were available to train. Importantly, it would receive more resources (e.g. money, ammunition, equipment) to train because once it finished its high readiness phase, it would deploy to one of the many ongoing or emerging missions.

In essence, the constraints placed on the Army by the fiscal austerity, as well as the overriding operational tempo, gutted its ability to train. Brigade concentrations and formation-level training became a thing of the past. Even Canadian Army bread and butter skills such as winter

Combat Camera.

A member of 2 RCR makes the acquaintance of a local child in the conduct of framework patrolling during OP UNAMEE.

warfare capability vanished. Completely unheard of in previous decades, units would have large numbers of senior NCOs who had never participated in a winter warfare exercise.

Larger problems still plagued the Army. The overwhelming tempo over the past decade had created a situation where the integrity of a unit was not protected. In order to send battle groups on operations, an ad hoc approach of stealing sub-units from other units to cobble together the necessary BG became a vicious compounding problem.[14] As the next BG was assembled to proceed on operations, the personnel and sub-units it had just provided to the previous BG could not be included, since they had just returned from a mission, and there was a standing one-year waiver for anyone who had just returned from an overseas mission before they could be compelled to deploy again. Therefore, the BG had to steal from other units to make up the requisite numbers. And with a seemingly neverending number of commitments, there was no breathing room to regroup. Therefore, units were consistently ripped apart to patch together the next BG going out the door.

Even with an ever-growing reliance on reservists, it was not always possible to fill the gap in required numbers. Nonetheless, the Army quickly became dependent on its reservists to provide the badly needed personnel, both overseas and at home, to fill regular force positions of those members sent overseas as augmentees. On the positive side, as the decade went on, the reliance on the reserve created a true total force with reservists who were well trained and very experienced, something that had eluded the CF throughout the Cold War.

The other major issue was the fact that the newly instituted Army Training Readiness Cycle (ATOC) was not working. Arguably, it just added to the stress that units and individuals were facing. For example, a unit on reconstitution, theoretically on a pause to refit and regroup, would be completely devastated. Its NCOs and junior officers would be tasked to instruct or take career courses, often taking them out of a unit and away from home for six to nine plus months of the year. For example, in 2001, 1 RCR was without over 60 percent of its senior NCOs and junior officers at any given point in time. In addition, despite a unit's limitations in personnel (specifically leadership) and money, the Army still had a large laundry list of individual training requirements it expected all units to complete. Added to the mandatory list of requirements and the national taskings was also the brigade and area headquarters, which would also unload unexpected tasks on the "reconstituting" units. As a result, by the end of reconstitution, a unit would be completely exhausted. Captain Gerry Byrne concluded, "the ATOC was the most demoralizing process the Army could have imposed on us. If you were in reconstitution you were nothing."[15] In the end, high readiness was easy — a unit had available personnel, resources, and a training focus. Conversely, "reconstitution" became a major leadership challenge.

The difficulties the Army was facing, however, were not lost on the senior leadership. As part of the strategy of pulling itself out of the "decade of darkness," the Army commander undertook a major transformational effort. In keeping aligned with the *1994 White Paper on Defence* and the more recent departmental strategy, *Strategy 2020,* the Army commander issued *Advancing with Purpose: The Army Strategy.*[16] His vision, which would guide The RCR and the rest of the Army, was clearly articulated:

> The Army will generate, employ and sustain strategically relevant and tactically decisive medium-weight forces. Using progressive doctrine, realistic training and leading-edge technologies, the Army will be a knowledge-based and command-centric institution capable of continuous adaptation and task tailoring across the spectrum of conflict. The cohesion and morale of our soldiers will be preserved through sharing a collective covenant of trust and common understanding of explicit and implicit intent. With selfless leadership and coherent management, the Army will achieve unity of effort and resource equilibrium…. As a broadly based representative national institution with a proud heritage, the Army will provide a disciplined force of last resort and contribute to national values and objectives at home and abroad.[17]

In essence, the Commander's intent was to unify the Army, revitalize and renew the emphasis on leadership, develop a modern and sustainable operational capability, and undertake an overarching cultural change.[18]

And so, as the Army worked hard at pulling itself out of its resource and organizational culture crisis, its personnel was already showing the positive effects of a decade's worth of operations in dangerous theatres. On return to regimental duty in 2000, as CO of 3 RCR, Denis Thompson noted, "the Army changed remarkably. It was a seasoned army."[19] He explained, "The Army evolved from focusing on buttons, bows and infrastructure to one that emphasized operations and having the right equipment."[20] He noted the senior leadership changed as well. "[Before in the 1980s and 1990s] you never saw senior Army officers. Prior to being a CO I never saw the Army commander once. Now you're tripping over senior leadership. They are more interested and engaged now."[21] Thompson assessed, "There was a big change. The army was all grown up — much more serious than it ever had been." Moreover, he believed, "The Sr NCOs knew their shit. They were hard and fit. There was no wastage; no fat — they were real soldiers."[22] He insisted, "The Sr NCOs were rock solid — younger, fitter, more mission focused than ever before."[23]

Thompson pointed to his RSM, Chief Warrant Officer David Preeper, as an indication of the new breed of senior NCO. He observed, "Preeper knew setting the proper attitude with the soldiers was not about painting rocks, shiny buttons and bows. It was no longer enough to say move now, more to follow. Everyone wanted to know why. The soldiers challenged leaders to think things through." Thompson asserted, "It was refreshing."[24]

Chief Warrant Officer Kit Charlebois agreed. He opined, "In the late 1990s, there was a noticeable shift in the 'personality' of the RSM. The old days of the RSM barking all the time and the soldiers giving a wide berth whenever the RSM would have been in close proximity changed." He explained, "The term 'soldiers first' became the common theme and the leadership placed emphasis on ensuring everything was done to look after the needs of the soldiers and their families." Charlebois added, "Emphasis was placed on duty with honour and ethics was applied from the highest ranks to the lowest. The majority of the troops joining the CF were well-educated and the education level for entering the Forces was a minimum of grade 10 where in the 1970s it was a minimum of grade 8." He also observed, "The new recruits were more techno savvy and were known as the Nintendo Generation. They didn't have the embedded hardness of their predecessors but could handle anything technical." He quipped, "Many of them had never been in the dark as they lived their whole lives in the city."[25]

Master Warrant Officer Keith Olstad reinforced the changes. "Soldiers," he insisted, "now had to be treated completely different than how I was treated." He recalled, "We couldn't push soldiers too hard to develop that mental toughness." Olstad conceded, "That was my hardest challenge — how to get the soldiers ready for operations where I thought they should be within the guidelines. It was difficult to provide the necessary challenge."[26]

Battalion mess life had changed as well. It was no longer a focal point for regimental members. "Other than being told by the DSM [Drill Sergeant Major] or RSM to be in the mess for an hour on Friday night," recalled Chief Warrant Officer Gravelle, "that was it." Tom France confirmed, "Mess life changed drastically in the 1990s. There was no smoking in the lines and there were new drinking policies." He explained, "the old army drinking mindset was phasing out." He remarked, "At the higher levels it was still there, but the younger generation was more of a Gatorade generation." Importantly, France reinforced, "We lost the concept of the Regiment as a family. Troops wouldn't go to the Mess anymore. They would stay in their rooms at night."[27] Olstad noted, "Conversations have changed. It use to be about girls and drinking, now it's about computers and games."[28] Gravelle observed, "People migrated more to their outside personal life. Even in quarters, you would only see new privates in the shacks." Gravelle added, "There were very few corporals or master-corporal living in. They would be renting or buying their own homes. This was a real change from the 1970s and 1980s."[29]

However, nothing would change the face of the CF, the Army, or The RCR more than an unfathomable terrorist attack in New York City. Few realized in the early morning hours of 11 September 2001 (9/11), that the world was about to change. The brazen attack by the terrorists, who, armed solely with cheap 99-cent box-cutters, hijacked fully fuelled commercial airliners and used them as precision munitions to strike not only the two separate towers of the World Trade Center in New York City, but also the Pentagon in Washington, D.C. A fourth hijacked jetliner heading for Washington, D.C., slammed into the ground in Pennsylvania short of its objective because of the bravery of its passengers. In total, almost 3,000 people were killed in the attacks.

The attacks stunned decision makers in both the U.S. and Canada. All air travel was immediately grounded as rumours of additional terrorists abounded. All three RCR regular force battalions were put on alert. Vehicles were loaded and troops sat on their rucksacks waiting for the order to deploy on vital point security tasks throughout Ontario. Little information seeped through the chain of command. It was as if higher headquarters at every level was gripped by a paralysis. At the unit level, Royals watched CNN to try and figure out what was going on. By 12 September the units were stood down.

Not surprisingly, Washington responded quickly to the 9/11 attacks to protect the American homeland and U.S. facilities and installations abroad. The Americans suspected that Osama bin Laden and his al-Qaeda (AQ) terrorist network, who were protected by the Taliban regime in Afghanistan, were responsible for the attacks. They also realized that they would need to strike their antagonists overseas. As such, on 14 September, the U.S. Congress authorized President George W. Bush to "use all necessary and appropriate force against those nations, organizations, or persons [who] planned, authorized, committed, or aided the terrorist attack on September or harboured such organizations or persons."[30]

The Americans also called on their NATO allies for help. As a result, NATO's North Atlantic Council met on 12 September to discuss the U.S. request to invoke Article 5 of the North Atlantic Treaty that defines "an armed attack against one or more of the Allies in Europe or North America" as "an attack against them all" and thereby, requiring each ally to "assist the Party that has been attacked by taking such action as it deems necessary."[31] This would be the first time that the Article 5 clause was invoked.

By 2 October the Americans provided their allies with "clear and compelling evidence" that AQ had in fact been behind the 9/11 attacks. Therefore, two days later NATO Secretary-General Lord Robertson announced that the alliance would indeed take collective actions to assist the United States.[32]

In addition, NATO, in accordance with treaty requirements, also notified the U.N. that it intended to invoke Article 5 under the framework of the United Nations Charter provision affirming the inherent right of member states to individual and collective defence. The U.N. Security Council had come to a similar conclusion, having also met to address the 9/11 attacks on 12 September. They subsequently urged all states to work together "to bring to justice the perpetrators, organizers, and sponsors of the attacks."[33]

Then, on 7 October 2001, the United States and the United Kingdom informed the security council that they were taking military action in self-defence, specifically that they were undertaking operations to strike at al-Qaeda and Taliban terrorist camps, training, and military installations in Afghanistan. That day Operation Enduring Freedom (OEF) commenced with the heavy bombing of Taliban bases and infrastructure throughout the country, as well as the 50,000 Taliban troops outside of Kabul manning the frontlines against the Northern Alliance (NA), which was a loose coalition of Afghan forces that were opposed to the Taliban.

Canada also reacted relatively quickly as its southern neighbour and its European allies mobilized for war. On 9/11 itself, Canada in accordance with its obligations under the North American Aerospace Defence (NORAD) treaty, became immediately involved.[34] Moreover, on 7 October, the day the Americans launched Operation Enduring Freedom, Canadian Prime Minister Jean Chrétien announced that Canada, "standing shoulder to shoulder with … the American people" would deploy sea, land, and air forces to assist the United States.[35] Shortly after the prime minister's announcement, the deputy chief of the defence staff responsible for CF operations issued his intent for Operation Apollo, the code name given to the CF's support to the American war on terror. Canada initially deployed a number of ships and aircraft.[36]

However, the Americans did not wait for the Canadian commitment to be fully mobilized. They quickly proceeded with their offensive. Approximately four weeks of bombing finally created the necessary effect. On 9 November 2001, the NA, who were now supported by U.S.

Special Forces (SF), CIA operatives, and American air elements, broke through the Taliban lines at Mazar-e-Sharif. The Taliban collapsed were was totally routed. Within the next three days all of northern, western, and eastern Afghanistan fell to the NA. The remaining Taliban forces fled south to Kandahar, the birthplace and headquarters of the movement. Throughout, they were harassed and pounded by U.S. air power.[37] On 5 December, Mullah Omar, the Taliban leader, surrendered Kandahar and fled to Pakistan.

Kabul fell to the Northern Alliance on 13 November. Priority then shifted to the south, namely the Taliban heartland of Kandahar. Within 63 days of commencing the offensive, the Americans and their Afghan allies captured Kandahar.[38] On 14 November, the day after the fall of Kabul, the U.N. Security Council had once again condemned the Taliban government "for allowing Afghanistan to be used as a base for the export of terrorism by the al-Qaeda network and other terrorist groups and for providing safe haven to Osama bin Laden." More important, to fill the imminent power vacuum, the U.N. now created a transitional government that would establish a "multi-ethnic and fully representative" government.[39]

As such, talks were held in Bonn, Germany, on 27 November 2001 from which was born the Bonn Agreement that called for an Interim Authority to be established in Afghanistan on 22 December 2001. This body was to provide leadership for Afghanistan until a representative government could be elected through free and fair elections. To ensure a smooth transition and to provide security until the Afghan National Security Forces (ANSF) could be established, UNSCR 1386 was tabled on 20 December 2001. The newest resolution called for a peacekeeping mission in Afghanistan to develop national security structures, assist in reconstruction, and organize and train future Afghan security forces. It also created the British-led International Security Assistance Force (ISAF), which was stationed in Kabul.[40]

However, Canada was not invited to participate. "The Europeans wouldn't let us join ISAF," revealed General Hillier, "Canada desperately wanted to join ISAF at the start of the war in Afghanistan, but we were shunned. Part of the reason was that the Europeans, the British in particular, remembered our risk-averse approach in Bosnia and had no faith that Canada would pull its weight, especially if things got tough. They did not want us as part of their alliance."[41] So instead, Canada opted to deploy a light infantry battle group based on the 3 PPCLI on 1 February 2002, to support American operations in the Kandahar area.[42]

Throughout the next six months, in support of the American initiatives to destroy Taliban and al Qaeda forces, members from 3 PPCLI and Canadian SOF conducted combat operations with their American counterparts in the Tergul Mountain range in the Sha-I-Kot valley in Eastern Afghanistan, as well as in the Gardez area, since a number of Taliban and AQ holdouts remained.

In fact, bin Laden and his senior AQ leadership and a large number of his forces dug-in at Tora Bora mountains in eastern Afghanistan. However, a concerted U.S. offensive forced them to abandon their positions and escape into eastern Pakistan. By early 2002, the Taliban and AQ in Afghanistan were largely defeated. Military estimates put the Taliban losses at 8,000–12,000 men, 20 percent of their total force. The wounded were estimated to number twice that, and a further 7,000 had been taken prisoner.[43] In the end, the Taliban lost over 70 percent of its strength.

As a result, by late July 2002, Canada redeployed its ground forces back home as the government felt the Taliban threat was largely eliminated. However, Canadian ground participation in Afghanistan quickly resumed when on 12 February 2003, Canada's European allies now with a change of heart, or perhaps because they had difficulty in attracting the necessary European participation, requested Canadian inclusion in ISAF for the U.N.-mandated mission in Kabul.[44] As a result, Canada, under the code name Operation Athena, once again deployed forces to Afghanistan, specifically, a battle group and a brigade headquarters for a period of one year, commencing July 2003.[45]

The task was to provide security in the Kabul area, reinforce the Afghan Transitional Authority, and assist, as well as facilitate, the rebuilding of the democratic process in Afghanistan. Army headquarters tasked 3 RCR with the mission. However, in keeping with the times, 3 RCR required to pull augmentees from its sister battalions to bring it up to strength for the mission. At the same time, "B" Coy, 1 RCR deployed with the RCD BG to Operation Palladium on what would be the last Canada BG rotation.

In addition, 2 RCR sent "I" Coy Gp to Operation Athena to provide security for the building of the Canadian camp in Kabul, dubbed Camp Julien. After the bus full of German soldiers was attacked by a suicide bomber on the way to the airport, they also became responsible for convoy operations to and from the airport, as well as transport for arriving Royals. In addition, during the summer of 2003, 2 RCR sent three rifle platoons to Camp Mirage in Dubai on consecutive two month tours from August to December to provide a defence and security platoon for that Canadian staging base.

Nonetheless, after a short period of theatre specific mission training, the 3 RCR BG deployed to Kabul, taking on the transfer of command authority (TOCA) on 21 August 2003. Lieutenant Jay Feyko, a platoon commander remembered, "Once we got there and had our feet on the ground we felt ready." He conceded, "We didn't know what to expect so we did a lot of continuation and refresher training in theatre."[46]

The Canadian base in Kabul, Camp Julien.

The key tasks of the 3 RCR BG were to:

a) assist in the maintenance of a secure environment for the Afghan Transitional Authority (AFA) in the ISAF AOR;
b) assist in the operation and the provision of local security for Kabul International airport;
c) execute ISAF force protection;
d) assist the U.N. in the disarmament, demobilization, and reintegration (DDR) process within the ISAF AOR; and
e) assist the international community effort to support the ATA in the establishment and training of the Afghan security forces.[47]

As such, the Royals conducted joint patrols and helped establish vehicle check points with the Kabul City Police (KCP). The 3 RCR BG also ran basic police training courses to assist with the professionalism of the KCP.[48] The BG engineers also disposed of over 2,000 unexploded ordnance (UXOs), cleared dozens of patrol routes, and responded to calls throughout the city for assistance with explosive ordnance disposal.

"Our mission," explained Feyko, "was to support the Afghan authorities, specifically the police and military to ensure they could support themselves; get back on their feet and do their job." He described, "We did this primarily through joint patrols and routine meetings with mayors and police chiefs. We tried to see how we could fit in and help." Feyko revealed, "Some police had one weapon between them. A lot of them were corrupt. They weren't being paid all the time so they did what they had to survive." He also added, "We were also trying to win the hearts and minds of the population. We were being friendly with everyone trying not to appear like an occupying force. We built schools and passed out shovels."[49]

"Daily operations," wrote Major Tom Mykytiuk, OC "N" Coy, "were largely at the section level." He explained, "the nature of the company's tasks necessitated maintaining a 24-hour presence of some kind within our AO." He noted, "we had to maintain the impression that ISAF could be everywhere and anywhere at any given time."[50] As a result, patrols avoided

Members of Para Company, 3 RCR conduct a patrol with an Afghan transitional authority policeman.

Para Coy, 3 RCR personnel on patrol in Kabul. The Queen's Palace is in the background.

routine, set routes or scheduled timings. Section patrols were up to 12 hours long. Not surprisingly, the foot patrols were the longest. "Each guy," stated Feyko, "had to carry up to 80 pounds of gear — protective plates, ammo and water."[51]

The CO, Lieutenant-Colonel Don Denne explained that "the threat in 2003–04 in Kabul was based upon the potential actions of any or all of the following groups: AQ, Taliban and Hebz-i-Islami Gulbuddin (HiG)." He noted that although there were AQ and Taliban sympathizers in the Kabul area, we were really up against HiG." Denne revealed, "We felt we were in a counter-insurgency right from the time we did our Transfer of Command Authority with the in-place German Battalion." He noted, "The threat to us was multifaceted: direct attack against a patrol with small arms and RPGs, rockets (107 and 122 mm) or mortars fired at the camp, mines, IEDs (including roadside bombs which had been tried a number of times previous to our deployment but not during) and suicide bombings, both person borne and vehicle borne (bicycle, moped, motorcycle, car, truck)." The CO explained, "I constantly reinforced a policy of vigilance right up to the point we were on the Hercules [aircraft] headed to Camp Mirage. We were not always sure we knew what we were looking for but it was likely something out of the ordinary."[52]

Not surprisingly then, with the start of 2004, the BG also took on directed operations in support of the KCP and the National Directorate of Security (NDS), which was the Afghan secret police. These operations demonstrated an evolution in the mission, as they were designed to take offensive action against confirmed security threats in the ISAF AO. They also required detailed planning, preparations, and intricate coordination between the various Canadian, ISAF, and Afghan organizations and agencies. This fostered greater involvement with external organizations, with all the attending frustrations, as well as benefits.[53] In sum, a number of successful operations resulted in the capture of criminals, weapons and explosives, narcotics, as well as information that could be processed into valuable intelligence.

The positive effects of 3 RCR BG's framework patrolling and directed operations became clearly evident. "The security situation got significantly better during our tour," noted Master-Corporal Josh Marian, "It was visually noticeable. Some side streets were barren when we arrived. By the end of our tour there were shops and people everywhere."[54] Jay Feyko agreed. "We saw a huge difference," he asserted, "By the end of the tour there was more traffic, more shops were open, there was music in the streets and there were women without burkas." He concluded, "It was the most rewarding experience of my life."[55]

The overall success of the tour, however, was marred by three tragic deaths. On 2 October 2003, a Para Coy patrol hit a TM-57 land mine in the Jowz Valley a few kilometres from Camp Julien, killing Sergeant Robert Short and Corporal Robbie Beerenfenger and wounding three others. Several months later, on 27 January 2004, Corporal Jamie Murphy became the first RCR to be killed by a suicide bomber.

The two-vehicle Para Coy patrol was en route to a meeting with local leaders when it had to slow down because of a small depression in the road. As the lead vehicle exited the depression and the second Iltis began to cross the obstacle, the bomber approached the slowed vehicle and detonated the suicide vest attached to his body. The hot

Photo by Master-Corporal Brian Walsh, Courtesy 3 RCR.

A detainee taken by 3 RCR during OP Tsunami in Kabul.

shrapnel showered the vehicle, killed Murphy, and severely injured the other three occupants.

The lead vehicle immediately stopped, took control of the scene and began to administer first aid. Within minutes, additional support arrived and the casualties were quickly evacuated to Camp Julien. Sergeant Jason Grapes recalled, "Our call sign (C/S) vehicle was the first to arrive when Murphy was hit. As we drove up we could see that the OC's vehicle was hit and that one of our guys was hurt but didn't think much of it. I saw the foot of the suicide bomber on the road and wondered what he was thinking. Then I saw Jamie [Murphy] slumped over in the jeep. Then it got real."[56]

Lieutenant Feyko was in the ill-fated patrol. He remembered:

> It was a cold morning with frost. I got the guys together since we were going to a meeting with the mayor. We were waiting for the OC to pull up. Everyone was looking forward to going home. Corporal Murphy was going home in nine days. He was planning to buy a home. It

A soldier's living space in Camp Julien.

was a two-vehicle convoy. We left at 0800 hours and the streets were particularly busy. I was the rear vehicle with three soldiers and myself. We were travelling north on Green Route. There were bumps in the road so traffic had to slow down. There was also a bus stop at the same place. I was watching my arcs and I could see a guy with his hands in his pockets trying to cross the road. I looked in his eyes and all I could feel was mistrust. I looked elsewhere for a second and then there was this huge explosion. I knew what happened right away. I was still conscious and I saw the driver moving. He was closest to the bomber. [Corporal] Murphy was the farthest away but he was sitting up. He took shrapnel to the brain stem. I could see right away by the blood that he was done.[57]

The incident simply reinforced the feeling of vulnerability many felt. Master-Corporal Marian recalled, "patrolling in the Iltis in town the first time was unnerving because you felt so exposed. Eventually you felt more comfortable."[58] He remembered, "Everyone seemed really friendly in the city. However, it was dicey after Murphy was killed." Major Jim McInnis concurred. "When the suicide bomber hit Murphy," he said, "we began to see things differently. We started going out the gate with a round up the spout."[59]

Much like the rest of the BG, the CO revealed, "I surely started to feel fear thereafter, personal fear and fear of losing more men, and had to summon different strategies to overcome that fear every time we left the relative safety of our Camp."[60] Marian acknowledged, "After the attack, we then rode in the back of LAVs." He conceded, "It really changed our perspective. It reminded us that we don't know who people are and what they are capable of."[61]

Despite the deaths, the tour was a success. Denne explained, "We had contributed significantly to the maintenance of security and stability in our AOR as part of the Kabul Multi-National Brigade (KMNB). I have no doubt about it!" He added, "We were a force to be reckoned with in

OP Parapet. 2 RCR mounted the Queen's Guard at Buckingham Palace, as well as providing the guard for the Crown Jewels at the Tower of London and the Queen Mother at St. James Palace. The tasking coincided with the 100th anniversary of The RCR's service in the Boer War.

Kabul during our time there and then Major-General Andrew Leslie, the Deputy Commander of ISAF called us the 800 pound gorilla — nobody was going to tangle with us, at least not head on." Peter Devlin, then the multinational brigade commander in Kabul noted, "3 RCR Roto zero above all established Canada and the CF as a nation of strength with a rare level of professionalism." He added, "They secured their sector, established relationships with military, police, civil authorities and power brokers in a skilful and honourable way."[62]

The CO, Don Denne explained how they achieved this effect:

> We were omnipresent, both by day and by night, and I have little doubt that this was a deterrent to insurgent activity. We made close relations with the Kabul City Police through open contact, mentorship, training and joint patrols and operations. We established very close and cordial relations with the local mayors, Maliks and Wakils through frequent meetings, CIMIC [civil military cooperation] projects and provision of whatever

assistance we could drum up including the distribution of materiel such as clothing, shoes, blankets, school supplies, toys and farming implements all sent from Canada.

We also noticed a couple of other things that led us to believe we were making a difference. First, the number of local weddings seemed to pick up during our tour and we were told that this happens during times when the economy is doing reasonably well and security exists. Second, the reconstruction that was going on in some parts of the city was remarkable. Considering the Mujahideen wars of the early 1990s pretty much destroyed south-western Kabul, and the Taliban did absolutely nothing to rebuild it when they took power in the vacuum that followed, construction was a good sign. Lastly, there appeared early in our tour on the side of a mountain in our Sector a makeshift Internally Displaced Persons camp. We certainly kept our eye on this and John's guys patrolled it frequently — we gave these folks whatever we could spare as they literally had nothing. We watched the Camp grow to a very large size by the time we departed, an indication that people felt it safe to return to Kabul and settle amongst the rocks — in the Canadian-patrolled Sector.

In addition, we conducted a series of Police Training Courses to take some members of the largely underpaid, inexperienced and untrained Kabul City policemen and have them at least look and try to conduct themselves as professionals instead of thugs in a rag-tag uniform. I believe this initiative, combined with mentorship, really started to have an impact as time wore on. It will take much more to professionalize a police force, starting with police officers training police officers, but I do believe we made a difference, however small.

Finally we paved the way for follow on elements of Canadian rotations by setting a strong and professional example in our AOR and within KMNB and ISAF, by assisting in getting our Camp sorted out as a firm base for future contingents, by breaking down initial barriers to getting business done within the AOR and by conducting an excellent handover with our replacements. I was very proud of the Battalion for all its accomplishments, tangible and intangible.[63]

Not surprisingly, while The RCR served in Afghanistan and Bosnia, those Royals still at home were called out on additional overseas service. In March 2004, elements of 2 RCR deployed to the violence ridden chaos that was Haiti. By January 2004, political violence in Haiti caused by allegations of governmental and police corruption rocked the small island country. Supporters of President Jean-Bertrand Aristide clashed with rival opposition members. In February, a rebel group called the Revolutionary Artibonite Resistance Front, led by a former police chief, Guy Philippe, seized Gonaives. By 22 February, the rebels had captured Cap-Haitien, the country's second largest city, effectively splitting the country in two. The rebels then marched toward the capital, Port-au-Prince, which was gripped by police corruption and criminal gangs. On 29 February Aristide fled the island.

By the beginning of March, Americans began to arrive in Haiti as part of the Multinational Interim Force (MIF), a U.N. Chapter VII peace-making mission that was created under UNSCR 1529. The American led MIF was a intervention force designed to enforce security and stability in Port-au-Prince. Canada contributed Combined Joint Task Force Haiti (CJTF-H) under Operation Halo. The intent was for the 500-person task force, formed on the nucleus of 2 RCR, to assist with the 90 day MIF mandate and prepare for the handover to the U.N. Stability Mission in Haiti (MINUSTAH), planned for April 2004.[64]

In the end, the Royals stayed for five months. Their stay was far from a Caribbean vacation. Port-au-Prince remained violent, and streets were unrecognizable because of mounds of garbage and sewage. David Lambert, then an OC, remembered, "It was the worst place you've ever seen. It was filthy. The sewers were clogged with plastic and garbage." He

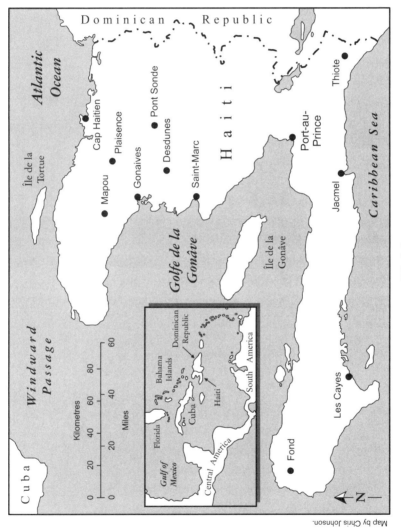

Map by Chris Johnson.

described, "One day we drove with the windshield down and we were black around our eyes and nose — it was dried fecal matter."[65] In addition, The heat was overpowering which added to the desperate living conditions. The troops lived in a field expedient camp and ate "Individual Meal Packs" (IMPs) throughout.

HQ CJTF-H allocated "I" Coy Gp, 2 RCR under operational control of the U.S. Marine Air Ground Task Force 8 (MAGTF 8). Its AO was in the southwest sector of Port-au-Prince centred on the expansive troubled communities of Carrefour, Martissant, and Grand Ravine, which had a combined population of approximately 800,000 people. The communities were poverty-stricken and governed by violent gangs. "It was a shit show," recalled Captain Marc Côté, "Dangerous patches of the city — basically crime orientated."[66]

"I" Coy immediately began to conduct framework patrols and vehicle checkpoints with the Haitian National Police (HNP) every day and night. The joint patrols increased HNP confidence and local security. "We did a ton of urban patrolling mostly police action," commented Côté, "Section and platoon patrolling with the odd company level operations."[67] He explained, "Our mission was presence and framework patrolling. We had two LSVW [Light Support Vehicle Wheeled] platoons and one LAV platoon in our company. The LAV platoon was held for the QRF [Quick Reaction Force] and big convoys and patrols. The LSVWs were used for persistent/presence patrolling." Côté noted, "You would be given a sector and the platoon commander would map out RV points and sections would break off and patrol and then meet at the RV locations."[68]

"It was a fantastic tour," assessed Côté, "We had all kinds of authority and autonomy. The command level gave us flexibility in planning operations and we could follow up on leads we found on earlier patrols." Moreover, the Royals had access to counter-intelligence/electronic warfare/intelligence enablers that were not normally available to conventional forces. "It gave us situational awareness to act, which combined with the authority and autonomy we had made us really effective," concluded Captain Côté.[69] He added, "We worked with the Haitian police as often as possible and forced them to be policemen. Like most shitty little countries the police were unpaid, unmotivated and unequipped."[70]

Members of 2 RCR conduct framework patrolling with a member of the Haitian national police.

Combat Camera.

The filthy state of Port-au-Prince created both operational and health challenges for the members of 2 RCR in Haiti.

Jason Guiney was more forceful. "Wherever we went," he asserted, "we grabbed the local police and built up their confidence."[71]

But the intent was more than just building local police capacity. Côté revealed, "We had a well developed bad guy list. Always a list of bad guys and we were always looking for them. Also, a lot of the patrols were used to find information on those on the list."[72] Besides the aggressive hunt for criminals, 2 RCR also had the advantage of the LAV. Jim Davis recalled, "The presence of the LAV had a profound effect on the criminal element of Port-au-Prince. So too did our soldiers operating at night with NVGs. Our ability to operate at night scared the shit out of the criminals and *shamirs* [insurgents]."[73] Not surprisingly, by mid-May the threat picture had altered substantially.

On 25 June 2005, MIF transferred responsibility to MINUSTAH. The arrival of a Brazilian brigade, effective that same date, freed 2 RCR personnel, now based on "H" Coy, to move 200 kilometres North to the city of Gonaives, which is seen as the "centre of gravity" for revolution in Haiti. The Royals relieved a French Foreign Legion company and began conducting cordon and search operations and presence patrolling immediately to deter criminal activity. Because of their night-vision technology, and the marked advantage that gave them, most operations were conducted at night.

The mission was closed out on 27 July 2004 and the Royals returned to Canada. "We made Haiti work," recalled Major Russell King, OC "H" Coy, "with presence and stability patrols, vehicle checkpoints to control the flow of arms, gradual disarmament of the people, and taking power away from armed gangs, while the diplomats, police, and aid workers tried to make the government work."[74] In the end, their contribution had been significant.

Along with the international deployments, there was major reform at home. In 2005, General Rick Hillier became CDS and accelerated the transformational process that was already underway by doing away with consensus-driven change models. Instead, he imposed his view of how the CF should be structured. "We need to transform the Canadian Forces completely, from a Cold War-oriented, bureaucratic, process-focused organization into a modern, combat-capable force, where the three elements — navy, army and air force, enabled by Special Forces — all worked together as one team to protect Canada by conducting operations effectively at home and abroad," he proclaimed. He added, "I envisioned a flexible, agile and quick-thinking military that would be able to bring exactly the right kind of forces to accomplish whatever mission they were given, whether it was responding to a natural disaster like a tsunami or an ice storm or fighting a counter-insurgency war in southern Afghanistan."[75]

As such, by February 2006, the CF was restructured with a Canadian Expeditionary Command (CEFCOM) that was responsible for all overseas operations and deployments, a Canada Command (CANCOM) for all domestic and continental U.S. operations, a Canadian Operational Support Command (CANOSCOM), as well as a Canadian Special Operations Forces Command (CANSOFCOM). The impact on the entire CF was dramatic. It changed reporting structures, increased personnel requirements, and created dissension in the different services. However, it

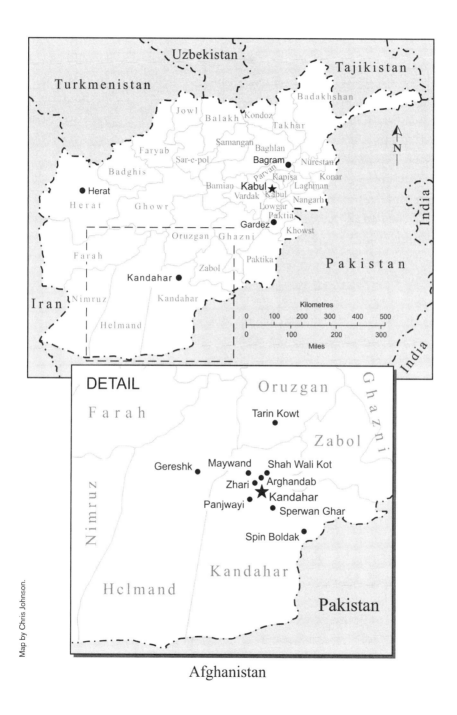

Map by Chris Johnson.

Afghanistan

also set a marker for decisive change. The long-term effects of the transformation are still to be seen.[76]

Back in Afghanistan, the mission was changing and it would have a dramatic impact on both The RCR and the rest of the CF. Increasingly, it became the focus of the Army. Over five successive six-month rotations, Canadian troops conducted foot patrols and surveillance tasks that established a presence and capability within the ISAF area of responsibility in Kabul. These tasks also generated intelligence and situational awareness. In addition, Canadian soldiers assisted and facilitated the rebuilding of the democratic process in Afghanistan.[77]

Then on 18 October 2005, Operation Athena came to an official end with the withdrawal of the last of the Canadians from the Kabul area.[78] But Canada did not leave Afghanistan. Rather it redefined its contribution as part of Stage 3 of ISAF's expansion across all of Afghanistan. Canada agreed to take responsibility for a "Provincial Reconstruction Team" (PRT) in the increasingly volatile and violent insurgent rich Kandahar Province. It assumed command of the PRT in August 2005.[79]

The 350-strong Canadian PRT represented the same multidisciplinary focus of the American PRTs that stressed development as well as security. It became a multi-departmental effort, employing personnel from DND, DFAIT, the Canadian International Development Agency (CIDA), the RCMP, and other Canadian police forces. Its mission was to help extend the authority of the Afghanistan government in Kandahar Province by promoting local stability and security, improving local governance structures, and engaging in reconstruction activities.[80]

Equally important to the Canadian commitment was the deployment in February 2006 of an infantry battle group of approximately 1,000 soldiers to work with the American forces to conduct stabilization and combat operations throughout Kandahar Province. The American forces were still operating under the framework of OEF, and the introduction of the Canadian battle group became an integral part of the transition from the American OEF framework to the ISAF Stage 3 transition of NATO control of Coalition forces in Afghanistan.[81] Subsequently, it fell to 1 PPCLI to conduct the combat tasks in Kandahar Province.[82]

For the Taliban, the transition from OEF to NATO control of Southern Afghanistan proved to be a golden opportunity to deepen and consolidate its control of Kandahar Province. They had begun their resurgence already in 2003. Once the Tora Bora battle was concluded, the Americans began to focus their attention on the impending invasion of Iraq and quickly pulled most their forces from Afghanistan, leaving largely a token conventional presence and a number of SOF, which focused almost entirely on hunting down AQ leadership. The Americans turned the task of rebuilding the country to the newly installed NA warlords, who were in large part the same corrupt, ruthless thugs who had created the conditions for the emergence of the Taliban in 1994 in the first place.[83] In addition, the Americans counted on their European allies and the newly created ISAF to provide some stability. However, ISAF focused almost exclusively on Kabul and other cities and had virtually no presence in the rural areas.

The expectations of Afghans that billions of dollars of U.S. and European investment to rebuild infrastructure, agriculture, and industry would flow into the country and improve their economy and standard of living failed to materialize. Instead, Afghans were once again terrorized by the same warlords and militias that the Taliban had routed years before, and the Kabul regime seemed distant and unresponsive to their needs. Additionally, the American presence that remained seemed only interested in bombing suspected Taliban and AQ targets and conducting night raids, all of which resulted in collateral damage and more Afghan resentment and anger.

Not surprisingly, the Taliban did not take long to take advantage of the situation. By the end of 2002, most its senior leadership had re-established itself in Pakistan, specifically in Quetta, hence the title the "Quetta Shura" for the senior Taliban decision-making body. It was this group that developed and leads Taliban strategy and direction, which they pass down to subordinate tactical commanders.[84]

The first overt signs of a Taliban resurgence came that same year, 2002, when *shabnamah* (night letters) began to appear warning citizens against co-operating with the government. In addition, Taliban fighters began to stockpile weapons in Afghanistan and develop supply lines from neighbouring Pakistan. By 2003, Taliban fighters were stopping traffic on main road networks and murdering Afghans and foreign aid workers. The first battles with U.S. troops also occurred that year and by the end of 2003, the Taliban had established almost complete control over Zabul and Helmand provinces.

The Taliban cleverly used the American preoccupation with Iraq to re-establish.[85] Moreover, they were astute in their efforts to exploit the rising popular dissatisfaction in the south with regard to high popular expectations of western economic assistance and the dismal reality of virtually no such support occurring. Small groups of Taliban fighters also conducted minor attacks in urban centres, such as Kandahar City, as well assassinations of pro-government mullahs, sporadic rocket and mortar attacks, and general intimidation of the population. These tactics, by the end of 2003, succeeded in driving most international non-governmental organizations, NGOs, out of the country, further exacerbating the dearth of Western aid.[86]

By 2004, the Taliban had developed solid lines of communication (LoCs) into Afghanistan from Pakistan and consolidated control over the mountainous region spanning the borders of Kandahar, Zabul, and Uruzgan. So confident were they with their advances that they attempted to advance against Kandahar City from their bases in Uruzgan, Zabul, and Shah Wali Kot. However, they were successfully blocked by a battalion of U.S. infantry that was deployed in Kandahar as part of Task Force (TF) Bronco.

Not to be deterred, the Taliban turned their focus westward. From such areas as Baghran and Sangin in Helmand, it hoped to penetrate into Panjwayi and Zhari. From here they desired to launch their campaign to control Kandahar City in 2006. The Taliban hoped to achieve this aim by isolating its objective and gaining control of the areas surrounding Kandahar City with targeted violence, to intimidate local leaders and the population. By the beginning of 2005, they started to murder police officers, government officials, "spies," and elders who were working with the Americans.[87] They also established a judicial system to increase the Taliban's legitimacy and began to infiltrate fighters into the area to challenge the government and ISAF for control of the physical terrain.

They had already infiltrated into the districts and created shadow governments that were effectively displacing the weak Government of the Islamic Republic of Afghanistan (GIRoA) structures in place. In addition, through a campaign of intimidation and fear, highlighted by night letters and selective assassination, they terrorized the population into submission. They now began to concentrate their fighters to openly challenge the Coalition and GIRoA. And, as the Taliban strength grew through the build-up of fighters, they became more and more aggressive.

By the Spring of 2006, much of the resurgent Taliban fighting fell to the Canadians. 1 PPCLI was responsible for covering an area of approximately 54,000 square kilometres. Adding to the huge task was the fact that another Canadian, Brigadier-General David Fraser, as part of the transition, took command of the southern region — including the province of Kandahar for which the PPCLI battle group was responsible. Fraser had jurisdiction for the other southern provinces, including the hot spots of Helmand and Uruzgan Provinces, an area measuring 220,744 square kilometres. Not surprisingly, Fraser leaned heavily on 1 PPCLI. In essence, the Canadians were the bridge between the U.S. led OEF mission and NATO's ISAF mission.

By June 2006, with the annual "fighting season" in full swing, the surge in Taliban activity became evident. In fact, it was indicative of a full-blown offensive. Between May and June there was an alarming increase in the number of enemy contacts. In addition, the Taliban began to confiscate cell phones from local nationals as a counterintelligence measure. They also established plans for setting up checkpoints and moving into Kandahar City itself. On 30 June 2006, the task force received reports indicating that the Taliban were issuing night letters directing Afghan locals to leave the Panjwayi and Zhari areas immediately, as Taliban elements were planning to engage GIRoA forces and CF elements.

The state of chaos and violence reached such levels that by June 2006 the Senlis Council reported, "Kandahar now is a war zone, with suicide bombings, rocket attacks, ambushes and repeated outbreaks of open warfare, resulting in numerous Canadian fatalities and many more injuries." They concluded, "Kandahar is a province at war: there is no peace to keep."[88] Statistics backed their assertions. By June 2006, there was a

"600% increase in violent attacks."[89] In that year the Taliban burned down 187 schools and murdered 85 teachers and more than 600 policemen.[90]

Consequently, the 1 PPCLI battle group focused its energies on security operations, specifically to find, fix, and destroy the enemy. In July, because of the increasing Taliban presence and activity, the CO developed a concept of operations that entailed concentrating his combat power in Pashmul to disrupt the Taliban. The Taliban, however, refused to go quietly, which meant they and the Canadians were involved in a constant state of combat. Embedded reporter Christie Blatchford summarized, "July was a daily diet of long battles that went on for hours and stretched the battle group thin over six hundred kilometres in seven separate districts over some of the most treacherous terrain in Afghanistan."[91]

By August intelligence reports continued to paint a grim picture of ongoing Taliban activity, namely key leader engagements and increasing numbers of "troops in contact" (TICs), all of which indicated that the enemy was massing forces in the Panjwayi valley. The Taliban focus on the area was not hard to understand. Panjwayi has always been critically important to the Taliban because it is a fertile, densely populated, and economically lucrative area. It has also been the traditional staging area for attacks against Kandahar City, as well as an area for resupply for troops staging in Zhari district.

In addition, Kandahar province and its capital, Kandahar City, have always been of interest to the Taliban because the region has consistently maintained a kind of autonomy from any of the various central governments in Kabul. It is also the second largest province in Afghanistan located in the harsh, barren, desert environment of the volatile southeastern corner of the country. It is bounded on the north and northeast by the mountainous Uruzgan and Zabul provinces and in the west by Helmand, and it shares a porous 402-kilometre border with the Pakistan province of Baluchistan. Kandahar City is situated at the junction of Afghanistan's main highways and is the major southern link to Pakistan. The highway system passes from Spin Boldak on the Pakistan border, through Kandahar City to Kabul.

In addition, Kandahar holds a seminal importance to the Taliban and its senior leadership. Many of them, including Mullah Omar, Mullah Osmani, and Mullah Obaidullah, were born and raised in the area. Furthermore, they preached Islam and fought in Kandahar. In fact, they hoped to repeat the success they achieved during the anti-Soviet jihad in the 1980s, when Panjwayi became the epicentre of resistance in the south. During the fall of 1982, mujahedeen fighters, with the support of the local population, and the expert use of the close terrain (i.e. canals, dense orchards, vineyards, walled compounds, fields of crops) had inflicted severe casualties on the Soviets and thwarted Soviet ability to exert control over the area. The Taliban believed they could once again prevail over an "occupying force" by utilizing the same ground and tactics as it had in 1982.

Moreover, Kandahar is the birthplace and continues to be the heartland of the Taliban itself. So, somewhat ironically, Kandahar had become a centre of gravity for both the GIRoA and the Coalition, as well as the Taliban, in the fight for the confidence and support of Afghans. Furthermore, NATO had begun to develop Afghan development zones (ADZ) to create secure bubbles around a nucleus where the GIRoA and NATO could push resources and redevelopment (i.e. "ink spot" method).[92] These efforts were all part of the governance, security, and reconstruction strategy for rebuilding a modern Afghanistan. Conversely, for the Taliban, victory in Kandahar Province would discredit the GIRoA and Coalition forces in the eyes of Afghans.

For all these reasons it became clear to Coalition commanders and GIRoA leaders that the Taliban were massing in Panjwayi to establish a permanent base of operations there, with a view to attacking Kandahar City. Further aggravating the situation, it was apparent that the Talibes were intent on winning. "The Taliban emptied Quetta and other centres to conduct offensive operations in Regional Command (South) (RC (S)) in 2006," confided one senior NATO staff officer. "It was a window of opportunity for them as we focused on elections and the hand-over from U.S. control in Kandahar to NATO control as part of Stage 3 expansion."[93] Lieutenant-Colonel Shane Schreiber revealed, "Our intelligence estimated that they [Taliban] brought in, as a minimum, 12,000 foot soldiers."[94]

In early August continuing reports of major enemy activity and massing of troops triggered yet another Coalition foray into the area. On 3 August 2006, 1 PPCLI BG found themselves in the Pashmul/Panjwayi area once again. After a vicious day-long combat that witnessed several armoured vehicles destroyed and many casualties, the BG was forced to pull back.[95] The size and defensive posture of the Taliban force made it clear that they intended to stay. Moreover, any attempt to remove them would need to be a brigade size operation.

Brigadier-General Fraser, the multinational brigade (MNB) commander for Regional RC (S) assessed that Panjwayi was going to be the Taliban's "major fight for the summer." He explained, "the third of August was the defining day that we knew exactly what we were facing, and what the enemy wanted to do, the enemy's intent."[96] In Fraser's estimation, the enemy's intent "was to isolate Kandahar City, not directly but indirectly, to demonstrate the weakness and the inability of the national Government to come after them with a conventional force."[97] He stated, "This also indicated to us that the Taliban were actually progressing with the evolution of their own operations to the next stage[98] where they thought they were capable enough to go and challenge the national government and coalition forces in a conventional manner."[99]

Fraser added, "We also assessed that their intent was to engage the international community in a battle of attrition on ground of their tactical choosing to cause as many casualties as they could to attack our centre of gravity (i.e. domestic public support)."[100] He concluded that the Taliban plan "was designed to defeat us from a 'political will' point of view; to illustrate weakness in the Government of Afghanistan and thereby set the stage where the Taliban could attack the city and defeat not only the provincial government there but also attack the national government in Afghanistan in a fairly sophisticated and substantive way."[101] As a result, Fraser briefed his plan to General David Richards, the British commander then in charge of NATO's ISAF forces in Afghanistan at NATO headquarters. "I said this is a fight we can't lose," remembered Fraser, "This is the main, main fight."[102]

And he was not wrong. However, the "main, main fight" would quickly become a fight The RCR would take on. And it was one they would not soon forget.

8

A Return to Combat Duty: Operation Medusa

The vicious and hard-fought combat engagements of the summer had clearly indicated to Canadian and NATO commanders that the enemy was skilled, tenacious, and well dug-in, in the Pashmul District. ISAF headquarters assigned to Fraser and his multinational brigade the mission of defeating the Taliban in Pashmul to set the conditions for the establishment of the Kandahar Afghan Development Zone (ADZ).[1] Subsequently, Fraser issued his intent to the Canadian BG, which was to disrupt the Taliban in the district; achieve security for the local population and freedom of manoeuvre for aid agencies; complete Quick Impact Projects (QIPs) to achieve rapid reconstruction; and subsequently develop the region's governance and economic capacity.

Fraser intended to shape the battlefield to disrupt Taliban forces through the conduct of leadership engagements; brigade manoeuvre, as well as the intensive application of air and indirect fires (e.g. fighter aircraft, Spectre AC-130 gunships, artillery); and to conduct operations (i.e. decisive strike; link-up; and secure the area of operations [AO]) to clear the enemy out of Pashmul/Panjwayi. His plan lacked one major component — combat forces.

The MNB operations officer Lieutenant-Colonel Schreiber acknowledged, "We were spread pretty thin on the ground between Martello, Spin

Courtesy 1 RCR BG.

Typical farmland in Pasmul showing the lush foliage, mud walls, and formidable and dominating grape-drying huts.

Boldak, Kandahar City and Panjwayi. Therefore, what we wanted to do was to concentrate the Canadian battle group and essentially fix the Taliban in Pashmul to make sure that they couldn't push any further into Kandahar or Highway 1." He described that they had hoped to use the coalition's superior ISR (intelligence, surveillance, reconnaissance) assets and firepower to "begin to pull apart the nodes and take apart the Taliban defense." Schreiber conceded, "We didn't have enough [combat power] to clear it." He observed, "At that point we assessed it would have taken a brigade attack and there was no way we were ever going to generate a four, or even a three battle group brigade to be able to do that." Schreiber quickly added, "nor did we want to because of the collateral damage that would have caused. So instead, what we decided to do was to defeat the Taliban build-up by isolating and disrupting and pulling the Taliban apart in chunks, hoping that at some point they would say 'okay it's not worth it.'"[2]

In essence, Fraser's intent was to separate the Taliban forces by putting deliberate kinetic and non-kinetic pressure on them. "We had them contained," he pronounced, "they were fixing themselves, or rather they had fixed themselves." Fraser explained, "They were bringing forces in from everywhere — infiltrating through the Reg[estan] Desert, up from Pakistan and they assembled a lot of commanders in the pocket."[3]

Remarkably, despite the abundance of historical data on insurgencies, the Taliban had chosen to build-up and posture themselves in such a way to directly challenge the GIRoA and NATO forces in a truly conventional manner, namely by digging in, building fortifications, and holding ground. Despite this brazen, but arguably foolish, decision (because of the Coalition's firepower) the Taliban were not about to make it easy to target them. The enemy operated in teams of roughly platoon equivalent size (i.e. 20–30 fighters) over which effective command and control was maintained. As they had already shown, and would further confirm, they were sophisticated enough to conduct tactical reliefs in place and coordinated attacks against their opponents. More important, their defences were prepared as strong points, which made extensive use of natural and man-made obstacles and all had interlocking arcs of direct fire with small arms, RPGs, and recoilless rifles. In addition, their indirect fire from mortars was responsive and well coordinated. Moreover, obstacles on roads were particularly prevalent with extensive use of pressure-plate IEDs. For example, in one area five such devices were found in a 50-metre span of road leading into a Taliban defensive position. In addition, they widened the existing canal with light equipment so that it could act as a tank trap.

Although NATO and the Canadians did not initially have a full picture of the Taliban defensive dispositions, no one was fooled by the effort it would take to clear the Taliban from the region. The challenge was imposing. "Essentially," conceded Schreiber, "especially after the 3 August attack we realized that we were facing a battalion size defensive position based upon complex obstacles covered by surveillance, indirect and direct fire and incorporating kill zones." He affirmed, "So this is what we faced, two company positions with strong points from which they [Taliban] would sally forth to conduct ambushes along Highway 1. We were having anywhere between three to five ambushes a day on Highway 1, every day late July and early August." Schreiber further declared, "and then they had another company defensive position to control the Arghandab River with a C2 [command and control] node in the middle."[4]

As a result of the apparent sophistication of the enemy, initially the brigade and battle group staffs devoted a great deal of effort planning and gathering intelligence. Subsequently, the emphasis shifted to "building up," specifically to assembling the combat forces and enablers (e.g. ISR platforms, aviation, close air support [CAS], direct- and indirect-fire assets), as well as the necessary logistical support to take out the Taliban completely.

But this would not be an easy task. The Taliban's excellent use of fieldcraft removed some of the vulnerability they imposed on themselves by engaging in a conventional battle of attrition. Trench lines were well prepared by hand and superbly concealed to evade detection by ground and airborne ISR assets. Trenches were tied into thick mud walls that proved extremely resilient against both direct fire weapons (i.e. 25 mm cannon and small arms) and C4 explosives. In fact, they had developed a sophisticated strongpoint replete with entrenchments that resembled a Soviet defensive position. Communications trenches were dug to connect the larger trench system and bunkers. Lieutenant-Colonel Schreiber concluded, "[the Taliban] had a battalion defensive position fully dug in with complex robust command and control capability with mutually supporting positions and advanced surveillance and early warning."[5]

The Taliban were highly motivated and fought in place. Their fire discipline was strictly imposed to draw Coalition forces into their kill zones, and they aggressively launched counterattacks from the flanks with small mobile teams to attack the depth of assaulting forces.[6]

Undeniably, the Taliban had chosen their ground well. Beyond the fortifications they had built, the natural lay of the land worked in their favour. Pashmul was a green belt with thick vegetation. Seven-foot (two metre) high marijuana fields hid movement and masked the thermal imagery of the LAV.[7] As one official report noted:

> The terrain was extremely difficult due to the combination of natural and built up features. Enemy defences were anchored on the Arghandab River that provided a natural impediment to high-speed manoeuvre to the

defensive position. Although dried up for the most part, the steepness of the banks canalized movement to fording sites where we were vulnerable to enemy direct and indirect fires. Canals criss-crossed the manoeuvre space and proved an impediment to off-road movement for LAVs. Corn and marijuana fields (with stalks extending to a height of 6–8 feet) limited visibility and provided excellent concealment for both TB [Taliban] fighters and natural obstacles. The most significant terrain features were arguably the mud walls and the vineyards. Mud walls approximately eight feet high and two feet thick dominated the terrain. In one case 10 blocks of C4 were required for a single breach. The vineyards covered earth mounds approximately 3–5 feet high with rows arranged every three feet.[8]

Fraser deployed his forces around the objective area to provide as much containment as he could. The containment force maintained a dynamic disposition to provoke the enemy to move inside the "circle so we could shape the battle and advantageously engage the enemy."[9] Coalition forces also dropped psychological pamphlets to warn and encourage non-combatants/civilians and less fanatical enemy personnel to vacate the area. "For the three weeks before we launched Operation Medusa, we talked to and gave money to every village leader in the area," revealed Fraser, "In exchange, we asked them to get rid of the Taliban." He conceded, "We had limited success."[10]

In the aftermath of the bloody August battle, Brigadier-General Fraser briefed General Richards on the plan for OP Medusa. In turn, the ISAF Commander confirmed to Fraser that Operation Medusa was the ISAF main effort. In fact, he went even further and pronounced that Operation Medusa was actually the "NATO main effort."[11] This sentiment was supported by NATO Secretary-General Jaap de Hoop Scheffer, who publicly announced, "If we fail and this nation becomes a failed state again, the consequences will be felt in Ottawa, in Brussels, in the Hague, in Madrid, in New York and elsewhere. That is what is at stake."[12]

Courtesy 1 RCR BG.

The twin peaks at Ma'Sūm Ghar that were focal points of the 19 August battle.

The stakes were clearly high. The fight for Pashmul, or more accurately for Afghanistan, as Brigadier-General Fraser and other senior NATO military leaders described it, no longer rested with 1 PPCLI. By early August they were already conducting a relief in place (RIP) with the 1 RCR BG or Task Force 3–06, as it was officially termed. At 1600 hours, 19 August 2006, a small ceremony to mark the transfer of command authority, or TOCA, between the outgoing and incoming units was taking place at Kandahar Airfield (KAF) between Lieutenant-Colonel Ian Hope and Lieutenant-Colonel Omer Lavoie, the CO of TF 3–06. Within hours of the TOCA, before Operation Medusa could even be launched, and with portions of his force having only been in theatre for a few weeks, Lavoie was fighting his first major battle.[13]

Reports from locals indicated a continuation of the infiltration of insurgent fighters, as well as new leaders, into the Panjwayi District. More troublesome was the reporting that a large portion of the reinforcements moving into Pashmul were assessed as the more experienced Taliban fighters from out of area who were likely augmented by foreign fighters. They continued to reinforce their defensive positions in Pashmul but also began conducting noticeably more and better coordinated attacks. They also demonstrated a large improvement in their use of fire and movement, and their ability to coordinate and concentrate their fires. The insurgents began to conduct almost daily ambushes along major routes targeting ISAF and ANSF elements.

The RCR reacted quickly and pushed out its companies to monitor enemy activity. On 19 August, Afghan Independence Day, with the TOCA ceremony barely finished, "A" Coy, 1 RCR BG, was deployed to the dominating high ground at Ma'Sūm Ghar to observe the enemy. The company arrived at 1730–1800 hours and linked up with the Afghan National Police (ANP) who maintained a presence on the high feature. This activity initiated a prompt response from the enemy. At approximately 1845 hours, the Taliban launched a major assault against the Bazaar-e-Panjwayi District Centre. "I had not anticipated," conceded Lavoie, "having my first command combat experience within hours of transfer of command authority."[14]

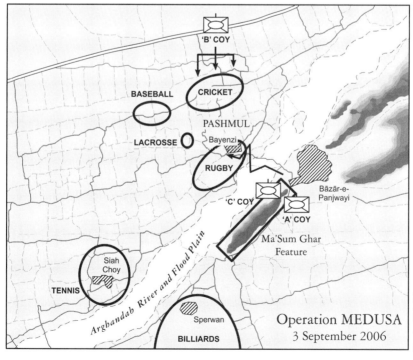

But he had no say in the matter as an estimated 300–500 insurgents armed with small arms and RPGs, and using disciplined section fire and movement, began to manoeuvre to overrun the ANP and "A" Coy positions on Ma'Sūm Ghar. Their assault entailed dismounted coordinated attacks from three different directions. Lavoie recalled, "Within a span of a few hours, 'A' Coy came under attack at night by an enemy that seriously outnumbered them."[15]

The assaulting insurgents proved to be nothing less than tenacious. The fight had lasted over three hours when "A" Coy pulled off the feature in darkness and under contact. "You just couldn't tell who was who," revealed Warrant Officer Mike Jackson, "And we were very lucky we didn't have any blue on blue [casualties]."[16] Moreover, "A" Coy could no longer secure their position and were running low on ammunition. Therefore, the OC, Major Mike Wright, decided to pull back to more defensible ground about three kilometres outside of Bazaar-e-Panjwayi to resupply and regroup.[17] At that point the "QRF" platoon from Patrol Base Wilson met up with the sub-unit and delivered the much needed ammunition. Wright then pulled back to the outskirts of Bazaar-e-Panjwayi and formed a leaguer for the last few hours of darkness.

In the end, the defence of Ma'Sūm Ghar, which represented the outer defensive perimeter of the district centre, had blunted the attack against the ANP headquarters inside Bazaar-e-Panjwayi. Coalition battle damage assessment indicated that approximately 80–100 insurgents were killed. In fact, local security forces recovered the bodies of at least 37 insurgents, a remarkable feat in itself, as the Taliban were always meticulous in policing the battlefield so as not to leave any indication of their losses.

Having beaten off the Taliban attack, Lavoie now focused his task force on the approaching mission. However, he still had to ensure the Taliban were kept in check until he was ready to launch Operation Medusa. As such, between 22–29 August, his task force undertook deterrence patrolling to prevent the Taliban from attacking the district centre. Meanwhile the planning for Operation Medusa was in its final stages.

Lavoie gave formal orders for Operation Medusa on 27 August 2006.[18] The CO outlined that he intended to achieve his mission by denying the enemy freedom of movement or action within the Panjwayi-

Zhari-Kandahar-Arghandab greenbelt, which had historically served as a significant sanctuary and transit route in past efforts to seize Kandahar City. The operation was to be a joint Afghan National Security Forces (ANSF)/ISAF initiative, with the ANSF leading wherever possible. Lavoie explained, "The key to success of this operation lies in our ability to match our strengths against enemy weaknesses in order to constantly disrupt his decision cycle and prevent his C2 assets from being able to react to our manoeuvre." As such, he directed that the battle group would "make maximum use of joint fires, ISR, EW, [electronic warfare] superior direct firepower capability, mobility and C2 to dominate the three dimensional battle space and overwhelm an enemy capable of operating on only one plane of the battlefield."[19]

Lieutenant-Colonel Lavoie planned on deceiving the enemy into believing that a major assault was imminent on their lines of communication, as well as on their command and control nodes. He hoped to achieve this by advancing aggressively from east to west on two separate axes with two respective balanced company group (Coy Gp) teams — one

Courtesy 1 RCR BG.

Aerial view of the Arghandab River watershed and surrounding Pashmul countryside.

advancing from the north and the other from the south. The plan was premised on the notion that once the Taliban understood that their critical vulnerabilities were being threatened by a major ground force, they would mass to defend themselves. This would allow ISAF assets to destroy them using precision fire from close air support, aviation, and artillery.

Lavoie and his battle group were originally given eight days to clear the objective. The precursor to the operation began on 1 September, when the Coy Gps moved to their waiting areas located close to their objectives and conducted battle procedure in preparation for their opening roles. "B" and Charles Coy groups were responsible for conducting feints north and south of Pashmul respectively with a view to drawing the enemy out of their defensive positions. Concurrently, "A" Coy Gp was to isolate Bazaar-e-Panjwayi to provide flank protection to Charles Coy Gp because of the nature of the threat and terrain. If successful in their actions, the enemy would be pummelled and annihilated by precision guided munitions and indirect fire.[20]

The following day, 2 September 2006, at 0530 hours, TF Kandahar manoeuvre elements deployed into their battle positions centred on enemy objectives in Panjwayi/Pashmul. Charles Coy, under command of Major Matthew Sprague, was responsible for seizing Ma'Sūm Ghar. Lavoie wanted to ensure he took possession of the high ground first, namely the Ma'Sūm Ghar feature, from which he could dominate the area by both observation and fire. Charles Coy did so without incident, arriving on the objective at 0600 hours, which was the intended "H-Hour."[21]

But the wild card remained — where exactly was the enemy? "We really did not have a good idea as to where each of the enemy positions were," conceded Major Greg Ivey, "in training it was very easy to see the figure 11 targets and vehicles and you knew where the left of arc and right of arc were, but I'll tell you, out there [Panjwayi] you didn't see people moving around very much. And when they did, we got on them right away, either with 25 mm cannon or with indirect fire."[22]

However, despite the provocation, or more probably as a direct result of the intimidating firepower, the Taliban chose not to show any reaction. The absence of any major enemy action or movement created impressions of weakness in the eyes of some Coalition leadership. The question became one of were the enemy already destroyed or effectively weakened? Or did the Taliban refuse to take the bait and instead remain safely hunkered down in their prepared positions?

The MNB commander, Brigadier-General Fraser, visited the forward Coy Gp in the early afternoon on 2 September at Ma'Sūm Ghar and decided that the task force would cross the Arghandab River without delay. Charles Coy Gp had already cleared two lanes from their battle positions on Ma'Sūm Ghar down to the river. They had taken their bulldozers and ploughed two widely dispersed lanes through the grape fields directly to the river flood plain. With these preparations already in place, at 1400 hours, the OC, his engineer detachment, and a security platoon conducted a reconnaissance (recce) to map out possible crossing points.

"I drove up and down the river bed," recalled Major Matthew Sprague, "still thinking we would have two and a half days of bombardment in accordance with the plan so we could do this [assault river crossing] in a deliberate fashion." He added, "No one had been down to the river yet — it was not an issue of getting across, but rather getting a foothold on the other side." Sprague further explained, "The enemy side of the river was steep and heavily covered with brush."[23] It became evident that the only clear flat crossing point was alongside the main road directly in line with the famous white school complex in the village of Bayenzi, which caused so much grief for the 1 PPCLI BG a month prior during the desperate combat of 3 August.[24]

"This was the ground the enemy had chosen to defend," acknowledged Brigadier-General Fraser, "[Objective] Rugby [the approximate area around the school complex] was where we assessed that the Taliban wanted us to fight them. That was their main battleground." The brigade commander elaborated, "Their whole defence was structured to have us coming across the Arghandab River in the south and fight into Rugby." He added, "And the schoolhouse was the area in the centre, where there were big killing fields to the east and the north."[25] Surprisingly, this also became the ground ISAF agreed to fight on.

Fraser ordered Sprague to push the security platoon across the river and leave them on the far side. "I was unhappy with this," acknowledged

Sprague, since they would be isolated in terrain that the Coalition neither controlled, nor would they fully understood exactly where or how large an enemy force was located there. Fortunately, Lieutenant-Colonel Lavoie was successful in arguing that there was no tactical advantage to leaving a platoon exposed on the edge of enemy territory and they were withdrawn as darkness fell.

Major Sprague was relieved when he was given permission to pull his platoon back to the friendly side of the river. However, his relief was shortlived. During the middle of the night, both the CO and OC were completely surprised by the ensuing orders from Brigadier-General Fraser. "At midnight I heard we had to cross the river," recalled a perplexed Major Sprague.[26] The brigade commander ordered the task force to conduct an assault river crossing at 0200 hours. Hard words were exchanged and Lavoie pushed back, concerned at the change in plan and lack of preparation. In essence, despite an apparently successful day of bombardment and cursory reconnaissance of the river, there were just too many unknowns. The crossing point was not marked; they had no data on flow rate or depth of the river; and, most important, they had little information on the enemy's disposition. Faced with these obstacles, Fraser relented and agreed to a first light attack.

Despite the change in H-Hour, however, the pressure to attack sooner than later was tangible. The MNB operations officer, Lieutenant-Colonel Shane Schreiber explained, "On 2 September, which was D-day, we spent most of the day pounding known Taliban positions in Objective Rugby and Cricket, especially a big bunch of buildings that became known as the white school. We pounded them for a good 12 hours. I mean it was a fire power demonstration."[27]

This impression was widespread. Not surprising then that conclusions were drawn on the effect of the actual bombardment. Moreover, impressions were reinforced with local perceptions. "We had reports that the Taliban were actually leaving," acknowledged Schreiber, "that they were actually running away." He added, "The locals said yeah, they're [Taliban fighters] abandoning their positions, they're leaving." Schreiber conceded, "And the enemy could get out, because they had covered routes in and out of the area."[28]

Courtesy 1 RCR

The infamous white school house that was the centre of the vicious combat on 3 September 2006 is pounded by indirect fire.

The prospect of the large concentration of Taliban fighters escaping unscathed concerned senior NATO commanders. Lieutenant-Colonel Schreiber revealed:

> When Major-General Benjamin Freakley [ISAF Deputy-Commander for Security] heard that the enemy may be escaping, he said "they're leaving, you're letting them out of the bag." That was his big fear is that the Taliban would get out of the bag and we'd have to fight them again later. So, he said "the Taliban are leaving so you have to get in there and get after them." Lieutenant-General Richards [the ISAF commander] agreed with him, so we started to get a significant amount of pressure to get in there and to actually find out what was going on in Objective Rugby.[29]

The pressure was then redirected to the battle group. "We [MNB] directed Omer [CO 1 RCR BG] to do the crossing earlier," asserted Schreiber, "We wanted him to go under the cover of darkness on the night of 2/3 September, [but] he wanted to wait until the morning of 3 September." The MNB operations officer acknowledged, "In the end, there was a bit of a compromise made. We originally said 0100 hours, Omer said 0600 hours, so we settled at 0400 hours." However, revealed Schreiber, "in reality by the time he started his crossing it was 0600 hours."[30]

The CO noted, "I was struck that morning by the sheer outward confidence in the plan displayed by the leadership of the BG, despite the fact that for most of them it was their first time experiencing a combat engagement." Lavoie revealed, "I am certain many of my officers shared the same misgivings I had. There was certainly huge risk in some areas of the plan, especially if we failed to surprise the enemy."[31]

Lavoie's misgivings were well founded. Nonetheless, based on the pushed timelines, Charles Coy Gp had no choice but to use the only existing crossing point which led into the killing fields that the brigade commander had previously described.[32] On 3 September 2006, at 0445 hours, engineer elements crept out to clear the route soon to be used by the infantry. A slight delay was experienced because of the darkness and the necessity to wait for the air support package. Sprague recalled, "I gave combat team orders on the fly over the radio." He lamented, "half of the combat team wasn't even with me at 0545 hours." The orders for the attack were basically "single file, order of march and follow me," stated the OC.[33] At 0620 hours, the leading elements of Charles Coy Gp crossed the Arghandab River under cover of A-10 "Thunderbolt" and B2 fighter bomber aircraft.[34]

They were also backed by overwhelming artillery support. The battery commander, Major Ivey stated: "We conducted a deliberate fire plan to get the guys across. The Charles Coy FOO was Captain Dan Matheson and he went across with Charles Company." Ivey and the CO, as well as an anchor OP, remained on the dominating ground of Ma'Sūm Ghar. "We had close air support basically for a 24-hour period starting 2 September basically prepping the enemy side of the obstacle [Arghandab River]," explained Ivey, "So we pounded the enemy position and then we pushed fires back into the enemy depth, into what we would have expected was their supporting positions." Ivey noted, "At H-hour on the 3 September, Captain Matheson used suppressant fires on that bank just to get the guys shaken out from their battle position on Ma'Sūm Ghar onto the Arghandab River. It was also used to suppress the enemy while they were actually crossing and conducting the actual breach." He added, "Once they gained lodgement on the far side or on the north side of the river, Captain Matheson pushed the fires back into the Taliban depth. He also had close air support at the same time to strike even deeper, probably about 1,000 metres or so."[35]

Under the cover of the overwhelming fire, the mission proceeded smoothly. "We crossed and got into a descent defensive posture and established a good foothold," explained Sprague, "we were in a half circle with 8 Platoon facing West, 7 Platoon facing North, the ANA and their American EMT [Embedded Mentor Training] team facing North-East and the engineer Zettlemeyer and bulldozer and other support elements in the flat area behind us."[36]

To Lieutenant Jeremy Hiltz, the 8 Platoon Commander, the whole scene upon crossing was eerie — the landscape was completely still. "We knew deep down inside," he revealed, "we knew they [Taliban] were there ... but it's still quiet and there's no indication that anything's wrong, except for guys are looking at each other, there's that feeling."[37] He added, "the guys were definitely on high, high alert and heightened senses, but to that point we weren't seeing any type of activity or any, anything that would indicate that there was any issues."[38]

To get through to the suspected enemy positions, however, Charles Coy Gp had to traverse a farmer's field that had been ploughed out. Furthermore, it had a series of ditches and berms that had to be breached. The ditches were approximately three to four feet deep and about eight feet wide in the middle of a huge marijuana field. The engineers took the dirt from the berms and simply filled in the ditches to make crossing points. Sprague sent 8 Platoon, dismounted, to clear some buildings on his left flank. He sent the ANA, also dismounted, off to his right flank to keep an eye on the main road. Shortly before 0800 hours, he then sent 7 Platoon, mounted in their LAV IIIs, straight up the middle through the breach. "Initially," conceded Sprague, "We all thought this is too easy."[39]

Despite the initial progress there were concerns. "Unfortunately, there was a lot of confusion due to lack of significant orders and being pushed forward quickly," asserted Lieutenant Hiltz, "It was my impression when we stepped across the river that we were to just push over onto the far side and secure it. And then all of a sudden it seemed like we were breaching and starting to push into Objective Rugby, significantly the white bunker, white school complex." Hiltz described, "The engineers were able to make their first breach and then they pushed forward with the bulldozers and started the breaching of the canal itself." He added, "They pushed through a second breach through the berm, down in between my Bravo and Charlie call signs [LAV IIIs] and then we again secured that." Hiltz confirmed, "the initial order was that 7 platoon would go through and with the engineers move in on the white school and bunker. They [7 Platoon] went across the canal and basically fanned out four abreast and advanced on the white school."[40]

Captain Derek Wessan, the 7 Platoon Commander, gave a quick set of orders to his platoon, who then moved through the engineer's breach and shook out into a battle line consisting of three 7 platoon, or call sign (C/S) 31, LAV IIIs (i.e. C/Ss 31A, B, C), and an engineer LAV C/S E32D. In addition, there was a LUVW (light utility vehicle wheel), the German-manufactured *Gelaendenwagon,* more commonly referred to as the "G" Wagon, in which rode the platoon second-in-command (2IC). The G-Wagon, C/S 31W, was jokingly referred to as 31 "Woof," since this "was the last noise you'd hear as the vehicle was engulfed in flames."[41]

Although the landscape was still as 7 Platoon worked its way through the final breach, the enemy had not been idle. A variety of surveillance assets, as well as the deployed troops themselves, began to report on Taliban activities in depth that began to respond to the initial stages of Charles Coy Gp's advance. Groups of 10–15 insurgents were reported moving about and occupying three- to five-man ambush positions that overlooked IEDs planted on the route leading to the enemy position. These targets were continuously engaged. In fact, it became clear that there were a lot of enemy and that Charles Coy Gp had stirred up a hornet's nest.

As 7 Platoon emerged on the other side of the breach, they found themselves in the middle of a marijuana field. There was an unnatural calm as the 7 Platoon LAVs pushed through the gap and took up an extended line facing the white school house complex approximately 50

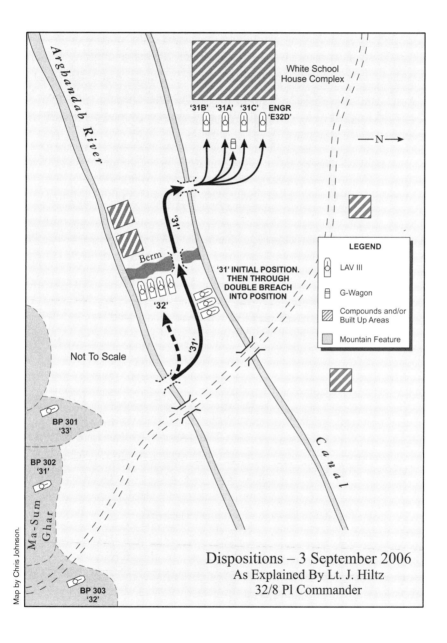

Map by Chris Johnson.

White School House Complex

'31B' '31A' '31C' ENGR 'E32D'

←—N—→

'31' INITIAL POSITION. THEN THROUGH DOUBLE BREACH INTO POSITION

'31'

Berm

'32'

'31'

Not To Scale

LEGEND

	LAV III
	G-Wagon
	Compounds and/or Built Up Areas
	Mountain Feature

Arghandab River

Canal

Ma-Sum Ghar

BP 301 '33'

BP 302 '31'

BP 303 '32'

Dispositions – 3 September 2006
As Explained By Lt. J. Hiltz
32/8 Pl Commander

303

metres away. The Platoon second-in-command, Warrant Officer Rick Nolan, pulled up in his G-Wagon and took up his position.

The enemy displayed remarkable fire discipline. They allowed the Canadians to approach extremely close before they opened fire. But when they did, it was with devastating effect. "It was dead quiet," remembered Master-Corporal Allan Johnson commanding the LAV III C/S 31A. Then he saw an enemy jump up on a roof and "all hell broke loose."[42] Corporal Justin Young recalled, "We pulled up through the breach and then when we shook out to extended line and then the rockets started flying."[43] Lieutenant Hiltz stated, "when 31 was approximately 50 metres from the white school, a pen flare went off and then it was a very concentrated, very rehearsed and well, well organized ambush, almost 360 degrees around us."[44]

Regardless of how the ambush was triggered, what is certain is that without warning, 7 Platoon was enveloped in fire from three directions. "The entire area just lit up," described Johnson, "We were taking fire from at least two sides, maybe three, with everything they [enemy] had."[45]

Charles Company combat team was now ensnared in a horseshoe ambush. Worst off was 7 Platoon, which found itself in the middle of an avalanche of enemy fire. Master-Corporal Justin O'Neil, the engineer field section 2IC recalled, "We crossed the Arghandab River, or dried riverbed, and put in two breaches heading towards the white school complex. My section was on the left-hand side of the breach behind the D6 dozer. The other engineer call sign, E32 Delta [C/S E32D], was behind the Zettlemeyer on the right side of the breach. I was in the air crew sentry hatch and had a pretty good view of the area. We pushed in towards the white school and then all hell broke loose — RPGs, small arms fire, everything. Then all the India call signs [infantry — Charles Coy Gp] started working their way up. We started pulling our heavy equipment guys out just because they were sitting there on the ground with no guns. I was watching C/S E32D starting to extract his section when I saw his LAV take a hit — a rocket in the turret."[46]

The engineer LAV, E32D, was the first vehicle casualty, hit by a munitions from an RPG or 82 mm recoilless rifle. Regardless, the heat round slammed into the turret ring of the LAV, spraying lethal shards of shrapnel everywhere in the interior. Sergeant Shane Stachnik, who was standing in the rear hatch, died instantly from a severed artery. Amazingly, the troop commander who was in the turret took a minor wound with some shrapnel in the shoulder, and his gunner beside him escaped completely unscathed. Both were leaning forward to look through their gun sights when the round came whistling in, just missing them by inches. The explosion also destroyed the radios so that neither the OC, nor the 7 Platoon commander knew what had happened to their engineer call sign.

Shortly thereafter, Warrant Officer Nolan's G-Wagon suffered a catastrophic hit. An RPG slammed into the unarmoured vehicle, penetrating the passenger windshield. "We rolled up, crossed the river, waited till the engineers formed a breach," recalled the driver Corporal Sean Teal. "Then we rolled through the breach with the LUVW behind the centre call sign," recounted Teal, "I was the driver, Warrant Officer Nolan was my front passenger, the doc [platoon medic] was behind him and the interpreter was right behind me." He continued:

> We sat there for a few minutes, we were joking around about, you know, kind of ironic that you're rolling into battle in a weed [marijuana] field, but immediately after that just a flash followed by just a big burst of heat, the big crush. And then everything went black. I was out the door. Grabbed my rifle. I didn't know at the time if anybody else was okay because I'm the tactical combat casualty guy as well. And I took a gander to the left, I yelled over to Corporal Reid that we got hit, which was obvious. I provided a small bit of suppressive fire and then got behind the G-wagon. The door swung open, the doc, the doc jumped out of the G-wagon. I pulled him behind the vehicle because he was really stunned. The interpreter fell out, landing on his head. And the warrant [Nolan] didn't come out. That's when I pretty much assumed that either he's probably unconscious because I knew that it had hit his side of the vehicle, actually it came through the windshield directly in front

of him. I told the doc to stay put, then I went around the passenger side, pushed the door open I took some pretty good enemy fire while doing so. The warrant was laying unconscious. There was a fire in the vehicle so I put it out, pulled him out and dragged him behind the vehicle. The doc couldn't give me a hand at that time because he was still pretty concussed. I made a quick assessment based on the severe wounds that he [Nolan] was a PRI 4 [priority 4 casualty, i.e. dead]. I went back and grabbed the warrant's weapon. I then butt stroked the doc and he then snapped out of his daze. He then confirmed the warrant was a PRI 4, which I had already told him.[47]

Corporal Richard Furoy, the medic or "doc," was sitting directly behind Nolan. "Everything in the world came down on us and then, whoomp, the G-Wagon went black," recalled Furoy. "I sort of lost consciousness," he explained, "[but] I could still feel the spray of gunfire; I could feel the concussion of the rounds inside my chest, but I couldn't hear anything."[48]

Everywhere individual battles of heroism and courage were played out in isolated dramas throughout the battlefield, which had become a cauldron of fire. Sergeant Derek John Scott Fawcett was surveying the ground from the rear sentry hatch of his LAV III, C/S 31C, when he ordered his driver to stop abreast of the other platoon vehicles as they approached to within 30–50 metres of the white school complex. Suddenly, Fawcett witnessed E32D and the G-Wagon get hammered by rocket fire in quick succession. He quickly reported the events to Lieutenant Wessan, who was riding in C/S 31C, since his own LAV was non-serviceable.

Next, Fawcett turned his attention to the G-Wagon, which was now a blackened and smoking wreck. However, behind it he could see Corporal Teal desperately signalling for help. Without hesitation Fawcett told Private O'Rourke and Corporal Funnel to follow him, and they exited the relative safety of their LAV and sprinted into the inferno outside. "Running through the marijuana towards the G-Wagon, the noise of the guns was deafening and the enemy fire was shredding the tall plants. It was raining marijuana on the sprinting soldiers."[49] Private O'Rourke recalled, "as we dismounted it was just like out of the movies, you hear the whizzes of the bullets and the RPGs — just wicked crazy sounds."[50]

Once they reached the G-Wagon, the gravity of the situation became clear. O'Rourke and Funnel began applying first aid to Furoy and the interpreter, who were both seriously hurt. Meanwhile Fawcett and Teal focused on engaging the enemy to relieve some of the pressure. Realizing the tenuous position they were in, Sergeant Fawcett ordered his soldiers to transport the wounded back to the LAV while he and Teal continued to provide covering fire. O'Rourke and Funnel twice traversed the bullet-swept field to evacuate the wounded, an act of bravery for which they received the Medal of Military Valour.

Meanwhile, the entire company was hammered by small arms and RPG fire. Even the Zettlemeyer front end loader to the rear of the fighting was quickly hit with an enemy 82 mm recoilless rifle and put out of action. Every weapon available fired in return, but no one could see their antagonists. Corporal Gary Reid insisted, "You couldn't see them. There was minimal movement but lots of rounds." He added, "There was small arms fire coming from everywhere, RPGs, everything that they had they threw at us. I think we spotted two guys and the rest was all spec[ulative] fire."[51]

Even the gunners in the hulking LAV IIIs had difficulty. The marijuana plants were so high that the gunners in the turrets failed to see any targets. Nonetheless, the barrels of the 25 mm chain guns soon glowed with heat as suppressive fire was rained down on the suspected enemy positions. Many of the guns jammed because of the incessant firing, and the pintle-mounted machine guns soon ran short of ammunition.

At one point in the desperate battle, the main gun of the LAV commanded by Master-Corporal Sean Niefer jammed after firing just a few rounds. Realizing the plight of his fellow soldiers caught in the open, Niefer stood up in his hatch, fully exposed, and began to lay down a barrage of fire using the pintle-mounted machine gun in the turret. To many who witnessed his selfless act of bravery to support those around him, his total disregard for the bullets and shrapnel whizzing through the air became representative of the vicious battle Charles Coy Gp found itself in.[52]

At the same time, 8 Platoon was fighting through a group of buildings on the left flank. Master-Corporal Ward Engley's section dismounted to secure a large ditch. "All of a sudden the whole world exploded around us," recalled Engley. RPGs, mortars, small arms, and machine-gun fire, seemingly coming from all directions, slashed the air. Nevertheless, the 1 RCR soldiers made their way to clear the complex array of compounds and buildings. They were required to go back and clear out buildings that had already been cleaned out, because the compounds had so many passages and tunnels that the enemy could use their greater knowledge of the terrain to re-infiltrate into the areas that had already been cleared out.

Adding to the problems of the 8 Platoon soldiers were malfunctioning grenades. As a result, the troops used their M72 66 mm rocket launchers to clear buildings. A door would be kicked in and the M72 tube punched into the room and fired. The effect of the blast and concussion gave the soldiers bursting into the room the necessary edge.

The platoon commander, Lieutenant Hiltz, by this time had dismounted and ran down the left flank to check on the progress of his soldiers. He explained, "I ran down to my left flank, the south side, and I pushed forward. I'd had several soldiers within my two section actually slightly concussed, knocked out by RPGs. They figure that they took no less than ten RPGs in their position alone that hit the buildings that they were around." He added, "They were able to push forward and hold that position."[53] Nonetheless, the incoming fire was heavy and Hiltz attempted to get assistance from 9 Platoon, which was deployed in a firebase on Ma'Sūm Ghar. He threw white smoke hoping that it would serve as a reference point. Unfortunately, from 8 Platoon's vantage point it was hard to tell whether the call for support fire was having any effect.

Concurrently, the ANA element assigned to the assault was also heavily engaged. The ANA were apparently fearless. Initially trailing behind Charles Coy Gp, as soon as the Taliban ambush erupted, the ANA troops "ran past us with their kit firing on the run," described Sergeant Donovan Crawford with admiration. "They raced up without hesitation," he added.[54] Lieutenant Ray Corby asserted "they [ANA] are quick, aggressive and eager."[55] Lieutenant Hiltz affirmed, "It was actually quite awesome to see that and it brought me back to grips with exactly what I was required to do. I needed to continue to push the platoon out and cover off and allow 7 platoon the ability to pull back."[56]

By this time Sergeant Fawcett and his soldiers had retrieved the dead and wounded occupants of the G-Wagon and returned to their LAV. But it appeared Charles Company Group could not catch a break. As the platoon began to withdraw from the trap, it found itself in the driver of C/S 31B backed into a ditch. Like a beached whale, the LAV was stranded and unable to move. Half suspended, its wheels were spinning wildly in the air. It now became a preferred target for the enemy, and RPG rounds sailed in, a number of them finding the target. The back door was hit, rendering it useless. Other rounds smacked into the vehicle — its armour saving those inside.

C/S 31C quickly came to the support of the stricken vehicle. Broadside to the enemy fire, the crew commander directed the soldiers in the back to take cover in the ditch, which provided greater protection until they were able to evacuate the troops from the back of the stranded LAV. In the ditch, one soldier "could hear the 'ting ting ting' as small arms fire hit the LAV, and he felt the vehicle rock as first one and then a second RPG slammed into the rear hatch area."[57]

The occupants of the stranded LAV now had to make their exit through the escape hatch, since the back ramp of the LAV had become inoperable due to the RPG strikes. One at a time the soldiers made the dash to the closest piece of shelter and provided covering fire for the next individual to run the enemy's gauntlet of fire. Once all were safely out, they loaded into C/S 31C, but space soon became an issue. "There was no room because we had approximately 12 to 13 guys in the back of a LAV III, which is in my eyes a miracle," commented Private O'Rourke. "I don't know how we fit so many people back there. But thank God for it."[58] Unfortunately, because of the lack of space, Sergeant Fawcett and Corporal Fields were on their own and had to make their way out of the death trap dismounted. Due to the circumstances, the body of the platoon warrant was initially left behind with the stranded LAV III in the ditch.

And the situation seemed to spiral out of control. At one point, it seemed that luck was simply not with Charles Coy Gp. A French Mirage jet zoomed in to deliver badly needed air support, but for some inexplicable reason, the 1,000 pound GPS guided bomb went off course and landed 20 feet from Major Sprague and his men. Sprague recalled, "the entire fire fight stopped as everyone watched this bomb bounce towards us." He recalled, "I thought we're fucked now." Corporal Rodney Grubb reminisced, "In the middle of all this chaos, we see this big, black fuck-off bomb coming towards us." He added, "it was like a big, black steel football. It hit the ground and bounced and bounced and bounced." Grubb hit the ground and concluded, "okay, we're done."[59] Fortuitously, the bomb never went off.[60]

As the recovery of vehicles continued, the fire fight intensified and Charles Coy Gp continued to be plagued by mishaps. The tow vehicle recovering the LUVW missed the breach and the G-Wagon fell into the ditch. After two and a half hours of attempting to recover it, Sprague made the call to blow-in-place (BiP) to deny any advantage to the enemy. One positive development occurred when the engineer LAV, C/S E32D, which had been struck in the opening salvo of the ambush, was also in the process of being recovered. As they began the recovery effort, the unconscious driver came to and was able to drive the damaged vehicle out of the trap.

Major Sprague now realized that there was not much more he could do, so he directed more fire forward and calmly organized the withdrawal of his forces, ensuring that neither casualties nor disabled vehicles were left behind. Warrant Officer Frank Mellish established a casualty collection point (CCP) behind the now disabled Zettlemeyer in a hollow in the ground. When Mellish discovered that the body of his best friend was still in the stranded vehicle, he grabbed Private Will Cushley to assist him retrieve the corpse. Before they could move, an 82 mm recoilless rifle round slammed into Zettlemeyer, spraying the area with hot molten shrapnel.

Lieutenant Hiltz recalled, "I was running in to check on my C-6 [General Purpose Machine Gun (GPMG)] team, and I vividly remember an RPG round heading directly towards me. And as I went down into the ditch where the C6 team was, it actually flew over my head." Hiltz remembered turning around and looking back and witnessing the tragedy about to unfold. "The round impacted on the Zettelmeyer and essentially the blast rained down right onto the group there," he explained. "It initially looked like everybody was okay but then I realized that there were quite a few of them that were wounded."[61]

Lieutenant Justin Bules, the 2 Platoon Commander stated: "My LAV was about 25 metres in front of the Zettelmeyer and my head was out of the turret and a recoilless rifle round came over my head, hit the Zettelmeyer and spalded."[62] Whether RPG or 82 mm recoilless rifle, the effect was the same. The impact of the round mortally wounded Mellish and Cushley.

On top of Ma'Sūm Ghar, a Canadian special operations forces (SOF) combat control team watched the tragedy unfold. "The LAVs were stuck in the field," described one SOF operator, "They were crammed in a little field and they had no mobility." He added, "We saw guys dragging bodies into a CPP and then there was a big explosion and then just guys laying there."[63] Another witness from the SOF team affirmed, "it was one of the most frustrating things I've ever had to watch."[64]

On the ground, the situation seemed tenuous. "It was total chaos," opined engineer Warrant Officer Roger Perreault.[65] Not surprisingly, it had become a fight for survival. As the battle continued to rage, 9 Platoon, located in a firebase position on Ma'Sūm Ghar, was frustrated at their lack of ability to fully support their sister platoons. Captain Rob Carey attested to the feeling of helplessness that C/S 33 experienced. "We just knew that they were under contact, they were in a kill zone and we knew that one of the vehicles had been hit by RPG and that there were casualties," explained Carey, "so we just started laying as much fire as we possibly could to their frontage." He added, "we had to be careful because there was quite a bit of confusion on the net and they were in the marijuana fields so they couldn't tell where the fire was coming from, they couldn't get a fix on the enemy."[66] Carey confirmed, "there was quite a bit of mayhem on the ground there."[67]

Sergeant Jamie Walsh noted, "After they got hit we tried to engage as best as we could." He emphasized, "We started engaging the schoolhouse and the bunker system right away."[68] But part of the problem was the limited arcs of fire that 9 Platoon possessed. "We couldn't fire at a lot because it would have been shooting right through [C/S] 31 and [C/S] 32's positions," conceded Sergeant Walsh. One of the SOF operators concluded, "The firebase was not far enough to the flank so they didn't have adequate arcs of fire so once across the river, 'C' Coy was on their own."[69]

Nonetheless, once the firebase heard that there were mass casualties, "we started to pound everything that we could," stated Sergeant Walsh.

"We called in for a reference, so one of the sections threw out white smoke and told us everything east of the white smoke was friendly, everything west was enemy," explained Walsh, "so we just used the white smoke as a reference point and just started hammering everything, trying to keep their [enemy] heads down to let [C/S] 31 recover their casualties and to be able to pull off the position."[70]

As Charles Coy Gp began its withdrawal, one issue still remained. Someone had to retrieve Warrant Officer Nolan's body. Sergeant Russell quickly stepped up. "Sergeant Russell pulled forward in his LAV and once he got the go ahead we fired at a rapid rate," described Lieutenant Hiltz, "it was complete mayhem as rounds were going in both directions all around them." The LAV pulled up to the stranded vehicle, and Russell and Private Spence dashed out, grabbed Rick Nolan's body and pulled him back into their LAV. "In a matter of two minutes they were back out and we covered them the whole time," assured Hiltz.[71]

Back at the CPP, Lieutenant Bules had backed up his LAV, lowered the ramp and began loading as many of the wounded as possible. "We backed up and put the ramp down near the CCP," stated Bules. He clarified, "I didn't have anyone in the back of my LAV that day so I had just put the back hatches down and we had gone in just with the crew for the battle."[72] By the time Bules was ready to pull out, he had 12 soldiers and the bodies of the deceased in his LAV III. He was unable to put his ramp up, and he had no chain, so "we just pretty much drove out of there with the ramp bouncing up and down every time we hit a bump," recounted Bules. He related, "I just kept telling my driver to go slow and he kept saying we got to get the hell out of here."[73]

Major Sprague now turned to his FOO to assist with withdrawal. "When the company commander was prepared to withdraw Captain Matheson brought in air burst rounds onto the marijuana fields and the corn fields, probably about 200 to 250 metres out in front of the company's dismounted troops to assist with the extraction," explained Major Ivey. He added, "At the same time, there were buildings in depth that we suspected the Taliban were using to fire RPGs and 82 mm recoilless rifles so as best as we could we used hellfire missiles from the attack helicopters, as well as 500 and 1,000 pound laser guided munitions to neutralize those areas." But Ivey clarified, "it was a tough slog because it was probably the first time that the FOO had been put in a situation like that where he was with the company commander conducting the fire plan, using the 25 mm cannon, controlling artillery at danger close distances under contact and his forward air controller [FAC] in the back [of his LAV] was controlling the aircraft all at the same time. So there was a lot going on."[74]

The withdrawal continued, and all the wounded and dead were pulled from the bloody field of battle. All the stranded vehicles that could not be recovered were "BiP'd" by close air support. Charles Coy Gp then regrouped. "We pushed back into the centre of the riverbed and just leaguered up and basically composed ourselves, and got all the casualties out," stated Master-Corporal O'Neil, "then we pushed back to battle position 302."[75]

The attempted assault on the enemy positions had been costly. The task force suffered four killed and eight wounded. "How more people weren't killed," pondered Sprague, "I don't know."[76] He asserted, "This wasn't some one-hour firefight we were in — we were fucking fighting for our lives, for seven hours."[77] Private Daniel Roasti asked the same question. "I'm convinced someone was watching over us," he added. "The amount of bullets that were flying, I just don't know why some of us are still here."[78] In the end, the action earned members of Charles Coy Gp six Medals of Military Valour and a Star of Military Valour.[79]

Once Charles Coy Gp moved back to battle position 302 on Ma'Sūm Ghar, "it was basically business as usual for us," commented Major Ivey. He explained:

> The offensive air support plan kept slogging along as intended and that night we had a significant amount of air based on the day's actions since we now had a pretty good idea where the enemy was. So, the FOO parties basically began trying to destroy as much of those compounds as they could and that happened all throughout the night. And I remember specifically, and I will never, ever forget this — that night just seemed to go on forever because we were on Ma Sūm Ghar and we kept dropping artillery and bombs anywhere from 1,000 to 3,000 metres

from our own location. And the echo of the bombs and the A-10 Thunderbolts and the other aircraft that we had just rang through the entire Arghandab valley. And, you know, we'd try and get to sleep as best we could behind the vehicles and the light from the explosions was so bright that it would go right through your eyelids as you were sleeping. And, you couldn't sleep because you could see the explosions go off, because we were up on top looking down into the valley and every strike would just light up the entire valley."[80]

By 1700 hours, 3 September, an intelligence report revealed, "the enemy believe that they are winning, and their morale is assessed as high." In fact, the Taliban quickly claimed victory following the withdrawal of Charles Coy Gp back to their battle positions on Ma'Sūm Ghar. Moreover, despite the loss of a significant amount of Taliban fighters, the intelligence report concluded that it did not have a demoralizing affect on the remaining Talibes. In fact, the defence of Pashmul became a rallying point for the local Taliban insurgents, and they began pushing reinforcements into the area and remanning many of the abandoned ambush positions.

Lieutenant-Colonel Schreiber, the MNB operations officer, took a stoic stance. "It was either a really good feint or an unfortunate attack," he proffered, "Either way, despite the loss of life, it worked like it had to happen, because it unmasked Taliban positions." He clarified, "So we sucked back, pounded it some more — we spent the remainder of that day pounding the hell out of them [Taliban] and Omer pulled back to set up and to try again the next morning.[81]

Charles Coy Gp now regrouped. "We pulled back to the battle position and we began to take stock and to start the healing process and start talking through some of the issues while still maintaining a strong force on the line," explained Lieutenant Hiltz.[82] Major Sprague spoke to the entire sub-unit about the day's activities then passed on the word that Charles Coy Gp was going back in the next morning to do a feint at approximately 0700 hours in the morning, following Bravo company's feint from the north, in an attempt to draw the Taliban out of their defensive positions. Hiltz asserted, "So the plan was that we would get everything ready to go that night. We would take a good night's rest and have a chance to suck back and take a breather and focus on what had happened and then realize that we had a job to get on with."[83]

For many in Charles Coy Gp, the prospect of going back into the grinder was daunting. The chaos at the white school complex was still fresh in their memories. Particularly unnerving was the fact that very few actually saw the enemy. Now, in the residual glow of the ongoing bombardment of the enemy positions, the soldiers prepared for another assault at dawn.

Misfortune, however, once again played its hand. As Charles Coy Gp awoke and began to prepare for another attack against the white schoolhouse, an American A-10 close air support aircraft that was called in to attack an enemy position across the river became momentarily disoriented and, before he realized his error, the pilot unleashed a partial burst of deadly fire from his seven-barrelled 30 mm Gatling gun, killing one Canadian and wounding 35 others, including the Charles Coy Gp OC.[84]

The latest calamity was disastrous. Having lost most of its command structure and almost a third of its strength in the friendly fire incident, Charles Coy Gp was now combat ineffective. "Twenty minutes away from an assault river crossing and Omer [Lieutenant-Colonel Lavoie] lost half a company," asserted Brigadier-General Fraser, "We delayed 24 hours but at the end of the day we had to get it done."[85]

The brief pause allowed Lieutenant-Colonel Lavoie the opportunity to recalibrate and amend the plan. He would no longer attack into the Taliban's kill zone. He now put the emphasis on the north and east, where he would conduct a deliberate push using overwhelming force through terrain of his choosing. The 1 RCR BG was now going to use three dismounted companies clearing from the east moving down the canals to get into the area and then clear out the enemy.[86]

After reallocating and reorganizing forces, the renewed push started on 6 September 2006, in the north by "B" Coy when they breached the tree line that marked the divide between friendly and enemy territory.

Courtesy "B" Coy, 1 RCR BG.

"Fix and load." Members of "B" Coy Gp prepare to take the next objective.

The 1 RCR BG now hit its stride. One sub-unit would move forward and dominate intervening ground and provide a firm foothold and act as a firebase. Artillery would then be called in to hammer the objective and then the next sub-unit would surge forward, break through the objective and fight through the target area.

The clearing of objectives seemed just like Cold War training designed to fight the Soviets, according to almost all who participated. What simplified matters was the fact that the objective areas were designated military targets, since the entire civilian population had been evicted by the Taliban and the area turned into a fortified defensive zone. As such, it became an exercise of unrestricted compound clearance. The soldiers would toss grenades into a building or room, then immediately upon the explosion, pour into it and hose it down with fire. Major Andrew Lussier acknowledged, "The Taliban did us a big favour; essentially they had kicked out all the civilians … It made life so much easier for us." He declared, "Essentially we just shot and bombed the crap out of these guys for the better part of four or five days while the battle group made their way from the north."[87]

Lavoie echoed these sentiments. "When the operation commenced, it seemed as if it were a Cold War training exercise," observed Lieutenant-Colonel Lavoie, There was nothing new in war fighting." He explained:

> We used air [support] to hit deep and danger close artillery at 300 yards or less. Dismounted infantry rushed in before the smoke cleared and seized the objective. Engineers cleared a route with bulldozers and dealt with IEDs. We pushed LAVs up to support infantry to the next objective and to the next bound. At night we conducted fighting patrols and Reconnaissance Platoon seized the line of departure for the next bound the next day. And much like predecessors in Vietnam who said they had to destroy the village to save it — we had to do the same.[88]

In essence, as the operation began to play out, it became increasingly "conventional" in nature. Fraser described it as "a conventional duke it out fight." He said, "The enemy wanted the ground and had prepared the area well for a defensive battle. In the end, it was all about putting the proper resources into the fight." The brigade commander asserted, "We knew we would win because losing just was not an option."[89]

Major Ivey concurred with the brigade commander's assessment. "We went right back to using conventional ammunition, high explosives," Ivey recalled. He continued, "The air burst we found was outstanding for neutralizing soldiers that we suspected were hiding under trees, using the shade as concealment or using the thick brush to move back and forth." He articulated, "So we used air burst a lot, as well as 155 mm delay ground burst to pierce through those complexes to get whatever effect we were trying to achieve, which was basically just to kill people and to destroy whatever bunkers they had." Ivey related that they also reverted to using smoke to blind the enemy, screen their movement, and mark targets for close air support.[90]

In essence, the choreography of the advance was in keeping with the conventional warfare playbook that most of the senior leaders in the

Members of 3 Section, 4 Platoon "storm the breach," 10 September 2006.

battle group had practiced since joining the army. "What we ended up doing was hours before the launch of an advance, each of the respective FOO parties with the two lead companies commenced their preparatory fires," explained Major Ivey. He added, "There was no flashes of brilliance — what we wanted to achieve was to destroy as much of the compound structures as we could that we thought were housing enemy OPs or firing positions and neutralize anybody and anything in the objective areas." As a result, higher headquarters pushed the necessary enablers (e.g. CAS, attack aviation, and guns) to the FOO parties so they could pound the Taliban into submission.

The Canadians quickly learned that the enemy was now pinned down because of the heavy fire and deliberate tactics. Moreover, the Taliban fighters were becoming extremely frustrated with their inability to fight back. Captured enemy communications revealed, "We cannot achieve our objective while we're getting bombarded."[91]

By 14 September 2006, the fight was largely over. 1 RCR BG elements pushing from the north linked-up with their sister elements pushing from

Combat Camera.

An enemy compound burns as members of TF 3-06 prepare to push through to the next objective.

the south. They had seized every last bit of ground from the Taliban, including the village of Bayenzi, which was the home of the infamous white school house complex that was at the centre of the death of so many Canadians.[92]

The two week ordeal, was in the words of Major Marty Lipcsey, the deputy commanding officer of TF 3–06, "quite a battle."[93] Lieutenant-Colonel Lavoie assessed, "the soldiers under my command have proven their courage and determination time and time again."[94] His sentiments were not based on false pride.

With the taking of Objective Rugby the combat phase of Operation Medusa was over. In the end, Fraser assessed, "after all that pressure, after all that time, the enemy just collapsed and they went to ground."[95] The brigade commander immediately ordered TF 3–06 to move from exploitation to reconstruction. By 16 September 2006, 1 RCR BG began to rotate its companies through KAF for rest and refit, maintaining two company groups on security and clearance operations in their area of responsibility. It seemed that by 17 September 2006, Operation Medusa, aside from

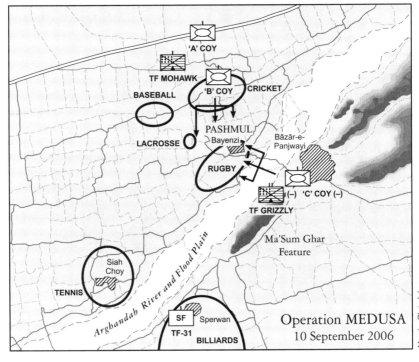

the non-kinetic reconstruction phase, was over. It appeared that the ISAF multinational brigade, but particularly the 1 RCR BG that bore the brunt of the fighting in the Pashmul area, had indeed defeated the Taliban.

The cost, however, was not inconsequential. In total, the Canadians had lost 5 killed and approximately 40 wounded. The fact that Canada bore the brunt of the fighting was not hard to discern. One reporter noted, "Canadians are getting killed at a rate five times the average for NATO and U.S. forces in Afghanistan, where Canada's soldiers have suffered more than one-quarter of the combat deaths in Afghanistan [in 2006]."[96]

The victory, however, was hailed as a monumental success. A NATO statement was swiftly broadcast announcing the victory:

> NATO launched its largest ever combat operation, against a well-prepared and determined enemy. It was fought to the south west of Kandahar City, in the Panshwaye and Zhari districts. It was here that the Taliban filtered in large numbers of insurgents in to first take and then, far more significantly, hold the area. It was a trial of strength that will have a lasting effect both militarily and on the hearts and minds of the Afghan people.[97]

Another NATO missive announced, "The operation has met its initial aims by dealing a severe blow to the leadership and forces of the extremists so that they are no longer a cohesive force and have had to dispense after suffering important losses."[98] A political official was less restrained. He remarked that Operation Medusa, "wiped the floor with the Taliban."[99]

Not surprisingly, NATO leadership used the success to push select messages. General James L. Jones, commander of Allied Command Operations cooed, "It has been necessary to fight in this instance to achieve the required effect. Importantly it has proved that NATO will not shirk from taking robust action where necessary and especially given the level of insurgent activity."[100] Similarly, ISAF Commander Lieutenant-General David Richards boasted:

>Operation Medusa has been a significant success and clearly shows the capability that Afghan, NATO and Coalition forces have when they operate together. I always said that I would be robust when necessary, and that is what I have done. The Taliban had no choice but to leave … Having created a secure environment in the area, it is now time for the real work to start. Without security, there can be no reconstruction and development. Without reconstruction and development there can be no long-lasting security.[101]

According to Lieutenant-General Richards, Operation Medusa was a key battle against the Taliban insurgency. "If Kandahar fell," he explained, "and it was reasonably close run last year, it did not matter how well the Dutch did in Uruzgan or how well the British did in Helmand. Their two provinces would also, as night followed day, have failed because we would have lost the consent of the Pashtun people because of the totemic importance of Kandahar."[102]

The Afghan government also hailed the success of Operation Medusa. Provincial Governor Assadullah Khalid stated on 17 September 2006, "Six nations fought side by side to inflict significant casualties on the entrenched insurgent forces, who could have avoided this sad loss of life by reconciling with the legitimate Afghan government."[103]

He added, "The ability of the Taliban to stay and fight in groups is finished. The enemy has been crushed."[104] Khalid assessed, "This operation in Panjwai and Zhari is one of very few successes in recent years."[105]

The rather effusive praise from senior NATO and Afghan leadership was echoed by some scholars and analysts. Author Barnett Rubin, a respected global authority on Afghanistan, credited "Canada's military for turning back 'a frontal offensive by the Taliban' in Panjwai last summer and for rescuing Afghanistan from what he considers 'a tipping point.'"[106]

The largely Canadian ground action did not go unheralded by its national command either. The CDS at the time, General Rick Hillier, asserted, "Afghan ministers will tell you that operation [Medusa] saved Afghanistan." He explained, "If Kandahar had been encircled, if Highway

1 had been shut down and if the Panjwai had been held by the Taliban, the government in Kabul would have fallen."[107] Hillier concluded, "By taking on the Taliban in the Panjwayi District of Kandahar and bloodying their noses, Operation Medusa saved the fragile government of Afghanistan and allowed it to continue to make progress."[108]

Brigadier-General Fraser revealed that "The ISAF commander was ecstatic." Fraser stated: "He [Richards] just could not believe what we were able to accomplish." The brigade commander elaborated, "He was very enthusiastic, I mean psychologically, what our troops did was impressive. They saved the city of Kandahar, arguably saved the country and they saved the alliance. They proved that NATO could fight as a coalition.[109] The MNB commander concluded, "We defeated the Taliban with only five of our casualties [killed]. Then the Taliban tried to bug out one night. Not many made it out. We saved the city, and in so doing, [we] saved the country."[110] NATO's initial assessment claimed 512 Taliban were killed and 136 captured.[111]

Lieutenant-Colonel Schreiber stated, "it is a conservative estimate that the Taliban suffered 1,500 casualties (1,000 wounded, 500 dead)."[112] Brigadier-General Fraser's assessment was similar. "We think we probably killed about 300 to 400 and captured 136, which includes the death of approximately five senior commanders on the ground." He added, "that is a significant defeat, the worst defeat the Taliban ever experienced in probably 40 years according to the Afghan Minister of Defence."[113] A strategist analyst concluded, "in all, the defense of Pashmul was an unqualified disaster for the Taliban."[114]

Operation Medusa proved to be a major turning point for both the Taliban and the CF. For the Taliban they learned they could not fight ISAF in a conventional manner and so they turned to asymmetric tactics. For the Army and The RCR, the war had now become its overwhelming core focus. Casualties, creeping force employment numbers, a nine- to 12-month "road to high readiness" (RTHR) training cycle to prepare battle groups to go overseas simply depleted Army numbers. Even the heavy reliance on reservists was not enough to assist with the crushing pressure on the Army to force generate the necessary troops to deploy overseas.

The voracious appetite of the war seemed endless. Moreover, the personnel cuts of the 1990s now came home to roost. The other services were pressed to provide personnel for base support functions at KAF. The Army's recruiting numbers were increased to grow the Army as well, and within the Army, personnel were taken from wherever they could be found to plug into a deployment hole.

Moreover, by 2007, promotions to fill leadership gaps had reached unheard-of numbers. For instance, in 1992 infantry promotions were frozen, and the following year only three captains were promoted to major. During the 1990s, 10 promotions at any rank level were seen as an exceptionally good year. By 2007–08, promotions from captain to majors were reaching into the 40s. Often, promotions would be curtailed because a regiment had already reached its lowest possible acceptable quality control line.

Training was also affected. Vehicle and equipment damage meant more and more stock had to be dispatched to theatre to ensure they had the necessary tools. According to an official DND report, "This has meant that all field force units with the exception of the infantry battle group training for the high readiness Afghan task have had to work with severely reduced equipment holdings to support the nominal individual and low level collective training that was authorized at their home units."[115] The high operational tempo in the Afghan Theatre of Operations (ATO) also resulted in a high demand for spare parts, which had a cascading effect on the availability of spare parts for the remainder of the field force in Canada. This resulted in high numbers of vehicles unable to be repaired at home, thus limiting training even further.[116]

In fact, by 2005, the Army introduced the Managed Readiness Training Fleet (MRTF), which was part of the Army's Whole Fleet Management process. This was a plan for the land forces to reallocate training and operational vehicles into strategically controlled fleets. In practice the formations and units were stripped of most of their tactical vehicles and equipment to create separate training fleets. The biggest fleet was held at the Combat Manoeuvre Training Centre (CMTC) in Wainwright. It consisted of enough major vehicles to equip a battle group undergoing training. It was estimated that this centralized fleet would save both time and money by reducing the vehicle and equipment transit costs. The other was in CFB Gagetown.[117]

In the end, a DND report concluded, "When a field force formation or unit is not the designated RTHR organization, they will only have a residual vehicle or equipment capability resident in their locations with which to train. To bring the training fleets up to their authorized strengths field force unit tactical vehicle and equipment holdings have been reduced to the point where some armoured reconnaissance squadrons and mechanized infantry companies lack vehicles to train on."[118]

The cost of the war did not escape The RCR. It paid the price in killed and wounded. In addition, the battalions became consumed in preparing to deploy; assisting those preparing to deploy; and providing individuals and sub-units to fill war time tasks either to other BGs, or to the PRT, or to the growing number of Operational Mentor Liaison Teams (OMLT) that were sprouting up to train, shadow, and mentor ANSF organizations.

And so, by mid-October the war was far from over. In fact, it became the preoccupation of the Army. Importantly, The RCR had fought NATO's first real ground battle and in the process signalled to the world that Canada was once again willing to commit its forces to combat, finally driving the "Canadian peacekeeper" myth into the ground. But the worst was not yet over. The Taliban had suffered a major defeat as a result of Operation Medusa, but they also learned from their failure. They now evolved into a much deadlier foe. For Royals serving in Afghanistan, the war was about to evolve into a much more complex and lethal conflict.

9

The Difficult War: Hard Service in Afghanistan

The hard-fought victory during Operation Medusa was applauded by Afghan, Canadian, and NATO commanders and officials. However, its enduring effect was fleeting. In fact, it was the period of reconstruction that proved to be deadlier than Operation Medusa itself, as a combination of roadside bombs, suicide bombers, as well as combat and mine strikes killed another 10 Canadian soldiers in the month that followed the capture of Objective Rugby.

As early as 18 September 2006, in an attempt to regain the initiative, the Taliban carried out three separate attacks, which to that point in time became one of Afghanistan's bloodiest days. In Kafir Band a suicide bomber hit a foot patrol, killing four soldiers from the 1 RCR BG and 24 children. In Kabul the same day a car bomber killed four ANP, and that night in Herat, another suicide bomber killed 11 people outside city's main mosque.[1] And the Taliban were certainly not prepared to surrender the Pashmul area to the GIRoA or Coalition forces. One Taliban fighter stated: "No Muslim wants the human garbage of foreign soldiers in Afghanistan." He explained, "We were ready to fight, but there was lots of bombs, lots of dust. It was hard to see. So we decided to fight somewhere else."[2]

In essence, realizing their error in attempting to fight in a symmetrical manner, the Taliban recalibrated their efforts and returned to their former methodology of intimidation, assassinations, and terror. But significantly, they also seemed to abandon any reservations they may have had about suicide bombers and the widespread, unrestricted use of IEDs. They now embraced whatever methods were required to beat their foe.

So, despite NATO's declaration of victory, there appeared to be some confusion as to the long-term impact or actual victory that was won as a result of the successful actions by the 1 RCR BG and Coalition forces in Pashmul between 3 and 14 September 2006. Although they had soundly defeated the Taliban's attempt at concentrating forces and holding ground, they had also pushed the Taliban to evolve into a much more dangerous and difficult foe to fight.[3] In essence, Operation Medusa forced the Taliban to adopt asymmetric attacks as their operational methodology. As such, the fight evolved into a much more complex, frustrating, and lethal war.[4]

The reality of the "long war" quickly made itself felt to the Royals.[5] The struggle now took on an exponentially more difficult and dangerous turn. The enemy faced with his lopsided defeat in Panjwayi learned the lesson that he could not face NATO forces in a traditional conventional attritional confrontation. As such, the Taliban transitioned to more asymmetric means, utilizing suicide bombers, IEDs, and intimidation of the local populace. "The Taliban reverted to their asymmetric tactics, which had made them far more dangerous," acknowledged Lieutenant-Colonel Schreiber, the MNB operations officer. "They've now re-infiltrated into this area [Pashmul], small groups of highly motivated fighters, tier one Taliban, many of them foreign fighters, Chechens, Tagiks, Arabs and they're now conducting a very effective asymmetric campaign that relies mostly on IEDs and IED ambushes."[6]

Intelligence officer and former Royal Captain Tim Button assessed, "Medusa achieved a 12 month effect. We watched how the Taliban changed the way they did business in a major way." Button emphasized, "We will never again see them mass together to attack. We drove their commanders underground and they were unable to openly exercise their command. But not concentrating force also makes it harder to find them. We reinforced their need to act asymmetrically." He concluded, "We don't see large opportunities to target them."[7]

Moreover, the Taliban also focused on disrupting reconstruction. In sum, the Taliban tactics were now more difficult to counter and made the struggle for the support of the local people increasingly difficult. Regardless, Afghan and NATO officials now pushed the 1 RCR BG hard to begin reconstruction. However, it was not as simple as that. Although reconstruction and development were key drivers to winning the support of the people or in the popular jargon, their "hearts and minds," the security problem was not yet solved. Lieutenant-Colonel Lavoie lamented, "we are under pressure to get on with reconstruction," yet the "fight isn't won yet." He explained, that the Taliban "was still very strong" and added that the enemy "must be defeated first for lasting reconstruction."[8]

What many unfamiliar with counterinsurgency fail to realize is that security and development are not mutually exclusive activities. Rather, they are mutually supporting. Quite simply there is no reconstruction and development without security, and no security without reconstruction and development. Each feeds the other. The local population must feel secure and safe from Taliban retribution if they are to assist the government and Coalition efforts. Without adequate protection they will remain neutral and aloof at best, or, at worst they will passively or actively support the insurgent efforts.[9] Afghan local Haji Gailani questioned, "You have planes. You can hear the Taliban on your radios. And still you cannot force them out of here. How can we?"[10] As one authoritative report concluded, "Security is the most basic precondition for civilian support of the government ... the motivation that provides the only real long lasting effect is the elemental consideration of survival."[11]

Without the support of the people, it becomes difficult, if not impossible, to gain intelligence on enemy activity and intentions. As such, much effort is spent on force protection that detracts from reconstruction and development, since there are only a finite number of resources in theatre. More important, it becomes extremely difficult to determine who is actually is the enemy. "We're trying to win the hearts and minds of the people," insisted Lavoie, "yet, we have to defend against the asymmetric threat."[12] Another Royal was more blunt. "We still think everyone approaching us wants to kill us," explained Captain Ryan Carey. "We have no choice but to plan for a fight right till we leave."[13]

A LAV III, from 7 Platoon, Charles Coy, 1 RCR provides security on Route Summit during its construction, October 2006.

For the Royals in the field, like those before them who struggled with counterinsurgency throughout history, it was the asymmetric nature of the conflict that created both frustrations as well as tangible delays in advancing the reconstruction and development agenda. Lavoie shrugged his shoulders as he admitted there was a full range of problems he and his troops faced. "The greatest source of frustration is intelligence," he conceded, "there is frustration working in an environment where it is so difficult to identify friend from foe." He explained, "within Patrol Base Wilson (PBW) we know there are Taliban operatives." Lavoie lamented, "when senior ANA or ANP officers in the headquarters are sending the Taliban information on our plans its difficult to operate." Moreover, he added, "in the field a farmer drops his shovel and picks up an AK-47 and transitions from a non-combatant to a combatant seamlessly."[14]

One young officer reinforced, "You don't know who your enemy is. One minute they will be walking down the street and have a woman and

Author photograph.

Warrant Officer Ray McFarlane coordinates between his platoon and a co-located ANA detachment in response to a reported Taliban incursion, October 2006.

children surrounding them and the next the woman and children will disappear and he [the enemy] will be firing at you."[15] Another NCO described:

> It was a real 360 degree battlefield out there. You never know where it is going to come from. The Taliban are quite good at getting behind you. Snap ambushes are what they are good at. We are getting dicked [informed on] all the time. They use a cordless phone with a 30 km range on it. As soon as we left somewhere and went anywhere, they knew about it. Their network was awesome and it aided them in laying ambushes and IEDs.
>
> They attack you when you are least expecting it. We made two mistakes and they punished us for that.[16]

But the pressures, strains, and realities of the soldier fighting the battle and those of their superiors are not the same. In fact, they are not even compatible, and the divergence between immediate interests and requirements grows wider as one rises up the hierarchal chain of command. To Lavoie and his soldiers, survival was one of the key, if not the primary, concerns. They fought the daily running battle with the Taliban and knew, regardless of the press reports and what their superiors were saying, the Taliban was still very much active and deadly in their area of operations.

However, Lavoie faced a cascading flow of scepticism and concern — starting from political masters in a number of NATO countries, including his own, down through their national, as well as NATO command chains. All were clamouring for results. It was not enough to declare victory in the press — NATO had to actually show it. Anxious to demonstrate that progress was being made to placate demanding national governments and politicians, the pressure on field commanders became enormous.

Lavoie constantly felt the pressure. "Its hard to convince headquarters of the reality on the ground," he bemoaned. "They've never been forward — they have not visited the troops forward, yet they don't believe I can't start phase IV reconstruction even though I've lost seven guys on this road [Route Summit]."[17] Lavoie's reference to Route Summit was a new road that he was now building between Highway 1 and Ma'Sūm Ghar in Pashmul to increase security and to provide a better road network to assist economic development in the area. The road project was a direct result of operations conducted during Operation Medusa.[18] The battle group had lost some soldiers on the existing road in Pashmul because it was narrow and cut through close country that was ideal for ambushes and IED placement. The governor had not come through with the promised ANA or ANP support to monitor the existing road so Lavoie decided to find an alternate route. He checked with brigade headquarters, and no one said no, so he promptly began to cut a great swath through the local cannabis fields.[19]

"I never thought I would be doing this," shrugged Lavoie. "We're supposed to be doing Phase IV Resettlement and Reconstruction and the ANA are supposed to do security but they haven't shown up." He pointed out, "Building the road is the only way to do it." He explained that it was short-term security for the region, his forward operating base (FOB) at Ma'Sūm Ghar, and long-term development and security for Pashmul, as it provided access on a defendable high speed road.[20]

But the project also had a negative side. With few ANSF to assist with the static defence and security of the road construction project, Lavoie was forced to use his battle group, which was already short-handed because of the casualties sustained during Operation Medusa, who had not yet been replaced, and the commencement of the home leave travel allowance (HLTA) rotation system, which was based on sending complete sections out of theatre at a time.[21] As such, low on personnel and with virtually no assistance from the ANSF, Task Force 3–06 was forced to take up static locations at various FOBs and strong points to defend the road construction.[22] With this approach, they surrendered the initiative and the ability to dominate the ground and became static targets tied to infrastructure.

To aggravate the situation even more, Lavoie noted that higher headquarters consistently tried to assign additional tasks, despite Lavoie's forces being stretched thin to provide security over the road construction and other FOBs within his AOR, all a direct result of a failure of host nation forces being made available to undertake static security tasks.[23] "NATO headquarters," Lavoie lamented, "often are unrealistic in their taskings — too often they have too great an appetite." He added, "I've had to say no on a number of occasions."[24] Lavoie sadly pointed out, "I've been forward on 15 of the 17 KIA [killed in action] to see the bodies being put into the body bags." He asserted, "That's a lot different than a casket being loaded on an airplane." With frustration, Lavoie insisted that "Higher HQ needs to see that." He explained that he was having difficulty convincing his seniors of the reality on the ground. "They've never been forward, the commander has not visited the troops forward, he hasn't seen the road," noted Lavoie. "I lost seven guys out here and he's never come," lamented the CO, "[yet he] doesn't believe we can't start Phase IV reconstruction."[25]

And so, with the kinetic phase of Operation Medusa behind them, the soldiers of the 1 RCR BG began transitioning into the "long war." Trying to both support reconstruction and development, as well as secure the wider area and fight the Taliban, TF 3–06 soon found themselves tied down in a static posture that gave the enemy the initiative. Embedded reporter Les Perreaux observed, "In those 19 days, soldiers attacked mercilessly to drive out Taliban forces and [then] watched helplessly as the Taliban drifted back in."[26] Not surprisingly, the Taliban seized on the opportunity and attempted to gain their own retribution for their costly defeat in September.

The daily routine soon turned into one of tedium punctuated by moments of terror. Soldiers endured the relentless heat and tolerated the irritating and constant dust churned up by any movement whether vehicle, human, or wind. The fine talcum powder–like sand covered everything, and it was impossible to keep anything clean. Adding to the misery were the unremitting sand fleas and flies that tortured the soldiers without pause.

Nonetheless, TF 3–06, which had an area of operations spanning approximately 60,000 square kilometres, found itself protecting Route Summit, which cut a 100-metre wide swath straight through the marijuana fields and grape vineyards. Its wide berth and straight trajectory provided easy observation, control, and security. More important, this easily accessible road, which would eventually be paved, would furnish local farmers with an excellent route that would allow produce and trade to transit quickly from the fertile Arghandab River valley to Highway 1, the major artery leading to Kandahar City and elsewhere.

The brunt of the defence of the road fell to Charles Coy Gp. They soon found themselves in a constant battle of wits with the enemy. The Taliban harassed the thinly stretched troops persistently. During the night they would stealthily plant IEDs and mines in the sandy furrow that currently represented the road. In addition, the Taliban deployed small teams that would attempt to surprise and ambush the Canadian troops. They had already immobilized two bulldozers and several other vehicles through IED and mine strikes.

The terrain once again assisted the insurgents. The tall marijuana fields and grape vineyards, interspersed with mud walls and sun baked mud huts that had the consistency of fortified strongholds, obscured visibility and allowed the Taliban concealed and protected manoeuvre space. Armed with the initiative and forgiving terrain, the Taliban kept up a constant pressure, hitting particularly hard on 14 October 2006, in an example of their increasing sophistication. The day started like so many others. Lieutenant-Colonel Lavoie rolled down the sandy strip that revealed the beginnings of a new road with his four vehicle convoy to coordinate with his sub-units and verify defences and progress being made. He quickly came across C/S 33A. Their LAV III, which was located half way between the 7 and 9 Platoons positions, had backed over an IED and the vehicle had become a mobility kill. Luckily, no one was injured. Unfortunately, the task force had just lost another precious vehicle that would be hard to replace.

Significantly, the IED had been placed in the middle of the unfinished road about 400 metres from 7 Platoon's defensive position, which was co-located with a small ANA detachment. Everyone was mystified as to how this had transpired. How had the "ghosts of Panjwayi" planted it without being seen? But an IED strike was not an uncommon occurrence, and efforts soon turned to recovering the vehicle back to Patrol Base Wilson.

As the morning wore on, members of 7 Platoon continued with their surveillance duty in the growing heat. Those not on duty within the LAV III or at sentry positions sheltered themselves under a tarp behind the protection of a low wall that was situated between two buildings that had been partially destroyed in recent fighting during Operation Medusa. On the opposite side of the wall ran a canal in which an ANA detachment had taken residence. The ANA operated several observation posts that were constructed to control the old road and the terrain to the West.

The members of the platoon had been in the field in this threat environment for 23 days straight. They slept, ate, and tried to relax in the filth that surrounded them. They slept on thermarest mattresses on the ground with their body armour at their side. Water was in short supply, and facilities lacking — washing clothes was unheard of and personal hygiene was limited. The incessant dust covered everything and made maintenance of weapons and vehicles a constant concern. Conditions were primitive.

At approximately 1100 hours, a radio message arrived stating that a group of three Taliban had been seen to the West of 7 Platoon's position.

Warrant Officer Ray McFarlane, the Platoon Warrant/second-in command (2IC), and Sergeant Donovan Crawford quickly coordinated with
the ANA detachment. After patiently spending time trying to convey
the message to the ANA leader who understood some English, and with
a large degree of innovative sign language, the message was passed and
the ANA mobilized. With members of 7 Platoon close by, with their 60
mm mortar ready to engage in the fight, the ANA sent a small patrol out
several hundred metres from the position to investigate the sighting.

A short time later excited voices could be heard close by, followed by
the "whoosh" and explosion of an RPG 7 rocket and the crack of some
small arms fire. Within minutes the ANA soldiers returned with great
big smiles gesturing with a wave of the hand and a simple "Taliban gone."
McFarlane was unable to ascertain whether the Taliban had been killed
or simply scattered. Each question elicited the same grunts and nodding
of heads from the ANA patrol. Nonetheless, the threat seemed to have
dissipated for the moment.

Meanwhile, several kilometres down the road to the South, 9 Platoon
(C/S 33) manned its position. It was given the designation Strong Point
Centre, aptly named since it was the middle position within the battle
group's defensive network that followed the path of the new road from
Patrol Base Wilson on Highway 1 to the imposing Ma'Sūm Ghar mountain feature, where "A" Coy, which had been seconded from the 2 PPCLI,
was constructing the new FOB Zettlemeyer, named after the engineer
vehicle that was struck on 3 September. Strong Point Centre was a formidable position based around an imposing mud structure built on a small
outcropping that dominated the road and the surrounding area.

The platoon used the natural lay of the land to anchor their defence.
Two LAV IIIs flanked the position and covered the western approach and
the road. To their front lay a 100-metre swath of sand and beyond that marijuana fields, grape vineyards, and an array of mud compounds and grape
drying huts. Visibility was limited. Sheltered behind the large mud building
that was the centre point of the defensive position and protected by a natural wall to its other side, another LAV III aimed its deadly 25 mm cannon
to the north covering the road approach. Finally, dug into the raised island
that was Strong Point Centre were two machine-gun pits. One faced south

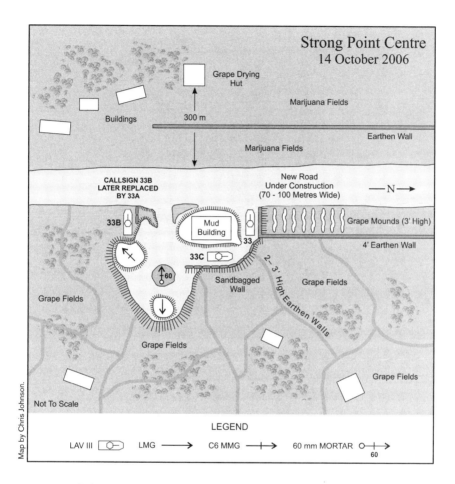

to control the road, while the other faced east to cover the close terrain, mainly grape vineyards, which bordered the defensive position. The platoon had augmented the natural fortress with a series of sandbagged walls.

Much like 7 Platoon, the soldiers rotated between sentry duty in the LAVs or in the machine-gun posts and catching up on sleep or a meal. Manpower was especially tight, since the section in the IED strike in the morning was back at PBW getting checked out medically for any injuries sustained during the blast. The incidents of the morning seemed to harbour no sinister omens and were largely forgotten. After all, those types of events were virtually everyday occurrences.

Back at 7 Platoon, at approximately 1430 hours, the gunner in the turret of the LAV covering south along the road and the vast fields to

A Charles Coy, 1 RCR LAV positioned in the heart of Strong Point Centre on Route Summit in the Panjwayi provides observation and security for the road development project.

A Royal on OP Dragon working through the Afghan challenge – close terrain, heat, and heavy loads.

the east, summoned Warrant Officer McFarlane. Out in the grape vine-yards, approximately 200–300 metres away, six men, ostensibly "farm-ers" as they carried no weapons, calmly walked south through the fields in single file toward a large grape drying hut located approximately 400 metres from 7 Platoon's position. RoEs forbade firing on unarmed civilians regardless of how suspicious they appeared. The Taliban were aware of this and used their ability to blend in with the normal farmers to their advantage. Identifying friend from foe was one of the great-est challenges in this environment. Royals had observed fighting age males in the fields on many occasions, but whether they were legiti-mate farmers or Taliban posing as such was difficult to ascertain. With cached weapons throughout the area, the enemy could transform from one to the other and back again very quickly. Determining who was the enemy, as well as being able to physically dominate the ground and sweep it for weapons, was almost impossible because of the shortage of personnel.

Unable to send soldiers on a patrol to investigate, McFarlane attempted to convince the ANA to follow-up; however, the ANA claimed they too lacked the troops to wander out into the fields to scrutinize the suspicious party. Quite simply, without direct Canadian participation, they would not venture out. As a result, McFarlane was forced to try and keep surveillance on the individuals as long as possible, since he was unable to take any other action. Not surprisingly, the "farmers" quickly melted away into the maze of walls, buildings, and vegetation.

At approximately 1450 hours, some visitors (i.e. members of the PRT and some local Afghan officials) started to congregate at the front of strong point centre. They were awaiting the CO's convoy for a ride back to PBW. Lieutenant Ray Corby, who had taken over as 9 Platoon commander three weeks earlier when casualties incurred at the start of Operation Medusa forced a reorganization, tried to speak to the visit-ing district chief but was brushed off. Corby then turned his attention to the Civil Military Co-operation (CIMIC) detachment commander, Chief Warrant Officer Fred Gratton. However, he was interrupted three times in a span of less than 10 minutes by the district chief who persis-tently asked when his ride would be arriving. During that same period the district chief received two phone calls on his cell phone and placed another call himself. He seemed desperately eager to leave.

The CO arrived at Strong Point Centre at approximately 1455 hours and dismounted to briefly discuss details of the earlier IED incident with Lieutenant Corby, while the visiting personnel at the location loaded onto the vehicles that made up the CO's tactical HQ (or 9er Tac). Just as the vehicles were in the midst of loading, a threat warning came over the air — "a Canadian position was in imminent threat of attack." The grid given was uncomfortably close to their current position. The soldiers had learned to dread these threat warnings — they were usually accurate. Inside Strong Point Centre, the warning was relayed verbally to Corby. As he formulated his next course of action, the initiative was wrested away from him. Less than a minute passed from the time he was given the notice to all hell breaking loose.

The initial barrage of enemy fire caught the soldiers of Charles Coy by surprise. The attack commenced with multiple RPGs being fired at the position. A minimum of three RPGs were fired in close succession, targeting C/S 33B, which was manning the southwest perimeter of the position, an empty trench on the western flank of the strongpoint, and the OP on the south east of the defensive position that contained a C-6 general purpose machine gun (GPMG). A high volume of small arms fire also hit the position. Some rounds impacted short and kicked up the dust on the new road while others cracked over the heads of the Charles Coy troops.

Lieutenant Corby was in the midst of discussing the platoon's course of action with Sergeant Jamie Walsh. As the RPG rockets and small arms fire rained in, reaction was immediate. Corby and Walsh dove for cover behind a small berm located behind C/S 33C, which was the LAV in the centre of the position. From this vantage point, looking toward the southwest, they could see smoke coming from the tree line and marijuana fields, as well as rounds splashing across the sand of the new road toward them. Visibility was quickly obscured as the dust was kicked up by the fire. Nevertheless, it seemed the concentration of the enemy attack was coming from the west. As such, the insurgents had the bright sun at their backs to mask their movement and blind the defenders.

Royals preparing to move into yet another objective.

The Canadians on sentry duty responded with alacrity. The 25 mm cannons on the LAVs, aided by their thermal sights that could see through the dust, thundered in reply, supported by light machine guns and GPMGs while the others quickly manned their fighting positions. When the storm struck, Private Jesse Larochelle was in the south-most machine-gun pit. The enemy attack washed over him like a rogue wave. His position erupted in explosions, as bullets and shrapnel hissed through the air around him. Larochelle thought he was hallucinating as he saw seemingly mini-explosions go off above his outpost. Little did he realize at the time that the enemy was using RPG munitions that emitted mini cluster rounds from their 75 mm warheads, which in turn exploded spraying deadly shrapnel much like an air-burst round. Despite the weight of fire, he continued to fire at his invisible antagonists, who were cloaked by the tree line.

Close by, the CO's tactical HQ had just started to roll when an RPG rocket swished to the rear and exploded in a ball of flame approximately 80 metres behind the convoy, where mere minutes prior, the CO, platoon commander, and others had been standing. The three LAVs and the

RG-31 Nyala armoured vehicle, which made up the tactical HQ, quickly swung around and immediately began to engage the enemy, adding an enormous amount of fire into the fields and buildings to the west from where the enemy assault was originating.

Unfortunately, it was a bit too late. As the "pum-pum-pum" of the 25 mm cannons echoed across the battlefield, the first SITREP cut through the noise of the battlefield and hit everyone as if they had been struck through the heart with a spike — "two VSA [vital signs absent], three wounded." Stark reality once again set in.

As Operation Medusa had shown, the Taliban are little match for the Western forces in either equipment or firepower. As a result, they rely on surprise, either through IEDs, mines, or ambushes. And they depend on achieving success in the first 30 seconds of the engagement before they become engulfed in return fire. Once again they got lucky.

The crew and section of C/S 33B were resting when the attack commenced. Private Jesse Kezar was in the driver's hatch and Corporal Jeremy Penney was in the gunner's seat when the initial barrage of fire hit. Penney attempted to fire the 25 mm gun, but the cannon jammed. Corporal Darryl Jones was in the process of moving into the turret from the rear of the LAV when the RPG round struck around the vehicle's laser warning tower. The resultant explosion showered the area with shrapnel, as lethal shards of metal and blast washed down through the rear air sentry hatch and over the back deck, killing one soldier who had been seated on the left bench and wounding another who was seated on the right bench. The same round also killed the section commander and wounded two others who were at the back of the LAV.

At exactly the same time, at 1500 hours, 7 Platoon was also hit. PKM machine-gun fire and RPGs engulfed the surprised troops. Bullets stitched their way along the wall that soldiers earlier had rested against, kicking up dirt and forcing all to find cover. The fire emanated from the grape-drying hut, where the six "farmers" were seen heading to earlier. The platoon replied in rapid succession, bringing all its firepower to bear, as well as that of the neighbouring ANA. During the contact, as many as 20–30 enemy were sighted in this area alone. Notwithstanding the enemy's strength, the situation was brought under control.

Back at 9 Platoon, Sergeant Walsh organized his section to better engage the enemy in their location. He placed Corporal Nick Damchuk, and Privates Jay Royer and Garret Achneepineskum behind a small berm directly behind his LAV, C/S 33C, where they laid down suppressing fire to the area west of the stronghold. Walsh then deployed Corporal Chris Saumure and Private Ed Runyon-Lloyd at the front of the LAV to observe for enemy activity to the east of the position. Corporal Mike Lisk was in the turret of C/S 33C, and he was soon joined by Master-Corporal Rob Murphy, who used the small escape hatch on the side of the LAV to crawl up into the turret. Because of the lack of enemy activity in their primary arcs to the northeast of the position, Murphy traversed the turret over the back deck of the LAV so that the cannon could be fired to the southwest. He then used the height of the pintle-mounted machine gun to fire over the high feature to their front to add extra firepower to the fight. All the while, Corporal Jeff Morin began redistributing ammunition to the section as the scale of the combat quickly depleted the immediate supply.

Simultaneously, Lieutenant Corby quickly moved to his HQ LAV that was sited on the north side of the position to ensure a contact report had been sent out. As he neared his vehicle, he could see the crew was busy engaging a large number of enemy directly to the west. Corporal Morgan Gonci had been in the driver's hatch before the attack. As the first few rockets exploded nearby, he could feel the LAV shake. Corporal James White, observing from the gunner's seat, also felt C/S 33 reel as an RPG rocket hit the front right side of the LAV, ripping off some of its up-armour plating. With the onset of the attack, Sergeant Craig Dinsmore crawled up through the rear of the vehicle into the crew commander's seat, and Corporal Gonci immediately began to provide target indication from the driver's hatch. At the same time Corporals Shane Robertson and Joey Paolini jumped into the back of LAV and raised the ramp. As Corby arrived, he banged repeatedly on the back door until it was opened. He then instructed Robertson and Paolini to provide security to the north of C/S 33 to ensure the enemy did not outflank their position.

Corby now took a headset and sent a supplementary contact report on the company net. He also requested a fire mission, sending his exact location, the distance to the enemy and the bearing of 4800 mils. Fortuitously,

Major Greg Ivey, G29 the CO's affiliated battery commander who travelled in the 9er Tac convoy, was already in the process of calling in artillery support. Within 10 minutes of the start of the engagement, 155 mm rounds exploded with an earth shaking "krummpp" 400 metres away, danger close, from Strong Point Centre. In addition, word was passed over the net that "AH" (Apache attack helicopters) were on their way.

Satisfied that the call for fire was taken care of, Corby now tried to raise his sections on the radio to get a more accurate read on the battle. He began with the OP with the GPMG, as it had the highest vantage point. He became concerned when he received no reply. His second call went to C/S 33B to the south of the position. Corby received a SITREP from Corporal Jones, who was in the turret of the 2 Section LAV. Jones informed the platoon commander that they had two casualties who were vital signs absent. He also requested a medic to look after the other three wounded soldiers. Corby questioned Jones on the extent of the other injuries and determined that they were not critical.

Luckily there was an advanced qualified soldier to administer first aid. However, he, Master-Corporal Jeremy Leblanc, was in dire need of additional medical supplies. As a result, Corby decided not to risk his only medic by sending her across exposed terrain in light of the heavy volume of enemy fire. Instead, Corby grabbed the medical bag and made his way to 2 Section's location himself.

Meanwhile Paolini and Robertson, on the outside of the HQ vehicle, were busy engaging the enemy. Between the two soldiers they saw two separate groups, five individuals in total, with small arms and RPGs engaging their position.

Out on the road, the CO's convoy continued to pour fire into the buildings, wood line, and marijuana fields. At about this time, Corby moved back to C/S 33C, which occupied the centre of the platoon position. He looked across at C/S 33B and could see that the turret was still firing. He quickly informed Sergeant Walsh of his plan to run the medical bag first to the OP and then to C/S 33B's location. Damchuk and Achneepineskum proceeded to lay down a wall of suppressive fire as Corby made his mad dash.

To get to 2 Section's LAV, he first had to pass by the southernmost OP. Corby did not expect to find anyone alive. As he arrived at the bowl in the centre of the strongpoint position, which was also the casualty collection point, he was able to get eyes on the OP. At first glance it had appeared that the OP had been struck hard. He could not see anyone, and the tarp that had been hung above the outpost to provide shade had been torn away by the fire, hanging in tattered rags. Close by he could see the empty casings of four M72 launchers.

Corby called out twice to the OP. He finally got a response. Private Larochelle poked his head up with his C-6 and confirmed he was "okay" and "by himself." The platoon commander then directed Larochelle to provide covering fire so he could enter the OP. Larochelle then pointed out where he had been engaging the enemy with his C-9 LMG, the C-6 GPMG, and the M72s. The firefight had been so brisk that Larochelle was down to his last half belt of 7.62 mm GPMG ammunition. He had weathered the storm and continued to fire at any movement or weapon signature he could see. He also maintained his discipline and continued to observe his arcs of fire to ensure no enemy was approaching from the east, even though he was taking heavy fire from the west.

Corby was humbled by the young soldier's valiant efforts.[27] However, he had no time to reflect on Larochelle's courage — there was work to be done. Corby now instructed Larochelle to lay down more fire so he could make his final way to 2 Section's (C/S 33B) LAV. Corby promised that when he returned he would bring additional ammo.

After the first deadly RPG strike, Corporal Jones had remedied the gun malfunction and started to return fire. A second RPG round then hit C/S 33B, setting off the automatic fire extinguishing system in the LAV. When Corby arrived, he quickly recognized that they had in fact suffered two killed. Master-Corporal Leblanc, who himself was wounded, had bandaged up the casualties, while the rest of the section were on the line busy returning fire from a sandbagged wall they had constructed next to the LAV position. Once patched up, Corporals Chris Dowhan and Chris Meace joined their section on the firing line.

By this time the Charles Coy soldiers were about 15–20 minutes into the fight. Corby now sent another SITREP to his company HQ. He learned that the company second-in-command was on the scene with numerous other LAVs to lend a hand. Corby then recommended that they form a firing line north of his position and orient themselves to the southwest so that they could assist in suppressing the enemy's heavy fire into Strong Point Centre.

As the battle dispositions were discussed, Jones reported a second stoppage of the cannon. Master-Corporal Leblanc, despite his wounds, switched places with Jones in an attempt to rectify the stoppage. However, becoming faint and weak from loss of blood, he was pulled from the turret, and Jones returned to do what he could.

Lieutenant Corby was happy to learn that 1 Section, which had hit the IED in the morning, was on its way back out with a replacement LAV, which had arrived into theatre fresh off the assembly line in London, Ontario. However, his morale took a hit when he heard that the Bison ambulance that accompanied it was now disabled because of a mechanical breakdown. As a result, he decided to use the battle damaged C/S 33B to evacuate the dead and wounded to PBW. This would get his soldiers back to PBW for medical attention quickly, and C/S 33A could provide the necessary reinforcements and added firepower

By now the Taliban were largely suppressed. The weight of fire and dreaded artillery, which impeded insurgent movement, swung the battle to the advantage of the TF 3–06 soldiers. But this was of no surprise to the Taliban. They were acutely aware of Coalition tactics, techniques, and procedures (TTPs), and knew exactly how long it would take for Coalition resources to be fed into the battle. To further complicate the response, the Taliban often coordinated attacks to buy themselves more time. Today, they hit simultaneously at five different locations throughout the AO.

With the enemy suppressed and the dead and wounded evacuated, Corby now put his thoughts to securing the position for the night. His position remained on "100 percent stand-to." To ensure he could hold the position, reinforcements and a resupply of ammunition were brought into the strong point. In addition, F-18 and F-16 fighter aircraft remained on station the entire night providing observation and fire when required. At one point an air strike lit up the darkness with a bright orange wall of flame — a beautiful sight in a rather macabre sort of way. To the soldiers holding the road, the sound of fighter aircraft streaking overhead was reassuring.

At 0700 hours, elements of 4 Platoon arrived to relieve the exhausted 9 Platoon, joining a 4 Platoon section that had come in during the night to reinforce the position. The relief in place went smoothly. The whole of 4 Platoon had already done a stint of duty at Strong Point Centre several weeks earlier. For 9 Platoon it was a bittersweet moment. They had weathered the storm well and shown resilience and courage. Tragically, they lost another two of their comrades.

The attack on 14 October 2006, was one of the larger attacks. But the war of the flea, continued with Taliban executing their incessant attacks against the Canadians who were stuck guarding infrastructure. By end November, approximately two months after the end of Operation Medusa, American SOF estimated the strength of the Taliban back in the Pashmul area at 800.[28] As a result, another operation was required to try and clear out the insurgents to allow for reconstruction and development.

Regional Headquarters (South) (RC [S]), which became the formal title of the formation headquarters, replacing the multinational brigade HQ title once NATO took full responsibility for Afghanistan in October 2006, set about preparing for another large operation. It assessed that a high level of insurgent activity continued to emanate from the Zhari/Panjwayi districts. The formation level staff officers claimed that although the local population was seeking an end to the violence, there existed "hard core" Taliban, assessed as "mostly foreign to the area," who still viewed the areas as a key battleground. As such, ISAF directed planners to create the conditions to force the enemy out of the area to allow the local population to take over responsibility for the first line of security reinforced by a smaller but enduring presence of ISAF and ANA troops. ISAF deemed this as a precondition for further development of the Kandahar ADZ.

The RC(S) assessment underlined what Lavoie had been trying to convince his superiors of for a long time. The formation intelligence officers noted that the insurgents continued to conduct reinforcing and resupply operations with relative ease into the Zhari/Panjwayi districts as a result of their rat lines emanating from the nearby Regestan Desert and other lines of communication to the west. The intelligence analysts concluded that the influx of weapons, particularly mortars, enabled the enemy to conduct frequent attacks against PBW and the other FOBs in the area. They

Courtesy 2 RCR.

India Coy soldiers on patrol during Operation Take-Out in Siah Choy, Zhari, May 2007.

further noted that Taliban had established an effective early warning network in the area and were capable of conducting coordinated ambushes at extremely short notice. Moreover, the insurgents could also count on drawing additional fighters from Uruzgan, Helmand, and other areas of Kandahar, as well as Pakistan to maintain relatively large force levels.

As a result, ISAF decided to build on the effects from Operation Medusa to establish an enduring stable environment within the Zahri/Panjwayi districts to enable the development of the Kandahar ADZ. A senior NATO commander stated the operation is a "show of unity and strength and a demonstration by ISAF of its ability to combat and defeat the Taliban."[29] As such, it ordered RC(S) to dislocate the "hard core" (Tier 1) Taliban by separating them from the "local Taliban" (Tier 2) and the local population on which they depend. This operation was predicated on engagement of local tribal elders to convince them to accept their role in the development of security. Manoeuvre elements would support this initiative by interdicting, disrupting, and destroying Taliban command and control nodes and fighters.[30]

As such, Operation Baaz Tsuka was born. Major-General Ton Van Loon, the Dutch ISAF commander, affirmed, "The aim of Baaz Tsuka is twofold, to destroy the Taliban's ability to mount a fresh offensive in the spring, and to encourage Afghan forces to take more control of security in the region." He revealed, "For me, success is when the elders can actually take responsibility for their own security when we can deploy police into the area as much as possible, when we can make sure the Taliban cannot use the window to build up for a spring offensive."[31]

Brigadier-General Tim Grant, the new commander of RC(S) who replaced David Fraser when he rotated out of theatre, insisted, "I'm still hopeful the plan laid out by General Van Loon will allow us to achieve the aim of dislocating the Taliban and have the village elders take more responsibility for influence and security with a minimum of fighting." Grant said, "the goal was to separate the hard line Taliban from those who are fighting mainly for the money."[32]

The colourful and gregarious Canadian chief of the defence staff, General Rick Hillier, was predictably more direct. He put the operation in

Courtesy Silvia Pecota.

Members of 3 RCR and their interpreter speak with locals during a patrol in Kandahar Province.

more understandable language. He stressed the principal aim of the operation was to kill Taliban commanders and suicide bomb makers. "One of the parts of this kind of operation," he explained, "is in particular to neutralize or take out the leaders who plan, prepare, facilitate; who get the money and get the vehicles for people" to conduct suicide bombings.[33]

The 1 RCR BG was once again a key component of the operation. "Having sat on Route Summit for the better part of two months now they're anxious to do something," opined Brigadier-General Grant. He ordered the 1 RCR BG to disrupt insurgent activity and set the conditions for the Kandahar City ADZ. The battle group, in concert with U.S. and ANA forces, assaulted from east to west to secure villages in the Panjwayi valley. 1 RCR BG specifically focused its operations around the hardened village of Howz-e-Madad and to the west, which was known as an insurgent transit area. Once the enemy was forced out of the valley, the emphasis then transitioned to humanitarian operations. Lieutenant-Colonel Lavoie clearly stated: "We're going to go in as soft as possible but as hard as necessary if they want to make it difficult on us." His hope was to conduct the operation "less kinetic than we did in Medusa."[34]

By 20 December, pronouncements emanating from RC(S) headquarters were positive. They assessed that Phases 1 and 2 of Operation Baaz Tsuka had significantly disrupted local insurgent command and control within the Zhari/Panjwayi region. Moreover, they received reports that insurgents were unsure of how to respond to the new offensive and that the will of the local fighters had started to wane. Intelligent analysts further assessed that insurgents were fleeing westward out of the AO.[35]

The operation once again seemed to provide the chimera of security in the area. It also provided the GIRoA and ISAF the opportunity to develop a series of fortified checkpoints, each operated by six to eight ANSF personnel, about five to seven kilometres apart along the main routes, as part of the long-term security program. But the long war continued.[36] There was no peace.

The inability of reconstruction and development to make significant inroads was as much a function of an inability to provide the necessary overarching security infrastructure as it was a failure of the Afghan government and the Coalition to ensure good governance. "The lack of

Afghan government presence and services, its inability to provide adequate security or improve the life of the average citizen with sufficient aid and revenues," counselled strategic analyst Anthony Cordesman, "[as well as] corruption and ethnic differences creates a vacuum threat forces can exploit." Cordesman concluded, "Rampant corruption, absence of rule of law, and failure of Government to provide equitable social services are rapidly undermining Afghan popular support for democratic governance model and possibly foreign military presence."[37]

Success in the long war depends on the ability of the government to be credible. But as the International Crisis Group reported, "Today, people are pulling back from a government that is failing them, if not preying on them." A poll taken on 7 December 2006, demonstrated that Afghan "public optimism has declined sharply across Afghanistan." Quite simply, public perception was that security was worsening and there was rising concerns about a resurgent Taliban, and decreasing faith in the government's effectiveness.[38] Two weeks later another poll revealed that only 62

Courtesy Silvia Pecota.

A gathering of the Royals. Brigadier-General Denis Thompson, Commander TFA, discusses next steps with 3 RCR CO, Lieutenant-Colonel Roger Barrett, and Major Rob McBride during OP Aray, October 2008, in Kandahar Province.

percent of Afghans believed that things were moving in the right direction in Afghanistan. Significantly, this was a dramatic 21 percent drop from the previous year.[39]

So who was winning the long war? "It's not a linear battlefield and it's much harder to measure progress," stated Lavoie, "The enemy has all the assets of an insurgent. One minute he has a hoe in his hand, the next minute it's an AK-47."[40] Ominously, the difficulty in measuring real success prompted some backward thinking. "We were asked to keep track of body counts of Taliban by higher HQ," revealed Lieutenant-Colonel Schreiber the operations officer at the RC(S) HQ, "We replied that this was meaningless — often inaccurate and it didn't matter anyways as it was not a measure of success. We were told to do it anyways because they needed something quantifiable to tell their higher."[41]

And so the long war dragged on. "The Taliban is learning from their experience [in conflicts with ISAF] in the same way we are and we see increasing use of heavier weapons on their part," stated Brigadier-General Joseph Votel, deputy commander of operations for ISAF's Regional Command East.[42] Another veteran commander conceded, "This is a thinking enemy and we ignore that at our own peril."[43]

"It's difficult, absolutely," confessed Major Todd Scharlach, "They [Taliban] are a smart enemy, they know what they have to do and they're trying everything they can to hurt us."[44] Brigadier-General Fraser agreed. "The enemy is adaptive and intelligent," he readily acknowledged.[45] So not surprisingly, the Taliban adjusted their methodology to maximize their tactical and strategic effect. For example, in 2005, there had been only 17 suicide attacks. "While there were just two suicide bombings in 2002, there is now one every five days," reported Elizabeth Rubin on 29 October 2006.[46] By the end of November, several months after Operation Medusa, there were a total of 106 suicide attacks.[47] One enemy fighter explained, "our resistance became more lethal, with new weapons and techniques: bigger and better IEDs for roadside bombings, and suicide attacks."[48] In December 2006, the Center for Strategic and International Studies in Washington, D.C. assessed, "the reconstituted enemy is more lethal and shows increased capacity for effective asymmetric warfare, including effective information operations."[49]

And so, Brigadier-General David Fraser, the brigade commander who was responsible for Operation Medusa, captured the frustration of the long war. He conceded, "The battle was hard, but the reconstruction was harder."[50] Nonetheless he insisted, "We're getting this right. We just have to persevere and stick it out."[51] Fraser warned, however, "the campaign to help build a nation will not be won this summer or next summer. It will take time." He rhetorically asked, "How much time?" and responded "As long as it takes."[52] Fraser emphasized, "Counterinsurgency is a marathon — this is really hard stuff."[53]

But to the soldiers the long war that played out after Operation Medusa boiled down to one simple realization. "You roll the dice with your life every time you go outside the wire," stated one Royal without emotion.[54] By the spring of 2007, the Taliban campaign strategy was designed to counter the Canadian presence in Zhari and Panjwayi. Strategist Carl Forsberg noted that the IED attacks became increasingly powerful and frequent. By April, the Taliban began rigging several bombs together effectively destroying the almost impregnable LAV IIIs

Courtesy 3 RCR.

Canadian and Afghan soldiers discover a major Taliban weapon cache in southern Kandahar Province during OP Aray, August 2008.

and inflicting fatal casualties on their crews. He assessed IED attacks became an almost daily occurrence on the section of Highway 1 running through the Zhari district.[55]

But the problem now belonged to Lieutenant-Colonel Rob Walker and his 2 RCR BG (TF 1–07) who had replaced 1 RCR. The TOCA occurred on 17 February 2007, by which time all 2 RCR BG sub-units had already arrived in place and had taken over security duties. Initially TF 1–07 picked up where the 1 RCR BG had left off, but they quickly shifted focus. "When we took over we had lost the initiative," conceded Walker. He explained, "1 RCR was working along 10 sq km. They got fixed on Route Summit to get it built and paved." The CO observed, "They lost the initiative. We intended to close down the FOBs and strong points on Route Summit as quickly as possible." Walker acknowledged, "The general impression with the guys was that they [FOBs and strong points] were a dumb idea." In the end, the withdrawal was done in March. Walker noted, "We secured the route by presence — rolling OPs and patrolling." He insisted, "We took back the initiative. We got off that damn road and had great success."[56]

The 2 RCR BG CO also clarified, "What we were trying to achieve in Zhari was to carry on with 1 RCR work in that Zhari and Panjwayi would not be a sanctuary where the Taliban could build up and plan attacks against Kandahar City." Walker noted, "The Taliban were still trying to cut-off and interdict, [but] we ensured it remained open." The CO grinned, "We mowed the grass. We dominated the area and we owned the night."[57]

This became key. The 2 RCR BG dismounted from their LAVs and conducted nightly patrols throughout their AO. "We did a lot of night patrolling," affirmed Captain Marc Côté. "We expanded our operations quite a bit to include night patrols in the grape fields — almost all dismounted patrols."[58]

In fact, the CO assigned a rifle coy to each of Zhari and Panjwayi districts to dominate the ground. Of equal importance was developing relationships with the local populace through low level *shuras* to work toward economic programs. But then again, this was the vital ground. In essence, destroying the Taliban was not their primary task. As part of Task Force Kandahar (TFK), the 2 RCR BG was responsible for securing, patrolling, and expanding the Kandahar ADZ, which included the city as well as the adjoining districts. The BG was also responsible for providing immediate reconstruction to communities as well as building governance capacity within the GIRoA.

To facilitate these tasks meant freedom of movement. For Lieutenant-Colonel Walker this was vital to achieve success. He explained that the BG was required "to ensure the safe flow of commercial traffic on Highway 1 between Kandahar City and Helmand Province to the west, and improve the flow of all civilian traffic." Quite simply, Walker believed "restoring civilian freedom of movement was key to getting life back to something like normal in Kandahar."[59]

One fundamental difference for the 2 RCR BG was that they were now partnered with an Afghan *Kandak* (battalion). The CO affirmed, "All our actions had an Afghan face — we did everything through the ANA." He reinforced, "All our operations were joint operations with the ANA and whenever we interfaced with the locals the key guy doing the talking was an ANA soldier." He concluded, "We tried to strip away the image of an occupying force."[60]

The partnership proved to be highly successful. "Throughout our ten operations our key issue was to promote the government of Afghanistan to the local populations," explained the CO. Although an effective relationship was developed between the 2 RCR BG and the ANA, no similar success was achieved with the ANP. Nonetheless, Walker concluded, "We demonstrated we could go anywhere, any time. We got out and talked to locals. We put on our human face." Walker assessed, "That alone had great impact with the locals. This allowed the PRT to go and start with meaningful work."[61]

Undisputedly, the Royals began to see a difference. "We achieved success," commented the CO. "We completed projects and we changed the attitude of the people. Walker noted, "OCs were sitting at district *shuras* along with the PRT guys to discuss economic progress. We were beginning to see a change in attitudes of the people." Walker explained, "We changed our presence and profile. With time we were told by our ANA and ANP partners that there was a softening in attitudes towards us by the locals."[62] And there were other indicators as well. Polls that were conducted in Kandahar showed that "70 percent of Afghans in the area showed hope for the future; 60 percent of the population did not support the Taliban (only 30 percent did); and most had a favorable impression of ISAF."[63]

The 2 RCR BG was somewhat fortunate in that the first few months of their tour was the winter season. As such, the Taliban were not excessively active, which allowed the Royals time to get to know their AO. With spring came a return of the fighting season, and the Taliban began to test the BG. However, it became known from the locals that the Taliban were not staying in the villages; rather, they were sleeping in the grape huts out in the fields. In addition, it appeared that there were only small numbers of foreign fighters.

The BG maintained its aggressive posture in an attempt to ensure the Taliban could not pose a significant threat to the Kandahar ADZ or its population. This, however, proved challenging, since the Taliban retained an impressive early warning system. Lieutenant-Colonel Walker explained:

> They focused on our vehicles so they could see us coming from kilometres away. The way we fought, we were tied to our vehicles. So we adapted. Vehicles would drop off dismounts [infantry soldiers] and keep on going. Guys would be in position in the morning moving into areas we knew they would be so when the Taliban woke up and moved we would already be there. We would then fix them with fire. Between May and July we killed at least 300 Taliban fighters. The Taliban would panic and attack but we held the key terrain so we could kill them. We also had the eye in the sky.[64]

Just as the Taliban were adapting so too were the Royals. Walker noted that in "previous tours it was a cycle of go in, fight, leave and then you'd have to go back in and fight again." He assessed that during "1 RCR's tour they stuck to the roads and used UAVs to try and hit the insurgents as they were going in or coming out of an area." Walker revealed, "I stuck my guys in the actual villages to clear the Taliban out and keep them out.

We got to the point where we could beat their early warning system."[65] Put bluntly, 2 RCR BG's strategy was to "own the night."

Moreover, the BG was proud of the fact they were not killing civilians. Walker insisted, "We were very discriminate and would rarely drop any ordnance on a compound. There were still families in the area."[66] The CO elaborated, "We stopped taking tanks into the grape fields as we tried hard not to destroy them." He believed they were more effective dismounted in any case. Walker assessed, "We were audacious in our control of the areas by day and night."[67] As opposed to 1 RCR's experience, Walker assessed that 2 RCR BG never fought more than 40 guys at one time.

Despite their best efforts, however, the 2 RCR BG could not completely eliminate the Taliban from their AO. Because of the tribal structure, it was difficult to know exactly what was actually happening on the ground. Nonetheless, Walker believed, "we achieved a disrupting effect. They could no longer build-up. We denied them a logistics base, sanctuary and the ability to interdict Highway 1." Importantly, he affirmed, "They were unable to project attacks into Kandahar City."[68] Walker opined, "We took it to them. Very rarely were we ambushed. We had five incidents and 18 killed. By exception we were caught out on the roads."[69]

Nevertheless, the Taliban's use of IEDs still proved to be lethal. For the Royals to clear areas within the Kandahar ADZ they had to travel by road and foot, there was simply no escaping it. And this, always made them vulnerable to a degree. Once such attack happened on 4 July 2007, when a catastrophic IED strike killed six BG soldiers, an Afghan interpreter, and wounded a number of others. The consensus was clear — it was the biggest IED seen to date in theatre, and no vehicle could have survived the blast. It was just another aspect of the struggle — as the Canadians and Coalition brought in better and more protected vehicles, the Taliban built bigger bombs. And so the long war continued.

By August, TF 1–07 had almost completed their tour. It had been an exhausting exercise in fighting Taliban, enabling governance as well as assisting reconstruction and development. Journalist Murray Brewster captured the essence of the Afghan experience. He wrote: "It has been a mad kaleidoscope of firefights, seemingly endless stretches of boredom, rocket attacks, unbearable heat, patrols, sweat, food in plastic bags, infrequent showers and more patrols."[70]

Important to note is that the members of the 2 RCR BG were not the only Royals in theatre. Many others served in the Canadian TFK HQ or Coalition headquarters in theatre. In addition, a number of Royals were part of the new Operational Mentor Liaison Team (OMLT) concept that began in 2007 and increasingly became a major focus of both Canada and NATO, as it was seen as an enabler to allow countries to eventually exit Afghanistan. The idea was simple. Western forces would be embedded with Afghan units at all levels to train and mentor the Afghan security forces. They would also act as liaison elements with Coalition forces. NATO commanders judged the expertise, training, and professionalism of the OMLT members to be a great mechanism to professionalize and increase the effectiveness of the ANSF.

But the OMLT task became yet another drain on limited personnel in the Army. By 2007/08, the war in Afghanistan became the primary focus of the Army and The RCR. Battalions were either getting ready to deploy as part of the "high road to readiness," just returning from deployment; shipping off individuals and/or sub-units to join other BGs, headquarters, or OMLTs to go into theatre; or training on the others to deploy. There was little scope for other substantive activities. And, as the Regiment entered its 125th year of service to the country, yet another RCR battalion was preparing to deploy.

The 3 RCR BG, commanded by Lieutenant-Colonel Roger Barrett arrived in theatre in September 2008. In many ways, not much had changed. The Canadians were still focused on fighting the Taliban for control of Zhari and Panjwayi districts. It remained a cat and mouse contest in which the Royals tried to root out the insurgents, and the enemy tried to inflict the greatest number of casualties possible, while at the same time discrediting the GIRoA and the coalition, and gaining the support of the people (through intimidation, terror, or other means).

The insurgent use of IEDs continued to increase. The Taliban ably realized the centre of gravity for the Western nations was casualties. The more they bled the Coalition forces, the greater the pressure on Western politicians to bring their troops home by the respective national populations. The trend was clearly visible in the increase in overall Coalition fatalities because of IEDs over time:

- 2002 — 4
- 2003 — 4
- 2004 — 12
- 2005 — 21
- 2006 — 42
- 2007 — 78
- 2008 — 152[71]

The 3 RCR BG now became the latest group of Royals to take up the sword. It was not long before they got involved in combat. The first platoons on the ground became involved in skirmishes immediately upon deploying to Zhari District. The first major BG operation occurred the next month. During the first week of October, 3 RCR BG and 42 Royal Marine Commando conducted Operation Aray and ventured into eastern Panjwayi, an area where there was still no permanent ANSF or Coalition presence.

The objective of the operation was to disrupt and dislocate insurgent activities and prevent enemy influence into Kandahar City. The BG went in heavy on LAV IIIs, working in conjunction with a squadron of Leopard main battle tanks. The overwhelming show of force prompted the insurgents to melt away. Once in situ, the area was flooded with dismounted patrols, which quickly made contact with the local population. Information was eventually received that led to a number of substantive finds. It became clear that the area was being used as a staging and transit area. A number of enemy caches were discovered that led to the capture of large amounts of IED equipment, explosives, weaponry, ammunition, and an estimated half million dollars of medical supplies. The munitions were blown in place and the medical supplies carried out of the area.

"Seizing this equipment will have a direct impact on the insurgent's ability to mount future operations," confirmed Lieutenant-Colonel Barrett. "We wanted to disrupt the enemy and learn about the area; six days later

Courtesy Silvia Pecota.

Soldiers from "N" Coy, 3 RCR prepare to blow a Taliban ammunition cache.

we have a much better understanding of the ground and we certainly disrupted and dislocated the Taliban."[72]

Later that month the BG struck another blow at the insurgents' ability to mount IED operations. In co-operation with the ANA, the 3 RCR BG launched Operation Artash in the Howz-e-Madad area of Zhari District. The intent was specifically to disrupt the resident insurgents who were responsible for a large number of IED attacks and ambushes. Once again, the insurgents fled prior to contact but left behind a quantity of equipment and munitions. We didn't find a lot," conceded Major Jason Guiney, "but just going there created a three week drop in IED activity throughout the area. That is a significant disrupt."[73]

Besides the disruption of the IED network, Major Rob McBride, OC "N" Coy, noted, "we have also proven once again that we are able to work effectively side-by-side the ANA to assert our presence in this area and deny the insurgents the freedom to carry out their activities."[74] Major Marc St-Yves agreed. "We're seeing," he confirmed, "an increase in the capability of the ANSF."[75]

For the next month, the BG focused on platoon and coy level framework patrolling, which included a constant dose of IED encounters, indirect fire, and firefights. St-Yves noted, "We own the night." He acknowledged, "The soldiers have an appetite to fight the big battle but we need to increase the security of the people."[76] And so the low level patrolling continued. However, the soldiers soon got their wish.

On 25 November 2008, the 3 RCR BG was ready to launch another BG level attack into the "heart of darkness" in central Zhari District. Operation Janubi Tapu 2 was designed to disrupt an insurgent safe haven where no GIRoA or Coalition troops had ventured for a long time. Lieutenant-Colonel Barrett planned to disrupt the insurgents in "order to reduce their ability to plan, coordinate, stage and conduct offensive operations in and around Kandahar City."[77] He also intended to go in with overwhelming combat power yet achieve surprise. Barrett did not mince words. "Let's be clear," he announced to his subordinate commanders, "we will not be welcome in this particular area, they control it, this is where their C2 and IED facilitators are, we are going in heavy to kill bad guys."[78]

Barrett was under no illusions. He had already informed his higher chain-of-command, "Everyone [Afghans] is connected or aware — to think otherwise is naive." The CO observed, "the AO is a mix of all [fighters]: foreign, hardcore, home-grown, coerced and simply for the money."[79] And in this particular area, the population was more inclined to support the enemy.

Nonetheless, the assault was a great success. "I" Coy conducted an airmobile assault and captured many insurgents on their objective. The insurgents were completely surprised by the speed with which the Royals had struck. "M" and "N" Coys had similar success with their rapid synchronized mechanized approach. Dismounting and fighting through their respective objectives they too inflicted a severe blow to the insurgents. The disruption desired certainly transpired as the Taliban were either killed in placed, captured, or forced to flee from an area they had considered a safe haven.

However, it did not take long for the Taliban to strike back. In December, nine Canadian soldiers were killed in two separate incidents, six of them Royals (three from 1 RCR and three from 3 RCR) on the infamous Highway 1 in the vicinity of Senjaray in eastern Zhari District. The latest attacks prompted 3 RCR BG to launch Operation Pancar, which was specifically designed to hunt down insurgent command and control (C2) facilities, as well as IED factories in eastern Zhari and Panjwayi Districts. The CO's intent was to enhance the security of the main supply routes. He identified IEDs as "deadly persistence" and he was intent on striking a blow to the insurgents' capacity to continue with their emplacement.

As such, Lieutenant-Colonel Barrett planned to hit known C2/IED nodes first and then conduct subsequent strikes based on the intelligence gathered from the initial assaults. On 18 December 2008, in coordination with a SOF operation, "M" and "N" Combat Teams penetrated their respective objective areas. Once again they were able to disrupt the enemy and destroy those who attempted to fight. "Their [Royals] tenaciousness to be successful was a true demonstration of their combat prowess," observed Chief Warrant Officer Ernie Hall, the BG RSM.[80]

His words were no idle boast. From arrival into theatre in September 2008 to the end of the year in December, the 3 RCR BG conducted five major BG operations, 26 coy level operations, over 550 platoon/troop

Courtesy 3 RCR

Members of 3 RCR involved in a firefight, August 2008.

patrols, and responded to over 100 Quick Reaction Force calls for assistance. Their message to the insurgents was clear — "We dictate the tempo, we dictate the fighting, and we will not let up in the winter months."[81]

And so, 3 RCR BG finished up the year continuing the fight in Afghanistan, demonstrating once again, that throughout 125 years of service to the country, Royals remained on the front lines in the service of the national interest and the people of Canada.

Conclusion

A s the Regiment completed 125 years of service, it could rightly be proud of all that it achieved. It had maintained a record second to none of its ability to rise to any challenge and to serve the nation with pride and professionalism. As this volume demonstrates, The RCR entered the Cold War undaunted by the nightmarish possibility of fighting on an atomic battlefield. Throughout the Cold War, it adapted and evolved to meet the changes in doctrine, equipment, tasks, and the realities of working within an alliance. Never did it waver and never did it fail to meet its responsibilities.

Equally, throughout that period, The RCR reacted to internal domestic requirements, whether it was providing aid to the civil power, or contending with administrative and organizational turmoil. With the backdrop of an ever decreasing defence budget and increasing fiscal pressures that provided the catalyst for, or necessitated, dramatic change such as the disbandment of regiments, battalions, and sub-units, to the unification of the CF, the regiment has always persevered, adapted, and set the example for others to follow.

The end of the Cold War did not change that. As the Regiment entered the 1990s with its panoply of change, chaos and crisis, The RCR remained a bedrock of stability for the nation. Serving on operations at home and abroad, it never wavered and it made the country proud. Its record of service and combat prowess was only strengthened as we entered the new millennium. A former colonel of the regiment remarked, "The focus is on operations. The missions are demanding now and will become more so. They will test our will as a nation, and the mettle of our army and our regiment."[1]

The Regiment has risen to the challenge. Continuous operational success in a brutal and savage war that continues at the time of writing with yet another RCR battalion in theatre, has proven once again The RCR is a regiment of warriors dedicated to their country. The price, however, has not been insignificant, as the Regiment has had to bid farewell to so many members of its family.

And so it continued, as The RCR moved forward to build on its legacy. But the Regiment, as was described in the introduction, is not a faceless entity. It is in fact the men and women, and their families who serve the Colours, directly or indirectly. They are the very life blood of the Regiment, that build its strength, character, and reputation. In turn, it is the Regiment that binds all as a family, provides strength, and reminds all that they belong to something bigger than themselves.

Pro Patria

Appendix A

Select Key Honorary and Regimental Appointments, 1953–2008

Colonels-in-Chief
FM HRH The Prince Philip, Duke of Edinburgh : 8 December 1953 — Present

Honorary Colonels
Brig The Hon M.F. Gregg: 31 January 1952 — 31 January 1958

Colonel of the Regiment
Gen C. Foulkes: 2 January 1959 — 26 May 1965
MGen D.C. Spry: 26 May 1965 — 10 July 1978
Brig T.E.D'O. Snow: 10 July 1978 — 7 July 1981
Col T.F.G. Lawson: 7 July 1981 — 26 July 1985
Col F. Klenavic: 26 July 1985 — 6 June 1989
Col A.S.A. Galloway: 07 June 1989 — 10 July 1993
Col R.M. Dillon: 10 July 1993 — 1 July 1997
LGen J.E. Vance: 1 July 1997 — 28 September 2002
MGen T.F. de Faye: 28 September 2002 — June 2006
MGen W.M. Holmes: June 2006 — July 2011

Commanding Officers

1st Battalion

LCol P.R. Bingham: 9 August 1950 — 31 July 1953

Maj F. Klenavic: 31 July 1953 — 27 December 1953

LCol T.R. McCoy: 27 December 1953 — 4 October 1957

LCol F. Klenavic: 4 October 1957 — 9 September 1960

LCol J.A. Johnston: 9 September 1960 — 24 January 1964

LCol T.D. Lafferty: 24 January 1964 — 24 November 1965

Temporary — Maj W.F. Stott: 25 November 1965 — 17 January 1966

LCol P.A. Labelle: 18 January 1966 — 29 July 1967

LCol J.J. Barrett: 29 July 1967 — 15 May 1969

LCol D.G. Loomis: 15 January 1969 — 21 February 1971

LCol J.C. Hayter: 21 February 1971 — 1 September 1972

LCol F.J. Norman: 1 September 1972 — 31 August 1973

LCol P.L. Spencer: 31 August 1973 — 11 June 1975

LCol W.J. Pettipas: 11 June 1975 — 27 July 1977

LCol C.E.S. Ryley: 27 July 1977 — 5 July 1979

LCol R.J.R. Gobeil: 5 July 1979 — 5 August 1981

LCol A.D. McQuarrie: 5 August 1981 — 14 July 1983

LCol L.C. Bowen: 14 July 1983 — 19 July 1985

LCol W.M. Holmes: 19 July 1985 — 26 June 1987

LCol B.M. Archibald: 26 June 1987 — 20 July 1989

LCol N.M. Pettis: 20 July 1989 — 11 July 1991

LCol W.N. Peters: 11 July 1991 — 9 July 1993

LCol M.S. Skidmore: 9 July 1993 — 6 July 1995

LCol T. Tarrant: 6 July 1995 — 4 July 1997

LCol P.J. Devlin: 4 July 97 — 25 June 1999

LCol B.N. Pennington: 25 June 1999 — 26 June 2001

LCol B. Horn: 26 June 2001 — 20 February 2003

LCol A.L. Kilby: 20 February — June 2003

Temporary — Maj S.G. Kooistra: June 2003 — March 2004

LCol O.H. Lavoie: June 2005 — July 2007

LCol J.S. Shipley: July 2007 — May 2008

LCol C.J.J. Mialkowski: May 2008 — July 2011

2nd Battalion

LCol R.A. Keane: 17 August 1950 — 2 January 1952
LCol G.C. Corbould: 2 January 1952 — 31 August 1957
Temporary — Maj J.W.P. Brian: 1 September — 30 November 1957
LCol D.E. Holmes: 1 December 1957 — 14 August 1960
LCol J.A. Clancy: 14 August 1960 — 20 May 1963
LCol J.W.P. Bryan: 20 May 1963 — 30 April 1964
LCol J.B.J. Archambault: 30 April 1964 — 15 July 1966
LCol B. Baile: 15 July 1966 — 27 July 1968
LCol J.A. Cowan: 27 July 1968 — 15 June 1970
LCol G.S. Morrison: 1 July 1970 — 30 July 1971
LCol I.S. Fraser: 30 July 1971 — 9 July 1973
LCol E.C. Quinn: 7 July 1973 — 13 June 1975
LCol D.A. Fraser: 13 June 1975 — 8 July 1977
LCol J.R. MacPherson: 8 July 1977 — 30 June 1979
LCol T.J. Kaulbach: 30 June 1979 — 25 July 1981
LCol M.G. O'Brien: 25 July 1981 — 20 July 1983
LCol W.J. Aitchison: 20 July 1983 — 19 July 1985
LCol J.L. Senecal: 19 July 1985 — 23 July 1987
LCol D.G. O'Brien: 23 July 1987 — 29 June 1989
LCol A.G. Mitchell: 29 June 1989 — 12 July 1991
LCol T.K.D. Geburt: 12 July 1991 — 27 June 1993
LCol C.T. Russell: 27 June 1993 — 21 July 1995
LCol P. Sweetnam: 21 July 1995 — 27 June 1997
LCol D.A. MacLean: 27 June 1997 — 30 September 1999
LCol J.B. Simms: 30 September 1999 — 17 August 2001
LCol J.H. Vance: 17 August 2001 — 18 July 2003
LCol J.P. Davis: July 2003 — June 2005
LCol R.D. Walker: June 2005 — August 2007
LCol G.S. Parker, CD: August 2007 — July 2008
LCol J.S. Fife: July 2008 — July 2011

3rd Battalion

LCol K.L. Campbell: 10 January 1951 — 21 July 1954

(Reformed 6 July 70)

LCol G.R. Cheriton: 6 July 1970 — 23 July 1971

LCol S.W. Spencer: 23 July 1971 — 7 August 1973
LCol G.L. Simpson: 7 August 1973 — 1 August 1975
LCol D.B. Ells: 1 August 1975 — 13 July 1977
LCol T.F. de Faye: 13 July 1977 — 5 July 1979
LCol R.P. Alden: 5 July 1979 — 16 July 1981
LCol J.P. Thompson: 16 July 1981 — 9 July 1983
LCol M.J.R. Houghton: 9 July 1983 — 27 July 1985
LCol J.S. Cox: 27 July 1985 — 15 March 1986
LCol A.A. Peterson: 15 March 1986 — 1 August 1986
LCol J.S. Cox: 1 August 1986 — 17 July 1987
LCol E.G. MacArthur: 17 July 1987 — 28 June 1989
LCol J.I. Fenton: 28 June 1989 — 10 July 1991
LCol R.A. Hatton: 10 July 1991 — 01 August 1993
LCol M.R. Sweeney: 1 August 1993 — 25 June 1995
LCol D.V. Pittfield: 25 June 1995 — 4 July 1997
LCol M.P. Jorgensen: 4 July 1997 — 29 June 2000
LCol D.W. Thompson: 29 June 2000 — 4 July 2002
LCol D.J. Denne 4: July 2002 — 12 June 2004
LCol R.R. Radford: 12 June 2004 — June 2006
LCol R.R. Barrett: June 2006 — June 2009
LCol K.I. Cameron: June 2009 — July 2011

4th Battalion and Precedents

The London and Oxford Fusiliers (3rd Battalion, The Royal Canadian
    Regiment) (designated 1 September 54)
LCol R.M. Dillon: 1 September 1954 — 21 October 1956
LCol D.B. Armstrong: 22 October 1956 — 25 April 1958

3rd Battalion, The Royal Canadian Regiment
(London and Oxford Fusiliers) (designated 25 April 58)

LCol D.B. Armstrong: 25 April 1958 — 01 May 1959
LCol S.G. Heaman: 1 May 1959 — 30 April 1962
LCol J.F. Leighton: 30 April 1962 — 27 January 1965
LCol A.R. McIntosh: 27 January 1965 — 26 May 1968
LCol A.J. Lawson: 26 May 1968 — 06 July 1970

4th Battalion, The Royal Canadian Regiment (London and Oxford Fusiliers) (designated 6 July 70)

LCol A.J. Lawson: 6 July 1970 — 9 May 1971
LCol W.G. Lindsay: 9 May 1971 — 16 September 1973
LCol M.W. Wood: 16 September 1973 — 14 February 1974
LCol W.G. Lindsay: 14 February 1974 — 15 June 1975
LCol D.J. Bonner: 15 June 1975 — 10 June 1979
LCol F.B. Graham: 10 June 1979 — 26 September 1982
LCol M.W. Wood: 26 September 1982 — 23 June 1985
LCol B.N. Smith: 23 June 1985 — 11 December 1988
LCol E.C. Quinn: 11 December 1988 — 30 May 1990

4th Battalion, The Royal Canadian Regiment (designated 30 May 1990)

LCol E.C. Quinn: 30 May 1990 — 10 June 1990
LCol D.N. Griffin: 10 June 1990 — 5 June 1993
LCol J.M. Walden: 5 June 1993 — 10 December 1994
LCol R.R. Bassarab: 10 December 1994 — 13 June 1997
LCol G.J.P. O'Brien: 13 June 1997 — 27 January 2000
LCol R.G.L. Holt: 27 January 2000 — 5 December 2002
LCol M.E.K. Campbell: 5 December 2002 — June 2005
LCol B.A. Millman: June 2005 — June 2008
LCol M. McDonald: June 2008 — June 2010

Home Station Commanders

LCol P.R. Bingham (Camp Petawawa): 25 February 1952 — 1 July 1953
Maj F. Klenavic: 1 July 1953 — 9 October 1953
LCol G.C. Corbould (Wolseley Barracks): 9 October 1953 —
    27 December 1953
LCol T.R. McCoy: 27 December 1953 — 2 November 1955
LCol G.C. Corbould: 2 November 1955 — 21 October 1957
LCol D.E. Holmes: 1 December 1957 — 14 August 1960
LCol J.A. Clancy: 14 August 1960 — 20 May 1963
LCol J.W.P. Bryan: 20 May 1963 — 30 April 1964
LCol J.B.J. Archambault: 30 April 1964 — 30 November 1965
LCol P.A. Labelle: 30 November 1965 — 28 July 1967
LCol J.J. Barrett: 28 July 1967 — 16 May 1969

LCol D.G. Loomis: 16 May 1969 — 21 February 1971
LCol J.C. Hayter: 21 February 1971 — 1 September 1972
LCol F.J. Norman: 1 September 1972 — 31 August 1973
LCol P.L. Spencer: 31 August 1973 — 11 June 1975
LCol W.J. Pettipas: 11 June 1975 — 20 July 1977
Col J.C. Hayter: 20 July 1977 — 27 August 1980
Col P.L. Spencer: 27 August 1980 — 8 July 1983
Col E.C. Quinn: 8 July 1983 — 10 September 1987
Col W.J. Aitchison: 10 September 1987 — 12 July 1991
LCol J.A. Boyd: 12 July 1991 — 24 June 1993
LCol A.G. Miller: 24 June 1993 — 17 August 1994
LCol M.S. Campbell: 17 August 1994 — 24 July 1998
LCol R.W. McBride: 24 July 1998 — 9 July 2001
LCol D.J. Denne: 9 July 2001 — 9 July 2002
LCol A. Bowes: 9 July 2002
LCol M.E.K. Campbell: July 2004 — 4 June 2005
LCol B.A. Millman: 4 June 2005 — 4 June 2008
LCol M.R. McDonald: 4 June 2008 — 15 May 2010

The Royal Canadian Regiment Depot (formed 19 March 1953 – disbanded 8 December 1968)

Maj E.L. Cohen: 15 June 1953 — 9 September 1956
Maj W.J. Jewell: 9 September 1956 — 4 October 1959
Maj H.V. Davies: 4 October 1959 — 18 March 1962
Maj S.G. Mackness: 18 March 1962 — 5 January 1964
Maj F.M. Vine: 5 January 1964 — 8 December 1968

The Royal Canadian Regiment Battle School (formed 1 May 1981 – disbanded 10 July 1997)

LCol J.V. Arbuckle: 1 May 1981 — 5 July 1982
LCol J.A. Boyd: 5 July 1982 — 5 July 1985
LCol R.M. Gray: 5 July 1985 — 24 June 1987
LCol M.R. Newman: 24 June 1987 — 25 June 1990
LCol S.T. Groves: 25 June 1990 — 4 July 1993
LCol S.D. Christensen: 4 July 1993 — 9 June 1995
LCol M.P. Zuwerkalow: 9 June 1995 — 10 July 1997

3 Airborne Commando (formed 29 June 1979 — disbanded 5 March 1995)

Maj I.A. Kennedy: 29 June 1979 — 26 August 1981
Maj B.M. Archibald: 26 August 1981 — 8 July 1983
Maj W.A. Leavey: 8 July 1983 — 5 July 1985
Maj E.P. Ring: 5 July 1985 — 31 July 1987
Maj J.P. Sweetnam: 31 July 1987 — 30 June 1989
Maj P.L. O'Brien: 30 June 1989 — 2 August 1991
Maj M.S. Skidmore: 2 August 1991 — 16 June 1992
Maj C.G. Magee: 16 June 1992 — 21 July 1993
Maj B. Horn: 21 July 1993 — 5 March 1995

Regimental Sergeants Major

1st Battalion

WO1 F.A. Burns: 1950 — 1954
WO1 G.M. Fox: 1955 — 1958
WO1 F.E. Lewis: 1958 — 1960
WO1 E.F. Keegan: 1 September 1960 — 9 March 1964
WO1 T. Slaney: 10 March 1964 — 31 May 1966
WO1 K.D. MacKenzie: 1 June 1966 — 16 October 1967
CWO R.W. Craig: 17 October 1967 — 1 August 1971
CWO B.C. Robinson: 1 August 1971 — 4 August 1975
CWO C.A. Girden: 4 August 1975 — 20 September 1978
CWO T.J. Shaunessy: 20 September 1978 — 20 May 1979
CWO J.D. Marr: 20 May 1979 — 1 September 1980
CWO V.A. Spicer: 1 September 1980 — 5 August 1981
CWO W.N. Northrup: 5 August 1981 — 22 June 1984
CWO M.G. MacDonald: 22 June 1984 — 27 July 1988
CWO H.J. Hickson: 27 July 1988 — 29 June 1990
CWO J.H. Fraser: 29 June 1990 — 11 July 1993
CWO J.H. Bentley: 11 July 1993 — 4 July 1997
CWO R.R. Hodgson: 4 July 1997 — 15 May 1998
CWO D. Mack (WSE, temporary): 15 May 1998 — 30 September 1998
CWO R.R. Hodgson: 1 October — 25 June 1999
CWO R.M. Carriere: 25 June 1999 — 26 June 2001
CWO S.M. Anderson: June 2001 — June 2004

CWO G.A. Cook: June 2004 — June 2005
CWO R.M.J. Girouard: June 2005 — November 2006
CWO M.H Miller: November 2006 — May 2008
CWO S.G. Hartnell: May 2008 —

2nd Battalion

W01 J.J.T. McManus: 9 August 1950 — 26 August 1953
W01 G.H. Fuller: 26 May 1954 — 1 September 1958
W01 H.A. Decemberoste: 2 September 1958 — 1 December 1961
W01 H.W.J. Leask: 2 December 1961 — 11 April 1965
W01 C.E. Hill: 12 April 1965 — 12 July 1967
W01 J.G. Juteau: 13 July 1967 — 31 August 1969
CWO D.C. Cox: 1 September 1969 — 30 June 1970
CWO D.B. Reekie: 1 July 1970 — 31 July 1971
CWO R.R. Semple: 31 July 1971 — 11 September 1972
MWO C.B. Myers: 11 September 1972 — 15 January 1973
CWO C.B. Myers: 15 January 1973 — 31 March 1976
CWO H. Clark: 16 August 1976 — 14 June 1979
CWO G.K. Zinck: 15 June 1979 — 15 June 1982
CWO B.J. Hurley: 15 June 1982 — 31 October 1983
CWO J.F. Carroll: 31 October 1983 — 17 July 1984
CWO J.A. O'Quinn: 17 July 1984 — 19 July 1987
CWO W.M. O'Hearn: 19 July 1987 — 13 August 1990
CWO J.R. Irvine: 13 August 1990 — 27 June 1993
CWO J.S. Mossop: 27 June 1993 — 15 March 1996
CWO J.H. Francis: 15 March 1996 — 5 May 1998
CWO E.J. Gapp: 5 May 1998 — 29 June 2000
CWO E. Christensen: 29 June 2000 — 18 July 2003
CWO M.R. Hornbrook: July 2003 — June 2006
CWO M.L. Baisley: June 2006 — June 2008
CWO K.V. Burgess: June 2008 — June 2010
CWO A.E. Penton: June 2008 —

3rd Battalion

W01 J.M. MacKay: September 1951 — March 1954
CWO C.J. Scott: 6 July 1970 — 1 September 1970
CWO R.A. Boyle: 2 September 1970 — 1 August 1973

CWO F.J. McLean: 6 August 1973 — 31 March 1976
CWO L.R. Dirks: 31 March 1976 — 15 July 1977
CWO R.A. McKinnon: 15 July 1977 — 23 June 1979
CWO A.L. Tompkins: 23 June 1979 — 1 July 1982
CWO H.L. Fife: 1 July 1982 — 27 July 1985
CWO J.P. Riley: 27 July 1985 — 16 July 1987
CWO L.R. MacDonald: 16 July 1987 — 6 July 1990
CWO S.G. Douglas: 6 July 1990 — 30 June 1993
CWO G.E. Vondrasek: 30 June 1993 — 24 June 1995
CWO G.A. Leach: 24 June 1995 — 4 July 1997
CWO F.W. Grattan: 4 July 1997 — 29 June 2000
CWO D.W. Preeper: 29 June 2000 — 28 March 2003
CWO D.R. Bradley: 28 March 2003 — 30 June 2005
CWO J.S. Sorbie: 30 June 2005 — August 2006
Temporary MWO T.L. Riddle: August 2006 — January 2007
CWO E.J. Hall: January 2007 — June 2009
CWO W.A. Bartlett: June 2009 —

4th Battalion and Precedents

The London and Oxford Fusiliers (3rd Battalion, The Royal Canadian Regiment)
WO1 H. Koenig: 1 September 1954 — 1955
WO1 A.J.C. Thorne: 1955 — 25 April 1958

3rd Battalion, The Royal Canadian Regiment (London and Oxford Fusiliers)

WO1 A.J.C. Thorne: 25 April 1958 — 1960
WO1 F.A. Burns: 1960 — 1962
WO1 R.H.J. Price: 1962 — 26 May 1968
CWO S.L. Ricketts: 26 May 1968 — 6 July 1970

4th Battalion, The Royal Canadian Regiment (London and Oxford Fusiliers)

CWO S.L. Ricketts: 6 July 70 — 1971
CWO D.T. Dingman: 1971 — 1974
CWO A.H. Boon: 1974 — 1980
CWO D.T. Dingman: 1980 — 1983
CWO D.A. Bell: 1983 — 26 October 1986
CWO M. Woods: 26 October 1986 — 4 November 1990
CWO S.J. St. George: 4 November 1990 — 15 February 1993

CWO R.R. Rennie: 15 February 1993 — 27 November 2002
CWO C.R.J. Gomes: November 2002 — October 2007
CWO D.A.C. Elyatt: October 2007 — June 2010

The Royal Canadian Regiment Depot

WO1 E. Tracz: 15 August 1953 — 6 January 1954
WO1 J.L. Goodridge: 6 January 1954 — 26 July 1955
WO1 F.A. Burns: 14 October 1955 — 2 August 1960
WO1 F.E. Lewis: 2 August 1960 — 03 December 1961
WO1 T. Slaney: 3 December 1961 — 9 March 1964
WO1 c.e. Hill: 10 March 1964 — 11 April 1965
WO1 K.D. MacKenzie: 9 November 1965 — 31 May 1966
WO1 D.M. Lee: 31 May 1966 — 10 June 1968

The Royal Canadian Regiment Battle School

CWO W. MacKay: 1 May 1981 — 1 August 1983
CWO J.P. Riley: 1 August 1983 — 27 July 1985
CWO H.L. Fife: 27 July 1985 — 30 May 1986
CWO C.A. Clayton: 7 July 1986 — 13 July 1988
CWO R.F. O'Quinn: 13 July 1988 — 29 August 1991
CWO D.R. Robinson: 29 August 1991 — 15 July 1994
CWO F.J. Grattan: 15 July 1994 — 29 May 1997
CWO J.T. Ginn: 29 May 1997 — 10 July 1997

Appendix B
Battle Honours

Note: Entries in italics are honours emblazoned on the Regimental Colours.

Northwest Canada

1. *Saskatchewan*
2. *Northwest Canada, 1885*

South Africa

3. *Paardeberg*
4. *South Africa, 1899–1900*

First World War

5. *Ypres, 1915*
6. Gravenstafel
7. St. Julien
8. Festubert, 1915
9. *Mount Sorrel*

10. *Somme, 1916*
11. Pozieres
12. Flers-Courcelette
13. *Ancré Heights*
14. Arras, 1917
15. *Vimy, 1917*
16. Arieux
17. Scarpe, 1917
18. *Hill 70*
19. *Ypres, 1917*
20. *Passchendaele*
21. *Amiens*
22. Arras, 1918
23. Scarpe, 1918
24. Droucourt-Queant
25. *Hindenburg Line*
26. Canal du Nord
27. Cambrai, 1918
28.*Pursuit to Mons*
29. France and Flanders, 1915–18

Second World War

30. *Landing in Sicily*
31. Valguarnera
32. Agira
33. Adrano
34. Regalbuto
35. Sicily, 1943
36. Landing at Reggio
37. *Motta Montecorvino*
38. Campobosso
39. Torella
40. *San Leonardo*
41. The Gully
42. *Ortona*

43. Cassino II
44. Gustav Line
45. Liri Valley
46. *Hitler Line*
47. *Gothic Line*
48. *Lamone Crossing*
49.Misano Ridge
50. *Rimini Line*
51. San Martino-San Lorenzo
52. Pisciatello
53. Fosso Vecchio
54. *Italy, 1943–45*
55. Apeldoorn
56. *Northwest Europe, 1945*

Korea

57. *Korea, 1951–53*

Notes

Introduction

1.   John A. Lynn, *Battle: A History of Combat and Culture* (Boulder, CO: Westview, 2003), 156.

2.   "HRH Prince Philip's Address, 23 October 1963," *The Connecting File: The Regimental Journal of The Royal Canadian Regiment* (henceforth *The Connecting File*), 1969, iv.

3.   "Remarks by MGen J.E. Vance on the Occasion of the Regimental Change of Appointment Parade of the Colonel of the Regiment," *Pro Patria: The Regimental Newsletter of The Royal Canadian Regiment* (henceforth *Pro Patria*), August 1981, Issue 46, 10.

4.   Captain J.A. Johnston, "A Year with the Royal Canadian Regiment," *The Connecting File*, Winter 1950–51, 54.

5.   D.G. Loomis, "Foreword," *Pro Patria*, Issue 1, June 1969, 1. Loomis also believed, "It is pride and trust rather than money which provides the basis of loyal, unflinching discipline in both war and peace. No one would disagree that the true Regiment, with our transcendental loyalties and carefully fostered codes of courage and sacrifice, can operate with men who are here today and gone tomorrow. The Regiment must have them and guaranteed continuity to train raw recruits into men such as we have — proud, tough soldiers — who draw spiritual strength and courage from

those who have gone before, from long friendships, from acts of proven and justified trust, from a sense of belonging to a great organization and from a feeling of devotion to our institutions which we have made such an integral part of our life and being." He added, "We all recognize that a strong regiment pays off in battle and in the nerve-wracking, frustrating duties of peacekeeping and internal security. It is our Regiment that demands the best from all of us and inspires us to give more than our mere pay cheques would demand of others in our society." Lieutenant-Colonel Dan Loomis, "CO's Remarks," *The Connecting File,* 1969, 8–9.

6. Arthur Bryant, "The Fate of the Regiment," *The Connecting File,* April 1948, 19. In 1953, Brigadier T.G. Gibson, Commander Western Ontario stated: "Notwithstanding the technical aspects of modern soldiering, the ancient and honourable qualities of the regular man-at-arms-the 'trusty and well-beloved servant' of the Crown — retain their primary importance. Personal integrity, physical fitness, unselfish loyalty and self-respect are simple virtues which in their very simplicity are often overlooked in this technological and materialistic era." He added, "Technical skills may be acquired and many desirable soldierly qualities developed, but the personal character of the individual is the real measure of his worth." Gibson concluded, "The regimental system which we enjoy in Canada provides the surest means of instilling in our infantryman the sense of teamwork that is essential in the field." He professed, "Well-trained officers and men bound together by pride of regiment and inspired by tradition are capable of great achievements." Brigadier T.G. Gibson, "Editorial," *The Connecting File,* Vol. 26, No. 1, Spring-Summer 1954, 4.

7. "HRH Prince Philip's Address, 23 October 1963," *The Connecting File,* 1969, iii.

8. Captain J.F. Farmer, "Members One of Another — For Country," *The Connecting File,* 1968, 5.

9. Editorial, *The Connecting File,* Fall-Winter 1953–54, 5. Along those same lines, Lieutenant-General Vance noted, "As a regiment we've taken to heart a kind of central need to be the nucleus on which to build a sense of professionalism for Canada's Army. We have almost from the beginning been the custodian of standards which are brought out, put to the test, demonstrated and talked about only when the chips are down. And yet, if those standards had not been there from 1885, where would they have been in 1899 when we set off for South Africa? Where would they

have been in 1914, or in 1939? But the point is somebody had to be really concerned about standards of professionalism. I think the thing that most characteristics RCR in this respect vis-à-vis the other regiments — has been its birthright almost certainly its lifelong preoccupation as the hearth keepers of professionalism in the Canadian infantry." Lieutenant-General Jack Vance, interview with author, 22 July 2005.

10. The term *Royal* is used throughout to describe members of The RCR. Although the historic, formal term (that is still used on parades) is *Royal Canadians*, the term *Royals* has been used since the Second World War to designate RCRs. It is recognized that *Royals* has also been used for members of the Royal Regiment of Canada.

11. Volume 1 is R.C. Fetherstonaugh, *The Royal Canadian Regiment, 1883–1933* (Fredericton, NB: The RCR, 1936). Volume 2 is G.R. Stevens, *The Royal Canadian Regiment, Volume Two 1933–1966* (London, ON: London Printing Co., 1967). Part 2, Volume 3, this volume, is entitled *From Cold War to New Millennium, 1953–2008*. Part 1, Volume 3, is Bernd Horn, *Establishing a Legacy: The History of The Royal Canadian Regiment, 1883–1953* (Toronto: Dundurn, 2009).

Chapter 1: Defending the Bastion of Freedom and Democracy

1. See Horn, *Establishing A Legacy*, for a detailed history of The RCR experience in the Korean War.

2. Canada, *House of Common Debates* [henceforth *Debates*], 5 February 1951, 77.

3. *Debates*, 12 February 1951, 267.

4. *Debates*, 8 May 1951, 2833. The paranoia included such claims by Parliamentarians as, "We also have no reason to believe that the Russians have not at this time, somewhere in the north, set up camouflaged rocket installations. It is not entirely beyond the realm of possibility;" and "We have no reason to believe they could not send suicide bombing missions, and if they did central Canada would make a beautiful target." *Ibid.*, 2834.

5. By 1953, the defence budget reached $1,907 million, a tenfold increase over 1947. Desmond Morton, *A Military History of Canada* (Toronto: McClelland & Stewart Inc., 1992), 238.

6. On 5 March 1946, at the request of Westminster College in the small

Missouri town of Fulton (population, 7,000), Churchill gave his now famous "Iron Curtain" speech to a crowd of 40,000. Besides accepting an honorary degree from the college, Churchill made one of his most famous post-war speeches. In this speech, Churchill gave the very descriptive phrase that surprised the United States and Britain, "From Stettin in the Baltic to Trieste in the Adriatic, an iron curtain has descended across the Continent." "Winston Churchill's Iron Curtain Speech," http://history1900s. about.com/library/weekly/aa082400a.htm (accessed on 29 August 2007). As early as 5 January 1946, Truman had said, "Unless Russia is faced with an iron fist and strong language, another war is in the making." James Chance, "The Day the Cold War Started," in Robert Cowley, ed., *The Cold War: A Military History* (New York: Random House Trade Paperbacks, 2006), 3. As of 18 December 1951, the Soviets maintained in their zone of occupation in Germany alone, 10 mechanized divisions, eight tank divisions, four rifle divisions, eight anti-aircraft divisions, and two artillery divisions, a total of 303,100 personnel. They also possessed a 15:1 advantage over NATO in fighter aircraft. Moreover, NATO planners believed the Soviets could reinforce their numbers with a further 60 divisions after initial mobilization. Sean Maloney, *War Without Battles: Canada's NATO Brigade in Germany 1951–1993* (Whitby, ON: McGraw Hill-Ryerson, 1997), 34.

7.   Canada carried out unprecedented peacetime military spending. On 5 February 1951, Brooke Claxton the MND announced dramatic rearmament initiatives; a division for the Army, 100 ships for the Royal Canadian Navy, and 40 squadrons for the Royal Canadian Air Force. This spending totalled $5 billion over the next three years.

8.   The MSF concept called for an airborne brigade group with forces drawn from Active Force units. Its mission was to counter enemy lodgements wherever they might take place in Canada, particularly in the North. For a detailed explanation see Horn, *Bastard Sons: The Canadian Airborne Experience 1942–1995* (St. Catharines, ON: Vanwell Publishing, 2001), 69–97; and Horn, *Establishing a Legacy*, 208–09.

9.   For a detailed explanation of the "exposed northern flank" issue and the consequent U.S./Canadian dynamic, see Bernd Horn, *Bastard Sons*, 69–97. By 1954, there were 30 radar stations strung out along the 49th parallel that made up the Pinetree line. The following year work began on the Mid-Canada line, which consisted of a series of radars along the 55th Parallel to provide additional warning. This was later reinforced by a line of radar

stations in the deep Arctic from Alaska to Baffin Island, making up the Distant Early Warning Line. It was completed in 1957. Collectively the belts of radar stations were designed to detect incoming Soviet bombers.

10. The DCGS anticipated that the long-term objective of forming the nucleus of the Active Force Brigade around three infantry battalions, trained in airborne/air-transported operations, would be realized by April 1951.

11. The concept for NATO originated in a 1948 British sponsored Treaty of Brussels, where a number of European countries formed an alliance to present a common front against the Soviet juggernaut. However, the scope of the threat necessitated bringing the U.S. and others on board. As a result NATO was formed, adding the U.S., Canada, Denmark, Iceland, and Italy to the original group of England, France, Belgium, the Netherlands, and Luxembourg.

12. Department of National Defence (henceforth DND), Directorate of History and Heritage (henceforth DHH), file 112.3M2 (D369), "Operational Requirement of Airborne Forces for the Defence of Canada," 3 December 1948.

13. James Eayrs, *In Defence of Canada, Volume Three: Peacemaking and Deterrence* (Toronto: University of Toronto Press, 1972), 100, 107, and 401. See also D.J. Bercuson, *True Patriot: The Life of Brooke Claxton, 1898-1960* (Toronto: University of Toronto Press, 1993), 195; and *Documents on Canadian External Relations, Vol. 11, 1944–45*, 1583. The case for a diversionary attack to tie up resources merits consideration. In the Second World War, the violation of American territory, namely the Aleutian Islands of Attu and Kiska, resulted in the investment of an Alaskan garrison of a quarter of a million troops. James Stokesbury, "The U.S. Army and Coalition Warfare, 1941–1945," in K.J. Hagan and W.R. Roberts, eds., *Against all Enemies*, (New York: Greenwood, 1986), 290.

14. DHH, File 112.3M2 (D369), "Composition of Mobile Striking Force for Defence of Canada," 3 December 1948; and "Appreciation on the Mobile Striking Force," 13 May 1949. See also DHH, File 112.3M2 (D400), "Appreciation on the Employment of the Active Force Brigade Group in Defence of Canada Operations," 1 November 1949.

15. Furthermore, it explained that the lack of a fighter escort would make sustained operations impossible. Even the use of the North for transitory aircraft operations was discounted. The Defence Cabinet Committee rationalized that "if the Soviets attempted to use a Canadian Arctic

station as a bomber base, warning would be received and it was expected that such a base, which would have immense supply problems, could be immobilized rapidly." More important, the official defence plan identified only Western Alaska and the Aleutian Islands as targets of potential enemy airborne forces. *Documents on Canadian External Relations, Vol. 17, 1951,* 1249. *Defence Scheme No. 3 — Major War,* Chapter 5; DHH, File 112.3M2 (D10), "The Direct Defence of Canada," 16 September 1948, Appendix A, 2 and 4. See also *Documents on Canadian External Relations, Vol. 15, 1949,* 1560–61. The Joint Intelligence Committee noted that "the radius of aircraft restrict area of operations to points in Alaska west of Fairbanks and Anchorage and to the extreme west of the Aleutian chain. DHH, File 112.3M2 (D400), "The MSF," 29 March 1950.

16. DHH, File 112.3M2 (D400), "The Employment of the MSF for Reduction of Enemy Lodgements in Canada," 2 May 1950.

17. Prime Minister Mackenzie King believed that the North did not represent a grave security risk. He endorsed the then Governor General's observation that stations in the Arctic "may become bases from which the enemy himself may operate were they not there." He subsequently formulated the strategy that "our best defence in the Arctic is the Arctic itself." Claxton reiterated this belief. He proclaimed, "In working out the doctrine of defence of our north, the fewer airfields we have, the fewer airfields we have to defend against the possibility of the enemy using them as stepping stones from which to leapfrog toward our settled areas. Indeed, were it possible the greatest single defence throughout our northland would be the rough nature of the ground and the extent of the territory itself." General McNaughton agreed with the concept that "ice is something of a defence in itself," and L.B. Pearson from the Department of External Affairs quickly dubbed the government's position the "scorched ice policy." Pickersgill, *Record, Vol. 3,* 370; and *Documents on Canadian External Relations Vol. 17, 1951,* 1249; Eayrs, *Peacekeeping and Deterrence,* 344; *Debates,* 15 April 1953, 3920; and Alan Harvey, "Scorched Ice Policy," *The Globe and Mail,* 27 November 1948, 17.

18. DHH, File 112.3M2 (D400), "The Employment of the Mobile Striking Force in the Reduction of Enemy Lodgements," April 1950; DHH, File 112.3M2 (D401), "MSF Plan for Reduction of Enemy Lodgements in Northern Canada," 23 August 1950; DHH, File 112.3M2 (D371), "MSF Directive," 14 August 1951; and DHH, File 112.3M2 (D388). It was

also decided that any enemy lodgement beyond the limits of Northern Continental Canada (the mainland) would be dealt with only by air strike. This was based on the premise that distances involved would make the mounting, particularly the enlargement of forward staging bases, of parachute operations to slow for timely response. A further pragmatic advantage was also considered. The smaller geographic area of responsibility made the employment of parachute forces more manageable. DHH, File 112.3M2 (371), "Mobile Striking Force Concept," 23 July 1951.

19. Warrant Officer D.J. Lacroix recalled how one morning in Brockville when the requirement to commence parachute and air-transportability training began rather suddenly with the arrival of the PPCLI para-instructors. "We couldn't get over how they doubled around camp whenever they went anywhere. We were told things like. "These guys are the toughest there are," and "You better do what you're told, these para instructors don't fool around." Lacroix added, "needless to say, we did and they didn't." WO D.J. Lacroix, "The End of An Era," *The Connecting File*, 1968, 12.

20. Interview with Ted Zuber, 30 July 2007.

21. Colonel Tim Riley, Letter to author, 5 June 2008.

22. Interview with Lieutenant-General (Retired) Jack Vance, 22 July 2005. Sergeant Bud Jones remembered, "When I returned to Petawawa from Korea, as soon as I walked in the door I was faced by a great big sergeant-major with a handlebar mustache who boomed 'Bud Jones are you going to be a jumper?' Although I always told myself there was no way I'm going to be a jumper I responded, You bet I am!'" Interview with Sergeant (Retired) Bud Jones, 12 November 2007.

23. Canada, *Canada's Defence Programme* (Ottawa: DND, 1956), 13.

24. 118. Defence spending, as a percentage of the Gross National Product, rose from 1.7 percent in 1947 to 7.6 percent in 1953. J.L Granatstein and D. Bercuson, *War and Peacekeeping* (Toronto: Key Porter Books, 1991), 2. The CGS planned for authorized Army strength to increase approximately 31 percent from 22,000 to 30,800 officers and men. *Documents on Canadian External Relations, Vol. 16, 1950,* 112. That same year the MND was able to report that military establishments had already increased by 40 percent. Library and Archives Canada (henceforth LAC), MG 32, Vol. 94, Box 5, Claxton Papers, "Memorandum to Cabinet," 7 August 1950.

25. The emphasis of military activity in the North shifted from a focus on active "defence" to one of simply "surveillance." This subtle shift was reflected

in DND annual reports. In the years between 1946 and 1957, the stated aim of Canada's defence program underwent a distinct evolution. Initially, the narratives contained in the publications, *Report on the Department of National Defence* and *Canada's Defence Program*, for these years defined the military's efforts in terms of "defence of Canada from direct attack." With the change of the threat assessment, the wording was amended to a more ambiguous "to provide for the security of Canada." Moreover, from 1949 to 1955, the Department of National Defence's annual summary, *Canada's Defence Program*, spoke of the need to repel "surprise attacks." In 1956, the wording was changed to reflect a scaled down level of direct danger to Canadian territory. The reports now noted that troops were required to deal only with "possible enemy lodgements." *DND Reports*, 1946–53 and *Canada's Defence Program*, 1949–57. Protection was never an issue. In later years the Parliamentary Special Committee on Defence noted the nation's irrefutable safety net. The Committee's report admitted, "the inviolability of Canadian territory is a sine qua non condition of the defence of the United States." *Special Committee on Defence: Proceedings*, 17 December 1963, 808.

26. George Kitching, *Mud and Green Fields: The Memoirs of Major-General George Kitching* (St. Catharines, ON: Vanwell, 1992), 260–61. See also DHH, File 112.3M2.009 (D264), "Army No Longer Smug in Arctic," *Winnipeg Free Press*, 8 December 1954.

27. Major-General C. Vokes, General Officer Commanding (GOC) Western Command, suggested that "a platoon or squad of fifteen men well-trained for northern operations would be a compact, hard-hitting group with greater mobility than one of normal strength." DHH, File 327.009 (D388), Letter, Vokes to the Acting VCDS, 22 August 1951. Vokes opined that "long range armed reconnaissance by the RCAF, should be adequate to eliminate lodgements immediately such are spotted, in the Barrenlands of Northern Canada and the Arctic Archipelago." *Ibid.* Similarly, the brigadier responsible for General Staff Plans, questioned the need for a large airborne force. He reminded staff of the director military operations and plans (DMO & P) that the resources of the Americans, namely two airborne brigades, should not be forgotten in planning for northern defence. He also remarked, "It would surely be more economical to use small parties of infantry carried in light craft to deal with enemy sea landings than the expensive parachutist." DHH, File 112.3M2 (D369). The RCAF insisted that in many cases "air

action alone might be sufficient to reduce an enemy lodgement." DHH, File 327.009 (D388), Letter, Acting VCGS to GOC Western Command, 14 August 1951. The nebulous nature of the threat prompted Western Command and the Tactical Air Group to demand: (a) further amplification on the three main reasons for an enemy lodgement with direction as to the degree of probability of each; (b) more detail as to how the enemy would make such a lodgement, its size, duration, and possible action after primary mission was completed; (c) The number of lodgements that might be expected simultaneously; and (d) most likely targets. DHH, File 112.3M2 (D264), "Estimate of Enemy Lodgements in Northern Canada," 2 September 1952.

28.   "Canadian Combined Forces Exercise Bulldog II, 1954," *The Polar Record*, Vol. 7, No. 51, September 1955, 492. The problems with aircraft were legion. Staff planners noted "that the serviceability figures for below 30 degree conditions on runways is very low, which is not surprising considering the serviceability rate in Montreal is only 50 percent." During the exercise, on the second attempt at a drop, only two of seven aircraft were capable of take-off even after a 1.5 hour warm-up. This was of little consequence, since the winds during the day were an average of 19 miles per hour, a full four miles per hour more than the permissible velocity. A night drop was out of the question since, as noted by the Director General of Army Plans and Operations, "we cannot drop at night because the night drop is no longer a part of the para course." He admitted, "If we can't drop in darkness, we might never get into certain places in the North at all." Not surprisingly, the press was asked not to publicize this point. Amazingly, they complied. DHH, File 112.3M2.009 (D264), Letter by Brigadier R.P Rothschild, 31 December 1954. See also Colonel W.N. Russel, "Airborne or Heliborne?" *CDQ*, Vol. 7, No. 3, 1978, 41.

29.   DHH, File 112.3M2.009 (D264), "Change Due in Arctic Warfare — The Lesson of Bulldog II," *Ottawa Citizen*, 10 December 1954. The final report of Exercise Bull Dog II recommended that "airlandings be practised on MSF exercises to determine whether this method might prove a more reliable means of delivering troops." *Ibid.*, "Airlandings — MSF Operations," 30 August 1956. Once again it was a question of threat. The unnamed officers stated the targets such as weather stations would not be worthwhile targets to an enemy.

30.   Interview with Lieutenant-General (Retired) Jack Vance, 22 July 2005.

31. See Maloney, *War Without Battles*, for the detailed history of Canada's NATO brigade in Europe.

32. "2nd Battalion The Royal Canadian Regiment," *The Connecting File*, Fall-Winter 1953–54, 81–82.

33. *Ibid.*, 81–82.

34. *Ibid.*

35. Interview with Lieutenant-General (Retired) Jack Vance, 22 July 2005.

36. *Ibid.* Sergeant Jones explained, "We went to Fort Lewis for pre-training and left right from Seattle for Germany. The families were shipped over separately." Interview with Sergeant (Retired) Bud Jones, 12 November 2007.

37. Interview with Lieutenant-General (Retired) Jack Vance, 22 July 2005.

38. *Ibid.*

39. Quoted in Jack Granatstein, *Canada's Army: Waging War and Keeping the Peace* (Toronto: University of Toronto Press, 2002), 340.

40. Interview with Lieutenant-General (Retired) Jack Vance, 22 July 2005.

41. Interview with Sergeant (Retired) Bud Jones, 12 November 2007.

42. Canada, *The Infantry Battalion in Battle (Motorized)* (Ottawa: DND, ND), para 101–02. The other roles were to gain information about the enemy by means of patrolling; to locate, contain and in conjunction with, or without nuclear weapons, destroy enemy penetration; to mop up; to form a mobile reserve; to form part of the advance guard in the advance to contact; to force the crossing of a defended obstacle; to close with and complete the destruction of the enemy; to maintain contact in the pursuit; to form part of the covering force in the withdrawal.

43. *Ibid.*, para 101–02.

44. Clearly the long-term effects of the different types of radiation were not known. During this period soldiers were also exercised in the Nevada desert to practice moving through the radiated battlefield following up atomic weapon detonations.

45. RCR Museum Archives, War Diary entry 21 August 1954. War Diary 2 RCR 1 August 54 to 31 August 54.

46. President Harry S. Truman stated on 30 November 1950, "We will take whatever steps are necessary to meet the military situation, just as we always have." In response to the question of whether this meant the use of the atomic bomb, he replied, "That includes every weapon we have … The military commander in the field will have charge of the use of the weapons, as he always has." President Eisenhower concurred. He dismissed the idea

of a "nice, sweet World War II type of war." He believed that if war came in any form, the United States would fight it with every weapon in its arsenal because the Soviet Union would surely do the same. Quoted in John Lewis Gaddis, *The Cold War: A New History* (New York: Penguin Books, 2005), 48 and 67.

47. "2nd Battalion The Royal Canadian Regiment," *The Connecting File*, Vol. 27, No. 1, Spring-Summer 1955, 52.

48. DHH, AHR, 2 RCR (1848) 1951, 1952, 1955–1957, Vol. 1, 2 RCR Historical Report, 31 December 1957.

49. Chief Warrant Officer John O'Quinn, interview with author, 23 March 2010.

50. Colonel Tim Riley, Letter to author, 5 June 2008.

51. DHH, File 325.009 (D840), Colonel N.G. Wilson-Smith, Directorate of Infantry, "Infantry Liaison Letter No. 10," 18 August 1958, 1.

52. *Ibid.*, Directorate of Infantry (DoI), Infantry Conference 1958, Conference Minutes, Serial 3, 2.

53. *Ibid.*, Serial 3, 4.

54. *Ibid.*, Serial 3, 3.

55. DHH, File 325.009 (D840), DoI, Infantry Conference 1959, Conference Minutes, May 1959, 10.

56. DoI, Infantry Conference 1958, Conference Minutes, Serial 3, 1.

57. *Ibid.*, Conference Minutes, Serial 3, 2.

58. *Ibid.*, Conference Minutes, Serial 5, 1. The director of infantry explained, "Modern war resembles two blind-folded heavy weights each with the capacity to deal a knock-out blow — if they can find a target. The first one to get his blind-fold off has a powerful, and quite likely decisive, advantage." *Ibid.*

59. John F. Guilmartin, "The ICBM and the Cold War: Technology in the Driver's Seat," in Cowley, *The Cold War*, 421.

60. DoI, Infantry Conference 1958, Conference Minutes, Serial 3, 1.

61. *Ibid.*, Conference Minutes, Serial 3, 1.

62. *Ibid.*, Conference Minutes, 8.

63. *Ibid.*, Conference Minutes, Serial 3, 2. This position overrode that taken earlier and captured in the 1952 publication *The Infantry Battalion in Battle (Motorized)*, which stated in the introduction, "Although the Infantry Brigade Group will not have an organic nuclear capability, they will almost always fight as part of a larger UK or US formation having such a capability. Nuclear support may come from a number of different

delivery systems not all of which are operated by artillery." By the end of the decade, the infantry corps saw itself needing an organic capability. As far as the division of responsibility in nuclear warfare, the director of infantry stated, "in so far as infantry is concerned our responsibilities, which are common to all corps, are as follows: a. radiation reconnaissance within unit areas; b. decontamination of personnel, equipment, ammunition, stores and ground unit capability; c. location and identification of nuclear bursts; d. protection against nuclear bursts; e. understand the effects of nuclear weapons to the extent of being capable of performing elementary nuclear target analysis; and f. analysis of any target to be engaged by the weapons available to the unit."

64. By mid-decade it was universally accepted by the government, military, and public, that the only probable method of attack, as highlighted in the 1954 Defence Program, was by air, specifically by the manned bomber. The Minister of National Defence bluntly affirmed "that in the final analysis the task of Canadian defence is defence against aerial attack over the north pole. We have to discard from any realistic thinking any possibility of an attack by ground forces on the area of Canada either by air or by sea." He also stated: "Anyone who has any knowledge of the terrain of the outlying parts of this country will realize that such an attempt would be worthless and useless and is not likely to be part of any aggressive plans which may be launched against Canada." The continuing belief was that "any attack on Canada will be in essence part of an attack on the United States." *Debates*, 17 June 1955, 4925. See also *Canada's Defence Programme* 1949–50; and A. Brewin, *Stand on Guard: The Search for a Canadian Defence Policy* (Toronto: McClelland & Stewart, 1965), 53–54.

65. DoI, Infantry Conference 1958, Conference Minutes, 4.

66. Warrant Officer Lacroix quipped, "Airportability consisted of manoeuvring jeeps and 1/4 tons into a mock-up of the C-47 Dakota. We squeezed each vehicle into and out of the mock-up a thousand times in the morning and a thousand times in the afternoon, it seemed." WO D.J. Lacroix, "The End of An Era," *The Connecting File*, 1968, 12.

67. DoI, Infantry Conference 1958, Conference Minutes, 3.

68. *Ibid.*, Conference Minutes, 3.

69. Brigadier T.G. Gibson, "Editorial," *The Connecting File*, Vol. 29, No. 1, Summer 1957, 5.

Chapter 2: An Era of Change

1. The Berlin blockade of 24 June 1948 to 12 May 1949 was one of the first major crises of the Cold War. In a bid to gain complete control of occupied Berlin, the Soviets blocked railway and road access to the other sectors of the city (i.e. American, British, and French sectors). The western powers organized an airlift of supplies that reached up to 927 aircraft, delivering approximately 6,393 tons of goods a day. In fact, by the spring of 1949, the airlift was supplying more cargo than had been previously delivered by rail. The Soviets subsequently lifted the blockade in May. The Warsaw Pact was the commonly known name given to the Soviet sponsored mutual defence Treaty of Friendship, Co-operation and Mutual Assistance that was established on 14 May 1955, as a counterpoint to NATO, specifically in response to the inclusion of West Germany into NATO. The member states at time of creation included Albania, Bulgaria, Czechoslovakia, East Germany, Slovakia, Hungary, Poland, Romania, and the U.S.S.R..

2. Approximately 3.5 million East Germans defected the Soviet-occupied territory before the Berlin Wall was erected.

3. Maloney, *War Without Battles*,159.

4. Quoted in Maloney, *War Without Battles,* 160.

5. On 15 October 1962, American intelligence personnel who were analyzing U-2 spy plane data taken over Cuba discovered that the Soviets were building medium-range missile sites on the island. The following day, President Kennedy convened an emergency meeting of his senior military, political, and diplomatic advisers to discuss the way forward. A surgical air strike against the missile sites was ruled out, and the president instead agreed to a naval quarantine of the island. Moreover, the U.S. demanded that the bases be dismantled and missiles removed. The naval blockade began on 23 October, and by the following day Soviet ships en route to Cuba capable of carrying military cargoes appeared to have altered, or reversed their course as they neared the American blockade line. On 26 October, the Soviets proposed a solution to end the crisis. They pledged to remove the missile bases in exchange for an American guarantee not to invade Cuba. Nikita Khrushchev announced the Kremlin's intent to dismantle and remove all offensive Soviet weapons in Cuba on 28 October, thereby effectively ending the crisis. The final agreement also included the removal of the U.S. Jupiter missiles stationed in Turkey.

6. Major-General (Retired) Tom de Faye, interview with author, 13 February 2009.

7. Brigadier-General Philip Spencer, interview with author, 18 March 2010.

8. Historian John Lewis Gaddis later noted that there was "a certain stability, even predictability, after 1962." He explained, "Neither side would ever again initiate direct challenges to the other's spheres of influence. Anomalies like a divided Germany and Korea — even absurdities like a walled capitalist West Berlin in the middle of a communist East Germany, or an American naval base on the territory of a Soviet ally just off the coast of Florida — came to seem quite normal." However, at the time, it seemed as if the world was teetering on the edge of war. Quoted in Cowley, *The Cold War*, xv.

9. Directorate of Infantry, "Infantry Liaison Letter No. 14," 27 October 1960, 3. DHH, File 325.009 (D840).

10. Major-General (Retired) Tom de Faye, interview with author, 13 February 2009.

11. Subjects of Discussion, Seminar of 1 Feb, Infantry Commanders' Conference 1960. DHH, file 325.009 (D840).

12. 1 RCR, Annual Historical Report for the Year Ending 31 December 1961, 22 January 1962. DHH, AHR, 1 RCR (1847), 1958–1965, Vol. 2.

13. Colonel Tim Riley, Letter to author, 5 June 2008.

14. Kitching, *Mud and Green Fields*, 268.

15. "Affiliated Officers' Conferences," *The Connecting File*, Vol. 33, No. 1, 1962, 19.

16. Pat Rossiter, interview with author, 6 April 2010.

17. Directorate of Infantry, "Infantry Liaison Letter No. 15," 12 June 1961, 3. DHH, File 325.009 (D840).

18. Major-General (Retired) Tom de Faye, interview with author, 13 February 2009. De Faye noted, "Equipment was very poor at the time. Second thing you did after settling in on arrival to Germany was to go downtown to Butzbach War Surplus and buy your kit — a U.S. surplus field jacket and U.S. rain jacket. That's how inadequate our kit was."

19. Lieutenant-General (Retired) Jack Vance, interview with author, 22 July 2005. Besides the focused mission, Vance also explained that there was also the exposure to Europe — the travel and personal experience, the different NATO nations, and the overall cultural experience.

20. "1 RCR — Training," *The Connecting File*, 1965, 25. "The training cycle," explained one Germany veteran, "was predictable — individual training

early spring; collective training and low level company training in the summer and then high level major collective training during 'fall ex.'"

21. Quoted in G.R. Stevens, *The Royal Canadian Regiment: Volume Two, 1933–1966* (London, ON: London Printing & Lithographing Co., Ltd., 1967), 329.

22. "Second Battalion, Training," *The Connecting File*, 1966, 30.

23. Lieutenant-General (Retired) Jack Vance, interview with author, 22 July 2005. Vance observed, "One of the bad side effects was that inevitably there was a kind of double standard in terms of which part of the army got the higher priority, whether it was who got the new equipment first and/or who got the extra money for more ammunition, or whatever it happened to be. So, fairly often the troops back home felt that they were being treated as sort of second-class citizens."

24. Colonel Joe Atchison noted, "I went to Germany to 2 RCR in 1968 and found the Germany NATO experience to be entirely different from soldiering in Canada. In many respects, the unit role was simpler — prepare to fight a nuclear battle against armour-heavy forces advancing on a broad front. There were no 'distractions' like Aid of the Civil Power, Civil Defense or parachuting. There was more equipment in the unit than in a Canada battalion. There were 18 M113 and one M548 plus a couple of 3/4 tons and a jeep in B Coy. Support Coy contained a mortar platoon of eight 4.2 inch mortars and an anti-tank platoon containing 12 106 mm RRs and some ENTAC ATGMs. When the unit moved or when it was laid out on the square for the annual Brigade Commander's Inspection, it was an impressive sight!" Colonel Joe Aitcheson, Letter to author, 17 December 2010.

25. DHH, AHR, 1 RCR (1847), 1958–65, Vol. 2, 1 RCR, Annual Historical Report for the Year Ending 31 December 1962, 31 January 1963.

26. "1 RCR — Three Years with 1 RCR," *The Connecting File*, 1965, 16.

27. "Second Battalion, Training," *The Connecting File*, 26.

28. Carson "Oscar" Lambert, interview with author, 24 February 2010.

29. Chief Warrant Officer Jay Gravelle, interview with author, 25 August 2009.

30. *Ibid.*

31. Gerald Skibinsky, letter to author, 26 March 2008.

32. D.C. Spry, "Editorial," *The Connecting File*, 1968, 2.

33. "Report on National Survival Activities," DSO&P Briefing, 4 January 1962, 2. RCR Museum Archives, Vol. 17, File 21, 2. As early as 1956, the reserve force was given the new role/task of civil defence. Three years

later the MND assigned tasks to the entire military in accordance with the Civil Defence Order — 1959. They were:

1. Provision of technical facilities and operation of a system to give warning to the public of the likelihood and imminence of an attack;
2. Determining the location of a nuclear explosion and the patterns of fallout, and giving the necessary warning of fallout to the public;
3. Assessment of damage and casualties from attack and fallout;
4. Controlling, directing and carrying out re-entry into areas damaged by a nuclear explosion or contaminated by serious radioactive fallout, decontamination work in those areas, and the rescue and provision of first aid to those trapped or injured;
5. Direction of police and fire services seriously damaged or contaminated areas that are the object of re-entry operations, including the control of traffic and movement of people in those areas;
6. Direction of municipal and other services for the maintenance and repair of water and sewer systems in seriously damaged or contaminated areas;
7. Provision of emergency support to provincial and municipal authorities in the maintenance of law and order and in dealing with panic or the breakdown of civilian authority; and
8. Maintenance and operation of emergency communication facilities.

34. See Horn, *Bastard Sons,* for details on the continuing debate on the "Arctic threat."
35. RCR Museum Archives, Vol. 17, File 21, "Report on National Survival Activities," DSO&P Briefing, 4 January 1962, 1, 3.
36. *Ibid.*
37. *Ibid.*
38. *Ibid.,* 4.

39. Bob Mahar, interview with author, 22 March 2010.

40. Carson "Oscar" Lambert, interview with author, 24 February 2010.

41. "Third Battalion," *The Connecting File*, Vol. 33, No. 1, 1962, 24.

42. "Civil Defence Stores Arrive with New Year," *The Connecting File,* Vol. 32, No. 1, April 1961, 11.

43. *Ibid.*

44. The mobile support column "is a military force designed primarily to carry out rescue operations during the re-entry phase of survival operations. It may also be used to restore order or guard essential installations or on any other appropriate task in survival operations. A column may also be used to assist civil authorities in national disasters such as explosions, fires, floods and hurricanes." Mobile Support Columns were designed to perform the following tasks: reconnaissance of damaged areas; radiation monitoring; decontamination; search and rescue; casualty collection and limited first aid; and police duties. Mobile support columns were task tailored forces designed to correspond to situation and location and intended for short-term operations. The doctrine stated: "Initially, the priority mission of columns will be the collection and evacuation of refugees followed by the rescue and collection of casualties. In the later stages of an operation, salvage, removal of health hazards and restoration of utilities will assume increased importance." In addition, the doctrine said that "the mobile support column will deploy on the outer edge of the area of damage and will work in towards the centre. First priority will normally be given to the areas of lighter damage since it is in this region that a concerted effort is likely to yield the largest saving of life." At all times the guiding principle is to use available effort in such a way as to produce the greatest possible saving of life." The RCR Museum and Archives, Vol. 17, File 17, "Training for national Survival — The Mobile Support Column."

45. "2nd Battalion," *The Connecting File*, Vol. 34, No. 1, 1963, 20.

46. At approximately the same time, the MND stated that the Army had four primary roles. In priority, he listed: (1) commitment of a brigade group in Europe and the maintenance of sufficiently trained groups in Canada in order to rotate that brigade; (2) the maintenance of a stand-by force on call to meet any further United Nations request; (3) the maintenance of a force capable of taking action against any possible commando-type raid in the Arctic or elsewhere in Canada; and (4) survival operations [nuclear war scenario].

47. "Force Structure — Mobile Command Guidelines." DHH, File 112.11.003 (D3) — Box 1.

48. DHH, File 112.012 (D1), *Debates*, 18 July 1958, 2363; *Special Committee on Defence: Minutes of Proceedings and Evidence*, 7 July 1960, 453; *ibid.*, 11 July 1963, 147; *ibid.*, 22 October 1963, 505.; and "Defence Achievements 1957–1960." See also Lieutenant-Colonel R.B. Tacaberry, "Keeping the Peace," *behind the headlines*, Vol. 26, No. 1, September 1966, 7. Lester B. Pearson, the Canadian secretary of state for external affairs and originator of the 1956 Suez Emergency Force concept, wrote of the need for countries to earmark small forces for U.N. duty to perform such functions as securing ceasefires that had been agreed upon by belligerents. See Lester B. Pearson, "Force for U.N.," *Foreign Affairs*, Vol. 35, No. 3, April 1957, 401. Brigadier-General Don Holmes stated: "We were the first genuine UN standby battalion — full strength, inoculated, and raring to go." "One Less Tiger," *Sentinel*, 1976/4, 8.

49. *Special Studies prepared for the Special Committee of the House of Commons on Matters Relating to Defence*, Supplement 1964/65, 84. The U.N. operation in the Congo (ONUC) was conducted from 1960 to 1964. Its function was to cover the withdrawal of Belgian forces and help the government maintain law and order with a view to maintaining the Congo's territorial integrity and political independence.

50. The agreement also provided for the creation of British Sovereign Base (SBA) areas on the island, namely Akrotiri SBA and Dhekalia SBA. Aside from the obvious problems created by two members of the alliance fighting (i.e. Greece and Turkey), Cyprus was also critical for NATO, particularly the Americans and British. The British kept a number of signals intelligence sites on the island (and post independence in the SBAs). In addition, both Britain and the U.S. flew U-2 reconnaissance aircraft sorties from the SBAs in the 1960s. Furthermore, the U.S. was concerned that Turkey remain a member of NATO, therefore, a solution to the Cypriot issue was very important. After all, the Americans kept many signals and electronic intelligence sites on Turkish soil, as well as nuclear munitions storage sites. In addition, they also flew reconnaissance aircraft from Turkish airbases. Therefore, much was at stake in Cyprus.

51. The RCR Museum Archives, 1 RCR Canadian Contingent Cyprus Force Structure Study, July 1970, para 118.1. War Diary of the 1st Battalion The Royal Canadian Regiment, Canadian Contingent, U.N. Force in Cyprus, from 1 September 1970 to 30 September 1970.

52. For a detailed account of the crisis, see Sean Maloney, *Canada and UN Peacekeeping: Cold War by Other Means, 1945–1970* (St. Catharines, ON: Vanwell, 2002), 187–221. By April 1964, UNFICYP had grown to nine infantry battalions and four armoured car squadrons.

53. "First Battalion, Commanding Officer's Comments," *The Connecting File,* 1966, 14.

54. *Ibid.*, 15.

55. The RCR Museum Archives, Vol. 23, File 4, 1 RCR "Operational Briefing," March 1967.

56. *Ibid.* 1

57. *Ibid.*

58. *Ibid.*

59. Major-General (Retired) Tom de Faye, interview with author, 13 February 2009.

60. 1 RCR, "Standing Operating Procedures for Kyrenia District," 17 October 1966, 209–10.

61. *Ibid.*, 203.

62. Interestingly, Balsam did not receive his chief of the defence staff commendation until 1976, 11 years after the event. At the time, senior commanders felt that the attendant publicity for the action might increase tension on the island. DND, New Release, 21 January 1976, reprinted in *Pro Patria*, Issue 28, May 1976, 55.

63. "First Battalion — Cyprus," *The Connecting File,* 1968, 9.

64. *Special Committee on Defence: Minutes of Proceedings and Evidence,* 22 October 1963, 507; and *Debates*, 8 May 1964, 3076.

65. *Special Committee on Defence: Minutes of Proceedings and Evidence,* 17 October 1963, 439; and *Debates*, 29 October 1963, 4141; and *ibid.*, 8 May 1964, 3076. Simonds argued that in terms of the country's size and financial burdens, this type of role would be "our most useful role within the alliance."

66. Already in 1956, General Maxwell Taylor, the American chairman of the Joint Chiefs of Staff, cautioned that "our program must provide for mobile ready forces prepared for rapid movement ... for use to resist local aggression in an unexpected quarter." He insisted that a strategy of "flexible response" was needed to provide a capability to react across the entire spectrum of possible challenge, for coping with anything from general atomic war to infiltrations. Maxwell D. Taylor, *The Uncertain Trumpet* (New York: Harper & Brothers, 1959), 191–96.

67. See Douglas Bland, *Chiefs of Defence: Government and the Unified Command of the Canadian Armed Forces* (Toronto: Canadian Institute of Strategic Studies, 1995), 63–90; and Douglas Bland, *Canada's National Defence. Vol. 1 Defence Policy* (Kinston: School of Policy Studies, 1997), 57–63.

68. *Special Committee on Defence: Minutes of Proceedings and Evidence*, 19 May 1964, 12.

69. Paul Hellyer, *Damn the Torpedoes: My Fight to Unify Canada's Armed Forces* (Toronto: McClelland & Stewart Ltd., 1990), 42–43.

70. "Defence," *Time*, Vol. 83, No. 14, 3 April 1964, 11–12. The new philosophy became enshrined in the *1964 White Paper* that captured the current emphasis on strategic mobility. Lieutenant-General Jean Victor Allard, then the Army commander, explained that "the [1964] White Paper subsequently set out a new concept for the utilization of our forces, based on their mobility, so that they could serve with the UN, with NATO, or within our own territory." General Jean V. Allard, *The Memoirs of General Jean V. Allard* (Vancouver: The University of British Columbia Press, 1988), 234.

71. The six functional commands were Mobile Command, Maritime Command, Air Defence Command, Air Transport Command, Material Command, and Training Command. In addition, eventually military training schools were streamlined from 91 to 32 and military trades cut down from 346 to 98.

72. *Debates*, 17 February 1966, 1417. See also *Special Committee on Defence: Minutes of Proceedings and Evidence*, 9 June 1966, 149.

73. D.C. Spry, "To All Ranks of the Regiment," *The Connecting File*, 1965, 8.

74. "RCR Depot," *The Connecting File*, 1966, 52.

75. Morton, *A Military History of Canada*, 254.

76. RCR Museum and Archives, Vol. 15, File 14, Letter, 1901–612 (RCG/RCR) "Contingency Plan Meeting — The Canadian Guards and the Royal Canadian Regiment," 5 April 1968.

77. *Ibid.*

78. The apparent gamble that a government or CDS would be unwilling to take on a regiment with Royal connection appears to be a classic failure to understand one's opponents. By 1968, the prime minister, Pierre Elliot Trudeau had little affection or time for traditional military trappings, and his French Canadian CDS, J.V. Allard, was intent on a program of increasing the number of French Canadian units in the CF. Given the choice, neither would disband Canada's oldest infantry regiment in favour of keeping a Guards regiment, with all the nuance and symbology that it entails.

79. Canada, *White Paper on Defence* (Ottawa: DND, March 1964), 13–14.

80. Paul Hellyer, *Address on the Canadian Forces Reorganization Act*, 7 December 1966, 6.

81. The RCR Museum Archives, Vol. 38, File 12, "1 RCR Airborne DCF Standing Operating Procedure," 20 November 1967, 2.

82. *Ibid.*, 2-s. The VCDS specifically directed that the RCR, PPCLI, and R22eR be responsible for maintaining the Army parachutist capability. LAC, RG 24, Acc 83–84/165, Box 34, File 2001–1/1, 3, "Proposed Reorganization of the Army Field Force," 18 March 1965.

83. *Special Committee on Defence: Minutes of Proceedings and Evidence*, 11 July 1963, 144. An Army assessment of the parachute capability in 1966, concluded, "Although three airborne company groups are under training at any one time, the operational effectiveness is frequently two or even one company group. This is caused by the rotation of infantry battalions between Canada and overseas. Furthermore, DCF units have been required to undertake other roles during summer months. The re-organization needed for these summer tasks greatly reduced their capability of mounting a DCF operation. It would be truthful to conclude that the effectiveness of the DCF parachutist element has been less than three company groups except possibly for a limited period during the winter months." AB Museum, File AB, "The Requirement for Parachutists in the Canadian Army," 14 February 1966, 2. CAR History (1966) Definition: Requirement SSB/AB Unit (Canadian Airborne Regiment Working Papers).

84. Interview with Major-General Walter Holmes, 17 July 1997.

85. Pat Rossiter, interview with author, 6 April 2010.

86. See Horn, *Bastard Sons,* 101–03

87. Interviews with author, Major-General Loomis, 11 December 1997 and Lieutenant-Colonel Swan, 16 August 1996.

88. Chief Warrant Officer John O'Quinn, interview with author, 23 March 2010.

89. RSM B.C. Robinson, interview with author, 21 September 1998.

90. *Special Committee on Defence: Minutes of Proceedings and Evidence*, 21 June 1966, 298–99.

91. *Ibid.*

92. For a definitive history of the Cdn AB Regt see Horn, *Bastard Sons.* The Cdn AB Regt was created with an airborne headquarters and signal squadron (80 personnel), two infantry airborne commandos (278 personnel

each), an airborne field battery (80 personnel capable of providing two, three gun troops of pack howitzers, or two groups of six medium (82 mm) mortars), an airborne field squadron (81 personnel), and an airborne service commando (i.e. combat service support and administration — 89 personnel). Lieutenant-General W.A.B. Anderson insisted, "The regiment will be kept in a constant state of combat readiness, available on a moment's notice for duty anywhere in the world as a fully trained, immediate-reaction parachute force for a wide range of commitments. It will be trained for defence, assault or peace-keeping missions in tropical and frigid climates and desert or mountainous terrain." Cited in W02 J.L. Wilson, "MOBCOM Briefing," *Sentinel,* February 1967, 2.

93. "Formation of the Canadian Airborne Regiment — Activation and Terms of Reference," 15 May 1967, 3.

94. WO D.J. Lacroix, "The End of An Era," *The Connecting File,* 1968, 12.

95. *Ibid.*

96. Captain R.H. Mahar, "2 Commando," *The Connecting File,* 1968, 69.

97. The Prague Spring refers to the period of political liberalization in Czechoslovakia that commenced 5 January 1968, under reformist leader Alexander Dubček. It ended 21 August, when the Soviet Union and Warsaw Pact allies invaded the country and stopped the reforms that included partial decentralization of the economy and democratization, which included loosened restrictions on freedom of speech, the media, and travel.

98. NATO created the ACE Mobile Force (Land) (AMF[L]) in 1964 as a means of dealing with the weakly defended northern flank.

99. Morton, *A Military History of Canada,* 255.

100. Major-General (Retired) Tom de Faye, interview with author, 13 February 2009.

101. Granatstein, *Canada's Army,* 363.

102. "HRH Prince Philip's Address, 23 October 1963," *The Connecting File,* 1969, iii.

103. Colonel P.R. Bingham, "Editorial," *The Connecting File,* 1967, 5.

Chapter 3: A Shift in Focus

1. Brigadier-General Jim Cox, interview with author, 27 April 2010.

2. Colonel Joe Aitcheson, Letter to author, 17 December 2010. Aitcheson also remembered, "that it was in this same timeframe that 1 and 2 RHC amalgamated and became 2 RCR and 2 Cdn Gds was redesignated 3 RCR. Maintenance of morale was a constant challenge. At the time, 2 RCR was referred to as the 'Cinderella' battalion — it turned into Black Watch at midnight! In fact, I was one of only three 'original' RCR officers in 2 RCR, the other two being Al Clarke and Garnet Smith. As Ian was himself a former Black Watch officer, it was not a surprise that we had classes in Scottish country dancing, carried ashplants and marched off to the 'Black Bear.' The duty piper piped the CO into the office every day and played all the calls — meals, defaulters, CO's orders etc. It was an interesting time to say the least."

3. "Commanding Officer's Introduction," *The Connecting File,* 1970, 28.

4. Master Warrant Officer John MacNeil, interview with author, 18 March 2010.

5. "Charlie Company," *The Connecting File,* 1970, 37.

6. Colonel Eric McArthur, interview with author, 17 January 2008. Feelings of the time were captured by Major Sandy Mitchell when he lamented, "In these days when old traditions and values seem to be assailed from so many directions, the purpose of the Association is significant." Letter, Major A.F. Mitchell, published in *Pro Patria,* Issue 6, November 1970, 10.

7. Letter, Commander FMC to VCDS, "Revision of Regimental Structure Mobile Command Units," 17 February 70, DHH, File 90/310.

8. There is a degree of "back to the future" involved with the most recent reorganization. The Regiment of Canadian Guards, consisting of four battalions, a depot, and a band were authorized on 16 October 1953. On 8 January 1954, the 2nd Battalion, The Canadian Guards (CG) was formed from members of 3 PPCLI, which was disbanded the previous day. Similarly, on 15 April 1954, the 1st Battalion, The CG, was formed from members of 3 RCR, which was disbanded on 14 April. A little over a week later on 22 April, the 1st Canadian Infantry Battalion Band was redesignated the CG Band. The CG Depot was activated on 1 September 1954. On 23 November 1954, the Governor General's Foot Guards was redesignated the 5th Battalion, The CG and on 3 January 1955, The Canadian Grenadier Guards was redesignated the 6th Battalion, The CG. The 3rd and 4th Battalions were disbanded on 31 March 1957 and the Depot was disbanded on 3 June 1968 and the Band 1 October 1968. In addition, that same date the 1st Battalion was reduced to nil strength and

placed on the Supplementary Order of Battle. On 1 August 1976 and 1 December 1976, the 5th and 6th Battalions, respectively reverted back to their original designations as The Canadian Grenadier Guards and the Governor General's Foot Guards.

9.   "3 Mechanized Commando," *The Connecting File,* 1970, 100.

10.   *Ibid.*

11.   3 Mech Cdo consisted of three rifle companies, a HQ company and a battalion HQ for a total of 33 officers and 540 other ranks. There was also a provision for 66 personnel for fly over for a total war establishment (WE) of 639. Weapons included: 12 ATGMs, 12 106 mm recoilless rifles (with a .50 cal spotting rifle attached), 66 84 mm Carl Gustav medium anti-tank weapons, 64 grenade launchers, 34 7.62 mm medium machine guns, 81 .50 calibre heavy machine guns, 12 60 mm light mortars, 8 81 mm medium mortars, 66 light auto rifles. Vehicles — 90 M-113A1s, 4 M-577A1s, 8 M-548A1s, 11 Lynx tracked recce vehicles, 14 jeeps, 14 3/4 tons, 20 2 1/2-ton trucks (195 vehicles altogether).

12.   Captain Bill Aikman, "3 Mechanized Commando. Born in a Storm," *Sentinel,* 1975/7, 7. The reference to the Devil's Brigade referred to the creation of The First Special Service Force (FSSF) during the Second World War. The FSSF was a joint U.S./Canadian formation made up of volunteers. As a result, in the initial days of its creation individuals wore their own regimental accoutrements and uniforms until all were issued a standard U.S. Army uniform.

13.   LAC, RG 24, Vol. 23571, File 1901–2, part 2, "Mobile Command Force Structure Conference 25–26 November 1969," Annex F, Appendix 1.

14.   The issue of 3 Mechanized Commando still raises conflicting perspectives depending on whether a member served in the unit or was a member of the Cdn AB Regt in Canada. To those in Canada it was seen as an anomaly. Its members wore the maroon beret, yet the vast majority of its personnel were not jump-qualified; the unit had no parachute role, and it never exercised in conjunction with the rest of the Cdn AB Regt. The paratroopers serving in Canada objected strenuously to the naming of 3 Mechanized Commando and argue it should never have been directly associated with the Canadian Airborne Regiment. According to them, it was an orphan and an embarrassment to the airborne ideal. Moreover, symbolized a retreat from the concept of a unique formation that provided adventurous and challenging training not found elsewhere. Furthermore, it represented a corrosion of the concept

of a pure airborne entity that was capable of swift global deployment. However, those who served in the unit insist that it was an integral part of the Cdn AB Regt. They argue that the mechanized unit made a conscious decision to be airborne and entered a partnership with a German jump battalion and the British Parachute Regiment, which allowed members of the unit to conduct continuation parachuting in Europe. It is interesting to note that the *Maroon Beret, 20th Anniversary Issue*, makes no mention of 3 Mechanized Commando. Obviously, the purists forgot that under the original "Forces Structure Study" each company, within each of the battalions/commandos was to be mounted in "ten Commando Armoured Personnel Carriers." Cost quickly relegated this idea to the dustbin. "The Canadian Airborne Regiment," *Forces Structure Study*, Chapter 7, April 1967, 1–2.

15. Letter, Lieutenant-Colonel J.A. Cowan, published in *Pro Patria*, Issue 3, 27 February 1970, 16. CFB Soest closed in April 1971. Baden-Soellingen had been a RCAF base since 1953 and as such was already well established as a Canadian enclave in southern Germany. Lahr, however, had been occupied by the French from 1946–67. The infrastructure was in deplorable condition and cost the Canadian taxpayers millions of dollars to make the Lahr facilities habitable. See Maloney, *War Without Battles*, 268–69. He notes that the "French took over pristine accommodations at the former RCAP Stations, Marville, Metz and Grostenquin."

16. Apparently progress was being made. By 1971, the number of U.N. troops had shrunk to 3,100 and the Canadian contingent was pared down from approximately 1,000 to 575 all ranks.

17. The RCR Museum Archives, 1RCR Canadian Contingent Cyprus Force Structure Study, July 1970, para 125.1. War Diary of the 1st Battalion The Royal Canadian Regiment, Canadian Contingent, U.N. Force in Cyprus, from 1 September 1970 to 30 September 1970. It also reiterated, "The basic agreement under which UNFICYP operates is the 'Mandate' of 31 Mar 64 and the Green Line Agreement." The Green Line Agreement delineates the limits of each side in Nicosia and vicinity. "There is no pattern to these agreements and understandings and none should be sought."

18. The RCR Museum Archives, "Standing Operating Procedures, Nicosia District, United Nations Forces in Cyprus," September 1970, para 303. War Diary of the 1st Battalion The Royal Canadian Regiment, Canadian Contingent, U.N. Force in Cyprus, from 1 September 1970 to 30 September 1970.

19. The RCR Museum Archives, "Standing Operating Procedures, Nicosia District, United Nations Forces in Cyprus," September 1970, para 105. War Diary of the 1st Battalion The Royal Canadian Regiment, Canadian Contingent, U.N. Force in Cyprus, from 1 September 1970 to 30 September 1970.

20. Letter, Warrant Officer D.J. Lacroix, published in *Pro Patria,* Issue 4, May 1970, 29.

21. In June a combined RCMP/QPP police anti-terrorist squad arrested 17 FLQ members responsible for the bombings. They were led by G. Schoeters, a Belgian trained in Cuba.

22. The anti-terrorist squad was able to shut down the cells in relative quick order and recover many of the stolen weapons. The leader of the cells was found to be F. Schirm, a Hungarian-born, ex–French Foreign Legionnaire.

23. The latest spate of violence was because of two different cells. One led by R. Levesque, a professional criminal, and the other by G. Gagnon a university professor and Pierre Vallieres, a journalist. Both cells were quickly rounded up by police.

24. Fortunately, only one of the four actually exploded.

25. DHH, File 1326–1847, Vol. 3, Report by First Battalion The Royal Canadian Regiment on Its Operations During the Emergency in Canada, October-November 1970, Appendix 3, to Annex B to 1 RCR Annual Historical Report 1970, 102.15.

26. *Ibid.,* 102.15–102.24.

27. They were released on bail and promptly disappeared.

28. Quoted in Dan G. Loomis, *Not Much Glory: Quelling the FLQ* (Toronto: Deneau, 1984), 29.

29. Loomis, *Not Much Glory,* 30.

30. Quoted in Sean Maloney, "A Mere Rustle of Leaves': Canadian Strategy and the 1970 FLQ Crisis," *Canadian Military Journal,* Vol. 1, No. 2 Summer 2000, 79.

31. DHH, File 1326–1847, Vol. 3, Report by First Battalion The Royal Canadian Regiment on Its Operations During the Emergency in Canada, Oct-November 1970, Appendix 3, to Annex B to 1 RCR Annual Historical Report 1970, 102.27.

32. Lt J. Collinson, "My Introduction to an Infantry Battalion," *The Connecting File,* 1970, 58.

33. *Ibid.*

34. 3 Platoon in Montreal 1970" *The Connecting File*, 1970, 58.

35. "Battalion Summary," *The Connecting File*, 1970, 29.

36. "Delta Company," *The Connecting File*, 1970, 43.

37. "Battalion Summary," *The Connecting File*, 1970, 29.

38. Granatstein, *Canada's Army*, 365. Public opinion polls across Canada and in Quebec showed a 90 percent approval rating for the government action. The murder of Laporte the following day seemed to confirm the requirement.

39. Quoted in Loomis, *Not Much Glory*, 139.

40. "Revolutionary Strategy and the Role of the Avant Garde," *The Montreal Gazette*, 31 October 1970.

41. *Ibid.*

42. In total, approximately 497 people were arrested under the War Measures Act. All but about 40 were released within one to 72 hours of being detained. Loomis, *Not Much Glory*, 141.

43. Quoted in Loomis, *Not Much Glory*, 144.

44. "Alpha Company," *The Connecting File*, 1970, 10.

45. Sixty-six percent of 1/4-ton vehicles and 90 percent of the 3/4- and 2 1/2-ton fleet were available in Ottawa within 24 hours of recall. DHH, File 1326–1847, Vol. 3, Report by First Battalion The Royal Canadian Regiment on Its Operations During the Emergency in Canada, Oct-November 1970, Appendix 3, to Annex B to 1 RCR Annual Historical Report 1970, 204.8.

46. *Ibid.*, 204.3.

47. *Ibid.*

48. 3 RCR later deployed for two additional seven-day tours to Ottawa on 23–30 November and 13–20 December.

49. The FLQ members flown out were Jacques Lanctôt, his wife Marie, and son Louise; Marc Carbonneau; Pierre Sequin; and Jacques and Louise Cossette-Trudel. See Major Guy Morchain, "Peace-Keeping At Home," *Sentinel*, February-March 1971, 7.

50. Lieutenant-Colonel Bev Totman, "Kingston Assist," *Sentinel*, July-August 1971, 23.

51. "'B' Company — Operation Pelican," *The Connecting File*, 1971 Edition, 94.

52. *Ibid.*, 93.

53. Lieutenant-Colonel Bev Totman, "Kingston Assist," *Sentinel*, July-August 1971, 23–24. One inmate was killed in the riot. On 10 July 1972, Royals would once again assist prison and police officials when 14 prisoners

escaped from medium security Millhaven Penitentiary. Penitentiary guards and Ontario Provincial Police (OPP) erected roadblocks immediately and two days later with no success, they requested CF helicopters. By day three, with the convicts believed to still be in the area, hundreds of troops from 1 and 3 RCR were called out to thoroughly search the area. They also relieved the OPP manning roadblocks along Highways 401 and 33. "It was laborious, mainly unrewarding work, beating through bush and pastures, vacant farmhouses or barns but the obvious relief of the citizens when the troops arrived compensated for much of its weariness." Eventually all but four of the escapees were caught. Troops returned to normal duty 24 July. Doug Steubing, "Millhaven Search," *Sentinel,* November-December 1972, 16.

54. Donald McDonald, *Defence in the 70s: White Paper on Defence,* reproduced in Douglas L. Bland, ed., *Canada's National Defence, Vol. 1 Defence Policy* (Kingston: School of Policy Studies, Queen's University, 1997), 144.

55. *Ibid.,* 130.

56. *Ibid.,* 134.

57. *Ibid.,* 135.

58. *Ibid.,* 139.

59. *Ibid.,* 140–41.

60. *Ibid.*

61. "'A' Company — Ex New Viking," *The Connecting File,* 1971 Edition, 91.

62. *Ibid.,* 92.

63. Private D. Lamb, "'O' Company," *The Connecting File,* 1973 Edition, 101.

64. Granatstein, *Canada's Army,* 373.

65. Although the government realized the importance of NATO to its foreign policy and began to reverse its marginalization of CF commitments to NATO in the late 1970s the numbers changed little:

    1976 — WE raised to 5,343 with an actual 3,212 deployed;
    1977 — WE 5,517 — 3,220 deployed; and
    1979 — WE 5,615 — 3,268 deployed.

66. The Soviet threat emanated from a NATO assessment that they would attack Northern Norway to: outflank the NATO defence system to weaken its lines of communications; to eliminate NATO surveillance of the Russia Northern fleet and to extend their own early warning system westwards; to

secure the approaches to the Barents Sea from North Cape to Spitzbergen; and to establish naval dispersal areas and forward air bases on the coast of Norway. DHH, 98/37, File 31, "Mobile Command Headquarters Minutes of the CAST Combat Group Study Period," 4–6 May 1971, Appendix I to Annex C, 3–4. DHH, 98/37, File 31.

67. *Ibid.*, Annex E, 1.

68. *Ibid.*

69. *Ibid.*

70. *Ibid.*

71. "Support Company — Ex Power Play," *The Connecting File,* 1971 Edition, 102.

72. DHH, 98/37, File 70, "Exercise WINTEREX 73 Mobile Command Post Exercise Report," 7 June 73, 3–5.

73. Maloney, *War without Battles,* 282.

74. Quoted in Maloney, *War Without Battles,* 309.

75. "Best Troops in Europe Easy Cdns," *Pro Patria,* Issue 12, May 1972, 37.

76. Captain D. Nolan, "3 Canadian Mechanized Commando," *The Connecting File,* 1973 Edition, 145. Tom deFaye recalled, "We worked in the towns, villages, forests and farmlands of central Germany. Despite the fact we must have been a tremendously disruptive factor in their lives, the people were incredibly kind and considerate." Major T.F. deFaye, "3 Canadian Mechanized Commando REFORGER 1975," *The Connecting File,* 1975 Edition, 146.

77. The RCR Museum Archives, David DeClerq, "Journal Excerpt — 1979 Reforger Exercise," letter to author.

78. Taskings, that is directives from higher headquarters to cut away personnel to do other tasks (e.g. provide instructors, cooks, drivers, enemy force, general duty personnel to schools, militia concentrations, or other CF events) was a continual and consistent scourge that plagued Army units in Canada.

79. Captain Bill Aikman, "3 Mechanized Commando. Born in a Storm," *Sentinel,* 1975/7, 8. Hohenfels was a major training area of the U.S. 7th Army that is located near the Czechoslovakian border.

80. "Wet and Cold in County Troms," *Sentinel,* November-December 1972, 7.

81. Major K.J.W. Reeves, "Diary of an Arctic Adventure," *Sentinel,* May 1971, 19.

82. "Norway," *Pro Patria,* Issue 8, May 1971, 28.

83. Major K.J.W. Reeves, "Diary of an Arctic Adventure," *Sentinel,* May 1971, 21.

84. John A. Robertson, *An Ageless Company: My Time in the Canadian Infantry* (Victoria: Trafford Press, 2007), 240.

85. Captain Bill Whitehead, "Hardly a Caper," *Sentinel,* June 1971, 32–34. The six-day jungle warfare course and subsequent counterinsurgency exercise was normally conducted in the Blue mountains. The climax of the training was usually held at the ancient site of Nanny Town, which was the scene of battle between runaway slaves and British forces in the 18th Century.

86. Captain Bill Whitehead, "Hardly a Caper," *Sentinel,* June 1971, 32–34.

87. The Regiment undertook the task of establishing and enforcing the demarcation line, providing organization and security for Prisoner of War (PoW) exchanges, and providing escorts for infrastructure repair. The Canadian troops assisted 20,000 refugees and delivered tons of food and supplies, tents, blankets, and cots before the arrival of the International Committee of the Red Cross (ICRC) and other agencies. In addition, they later delivered ICRC family messages to villages. The "can do attitude" and efforts of the paratroopers was noted by the Cypriots. A sign was erected outside one of the refugee camps in the Canadian sector with a hand drawn paratrooper under full canopy with the words, "All Canadians welcome." The Canadian Airborne Regiment, "The Regiment in Cyprus," *The Maroon Beret,* January 1975, 28–40.

88. Annex A to 1326-1(10), Canadian Airborne Regiment Historical Report, dated 8 February 1995. CAFM.

89. The RCR Museum Archives, War Diary of the 1st Battalion The Royal Canadian Regiment, Canadian Contingent, U.N. Force in Cyprus, from 1 December 1974 to 31 December 1974. War Diary — December 1974 overview, 13 January 75, 1.

90. *Ibid.,* War Diary — December 1974 overview, 13 January 75, 2.

91. *Ibid.,* War Diary — December 1974 overview, 13 January 75, 3.

92. *Ibid.,* War Diary — December 1974 overview, 13 January 75, 5.

93. There was one exception dealing with property East of Larnaca Road. The Turkish-Cypriot Ministry of Defence refused access to guarantee security, as they deemed it a military sensitive area. The RCR Museum Archives, War Diary of the 1st Battalion The Royal Canadian Regiment, Canadian Contingent, U.N. Force in Cyprus, from 1 December 1974 to 31 December 1974, War Diary — December 1974 overview, 13 January 75, 5.

94. *Ibid.,* from 1 January 1975 to 31 January 1975, War Diary — January 1975 overview, 10 February 1975, 1.

95. Unofficial Duty Log kept by "B" Coy, 1 RCR during their 1974/75 tour. It was provided by Jerry Thompson. He explained, "the B Coy Duty officers including the senior NCOs, WOs and the CSM started to keep an unofficial diary that became a daily source of entertainment and comment within the company. No one was safe from the pen of the writer. The chief source of comment was the company operations warrant, WO Bernie Hurley who ensured the safe keeping and integrity of the diary."

96. The RCR Museum Archives, War Diary of the 1st Battalion The Royal Canadian Regiment, Canadian Contingent, U.N. Force in Cyprus, from 1 April 1975 to 30 April 1975, War Diary — April 1975 overview, 13 May 1975, 1.

97. Brigadier-General Philip Spencer, interview with author, 18 March 2010. He also noted, "Prior to going over we did lots of training. We didn't know what exactly to expect so we trained for war. It was a great decision." The unofficial diary for 31 March 1975 captured the events of one such escalation of fire. It revealed, "All hell broke out at midnight, the Gks opened up with everything to celebrate EOKA day. Both radio nets were just buzzing. Operations B (intelligence) got into the act as the coy comd was under fire. He wanted to know all the numbers, ranks and names of everyone firing along the DML as if we knew everyone by sight. Cpl Vincent looked a little pale when he returned with the OC. I guess bullets were bouncing all around the vehicle. We finally got the shooting stopped at 0245."

98. Lieutenant-Colonel R.J. (Bob) Mahar, interview with author, 23 March 2010.

99. D.W. Middlemiss, and J.J. Sokolsky, *Canadian Defence: Decisions & Determinants* (Toronto: Harcourt, Brace, Javonovich, 1989), 39.

100. Gerald Porter, *In Retreat: The Canadian Forces in the Trudeau Years* (Toronto: Deneau & Greenberg, 1980), 165. The reversal is dramatic. A government report captured the essence of the government's original intent. It recorded, "In April 1969, Prime Minister Trudeau announced changes in defence policy which had a major effect on the land forces. It was decided to reduce the troops in Europe by roughly half. In 1971, a new Defence White Paper elaborated on these changes as well as giving greater emphasis to the protection of Canadian interests at home as a way of 'fostering economic growth and safeguarding sovereignty and independence.' It was also proposed that the Europe-based land force be reconfigured to give it a higher degree of mobility and greater compatibility with Canada-based forces — in short, 'a lighter, more mobile land force capable of a wide

range of missions.' This involved, among other things, plans to abandon the main battle tank — a policy which, in fact, never materialized." Canada, *Report of the Special Committee of the Senate on National Defence, Canada's Land Forces,* October 1989, 3.

101. DHH, File 76/89, Address by General J.A. Dextraze, CDS to the Conference of Defence Associations, 16 January 1976, 11.

102. *Ibid.,* 12.

103. DHH, File 77/186, Address by General J.A. Dextraze, CDS to the Conference of Defence Associations — 40th Annual Meeting, 13 January 1977, 9; and DHH, File 77/31, "Text of CDS Speech to Press," Message CDS 424, 081800Z December 1976.

104. DHH, File 77/186, Address by General J.A. Dextraze, CDS to the Conference of Defence Associations — 40th Annual Meeting, 13 January 1977, 10.

105. The establishment of the SSF and the requirement to move the Canadian Airborne Regiment from Edmonton to Petawawa to facilitate its establishment created enormous antipathy by many towards Dextraze. The reasons for the hostility to Dextraze's scheme went well beyond the simple fact that the Cdn AB Regt had grown "roots" in Edmonton and was accepted as a valued member of that community. The decision was not only extremely unpopular but operationally unsound. There were a large number of operational concerns that had not been adequately addressed. Petawawa did not have parachute training equipment or facilities, nor did it have a close accessible airfield to allow for rapid deployment. Another concern was the fact that the Parachute Maintenance Depot, where all parachutes were checked and packed, remained in Edmonton. Colonel Fraser was horrified at all of this because: "In Edmonton, we had one of the finest combined operation establishments located anywhere in the world. We were co-located on a major air base with a resident C130 Squadron, a resident Helicopter Squadron and a resident Air Reserve Squadron. The Canadian Forces Parachute Maintenance Depot and the Tactical Air Lift School were in the same barrack lines, as was the Canadian Airborne Centre. One of the largest supply depots in Canada was less than a mile away." RUSI Presentation, Fraser Papers, 17. For a detailed account see Horn, *Bastard Sons,* chapter 6.

106. DND Information pamphlet, "Special Service Force," no date (ND).

107. Captain Bill Aikman, "Beginnings," *Sentinel,* 1977/1, 6.

108. DHH, 98/37, File 97, "Operation Gamescan 76. Operation Order 2/76 2 Combat Group," 17 March 76.

109. CF undertook a wide range of tasks that included: assistance in conduct of competitions; field engineer support; aerobatic displays; logistic support including medical, transportation, and supply; computer results system; communications support; protocol duties and ceremonial activities; medal control system; liaison officers; and assistance in managing of Olympic villages. DHH, 98/37, File 97, "Operation Gamescan 76. Operation Order 2/76 2 Combat Group," 17 March 76.

110. Letter, Lieutenant-Colonel W.J. Pettipas to RHQ, published in *Pro Patria,* August 1976, Issue 29, 3.

111. All personnel on duty on security tasks carried loaded magazines on their weapons, however, the weapons were not readied (i.e. there was no round in the chamber).

112. "Olympic Regatta Kingston," *Sentinel,* 1977/1, 36.

113. *Ibid.,* 36. The CO, Lieutenant-Colonel D.B. Ells stated: "We were responsible for the security of the Olympic athletes in their village and the officials as well. We had a full company committed to vital points; mainly Hydro and public utility installations. We assisted the RCMP in the protection of VIPs and we had a standby company on various degrees of notice to assist any of the police agencies in Kingston." There were no major incidents and the CO felt that the battalion had served as a "deterrent." Letter, Lieutenant-Colonel D.B. Ells to RHQ, published in *Pro Patria,* August 1976, Issue 29, 8.

114. "Airborne: Task Force 3," *Sentinel,* 1977/1, 25.

115. Letter, Lieutenant-Colonel Roger MacPherson to author.

116. During the tour one major event occurred. In January 1978, the U.N. Secretary General, Kurt Waldheim, visited the island for talks with the leaders of the two communities. The Nicosia airport, which had been closed since 1973, was used for his arrival and departure. 2 RCR provided the necessary security at the airport and for meetings at the Ledra Palace Hotel. Media access was tightly controlled. At times there was no access at all. During one such black-out, a carload of Turkish-Cypriot journalists arrived late and attempted to force their way through the checkpoint. Private H.H. Donnelly, from "H" Coy, stood his ground. The car continued to force its way through to the extent the vehicle physically hit Donnelly. At that point he and the other sentry took deliberate aim at the driver, who proceeded to back away. Private Donnelly was later awarded a CDS Commendation for his actions. Letter, Lieutenant-Colonel Roger MacPherson to author.

117.   DND News Release, 18 February 1977, AFN 40/77.

118.   See Message, "Land Force Restructuring," NDHQ Ottawa, CDS 220 301905 July 77; and DHH, File 77/420, Letter, CDS to MND, "Land Force Restructuring," 11 January 1977.

Chapter 4: The Last Hurrah

1.   Chapter VI is commonly used to refer to traditional U.N. peacekeeping operations under the U.N. Charter, i.e. "Chapter VI: Pacific Settlement Of Disputes." In the 1990s reference to Chapter VII or peacemaking operations was made referring to "Chapter VII: Action with Respect to Threats to the Peace, Breaches of the Peace, and Acts of Aggression," which allowed U.N. forces to use much more robust rules of engagement that permitted the use of force to achieve desired results.

2.   Training can be largely defined as a predictable response to a predictable situation as opposed to education, which is a reasoned response to an unpredictable situation — i.e. critical thinking in the face of the unknown.

3.   Hillier concluded, "We paid a high price for that mindset later, because it led directly to some of the challenges that we faced in the 1990s and early 2000s." General Rick Hillier, *A Soldier First: Bullets, Bureaucrats and the Politics of War* (Toronto: HarperCollins Publishers Ltd., 2009), 92. Brigadier-General Denis Thompson, then a subaltern, noted, "Culture of the 1980s was more routine, family orientated. It was a lot less serious than today — we weren't involved in a knock them down insurgency." Brigadier-General Denis Thompson, interview with author, 14 July 2008.

4.   Chief Warrant Officer C.Y.M. (Kit) Charlebois, letter to author, 30 December 2010.

5.   Chief Warrant Officer Jay Gravelle, interview with author, 25 August 2009.

6.   Master Warrant Officer Rob Douglas, interview with author, 11 August 2008.

7.   Chief Warrant Officer Dave Preeper, interview with author, 8 July 2009.

8.   Brigadier-General Denis Thompson, interview with author, 14 July 2008.

9.   Lieutenant-Colonel Bill Bentley, interview with author, 3 June 2010.

10.   Brigadier General Jim Cox, interview with author, 27 April 2010.

11.   Chief Warrant Officer John O'Quinn, interview with author, 23 March 2010.

12.   Colonel Don Denne, letter to author, 12 September 2010.

13.   Colonel Bill Peters, interview with author, 11 December 2010.

14. Master Warrant Officer Rick Duncan, interview with author, 15 April 2008.

15. Chief Warrant Officer C.Y.M. (Kit) Charlebois, letter to author, 30 December 2010.

16. R.I. Stewart, "Discipline, Soldierly Behaviour and Leaders Responsibilities," 7 May 1984. Accessed from Major-General Stewart's personal papers [henceforth referred to as Stewart Papers].

17. Chief Warrant Officer Jay Gravelle, interview with author, 25 August 2009.

18. Major-General Denis Tabbernor, interview with author, 20 January 2009.

19. Lieutenant-Colonel Rusty Bassarab, interview with author, 7 October 2009.

20. Colonel Doug Maclean, interview with author, 2 July 2009.

21. Brigadier-General Denis Thompson, interview with author, 14 July 2008.

22. Master Warrant Officer Tom France, interview with author, 1 May 2009.

23. Brigadier-General Denis Thompson, interview with author, 14 July 2008.

24. *Ibid.*

25. Major-General Tom de Faye, interview with author, 13 February 2009.

26. For instance, the Strategic Defence Initiative (SDI) challenged the argument that vulnerability could provide security. "It called into question the 1972 Anti-Ballistic Missile Treaty, a centerpiece of SALT I. It exploited the Soviet Union's backwardness in computer technology, a field in which the Russians knew that they could not keep up. And it undercut the peace movement by framing the entire project in terms of lowering the risk of nuclear war: the ultimate purpose of SDI, Reagan insisted, was not to freeze nuclear weapons but rather to render them 'impotent and obsolete.'" Gaddis, *The Cold War*, 48.

27. National Defence, *Challenge and Commitment: A Defence Policy for Canada.* 1987, 5. By 1983, the Cold War represented a very real threat. The DND strategic assessment pronounced, "The two-fold concern for the West throughout 1983 remained how to maintain a credible deterrent against a large and growing military power which holds intrinsically hostile and conflicting ideological values, without at the same time unduly provoking its deep-seated and largely self-created sense of insecurity." Canada, *Defence 83* (Ottawa: DND, 1984), 3.

28. National Defence, *Challenge and Commitment: A Defence Policy for Canada.* 1987, 10.

29. *Ibid.*, 11.

30. *Ibid.*, 21.

31. In 1982, the Warsaw Pact (WP)/NATO power balance in Europe was as

follows: tanks — WP 42,500 to 13,000; artillery pieces — WP 31,500 to 10,700; APC — WP 78,800 to 30,000; Attack Helicopters WP 700 to 400. Quoted in Granatstein, *Canada's Army,* 376.

32. In total, Warsaw Pact active and reserve forces worldwide comprised 246 divisions and 29 brigades, with 61,000 main battle tanks and air forces equipped with nearly 13,000 aircraft. NATO, *NATO and the Warsaw Pact: Force Comparisons* (NATO Information Service: Brussels, 1984), 4.

33. There were also nearly 400,000 other militarily trained personnel, such as Home Guards and Gendarmerie. Total active and reserve forces belonging to NATO nations, but not all committed to NATO, included 82 Divisions and over 180 independent brigades with about 25,000 main battle tanks and approximately 11,200 combat aircraft. NATO, *NATO and the Warsaw Pact,* 4.

34. *Ibid.,* 7.

35. National Defence, *Challenge and Commitment: A Defence Policy for Canada.* 1987, 12.

36. Maloney, *War Without Battles,* 360.

37. Former 4 CMBG Commander Brigadier-General Richard Evraire confided to an American commander that the force was not equipped for the new battle concept. He believed "the best use he could make of 4 CMBG was to make sure it was in a fairly static defensive positions with the possibility of counterattacking here or there but not as an offensive weapon." He conceded, "I know this did not please too many people, but it was hardly the place to be untruthful." Quoted in Granatstein, *Canada's Army,* 376.

38. Maloney, *War Without Battles,* 367.

39. "3rd Battalion," *The Connecting File,* 1989 edition, 13.

40. *RCR Chronological Summary 1 Jan to 31 Dec 88.* Annex C. To 3 RCR/1325–2 (IO), dated March 89, 3.

41. Brigadier-General Denis Thompson, interview with author, 14 July 2008.

42. Information that has come to light since the end of the Cold War confirms that the use of nuclear weapons was incorporated into all Warsaw Pact exercises in the 1980s. It appears that the Soviets were prepared to go nuclear on any indication that NATO was preparing to use nuclear weapons at any level. See Maloney, *War Without Battles,* 379.

43. Major-General Denis Tabbernor, interview with author, 20 January 2009.

44. Master Warrant Officer Rick Duncan, interview with author, 15 April 2008.

45. There was a down side of course to the scripted exercises, normally in

the same regions. Master Warrant Officer Duncan observed, "After my second scripted AMF (L) exercise, I felt really sorry for the guys who were there for their 13th time." I had a similar experience. As a young second-lieutenant I was excited at the prospect of an upcoming Norway deployment. When I questioned a grumpy warrant officer why he wasn't thrilled about the impending exercise, his condescending reply was simply, "Sir, I too was really excited about my first 11 trips to Norway."

46.   Ian Thomson, "The Ace up NATO's Sleeve," *Sentinel*, Vol. 10, No. 4 (1984), 11. Thomson explained, "The three infantry battalions [within AMF(L)] provide 'Key Companies' which carry out the deterrence phase of an AMF deployment. It is this deterrence phase that will make or break the operations of AMF whether they are deployed to north Norway or to eastern Turkey."

47.   Ian Thomson, "The Ace up NATO's Sleeve," *Sentinel*, Vol. 10, No. 4 (1984), 11. Lieutenant-Colonel Rusty Bassarab stated: "They told us our job was to go there to die so all [NATO] countries would be committed. In short, the role of AMF(L) was to commit other nations." Lieutenant-Colonel Rusty Bassarab, interview with author, 7 October 2009.

48.   Ian Thomson, "The Ace up NATO's Sleeve," *Sentinel*, Vol. 10, No. 4 (1984), 13.

49.   DND News Release AFN 07/80, 13 February 1980.

50.   Ian Thomson, "The Ace up NATO's Sleeve," *Sentinel*, Vol. 10, No. 4 (1984), 12. One recurring theme during all the exercises was the mountains. "The principal reactions appear to have been centered on the height of the mountains (and the consequent difficulty of climbing them) and the thickness of the swamps (and the consequent difficulty of crossing them)," according to then Lieutenant-Colonel Joe Aitchison, the CO of 2 RCR. Letter, Lieutenant-Colonel W.J. Aitchison to Colonel of the Regiment, November 1984, published in *Pro Patria*, Issue 56, December 1984, 5.

51.   Master Warrant Officer Rick Duncan, interview with author, 15 April 2008.

52.   *Ibid.*

53.   Brigadier-General Denis Thompson, interview with author, 14 July 2008.

54.   "Oh … What A Lovely War," *Sentinel*, Vol. 25, No. 5 (1981), 4.

55.   Letter, Lieutenant-Colonel W.T.J. Kaulbach, to Colonel of the Regiment, published in *Pro Patria*, Issue 46, August 1981, 25.

56.   Canada, *Defence 83* (Ottawa: DND, 1984), 40; and Richard Moore, "CAST

of thousands on the Western Front," *Sentinel,* Vol. 19, No. 4 (1983), 3. The exercise cost $7.5 million.

57. Richard Moore, "CAST of thousands on the Western Front," *Sentinel,* Vol. 19, No. 4 (1983). 3.

58. *Ibid.*

59. Canada, *Defence 85* (Ottawa: DND, 1986), 45–46.

60. Letter, Lieutenant-Colonel Larry Bowen to Colonel of the Regiment, July 1985, published in *Pro Patria,* Issue 58, August 1985, 4.

61. Richard Moore, "Lightning Strike," *Sentinel,* Vol. 24, No. 2 (1988), 6.

62. See Horn, *Bastard Sons,* for a detailed history of Canadian concerns with regard to the North.

63. Director General Policy memorandum, "CANUS Int Estimate 1979," 12 July 1979. DHH — NDHQ files on Canadian Airborne Regiment, not yet filed at time of use.

64. Proceedings of the Special Committee of the Senate on National Defence [henceforth Senate Defence Committee], 31 October 1989, 4:180; and Colonel J.M.R. Gaudreau, Letter, 3120–1 (R Comd), dated 17 March 1986, "Operational Concept For the Canadian Airborne Regiment to Defeat the Wartime Land Threat to CDA," 4–5. The appreciation astutely noted, "Based on the historical experience of the Second World War, the Canadian government or the Canadian people will be most unwilling to allow our ground forces to deploy out of country — Europe — until we have satisfactorily dealt with an enemy presence on our sovereign territory." However, threat must be balanced against enemy intention and probability of occurrence.

65. Senate Defence Committee, 26 January 1988, 12:30.

66. *Ibid.,* 31 October 1989, 4:178; and *Canada's Land Forces,* 71.

67. Senate Defence Committee, 31 October 1989, 4:181–82; *Canada's Land Forces,* 72–73; Gaudreau, "Operational Concept For the Canadian Airborne Regiment to Defeat the Wartime Land Threat to CDA," 2; M.J. Goodspeed, "SPETSNAZ: Soviet Diversionary Forces Checkmate in Two Moves?" *CDQ,* Vol. 18, No. 1, Summer 1988, 44; and William Baxter, "The Soviet Threat from the Sky," *Army,* Vol. 31, No. 4, April 1981, 42–43.

68. Senate Defence Committee, 31 October 1989, 4:182.

69. Richard Moore, "Lightning Strike," *Sentinel,* Vol. 24, No. 2 (1988), 8.

70. *Ibid.,* 5. In 1988 alone, besides Ex Lightning Strike, five company-size exercises took place in Canada's far north. DND assessed, "These exercises

provided essential training for northern operations and allowed Mobile Command to contribute to the department's renewed emphasis on establishing a visible presence in the North." Canada, *Defence 88* (Ottawa: DND, 1989), 44.

71. National Defence, *Challenge and Commitment: A Defence Policy for Canada*. 1987, 23–24. The new Conservative government initiatives as part of their new 1987 defence white paper, *Challenge and Commitment*, included the North American Air Defence Modernization Program (North Warning System), a proposed new Northern (Army) Training Centre, the designation of five northern airfields as forward operating locations (FOLs), the construction of the *Polar 8* icebreaker, and a new fleet of nuclear submarines. The programs were designed to provided increased presence to survey friend and foe alike. However, NDHQ focused largely on an air force and naval presence. Erik Nielsen (MND 1985) stated: "I want to emphasize the importance of fully exercising sovereignty in our north. The DEW Line has served Canada well, but Canadians do not control it … The North Warning System will be a Canadian-controlled system-operated, maintained and manned by Canadians. Sovereignty in our north will be strengthened and assured for the future." *Challenge and Commitment*, 50–55, and 60; R.B. Byers and M. Slack, eds., *The Canadian Strategic Review, 1985–1986* (Toronto: CISS, 1988), 128–31, and *1987*, 106; and *Debates*, 13 March 1985. Beatty claimed the FOLs would "enhance the Canadian Armed Forces ability to ensure Canada's northern sovereignty." DND News Release, 11 March 1987 as quoted in Byers, *Canadian Strategic Review, 1987*, 106. The white paper also noted that technology had nullified the Arctic Ocean as a historic buffer between the superpowers and had made the Arctic more accessible. It stated: "Canadians cannot ignore that what was once a buffer could become a battleground." (*Challenge and Commitment*, 6). The underlying motive was explained by Perrin Beatty, the MND. He admitted, "Our sovereignty in the Arctic cannot be complete if we remain dependent on allies for knowledge of possible hostile activities in our waters, under our ice and for preventing such activities." (Paul George, "Arctic defence too hard to handle?" *The Globe and Mail*, 12 March 1987, A7). The expressed concern was used as an attempt to justify the cost of a fleet of nuclear submarines. It was not in response to the belief in a potential Arctic battleground. This point of view is shared by Canadian military strategists who "have privately mused

that ... it seems safe to assume the threat of attack on or through the ice of the Arctic Ocean against Canada is indeed negligible." Joseph Jockel asserted that, "It is important not to overrate the importance of Canadian Arctic waters, a tendency that sometimes emerged in the Canadian SSN debate ... To the north, there are very substantial limitations to the firing positions SLCM-carrying submarines could take up." (Jockel, *Security to the North*, 162). For a description of the difficulties of submarine operations in the North see W.G. Lalore, "Submarine Through the North Pole," *The National Geographic Magazine*, Vol. 115, No. 1, January 1959, 2–24; and J.F. Calvert, "Up Through the Ice of the North Pole." *The National Geographic Magazine*, Vol. 115, No. 1, July 1959, 1–41.

72. A "renewed" focus on the Arctic whenever a perceived threat to Canadian sovereignty emerges is a recurring national reality. Fiscal pressures and the end of the Cold War quickly dampened the Conservative government surge of interest in the Arctic. Many of the programs proposed, such as the fleet of nuclear submarines, the northern training centre, and the *Polar 8* icebreaker were never implemented. Nevertheless, six years later the *1994 Defence White Paper* still echoed the sentiments of its predecessors and emphasized that "sovereignty is a vital attribute of a nation-state." Canada, *1994 Defence White Paper* (Ottawa: DND, 1994), 15. It also expressed a consistent and historic theme, namely that Canada faced no direct threat. The underlying necessity was clearly the ability to protect its sovereignty. This theme has remained consistent. The *Defence Planning Guidance* 1998 (DPG 1998), stated that "while Canada faces no direct military threat at present ... Canada must have the ability to protect its sovereignty." Canada, *Defence Planning Guidance 1998* (Ottawa: DND, 1997), 1–1. The recent summer 2010 Arctic tour by Prime Minister Stephen Harper also reinforced this theme.

73. Byers, *Canadian Strategic Review, 1985–1986*, 126–28; Sokolsky, 13; and J.T. Jockel, *Security to the North: Canada-U.S. Defence Relationships in the 1990s* (East Lansing: Michigan State University Press, 1991), 30–31.

74. Master Warrant Officer Rick Duncan, interview with author, 15 April 2008. One officer observed with regard to operating north of the 60th parallel, "Everything that's done in these regions takes a lot of energy. Things also tend to take a lot longer to get done. To avoid sweating, dehydration and hypothermia, we move a lot slower. We also consume more food up here. It comes down to a balance between survival and maintaining basic

operational capability." Richard Moore, "Lightning Strike," *Sentinel,* Vol. 24, No. 2 (1988), 7–8.

75. Chief Warrant Officer John O'Quinn, interview with author, 23 March 2010.

76. Richard Larouche, "Arctic Battle: Exercise Sovereign Viking," *Sentinel,* Vol. 18, No. 6 (1982), 6.

77. *Ibid.,* 7. The reality of the conditions also meant that in a blizzard, "you can barely see the end of your nose. You have to stay in one place or risk getting lost."

78. By the end of the decade, the role had not changed for UNFICYP in Cyprus. It was still "to contribute to the maintenance and restoration of law and order and a return to normal conditions." "1st Battalion," *The Connecting File,* 1989 edition, 7.

79. Al Ditter, "Cyprus ... 20 Years and Counting," *Sentinel,* Vol. 10, No. 6 (1984), 4.

80. *Ibid.,* 4.

81. Brigadier-General Denis Thompson, interview with author, 14 July 2008.

82. *Ibid.*

83. Chief Warrant Officer C.Y.M. (Kit) Charlebois, letter to author, 30 December 2010.

84. Chief Warrant Officer John O'Quinn, interview with author, 23 March 2010.

85. Lieutenant-Colonel Colin Magee, interview with author, 23 November 2010.

86. Master Warrant Officer Tom France, interview with author, 1 May 2009.

87. Letter, Major B.M. Archibald to Colonel of the Regiment, printed in *Pro Patria,* Issue 50, November 1982, 47.

88. Letter, Major-General Bob Stewart to author, 1 July 1998.

89. "Manning — Canadian Airborne Regiment," Commission of Inquiry into the Deployment of Canadian Forces to Somalia. In *Information Legacy: A Compendium of Source Material* [CD-ROM] [henceforth *Information Legacy*] (Ottawa: Canadian Government Publishing, 1997), Evidentiary Exhibits, 9 October 1985.

90. *Ibid.* Certain steps were already in place to assist with the personnel short-ages. First, any volunteer for the basic parachutist course was required to sign a waiver stating that he would serve in the airborne regiment if called to dos so. Failure to fulfil this contract could, and did, result in the loss of the right to wear the distinctive parachutist qualification badge

(commonly referred to as "wings"). Second, the parent regiments and their battalions often directed posted individuals to the airborne whether they volunteered or not. As will be discussed, often the airborne was used to discard those individuals who were viewed as undesirable. Colonel Rick Hatton candidly asserted that an ongoing fallacy is the notion that everyone who served in the airborne volunteered to do so. Interview with author, 16 December 1998.

91. See Horn, *Bastard Sons*, for the detailed history of the Canadian Airborne Regiment; and *Commission of Inquiry into the Deployment of Canadian Forces to Somalia* (henceforth *Somalia Commission*), Transcript of Policy Hearing, Vol. 4, No. 21, June 1995, 620, and 5 October 1995, 409; and the Canadian Forces Board of Inquiry — Canadian Airborne Regiment Battle Group, Phase I, Vol. 11, H-1/6 (henceforth referred to as BOI — Cdn AB Regt BG).

92. Letter, Lieutenant-Colonel T.J. Kaulbach, to Colonel of the Regiment, published in *Pro Patria,* Issue 44, November 1980, 18.

93. Brigadier-General Denis Thompson, interview with author, 14 July 2008.

94. Letter, Lieutenant-Colonel A.D. McQuarrie, to Colonel of the Regiment, March 1983, published in *Pro Patria,* Issue 51, April 1983, 7.

95. Peter Haydon in John Wood (ed.), *Talking Heads Talking Arms: No Life Jackets* (Toronto: Breakout Educational Network, 2003), 53.

96. "An Interview with the Honourable Perrin Beatty, Minister of Defence," *Defence in Canada,* Special Issue, Vol. 33, 1988, 20.

97. The strength of the CF at the end of 1985 was 83,910 regular force and 24,548 reserve force personnel. Canada, *Defence 85* (Ottawa: DND, 1986), 10.

98. Canada, *Defence 85* (Ottawa: DND, 1986), 1.

99. National Defence, *Challenge and Commitment: A Defence Policy for Canada.* 1987, 43.

100. The white paper noted, "In 1962–63, more than 20 per cent of the budget was spent on capital projects. This level generally declined throughout the 1960s until it reached a low point of about 9 per cent in 1972–73. It began to increase thereafter, but it was not until 1982–83 that it went above 20 per cent again. In 1985, NATO countries spent, on average, about 25 per cent of their defence budgets on equipment acquisition." National Defence, *Challenge and Commitment: A Defence Policy for Canada.* 1987, 43.

101. Canada, *Defence 85* (Ottawa: DND, 1986), 1.

102. At the time the CDS stated: "The purpose of the exercise is not to verify the

feasibility of the policy, the concept, or Canada's commitment to the northern flank of NATO. The purpose is to train and to demonstrate, both to our allies and our potential adversaries, that Canada has the will, the intention and the solidarity with our allies to deploy troops on NATO's northern flank when required in time of crisis." The reality, or at a minimum consequence, of the exercise, would prove otherwise. Louis Mackay, "Brave Lion: Troops Deploy to Norway," *Sentinel*, Vol. 23, No. 1 (1987), 6.

103. Canada, *Defence 86* (Ottawa: DND, 1987), 13–14.

104. "An Interview with the Honourable Perrin Beatty, Minister of Defence," *Defence in Canada*, Special Issue, Vol. 33 1988, 20.

105. National Defence, *Challenge and Commitment: A Defence Policy for Canada*. 1987, 61.

106. *Ibid.*, 62.

107. *Ibid.*, 63.

108. Canada, *Defence 89* (Ottawa: DND, 1987), foreword.

109. The change in attitude resulted in Canadians utilizing "Manoeuvre Damage Control" teams that followed 4 CMBG and made repairs on the spot, conducted investigations on claims made, and doled out cash where circumstances warranted.

110. Lieutenant-General Jack Vance, interview with author, 22 July 2005.

Chapter 5: The New World Order

1. On 27 April 1989, the provincial and federal governments, under pressure from the Mohawks, directed that a moratorium on construction be put into effect until 21 August. The situation was exacerbated by a SQ raid on 29 September. During negotiations over the golf course expansion, approximately 50–75 SQ members, supported by a helicopter, raided the Kanesatake Riverside Bingo. The raid resulted in seven arrests and instigated eight additional search operations. The moratorium was eventually renewed until December 1989, but then lifted on 9 March 1990. Mohawk representative Elen Gabriel stated: "That [8 March] is when the fishing shack went up. There was no barricade, but the fishing shack and observations on whether workers were going to come in and start cutting trees." Cited in Timothy C. Winegard, *Oka: A Convergence of Cultures and the Canadian Forces* (Kingston: CDA Press, 2008), 69. This was the beginning of the Oka Crisis.

2. The Mohawk or *Kanien'keha:ka* translated to "People of the Flint."
3. The struggle over illegal activities was immense. There were 8,500 Mohawks living on the Akwesasne Reserve at the time. Violence between the pro- and anti-gambling factions, as well as conflict with the New York State Police; the Ontario Provincial Police; the Royal Canadian Mounted Police; and the Federal Bureau of Investigation, prompted approximately 2,000–4,000 Mohawks to leave the reserve by April 1990. Cited in Winegard, *Oka*, 72–73.
4. Winegard, *Oka*, 76–77.
5. Operations Order, Operation Feather, dated 2 May 1990.
6. *Ibid.*
7. *Ibid.*
8. Quoted in Winegard, *Oka*, 87. Norris noted, "It has taken days to develop mutual trust and understanding."
9. The Municipal Council sent a letter to the Director-General of the SQ, Robert Lavigne, stating, "We ask you … to put a stop to the various criminal activities currently taking place on the Chemin du Milieu and to arrest the authors of the crimes so that we can proceed with the re- establishing the recreational use of the occupied lands … but we will not be able to do so until you have restored public safety in the occupied territory. We are counting on you to settle the issue without further delay and without further requests from us." Quoted in Winegard, *Oka*, 104.
10. A subsequent Coroner's Inquest that was made public in 1995, determined that Corporal Marcel Lemay was killed by a bullet fired by the Mohawks. The report also revealed, "beyond a shadow of a doubt that the first shot was fired by the occupants [Mohawks]," at the request of Warrior Dennis "Psycho" Nicholas. Coroner Guy Gilbert concluded in his report that, "it was a mistake to intervene on the morning of July 11, 1990." One CF intelligence operator who was on the scene revealed the SQ raid turned into "a comic opera farce." He noted, "It is one thing for a police SWAT team to corner a couple of punks in the corner grocery. It is another thing to take on determined men who are fully armed and prepared to defend themselves. The Mohawks routed the police, there is no question." See Winegard, *Oka*, 108.
11. The Mercier Bridge was a vital commuting link for over 60,000 vehicles a day, representing an approximate 200,000 passengers.
12. Intelligence gathered by the CF indicated, "We had found evidence that the closure of the bridge was already planned and [events on] 11 July hastened it or was the perfect excuse." Winegard, *Oka*, 111.

13. Letter, Sam Elkas (Quebec Attorney General) to General John de Chastelain, 6 August 1990.

14. "Annual Historical Report — 2nd Battalion, The Royal Canadian Regiment," 12 June 1991, 2. Within days, elements of the Combat Training Centre (CTC), Armoured School, 22 Field Engineer Squadron and "W" Battery, 1 RCHA were placed under command and 2 RCR became a battle group.

15. "OP Salon Summary Record of Decisions, 7–9 August 1990." On 8 August, the prime minister had already announced publicly the appointment of Alan Gold, chief justice of the Superior Court of Quebec, as the federal negotiator and mediator between all parties concerned. He also made reference to the possible intervention of the CF.

16. Lieutenant-Colonel Colin Magee, interview with author, 23 November 2010.

17. Quoted in Winegard, *Oka*, 129.

18. It was an integrated approach. Agents from the CF, the RCMP, the SQ, the DND Special Investigative Unit (SIU), as well as the Canadian Security Intelligence Service (CSIS) were all active. A joint Intelligence Collection and Analysis Centre (ICAC) was created at FMC HQ in St-Hubert to collect and collate information from all the mentioned agencies. There were at least three trained intelligence operators fluent in Mohawk dialect who posed as journalists and worked behind Warrior lines at both Kanesatake and Kahnawake. In addition, Mohawks opposed to the Warriors also supplied government agencies with information on weapons caches and Warrior activities and plans.

19. Intelligence assessment noted that a minimum of 20 Warriors had seen combat action in Vietnam, six were ex-members of the CF, and 10–20 Mohawks had U.S. military training. Others had received some training in basic military skills and tactics.

20. Gerald Baril, "Mission Accomplished," *Sentinel*, Vol. 26, No. 6 (1990), 3.

21. Winegard, *Oka*, 142. It appeared that the true motives started to emerge. The crisis was more about a struggle over control of power and money than it was about saving the "the Pines." In fact, the Warriors cut down 155 of the "sacred trees" to build barricades and bunkers.

22. Quoted in Winegard, *Oka*, 143–44.

23. *Ibid.*, 145.

24. What was not made public was the fact that the government feared that the Warriors had wired the Mercier Bridge for demolition. Although

whether or not they had accomplished this was unconfirmed, what was known was that there were trip-wired booby-traps underneath the Mercier Bridge, as well as on the railway bridge. Another concern was the amount of Native sympathy and support across the country. There were many protests and "copy-cat" barriers erected on reserves across the country. There was also serious violence and sabotage. For example, the Ojibwas in northern Ontario blocked a main railway line and the Trans-Canada Highway. Natives near Matapedia in Quebec blocked a rail line and dug up a section of track. In addition, five hydro towers were toppled and a bridge burned near London, Ontario.

25. CBC Newsworld, *This Country: Special Report, Brian Mulroney Press Conference* (Ottawa: Media Tapes and Transcripts Ltd., August 1990).

26. Quoted in Winegard, *Oka,* 159. The bridge was actually surrendered to the CF in the early hours of 1/2 September 1990. It was not until 2115 hours on 3 September that the Mercier Bridge was declared safe and free of any explosive devices. It was open to public traffic on 6 September 1990.

27. On 30 August CF officers met with Jack LeClerc, the Mohawk representative to clarify the situation and arrangements. Mohawk conditions stipulated that the military could enter the reserve but only in groups of 10 or less; military engineers would supervise all road work; routes would be patrolled by military personnel who would be accompanied by unarmed Mohawks; APCs, less .50 calibre machine guns, could enter the reserve, no SQ on the reserve, and there would be free passage of supplies onto the reserve.

28. "Van Doo" (English pronunciation for *vingt-deux* [22])) is a nickname for the R22eR.

29. It is interesting to note that Operations Salon and Akwesasne completely depleted the supply of concertina wire across the entire CF.

30. War Diary of the 2nd Battalion The Royal Canadian Regiment [henceforth 2 RCR War Diary], 3 September 1990.

31. Lieutenant-Colonel Bassarab recalled, "As soon as they saw us coming they would pull back the armed warriors and bus in women and children, so we always faced something different than we expected or were armed to deal with." Lieutenant-Colonel Rusty Bassarab, interview with author, 7 October 2009.

32. 2 RCR War Diary, 3 September 1990.

33. *Ibid.*

34. "Annual Historical Report — 2nd Battalion, The Royal Canadian Regiment," 12 June 1991, 2. The actual seizure of $750,000 worth of contraband cigarettes resulted from an inside tip by members of the reserve. The DCO, Rusty Bassarab revealed, "They deliberately fed that to us because he wasn't paying his 10 percent cut to the band. We were doing their work." Lieutenant-Colonel Rusty Bassarab, interview with author, 7 October 2009. At the same time as the longhouse was being searched, a vehicle attempting to smuggle out weapons from the area was stopped. One of the Natives pulled a knife, but was quickly subdued and arrested.

35. "Annual Historical Report — 2nd Battalion, The Royal Canadian Regiment," 12 June 1991, 2.

36. Winegard, *Oka*, 177.

37. The action was extremely immature and poorly thought out. It led to 2 RCR commanders fearing that the Natives had captured an APC with all of its weaponry. They were in the process of targeting the vehicle to destroy it, when, fortunately, they discovered what had transpired. The officer was relieved of his platoon command, sent home, and later charged.

38. Quoted in Winegard, *Oka*, 179. Up until that point the dress policy stipulated that officers wore berets and all other ranks wore helmets. That policy was subsequently changed.

39. For instance, one soldier was beaten unconscious with his own helmet and another had to have his ear surgically reattached.

40. "SIU Report, 19 September 1990."

41. Gerald Baril, "Mission Accomplished," *Sentinel*, Vol. 26, No. 6 (1990), 7–8.

42. *Ibid.*

43. Lieutenant-Colonel (then Captain) Pat McAdam stated: "Instances like the Diome house and Tekakwitha Island, they [SQ] said they would not come in. We lost faith in their ability to support us and carry out their functions. So we were forced to because they would not react." Quoted in Winegard, *Oka*, 182.

44. The RCR Museum Archives, "Statement of Sgt I.A. MacGillivary, Concerning Events of 26 September 90."

45. 2 RCR War Diary, 26 September 1990;" and Annual Historical Report — 2nd Battalion, The Royal Canadian Regiment," 12 June 1991, 2.

46. Approximately 28 proposed citations ranging from medals of bravery to FMC commendations were written up for the exceptional acts of bravery,

courage, and professionalism. None were awarded because of the domestic context.

47. Lieutenant-General Kent Foster cited in Gerald Baril, "Mission Accomplished," *Sentinel*, Vol. 26, No. 6 (1990), 7.

48. Lieutenant-Colonel Colin Magee, interview with author, 23 November 2010.

49. There was another variable at play consistent with the times. "The troops did not trust the Army to back them up," revealed the DCO. He added, "The restraint was not due solely to discipline. It was because they knew that the government/Army wouldn't back them up or support them if something happened." Lieutenant-Colonel Rusty Bassarab, interview with author, 7 October 2009.

50. Lieutenant-Colonel Greg Mitchell cited in Gerald Baril, "Mission Accomplished," *Sentinel*, Vol. 26, No. 6 (1990), 8. Well-known journalist Peter Worthington acclaimed that the Army, "is, literally, the world's expert in easing tense, volatile situations … without fanfare or fuss, mostly on their own judgment and initiative." Granatstein, *Canada's Army*, 380.

51. A series of U.N. Security Council resolutions were imposed: Resolution 660 — condemning the invasion and demanding a withdrawal of Iraqi troops; Resolution 661 — imposing economic sanctions, and Resolution 665 — authorizing a naval blockade to enforce the economic sanctions.

52. The U.S. launched Operation Desert Shield on 7 August 1990, to protect Saudi Arabia from potential Iraqi invasion. Hussein had also demanded that Saudi Arabia forgive Iraqi debt accrued during its long-standing war with Iran. In addition, following the conquest of Kuwait, Hussein began to assail the American-supported Saudi kingdom, saying it was an illegitimate and inadequate guardian of the Islamic holy cities of Mecca and Medina.

53. There has been great debate on the failure of Canada to send ground combat forces to the first Gulf War. As always, the government's fear of casualties had its effects, particularly in light of the ominous predictions by strategic analysts and media pundits on the nightly news of how deadly any offensive against a dug-in enemy would be. However, the greater burden of blame lies with the CF. Inter-service disputes, budgetary constraints, and a desire to use the current conflict to replace aging equipment all played their part. The Army's cost estimate of sending and sustaining a brigade-sized force became simply untenable. As a result, the Army played only a supporting role. See Maloney, *War Without Battles*,

449–59 for details on the analysis of OP Broadsword, which was the staff check on deploying ground forces to the Gulf.

54. *"Mike" Company in the Persian Gulf: 3rd Battalion, The Royal Canadian Regiment Support of Operation Scimitar.* Annex A to 3 RCR /1325-2 (IO), Dated 31 March 1991, 1–4.

55. *Ibid.*

56. SCUD refers to a type of tactical ballistic missile developed by the Soviets during the Cold War. It was exported to a large number of countries worldwide. At the start of the Gulf War, Iraq had an effective (SCUD) missile force. They utilized these to strike at coalition forces that were building up in neighbouring countries, and strike at Israel (42 times) in an attempt to lure them into the war, which most believed would have destroyed the American-built coalition. In the end, SCUD missiles were responsible for the deaths of 28 U.S. servicemen when a missile struck their barracks in Dhahran, Saudi Arabia.

57. On 1 March a Challenger jet left Bahrain with a small contingent of military personnel and the Canadian ambassador to Kuwait. Among the group was Warrant Officer Joe Parsons of 12 Platoon. His job was to search the embassy for booby-traps so that the ambassador could enter the building and raise the Canadian flag. The embassy was in a shambles, making Parsons's job even more difficult. Nonetheless he cleared the way up to the roof, enabling the Canadian flag to once again fly over Kuwait City.

58. The Canadian Army support also included turning over 4 CMBG's entire war stock of 155 mm ammunition to the British as well as providing all heavy Canadian lift in Germany to the Americans to support the logistical effort.

59. Quoted in Maloney, *War Without Battles*, 459–60. They remained on this level of alert for over four weeks.

60. The close-out actually took approximately 18 months. The final farewell "celebration" took place in Soest on 16–17 May 1993. At the same time, the Canadians exercised the Freedom of the City of Soest for the last time, having first been granted to The RCR in 1964.

61. The six republics were Serbia, Croatia, Slovenia, Bosnia-Herzegovina, Macedonia, and Montenegro. See Robert F. Baumann, George W. Gawrych, and Walter E. Kretchik, *Armed Peacekeepers in Bosnia* (Fort Leavenworth, KS: Combat Studies Institute Press, 2004) for an excellent source on the war in the Former Yugoslavia.

62. Baumann, 22.

63. The JNA terminated military operations after only 10 days of fighting. Casualty rates were relatively modest: JNA — 43 killed and 163 wounded; Slovenia — 12 killed and 144 wounded.

64. Baumann, 23.

65. The ECMMY included 15 Canadians. They were unarmed. The first teams arrived in theatre in September 1991.

66. The UNPROFOR commander was Indian Lieutenant-General Nambiar; the deputy commander was French Major-General Morillon, and the Chief of Staff, was Canadian Brigadier-General Lewis MacKenzie. UNPROFOR itself was a multinational peacekeeping force, initially consisting of 12 infantry battalions drawn from Canada, Argentina, Belgium, Czechoslovakia, Denmark, France, Jordan, Kenya, Nepal, Nigeria, Poland, and Russia. In addition, Canada provided an engineer regiment, the Netherlands provided a signals battalion, the British a medical battalion, the Finns construction engineers, and the Norwegians a movement control unit. National contingents and tasks changed with the evolution and the conflict and the rotation of units.

67. See Maloney, *War Without Battles,* 468.

68. The U.N. imposed limit for the infantry battalions was 860 personnel. After the commander's recce in theatre, Lieutenant-Colonel Michel Jones decided that instead of four rifle companies of 117 soldiers each, he would opt for a BG structure of a Headquarters Coy, "A" Coy, and Administration Coy from 1 R22eR, and "N" Coy and Recce Platoon from 3 RCR.

69. DHH, AHR, 3 RCR (1576) 1991–94, Vol. 2, Annual Historical Report 1992- 3rd Battalion, The Royal Canadian Regiment (UIC 1576), 29 January 1993, 2.

70. Quoted in Maloney, *War Without Battles,* 470.

71. DHH, AHR, 3 RCR (1576) 1991–94, Vol. 2, Annual Historical Report 1992- 3rd Battalion, The Royal Canadian Regiment (UIC 1576), 29 January 1993, 2.

72. Baumann, 24.

73. The Americans recognized Bosnia-Herzegovina as an independent state on 7 April 1992.

74. The UNPROFOR headquarters had just finished its move from Sarajevo to Belgrade when the decision to open up the airport occurred. In

addition, the BG CO's request for TUA and mortars was turned down by the U.N. because they felt it would appear too warlike.

75. Lieutenant-General Peter Devlin, interview with author, 9 November 2010.

76. Annual Historical Report 1992 — 3rd Battalion, The Royal Canadian Regiment (UIC 1576), 29 January 1993, 3. DHH, AHR, 3 RCR (1576) 1991–94, Vol. 2.

77. *Ibid.*

78. Hillier, *A Soldier First*, 185.

79. K.M. Boughton, "Germany Remembered," Pro Patria, Issue 75, August 1993,12. In total, 2 RCR served seven years in Germany at Fort York, 1953–55 and 1965–70; 1 RCR served five years, 1955–57 and 1962–65, also in Fort York; and 3 RCR served 12 years in Germany in Baden, 1977–84 and 1988–93.

80. Of the these, 52 Regular and nine Class B/A positions were allocated to Borden and the remaining 32 Regular/31 Class B/As were employed with the four affiliated infantry units.

81. Lieutenant-Colonel Mike Sweeney, interview with author, 23 November 2010.

82. *Ibid.*

83. *Ibid.*

84. Colonel R.M. Dillon, "Colonel of the Regiment," *The Connecting File,* 1993, 4.

85. Canada maintained a single staff position at UNFICYP HQ.

Chapter 6: Into the 1990s

1. Granatstein, *Canada's Army,* 382.

2. Major David DeClerq remembered working as a staff officer on disarmament in the late 1990s speaking to former Warsaw Pact officers. They all reached a strange consensus. He recalled, "We all talked about the good ole days of the Cold War when everyone knew the rules; how far you could push and everything was predictable. Everything was ritualized." Major David DeClerq, interview with author, 12 March 2010.

3. This is easily explained. The often tense but always stable standoff between superpowers in Europe and elsewhere in the world was contained in a framework where players were clearly delineated and rules universally understood. The Cold War, in many respects, artificially divided much of

the world into two distinct camps aligned with one or the other superpower. As such, states were often artificially propped up and maintained through the provision of economic and military assistance. These tools were both the carrot and stick used to keep proxies and allies in line. However, with the fall of "the Wall" in 1989–90, many of these states were abandoned, and thus they drifted toward total collapse. The resultant chaos transformed the international security environment. Where conflict in the Cold War was based on an interstate paradigm, it now took on an intrastate posture. Failed states spiralled into anarchy creating a vacuum of power that was often filled by warlords, paramilitary gangs, and criminal organizations. The civil wars and incidents of unrest that followed were incredibly savage and frequently threatened to spill over borders. In 1995, Boutros Boutros-Ghali, the secretary general of the United Nations, wrote, "the end of the cold war removed constraints that had inhibited conflict in the former Soviet Union and elsewhere … [There] has been a rash of wars within newly independent States, often of a religious or ethnic character and often involving unusual violence and cruelty." Boutros Boutros-Ghali, *An Agenda for Peace 1995, 2nd ed.* (New York: United Nations, 1995), 7.

4. From 1989–2001 the CF deployed on approximately 67 missions compared to 25 missions during the period 1948–89.

5. Hillier, *A Soldier First*, 92.

6. Baumann, 26.

7. On 9 October the U.N. Security Council pass Resolution 776, which banned military flights (other than UNPROFOR) over Bosnia.

8. WO Grant Gervais, "A Soldier's Perspective: Where Do We Stand?" *Pro Patria*, Issue 74, April 1993, 18.

9. Major Bernd Horn, "Impressions of a Foreign Land," *Pro Patria*, Issue 74, April 1993, 19.

10. Jordie Yoe, in John Wood, ed., *The Chance of War: Canadian Soldiers in the Balkans, 1992–1995* (Toronto: Breakout Educational Network in association with Dundurn Press, 2003), 216.

11. Lieutenant-Colonel Tom Geburt, 2 RCR Operation Cavalier Scrapbook, 1993, 1. The move was by vehicle from Lipik to Daruvar, by rail to the port city, Rijeka, by ferry to Split, and then by vehicle to the camps. The entire move took place between 18 February to 3 March 1993.

12. 2 RCR BG, "Handover Notes for Ops O 2 R22eR BG, OP Cavalier," ND, 6. The RCR MA.

13. Jim Davis, in Wood, *The Chance of War*, 39.

14. For a detailed account of the mission to Srebrenica, see Bernd Horn, "Verging on the Absurd: The Srebrenica Relief Convoy," in Bernd Horn, *In Harm's Way — On the Front Line of Leadership* (Kingston: CDA Press, 2006), 16–38.

15. Letter, P. Morillon to Major-General J.M.R. Gaudreau, April 1993.

16. Major Tom Mykytiuk, "The Srebrenica Seven," unpublished article, The RCR MA.

17. Baumann, 45.

18. The U.N. subsequently declared the cities of Tuzla, Zepa, Gorazde, Bihac, and Sarajevo as safe areas as well.

19. 2 RCR, "Estimate on Deployment Coy Gp Deployment to Srebrenica, BH," ND, 1. The RCR MA.

20. *Ibid.*, 2. The U.N. forces aside from the 2 RCR, "G" Coy Gp included: nine UNCIVPOL, four UNMOs, one UNHCR representative, three International Committee of the Red Cross (ICRC), and one Medecin Sans Frontier (MSF) representative.

21. Lieutenant-Colonel Perry Poirier, interview with author, 19 October 2009.

22. Mykytiuk, "The Srebrenica Seven."

23. Lieutenant-Colonel Perry Poirier, interview with author, 19 October 2009.

24. Despite the declaration, all suspected that the Bosnians had simply handed in their older weapons and kept their newer ones, just in case.

25. Peter Vallee, in Wood, *The Chance of War*, 207.

26. Lieutenant-Colonel Rob Walker, interview with author, 5 October 2008.

27. Jordie Yoe, in Wood, *The Chance of War*, 221.

28. Kurt Grant, *All Tigers, No Donkeys* (St. Catharines, ON: Vanwell, 2004), 80.

29. *Ibid.*, 143. Grant commented, "I have yet to see a single homeless or starving person. The farmers are doing well and the city folk are holding their own. Life goes on. For a country under a fuel embargo, there are a remarkable number of vehicles on the road."

30. *Ibid.*, 205.

31. Master Warrant Officer Tom France, interview with author, 1 May 2009.

32. Hillier, *A Soldier First*, 155.

33. Baumann, 40.

34. MacKenzie, in Wood, *The Chance of War*, 81.

35. Major Tony Balasevicius, interview with author, 27 July 2009.

36. Brigadier-General Denis Thompson, interview with author, 14 July 2008.

Thompson stated: "We were more serious than previous era but not as serious as today [fighting the insurgency in Afghanistan]."

37. "DND Press Announcement — Canadian Airborne Regiment Going to Somalia," *Information Legacy*, 2 September 1992, DND Document Control No. 111796, p 107509. UNOSOM was created on 24 April 1992, through U.N. Resolution 751, in response to the continuing deterioration of the situation in Somalia. The military/civilian operation was envisioned as a multinational force of over 4,000 personnel. The military was assigned the task of monitoring the ceasefire in Mogadishu, and securing human aid and ensuring its safe delivery to distribution centres as well as protecting U.N. personnel. UNOSOM was overtaken by the U.S. led UNITAF on 4 December 1992.

38. U.N. Department of Information, *The UN and the Situation in Somalia*, Reference Paper, 15 December 1992, 4–7; BOI — Cdn AB Regt BG, Phase I, Vol. XI, A-1/33; and Dan Loomis, *The Somalia Affair: Reflections on Peacemaking and Peacekeeping* (Ottawa: DGL Publications, 1996), 115. The UNITAF operational concept was based on a four-phase scheme designed to restore stability to Somalia. Phase One was the initial landing by American forces to secure the port and airport at Mogadishu, and the airfields at Baledogle and Baidoa. Phase Two was the securing of the port and airfield at Kismayu, and airfields at Hoddur, Bardera, Gialalassi, and Belet Huen. The final objective of this phase was the securing of the port of Marka. Phase Three envisioned the expansion of security and relief operations throughout the Humanitarian Relief Sectors, and Phase Four was the transition of command and control from UNITAF to UNOSOM II.

39. *Somalia Commission*, Transcript of Policy Hearing, Vol. 2, 19 June 1995, 269–72.

40. Loomis, *The Somalia Affair*, 293. This aspect of the mission has been totally lost in the post-Somalia sequence of events. The Somalia Commission's final report noted, "The mission called for troops who were well led, highly disciplined, and able to respond flexibly to a range of tasks that demanded patience, understanding, and sensitivity to the plight of the Somali people. Instead they arrived in the desert trained and mentally conditioned to fight." Executive "Summary — Training," *Information Legacy*. The first phrase is required of all U.N. missions or operations. The second was specifically required by this mission based on the mandate of UNITAF.

41. *Somalia Commission*, Transcript of Policy Hearing, Vol. 2, 19 June 1995, 273; and Canadian Joint Task Force (CJTF), *In the Line of Duty* (Ottawa: DND, 1994), 16. To accomplish their assigned mission the Airborne Battle Group divided the Canadian Humanitarian Relief Sector, also known as the Belet Huen HRS, into four security sectors, which in turn were assigned to the sub-units of the battle group. The town of Belet Huen was designated as Zone 2 and was the responsibility of the dismounted 2 Commando (reinforced by the 1 RCR Mortar Platoon). The southeastern section of the HRS was designated as Zone 1, and the southwestern portion Zone 3. The Shabelle River separated the two sectors that were the responsibilities of 1 and 3 Commandos, respectively. Both of these sub-units were mounted in the Grizzly AVGP. The northeastern area was designated Zone 4. This area was considered the most complex of the four zones because it contained two hostile Somali factions, the Ethiopian border, and an exposed flank to the still unstable central regions of Somalia. This sector was the responsibility of A Squadron, the RCD, which operated out of the town of Matabaan, located approximately 80 kilometres northeast of Belet Huen.

42. BOI — Cdn AB Regt BG, Phase I, Vol. 11, A-4/33. The Airborne Battle Group consisted of regimental headquarters based on headquarters commando (and included a reconnaissance platoon and a direct fire support platoon; 1 and 3 Commando mounted in Grizzly AVGPs; 2 Commando as a dismounted infantry company reinforced by mortar platoon from 1 RCR; "A" Squadron RCD mounted in Cougar (armed with a 76 mm gun) AVGPs; a close support engineer squadron from 2 CER; and Service Commando reinforced by surgical and dental teams.

43. BOI — Cdn AB Regt BG, Phase I, Vol. 11, A-3/33. The living conditions were particularly primitive as the paratroopers had only the most basic of necessities. Soldiers were given six litres of water a day per man for consumption, and it was only after three weeks that a five gallon jerry can of water was made available per section for washing of oneself or one's laundry. Corporal Ed Ormond captured the attitude when he stated: "You had to be an airborne paratrooper to survive the harsh conditions we endured while there … no showers or any way to get clean at all, living in trenches and eating dirt for two months." (Submission to author, April 1995). Sergeant Mark Godfrey testified at the Somalia Commission, "we were living in a hole and every night it would fill up with various insects

... we were limited to one jerry can of water per man per day. So you had to either eat with it, drink with it or wash with it. It was harsh conditions." (*Somalia Commission*, Hearing Transcripts, 3 April 1996, 10823).

44. Letter, Lieutenant-General R.B. Johnston, commander UNITAF to Admiral J.R. Anderson, CDS, 1 May 1993, 1.

45. *Ibid.*, 2–3; and BOI — Cdn AB Regt BG, Phase I, Vol. 11, A-11/33 to A-16/33. The incessant patrolling and continuous presence of paratroopers within in Belet Huen earned them the nickname the "Clan who never sleeps" from the Somalis. Canadian Joint Task Force, *In the Line of Duty* (Ottawa: Department of National Defence, 1994), 18.

46. Letter, Robert B. Oakley, (Special Envoy to Somalia), to the Minister of National Defense, dated 11 May 1993, 2; and BOI — Cdn AB Regt BG, Phase I, Vol. 11, A-2/3. The Canadian HRS was declared secure 28 March 1993.

47. Loomis, *The Somalia Affair*, 410.

48. *Ibid.*, 439.

49. *Somalia Commission*, Transcript of Policy Hearing, Vol. 2, June 19, 1995, 284.

50. Beno Papers, Letter, W.B. Vernon (Commander LFCA) to DCDS, 13 May 1993, 2.

51. Major-General (Retired) Lewis MacKenzie, "In Defence of Matieu and the Airborne," *Toronto Star*, 22 July 1994, A21.

52. *Information Legacy*, Hearing Transcripts, Vol. 52, 1 April 1996, testimony of Captain Jacques Poitras, CJFS Public Affairs Officer in Somalia, record 88361–88374.

53. Colonel Serge Labbé, *Canadians in Somalia — Setting the Record Straight or Somalia Cover-Up* (Private Printing, 1994), 363. Colonel Labbé's well-written book is a comprehensive catalogue of the humanitarian effort conducted in Somalia. However, it is completely uncritical of the mission. Furthermore, there is a painful absence of clarification or even mention of the controversial aspects of the tour. Despite the book's 556 pages, there is only a single paragraph in which the "unfortunate deaths" of Somalis under Canadian custody is mentioned. Likewise, there is the briefest of remarks on subjects such as RoE and no reference of the confusion following the March killings. The unbalanced account detracts from the credibility of an otherwise insightful look into the Somalia mission.

54. Letter, Oakley to the MND, 11 May 1993, 4. Major-General Lewis MacKenzie stated: "When I went to Somalia in 1992, Lieutenant-General Johnson, who was the overall force commander, an American, told me that the Canadian troops were the best in his 14,000-person force." Lewis MacKenzie in Wood, *The Chance of War*, 77.

55. According to the report of Major Armstrong, "the deceased had been first shot in the back and subsequently 'dispatched' with a pair of shots to the head and neck area. Major Armstrong considered that the wounds were consistent with the Somali being shot as he lay wounded on the ground." "Report of the Commission of Inquiry, Executive Summary — Mission Aftermath," *Information Legacy*, Record 2874. Master-Corporal Petersen testified that he observed that "the dead Somali's neck was blown out, his head was gaping open at the back of the skull and his face was sagging to one side." "Report of the Commission of Inquiry, Vol. 1 — March 4 Shooting," *Information Legacy*, Record 2871. The officer in charge of the operation was Captain Rainville. His posting to the Regiment, as well as deployment to Somalia was questioned by the SSF commander because of Rainville's existing "Rambo" reputation.

56. "Report of the Commission of Inquiry, Vol. 5, 4 March — Findings," *Information Legacy*, Record 9569. The commission was scathing in its comments of the handling of the incident. It asserted that actions both within theatre and by the command structure in Canada were negligent in ensuring a proper investigation was conducted. See also Coulon, 97.

57. Peter Worthington, *Scapegoat: How the Army Betrayed Kyle Brown* (Toronto: Seal Books, 1997), 116–35; Peter Worthington, "Private Brown," *Saturday Night*, September 1994, 35–36; Brian Bergman, "A Night of Terror," *Maclean's Magazine*, 28 March 1994, 26–28; and "Brutal Allegations," *Maclean's Magazine*, 7 March 1994, 13.

58. General M. Baril, "Officership: A Personal Reflection," in *Generalship and the Art of the Admiral*, eds. Bernd Horn and Stephen Harris (St. Catharines: Vanwell Ltd., 2001), 138.

59. See "Court Martial Held Without Public Notice," *The Globe and Mail*, 9 July 1997; *Report of the Board of Inquiry into the Command, Control and Leadership of CANBAT 2*, dated 15 November 1996; Scott Taylor and Brian Nolan, *Tarnished Brass* (Toronto: Lester Publishing Ltd., 1996); and Taylor, Scott and Brian Nolan. *Tested Mettle: Canada's Peacekeepers at War* (Ottawa: Esprit de Corps Books, 1998); "Shamed In Bosnia," *Maclean's*

Magazine, 29 July 1996, 10–12; Worthington, *Scapegoat,* 314–15; Peter Desbarats, *Somalia Cover-Up: A Commissioner's Journal* (Toronto: McClelland & Stewart, 1997), 4–5; and Winslow, 72–74. *Esprit de Corps* magazine also ran a running critique of any and all foibles present in the CF in virtually every issue of its publication from 1993 to the present.

60. For example see DND News Release NR-96.111, 27 December 1996; "The Rise and Fall of an Officer," Ottawa Citizen, 10 April 1998, A4); Jack Granatstein, *Who Killed the Canadian Military?* (Toronto: HarperFlamingoCanada, 2004),155; John A. English, *Lament for an* Army (Concord, ON: Irwin Publishing, 1998), 7, 64–65; and Scott Taylor and Brian Nolan, *Brass* (Toronto: Lester Publishing Ltd., 1996); Major Robert Near, "Devining the Message: An Analysis of the MND and Somalia Commission Reports," in Bernd Horn, ed., *Contemporary Issues in Officership: A Canadian Perspective* (Toronto: CISS, 2000), 65–91; and previous endnote.

61. *Somalia Commission Report,* Executive Summary, S-4. See also Desbarats, 3–4.

62. Rodal, 73. See also Canada. *Debrief the Leaders Project (Officers)* (Ottawa: DND, 2001); and Allan D. English, *Understanding Military Culture: A Canadian Perspective* (Kingston: McGill-Queen's Press, 2004), 104–08.

63. One warrant officer captured the general sentiment. He stated: "There's not a lot of trust out there between the frontline units and the Puzzle Palace [NDHQ]. There's a huge gap. It's like a black zone and they have to do something to correct it." Matt Stopford, in Woods, 129. Another senior NCO captured the sentiments of his peers when he bluntly told a general who had come to bid them good luck on their impending tour to the Former Yugoslavia, "We do not trust you or the other officers to back us up if we make a decision that does not play well back in Canada." He continued, "We think that your kind will be there to bask in the reflected glory if things go well but that we and our troops will be hung out to dry if politicians or the public sitting safely in Canada do not like the response we make in the heat of the moment." Quoted in J.L. Granatstein, *A Paper Prepared for the Minister of National Defence by J.L. Granatstein,* Canadian Institute of International Affairs, 25 March 1997, 15.

64. Doug Young, MND, *Report to the Prime Minister on the Leadership and Management of the Canadian Armed Forces* [henceforth *MND Report*] (Ottawa: DND, 1997), 1. In the DND commissioned Pollara survey titled *Canadians' Opinions on the Canadian Forces (CF) and Related Military*

Issues, dated December 1998, only 52 percent of respondents agreed with the statement "The quality of leadership among CF senior officers is high." Only 35 percent agreed with the statement "The CF leadership is honest when making statements to the public." A Philips Employee Feedback Survey conducted by DND was even more damning. The poll showed that only 15 percent of the civilian and 17 percent of the military respondents expressed "confidence in the most senior levels of the Department." This is even more damning since the senior and general officer and civilian managers were over represented in the survey. See Bernd Horn, "Wrestling with an enigma," in Lieutenant-Colonel Bernd Horn, ed., *Contemporary Issues of Officership: A Canadian Perspective* (Toronto: Canadian Institute of Strategic Studies, 2000), 133–35.

65. See Jan Willem Honig and Norbert Both, *Srebrenica: Record of a War Crime* (London: Penguin Books, 1996).

66. The Americans blamed the Bosnian Serbs, however, international experts believed that the evidence pointed toward Bosnian-Muslim forces, who targeted their own people so that they could blame Serb forces and garner international outrage and support. See Baumann, 43; and Roy Rempel, *The Chatter Box: An Insider's Account of the Irrelevance of Parliament in the Making of Canadian Foreign and Defence Policy* (Toronto: Breakout Educational Network, 2002), 160.

67. The airstrikes prompted the Serbs to take UNMOs as hostages and use them as human shields to protect military installations. Contingency plans were drawn up to provide an international force to assist with the extraction of U.N. forces from the former Yugoslavia should hostilities break-out. One of the designated units to prepare for this eventuality, which was code-named contingency operational plan (COP) Cobra, was 2 RCR. As part of the preparation, the unit conducted company and battalion exercises and participated in brigade work between August and September 1995. Preparations continued into January 1996 with a major command post exercise.

68. BiH was divided into three division-plus size sectors: the American-led Multinational Division North (MND-N) stationed out of Tuzla; the British-led Multinational Division Southwest (MND-SW) centred in Gronji Vakuf and later transferred to Banja Luka; and the French-led Multinational Division Southeast (MND-SE) located in Mostar.

69. Brigadier-General Denis Thompson, interview with author, 14 July 2008.

70. *Ibid.*
71. *Ibid.*
72. Baumann, 114.
73. "3rd Battalion," *The Connecting File,* 1998, 21.
74. Major Matthew Sprague, interview with author, 19 October 2007.
75. Master Warrant Officer Rick Duncan, interview with author, 15 April 2008.
76. Lieutenant-Colonel Rob Walker, interview with author, 5 October 2008.
77. Chief Warrant Officer Jay Gravelle, interview with author, 25 August 2009.
78. *Ibid.*
79. Colonel Jim Davis, interview with author, 9 July 2009.
80. Captain Piers Pappin, interview with author, 14 July 2008.
81. Quoted in Baumann, 160.
82. Drago Tokmakcija, the deputy mayor and president of the local HDZ, held real political and economic power, much like a Mafioso. He had strong ties to the military and controlled the police.
83. Baumann, 161.
84. Quoted in Baumann, 149.
85. Master Warrant Officer Rick Duncan, interview with author, 15 April 2008. SFOR headquarters admitted in a press conference a few days later that the riot represented "a tragic reversal of the progress made in Bosnia since the end of the war." SFOR reiterated that its mandate was not to stop the initial incidents. That responsibility fell squarely on the shoulders of the civil authorities. SFOR's task was to prevent any escalation and limit the loss of life and property. The Drvar police, however, had fallen far short of their responsibilities. They had failed to respond to the riot and might have even been accomplices to the event. The SFOR briefer confessed to some mistakes having been made by the international community. The town's police force, for example, had been left completely in the hands of Croats. SFOR addressed this problem immediately by setting a 48-hour deadline for the appointment of a Serb as deputy chief of police and for the assigning of 15 Serbs to the police force. The presence of Serb police would help calm some fears among the Serbs living in the Drvar region. In the press conference, the official from the Office of the High Representative noted that the percentage of returnees in Drvar had been high compared with other localities, and that this had resulted in "a lot of

incidents" before the riot itself. The Canadians had been right in urging a slowdown in the rate of returnees. On 28 April, just four days after the riot, officials of Canton Ten signed an agreement in Livno for creating a multi-ethnic police force. Baumann, 166

86. "Annual Historical Report — 1st Battalion, The Royal Canadian Regiment," 1 November 1999, 6.

87. Colonel Jim Davis, interview with author, 9 July 2009.

88. Master Warrant Officer Rick Duncan, interview with author, 15 April 2008.

89. Chief Warrant Officer Jay Gravelle, interview with author, 25 August 2009. In April 2004, Canada cut its 1,200 personnel force to 650. Six months later it reduced its commitment to 85, and by end year had shut down the mission entirely.

90. Captain Piers Pappin, interview with author, 14 July 2008.

91. The MND announced the disbandment on 23 January 1995, however, the actual ceremonies did not transpire until the weekend of 4/5 March 1995.

92. Designation given to the remaining elements of the Canadian Airborne Regiment, effective 6 March 1995 (the day following official disbandment). The Canadian Airborne Holding Unit ceased to exist as of 1 September 1995 when it was absorbed by 3 RCR upon its move from CFB Borden to CFB Petawawa.

93. Message — LFCHQ COS 030, dated 032145Z March 95, "Disbandment Cdn AB Regt." A 1994 Land Forces Command estimate concluded that "within the Land Force the only high readiness force that is capable of conducting land operations expeditiously into any condition of climate and terrain is the Canadian Airborne Regiment." The report noted that the regiment was ideally suited to conduct expeditionary, contingency and vanguard operations that ensured a military presence, by parachute if necessary, which in turn would enable the follow-on deployment of slower, less mobile conventional forces. It further declared that "the Regiment, in conjunction with the required tactical airlift, constituted the national strategic reserve that underpins the credibility of Canadian sovereignty operations." LFC, "Justification for an Airborne Capability in the Canadian Forces," 19 April 1994, 4.*Ibid.*, 4. See also "The Requirement for an Operational Parachute Capability in the Canadian Forces Structure," 21 February 1994, 4–11.

94. LFCHQ, "Operational Enhancement of the Land Field Forces and Maintenance of a Parachute Capability," 13 March 1995, 2 and 5.

95. SSFHQ, "Maintenance of an Interim Airborne Capability," 5 April 1995, 2.

96. *Ibid.*

97. The CO of the 10/90 was somewhat indignant about the decision. "We were never fully allowed to finish," he revealed, "People were just posted away because of a higher decision to re-establish 3 RCR/light infantry battalions once the Cdn AB Regt was disbanded." Lieutenant-Colonel Mike Sweeney, interview with author, 23 November 2010.

98. *Somalia Commission Report,* Transcript of Policy Hearing, Vol. 2, 19 June 1995, 281–82. See "Canadian Troops Don't Need Enemies," *London Free Press,* 28 July 1999, and "Military Cover-up Inquiry Sounds Like Somalia Mess," *The Guardian* (Charlottetown), 28 July 1999; and James Cudmore, "Cogs in the Military," *National Post,* 31 July 1999. See also editorials in the *Toronto Star,* 28 July 1999; *The Globe and Mail,* 30 July 1999; and the *Hamilton Spectator,* 30 July 1999, all of which questioned the ability of the CF to conduct a fair and impartial inquiry.

99. *Somalia Commission Report,* ES-46; Vol. 5, 1450.

100. Of the 65 recommendations contained in the MND Report, 22 dealt with military leadership.

101. Canada. *Minister's Monitoring Committee on Change in the Department of National Defence and the Canadian Forces: Final Report- 1999* (Ottawa: DND, 1999), iii.

102. General Ray Hennault later acknowledged that "Somalia had been a dramatic wake-up call — a rude awakening that something was amiss." He further commented that "it wasn't just Somalia, it was a build up of incidents." He also noted that it was clearly a military leadership failure. General Ray Hennault, interview with Bernd Horn and Bill Bentley, 9 November 2010.

103. See Canada. *Duty with Honour: The Profession of Arms in Canada* (Ottawa: DND, 2003), 6–7 and 25.

104. See for example: DND News Release NR-96.111, 27 December 1996; "The Rise and Fall of an Officer," Ottawa Citizen, 10 April 1998, A4); Granatstein, *Who Killed the Canadian Military?,* 155; English, *Lament,* 7, 64–65; "Court Martial Held Without Public Notice," *The Globe and Mail,* 9 July 1997; *Report of the Board of Inquiry into the Command, Control and Leadership of CANBAT 2,* dated 15 November 1996; Taylor, *Tarnished Brass*; and Taylor, *Tested Mettle*; "Shamed In Bosnia," *Maclean's Magazine,* 29 July 1996, 10–12; Major Robert Near, "Devining the Message: An Analysis of the MND and Somalia Commission Reports," in Bernd Horn, ed., *Contemporary Issues in Officership: A Canadian Perspective* (Toronto: CISS, 2000), 65–91; Editorial,

Esprit de Corps, Vol. 4, No. 2, 9. See also Peter Worthington, "A blind eye to a regiment's sins," *Ottawa Sun,* 1 August 1996, 11; and *Esprit de Corps* magazine also ran a running critique of any and all foibles present in the CF in virtually every issue of its publication throughout the 1990s.

105.   Sadly, although this senior infantry officer openly admitted that he was conversant with the problem, he did nothing to ensure fairness for everyone. In fact, he is remembered by many as one of the most careerist, deceitful moral cowards of the period.

106.   Colonel Jim Davis, interview with author, 9 July 2009. Colonel Rick Hatton had a similar recollection. "I remember," he stated, "the Somalia era as dark, dark years. I believe the population and government lost faith in us. It was a bad, bad time." Colonel Rick Hatton, interview with author, 28 February 2008.

107.   Hillier, *A Soldier First,* 93.

108.   In 1989 the Canadian Human Rights Tribunal ordered that women be integrated into all military occupations by 1999.

109.   Major Jay Feyko, interview with author, 28 January 2009.

110.   Captain David Garvin, interview with author, 10 January 2009.

111.   Master Warrant Officer Tom France, interview with author, 1 May 2009.

112.   Lieutenant-General Andrew Leslie, Land Staff Prayers, 15 June 2009.

113.   Canada, *Chief Reserve Services Evaluation of Land Force Readiness and Training* (Ottawa: DND, August 2010), 9. The report also noted, "There have been no common applied standards, and few training events have caused the Army to reconsider or change its doctrine. The Army has failed to make maximum use of training to facilitate learning."

114.   Colonel R.M. Dillon, "Colonel of the Regiment," *The Connecting File,* 1993, 5.

115.   Colonel R.M. Dillon, "Colonel of the Regiment," *The Connecting File,* 1994, 3.

116.   Lieutenant-General (Retired) J.E. Vance, "Colonel of the Regiment," *The Connecting File,* 1997, 4.

Chapter 7: The New Millennium

1.   "Gen. Hillier speaks to the Globe on Afghanistan," edited transcript, http://www.theglobeandmail.com/servlet/story/RTGAM.20060302. whilliertrans0303/BNStory/Front (accessed 3 March 2006).

2.   Hillier, *A Soldier First*, 93.

3.   *Ibid.*, 262.

4.   General M. Baril, "Officership: A Personal Reflection," in *Generalship and the Art of the Admiral*, eds. Bernd Horn and Stephen Harris (St. Catharines: Vanwell Ltd., 2001), 138.

5.   Lieutenant-General Mike Jeffrey, Keynote Address, Commanding Officer Course, 21 June 2001.

6.   See MND Report, *Leadership and Management of the Canadian Forces*, 7–39; MND Report, *Compendium of Changes in the Canadian Forces and the Department of National Defence*, 1–12; and Minister's Monitoring Committee on Change (henceforth MMC), Final Report 1999. Fundamental to the transformation was a CF ethos statement put out in 1997, which outlined three key principles: respect the dignity of all persons; serve nation before self; and obey and support lawful authority. This statement was incorporated into all recruiting, training, and professional development.

7.   Major R.J. Martin, letter to author, 16 December 2010.

8.   Brigadier-General Jim Cox, interview with author, 27 April 2010.

9.   Colonel Jim Davis, interview with author, 9 July 2009.

10. The LAV III is a 17-ton, eight-wheeled armoured personnel carrier built in London, Ontario, by General Dynamics Land Systems. It is approximately seven metres long and 2.81 metres high. The vehicle has a crew of three and carries seven soldiers with all their equipment. With a top-end speed of 100 kilometres per hour, it has a range of 500 kilometres. The LAV III is also heavily armed. It boasts a 25 mm Bushmaster chain gun, a 7.62 mm general purpose machine gun (GPMG), a 5.56 mm pintle-mounted machine gun, and eight smoke grenade launchers.

11. This was the first Canadian operational deployment of the LAV III. It was rated as outstanding by the troops for its mobility, endurance, and protection. A land-mine strike disabled a LAV with minor damage, but, more important, without hurting anyone.

12. The Canadian contribution consisted of a LAV coy, a recce platoon, an engineer troop and a combat service support platoon, and coy headquarters. In essence, it was a Coy Gp organization that was integrated into a Dutch marine battalion in Eritrea.

13. Colonel Bill Peters, "Director Land Strategic Planning & Director of Infantry," *Pro Patria*, Issue 83, October 2001, 3.

14. For example, Colonel Bill Peters described, "In 1 RCR for instance we had soldiers serving in four different continents. It exemplified an army tugged in every different direction. We were trying to do all these things for politicians in far flung regions of the world. As a result, the Army tried to control everything from a very high level, and this resulted in a lack of respect for the integrity of battalions." Colonel Bill Peters, interview with author, 11 December 2010.

15. Captain Gerry Byrne, interview with author, 5 January 2009.

16. Strategy 2020 contained eight departmental change objectives: 1. Innovative Path — create an adaptive, innovative and relevant path into the future; 2. Decisive Leaders; 3. Modernize; 4. Globally Deployable; 5. Interoperability; 6. Career of Choice; 7. Strategic Partnerships; 8. Resource Stewardship.

17. Canada, *Advancing with Purpose: The Army Strategy* (Ottawa: DND, 2002), 13.

18. Canada, "Land Force Strategic Direction and Guidance," *Strategic Operations and Resource Plan* (Ottawa: DND, 2000), 1/3–9.

19. Brigadier-General Denis Thompson, interview with author, 14 July 2008.

20. *Ibid.*

21. *Ibid.*

22. *Ibid.*

23. *Ibid.*

24. *Ibid.*

25. Chief Warrant Officer C.Y.M. (Kit) Charlebois, letter to author, 30 December 2010.

26. Master Warrant Officer Keith Olstad, interview with author, 11 January 2009.

27. Master Warrant Officer Tom France, interview with author, 1 May 2009.

28. Master Warrant Officer Keith Olstad, interview with author, 11 January 2009.

29. Chief Warrant Officer Jay Gravelle, interview with author, 25 August 2009.

30. Quoted in United Kingdom, Parliament, House of Commons Library, International Affairs & Defence Section, Research Paper 01/72, 11 September 2001: the response, 31 October 2002, 17, http://www.parliament.uk/commons/lib/re-search/rp2001/rp01–112.pdf (accessed 7 March 2007). The history between the Americans and Osama bin Laden and al-Qaeda (AQ) went back a long way. They had tracked bin Laden from Sudan to Afghanistan. On 28 August 1998, the Americans were able

to convince the U.N. Security Council to pass UNSCR 1193 demanded that "Afghan factions … refrain from harboring and training terrorists and their organizations." More specific UNSCR 214, passed on 8 December 1998, affirmed that the Security Council was "deeply disturbed by the continuing use of Afghan territory, especially areas controlled by the Taliban, for the sheltering and training of terrorists and the planning of terrorist acts" and reiterated that "the suppression of international terrorism is essential for the maintenance of international peace and security." The Americans continued their U.N. offensive. On 15 October 1999, the U.S. secured the adoption of UNSCR 1267, which expressed concerns about the "continuing violations of international humanitarian law and of human rights [in Afghanistan], particularly discrimination against women and girls," as well as "the significant rise in the illicit production of opium." Importantly, the Resolution specifically criticized the Taliban for offering "safe haven to Osama bin Laden and to allow him and others associated with him to operate a network of terrorist training camps … and to use Afghanistan as a base from which to sponsor international terrorist operations." As such the Security Council demanded "that the Taliban turn over Osama bin Laden without further delay" so that he could be "effectively brought to justice." The council also instituted the same economic and financial sanctions on the Taliban regime that had been recently imposed by the United States. The Taliban failed to comply, and on 12 October 2000, the AQ attacked the USS *Cole* in the harbour at Aden, killing 17 U.S. sailors and wounding 39. To exacerbate the looming showdown, bin Laden took full credit for the operation, prompting the Security Council to pass UNSCR 1333 on 19 December 2000. This resolution reaffirmed the charges made just a year earlier and added the stipulation that the Taliban were to ensure the closing "of all camps where terrorists are trained." In addition, economic sanctions were strengthened, Taliban offices were to be closed in the territory of member states, landing rights for Afghan national airways was revoked, and all assets linked to Osama bin Laden and al-Qaeda were frozen. Once again the Taliban regime did nothing As a result, yet another UNSCR was passed on 30 July 2001, which described "the situation in Afghanistan … as a threat to international peace and security in the region." As such, in the weeks leading up to 9/11 Afghanistan had already been identified as a major threat centre for American national interest. See *United Nations Security*

Council Resolution 1193, 28 August 1998; *Resolution 1214,* 8 December 1998; *Resolution 1267,* 15 October 1999; *Resolution 1333,* 19 December 2000; *Resolution 1363,* 30 July 2001; and Ahmed Rashid, *Taliban: Militant Islam, Oil and Fundamentalism in Central Asia* (New Haven: Yale University Press, 2001), 80; Daniel Benjamin and Steven Simon, *The Age of Sacred Terror* (New York: Random House, 2002), xiii and 289. See also Steve Coll, *Ghost Wars* (New York: Penguin Books, 2004) for a comprehensive account of the U.S./bin Laden/AQ interrelationship.

31. North Atlantic Council Statement, 12 September 2001, Press Release (2001)124, http://www.nat.int/docu/pr/2001/p01–124e.htm (accessed 7 March 2007); and NATO, *NATO Handbook* (Brussels: NATO Office of Information and Press, 1995), 232.

32. Statement by NATO Secretary-General Lord Robertson, 4 October 2001, http://www.nato.int/docu/speech/2001/s011004a.htm (accessed 7 March 2007). See also Tom Lansford, *All for One: Terrorism, NATO, and the United States* (Aldershot: Ashgate Publishing, 2002), 126.

33. See *United Nations Security Council Resolutions 1368,* 12 September 2001 and *UNSCR 1373,* 28 September 2001. Interestingly, the U.N. had already in essence given its approval to NATO on 28 September when they invoked Chapter VII of the United Nations Charter, which authorized the use of military force.

34. See Janice Gross Stein and Eugene Lange, *The Unexpected War: Canada in Kandahar* (Toronto: Viking Canada, 2007), 2–34.

35. Jean Chrétien: "Canadian troops 'will do Canada proud,'" 7 October 2001, http://www.ctv.ca/servlet/ArticleNews/story/CTVNews/1025062429054_20471629 (accessed 7 October 2001). The Standing Committee on National Security and Defence affirmed, "In those early days the Committee saw two good reasons for Canada to play a role in Afghanistan. One was supporting our long-time American ally in a time of need. The second was that any initiative that our Government could take to counter international terrorism, as called upon by the United Nations, had merit." Canada, *How are We doing in Afghanistan?* Report of the Standing Senate Committee on National Security and Defence," June 2008, 1.

36. DND's initial contribution included: a naval task group of two frigates (HMCS *Charlottetown* and HMCS *Halifax*), one destroyer (HMCS *Iroquois*), one replenishment ship (HMCS *Preserver*), and five maritime helicopters as of 10 November 2001; one frigate (HMCS *Vancouver*)

(with 1 maritime helicopter) to augment U.S. Carrier Battle Group (CBG) USS *John C. Stennis*; an air lift task group (ALTG), comprised of three C-130 Hercules and one C-150 Polaris aircraft; a long range patrol task group (LRPTG) consisting of two CP-140 Aurora patrol aircraft; and a national command element (NCE) located with U.S. Central Command (CENTCOM) headquarters in Tampa, Florida. The CDS provided a clear mission for the deploying troops. He affirmed that the "CF will contribute to the elimination of the threat of terrorism as a force in international affairs by contributing [Canadian] Joint Task Force South West Asia (CA JTFSWA) to the commander-in-chief (CINC) CENTCOM in support of the USA led campaign against terrorism in order to protect Canada and its allies from terrorist attacks and prevent future attacks." His intent was to support the international campaign through an initial six-month commitment of military forces, the role of the CF being further refined as the Coalition military campaign plan evolved and matured.

37.   Maulvi Mohammad Haqqani, a Taliban fighter at the time, conceded, "I never thought the Taliban would collapse so quickly and cruelly under U.S. bombs." He lamented, "The bombs cut down our men like a reaper harvesting wheat." Maulvi Abdul Rehman Akhundzada cited in Sami Yousafzai and Ron Moreau, "The Taliban in their Own Words," *Newsweek. com*, 5 October 2009, 36.

38.   The multinational forces took control of Kandahar on 7 December 2001. American efforts then shifted to tracking down Osama bin Laden and his top AQ leadership. Canadian air, sea, and SOF elements remained to support the ongoing Coalition force efforts.

39.   *United Nations Security Council Resolutions 1378,* 14 November 2001.

40.   The first of the ISAF troops deployed to Kabul on 22 December 2001. General Hillier believed that "NATO never really wanted to get into Afghanistan — it backed into it, largely against the will of many members, though all did acquiesce. The first tentative step was taking over the ISAF mission in and around Kabul." He insisted, "NATO ended up taking an incremental approach into the mission, agreeing to take responsibility for ISAF and then trying to get member nations to deploy the troops and equipment to do it. One result of this was the idea of provincial reconstruction teams, which were seen as a way for the alliance to expand the ISAF mission throughout the rest of Afghanistan without any need for the large numbers of troops that it didn't have committed. Some NATO

members were already leery of sending their soldiers to Afghanistan, and many were not eager to allow their soldiers to engage in anything resembling combat." Hillier, *A Soldier First,* 473 and 281–82.

41. *Ibid.* General Hillier elaborated, "As far as they were concerned, Canada could not be relied upon to do the tough stuff and was therefore of no use. The British Command structure remembered the years in the former Yugoslavia when 'Can'tbat' — Canada's contribution to the U.N., and later to NATO, forces — needed days or even weeks to get approval from Ottawa before we would take on an operation, assuming we were even allowed to do so. The Canadian government, which desperately wanted to join the ISAF operation, was paying the price for its risk-averse, micro-managing approach to military overseas operations." *Ibid.,* 473.

42. During their six months in Afghanistan, the 3 PPCLI Battle Group performed tasks ranging from airfield security to combat operations. By this time Canada had also deployed a JTF 2 assault troop.

43. Rashid, *Taliban,* 220.

44. ISAF was authorized under UNSCRs 1386, 1413, 1444, and 1510. UNSCR 1386 (20 December 2001), as well as UNSCR 1413, authorized ISAF to operate under Chapter VII of the U.N. Charter (peace-enforcing). Furthermore, under UNSCR 1444 (27 November 2002) the role of ISAF remained to assist in the maintenance of security and to help the Afghan Transitional Authority (Afghan TA) and the initial activities of the U.N. in Kabul and its environs — nowhere else. However, UNSCR 1510 (13 October 2003) authorized the expansion of the ISAF mandate beyond the original provision of security in the Kabul area into the rest of Afghanistan. The first ISAF troops deployed as a multinational force (without Canadian participation) initially under British command on 4 January 2002.

45. John McCallum, the MND, told the House of Commons: "Canada has been approached by the international community for assistance in maintaining peace and security in Afghanistan for the UN mandated mission in Kabul. Canada is willing to serve with a battle group and a brigade headquarters for a period of one year, starting late this summer." Canada, *Canadian Forces in Afghanistan.* Report of the Standing Committee on National Defence, June 2007, 39; and John McCallum, "Stepping up to the plate," *The Washington Times,* 31 July 2003.

46. Major Jay Feyko, interview with author, 28 January 2009.

47. "Commander Task Force Kabul (TFK) OP O 9800 (001/03) — OP ATHENA — CA Contribution to International Security Assistance Force (ISAF) in Afghanistan," 17 1715Z August 03.

48. The courses were developed by the Germans and focused on basic procedures such as: road blocks, traffic control, vehicle check points; incident scene management; and general conduct of police patrols.

49. Major Jay Feyko, interview with author, 28 January 2009. Feyko stated: "My impression of Kabul was, what a horrible place. It was nothing you could imagine, the smells and the heat. I couldn't understand how you could live in such poverty with no connectivity to the outside world. All the women were in burkas and there were open sewers everywhere."

50. Major Tom Mykytiuk, "Company Command in the Three Block War: November Company, Task Force Kabul, Rotation) — Operation Athena," in Horn, *In Harm's Way — On the Front Lines of Leadership*, 131–32.

51. Major Jay Feyko, interview with author, 28 January 2009.

52. Colonel Don Denne, letter to author, 12 September 2010. Denne stated: "We did not entirely dismiss the influence of the warlords which was considerable as they were paying lots of men to bear arms. We maintained contact with all of them and had very cordial relations. They never positioned themselves to confront us at any time and if anything, wanted to help. In short, with the exception of Abdul Sayyaf, a former Afghan prime minister who lived up in a fortified villa in Paghman District, they all seemed fairly benign."

53. One of the frustrations, which would be felt later in spades, was the question of operational security (OPSEC). The police were often not above suspicion of being involved in criminal activity. As such, to bring them in on the planning too early would jeopardize the mission, yet to hold off to long would appear as if ISAF was marginalizing, if not ignoring, the transitional government authorities.

54. Master-Corporal Josh Marian, interview with author, 15 July 2008.

55. Major Jay Feyko, interview with author, 28 January 2009.

56. Sergeant Jason Grapes, interview with author, 20 July 2008.

57. Major Jay Feyko, interview with author, 28 January 2009. Feyko described, "There was a lot to look for. We had a conception of what a suicide bomber looked like, but we weren't sure. We didn't know where the threat would come from."

58. Master-Corporal Josh Marian, interview with author, 15 July 2008.

59. Major Jim McInnis, interview with author, 7 August 2009.
60. Colonel Don Denne, letter to author, 12 September 2010.
61. Master-Corporal Josh Marian, interview with author, 15 July 2008. The ironies of military life also made Marian ponder the logic of some decisions. "After Murphy's death we were told the Iltis isn't safe so, we have to ride in LAVs. But then, the Iltis was brought back." Marian posed the logical question, albeit rhetorically, "So, the Iltis was now safe?"
62. Lieutenant-General Peter Devlin, interview with author, 9 November 2010.
63. Colonel Don Denne, letter to author, 12 September 2010.
64. MIF force strength was approximately 3,000. MINUSTAH was allocated 6,700 troops and 1,622 civilian police.
65. Lieutenant-Colonel David Lambert, interview with author, 9 October 2009.
66. Captain Marc Côté, interview with author, 17 September 2009.
67. *Ibid.*
68. *Ibid.*
69. *Ibid.*
70. *Ibid.*
71. Major Jason Guiney, interview with author, 10 January 2009.
72. Captain Marc Côté, interview with author, 17 September 2009.
73. Colonel Jim Davis, interview with author, 9 July 2009.
74. Quoted in Lee Windsor, David Charters, and Brent Wilson, *Kandahar Tour: The Turning Point in Canada's Afghan Mission* (Mississauga: John Wiley & Sons Canada, Ltd., 2008), 19.
75. Hillier, *A Soldier First*, 323.
76. See Lieutenant-General Michael Jeffrey, *Inside Canadian Forces Transformation: Institutional Leadership as a Catalyst for Change* (Kingston: CDA Press, 2009) for a detailed account of the process. In 2009, the new CDS announced yet another round of "transformation" intended to consolidate changes made and to implement corrections based on experience and the changing fiscal climate.
77. On 9 October 2004, Afghanistan held presidential elections. Hamid Karzai won 55.4 percent of popular vote and became president. More than 10 million Afghans registered to vote. Parliamentary and provincial council elections were held on 18 September 2005 and 6.8 million Afghans participated. On 19 December 2005 the national assembly

composed of 249 members of the Wolesi Jirga (lower house), all elected, and 102 members of the Meshrano Jirga (upper house), some appointed, stood up. Canada, *Canada's Mission in Afghanistan: Measuring Progress.* Report to Parliament, February 2007, 11.

78. The last Canadian material assets were moved and shipped to Kandahar on 29 November 2005, and Camp Julien, the Canadian base in Kabul, was officially handed over to the Afghan Ministry of Defence.

79. On 17 May 2006, Parliament voted to extend the Canadian military mission in Kandahar Province as well as the work of the PRT up to February 2009. The Americans created the PRT construct in November 2002, as part of OEF. It became a critical component of the U.S. efforts to stabilize Afghanistan. PRTs were conceived as a way to integrate diplomats, development officials, military assets, and police officers to address the causes of instability, namely, poor governance, weak institutions, insurgency, regional warlords, and poverty. Canada, "An Interim Report of the Standing Senate Committee on National Security and Defence," *Managing Turmoil: The Need to Upgrade Canadian Foreign Aid and Military Strength to Deal with Massive Change* (henceforth *Managing Turmoil*), October 2006, 150. See also Michelle Parker, "Programming Development Funds to Support a Counterinsurgency: A Case Study of Nangarhar, Afghanistan in 2006," Case Studies in National Security Transformation, Number 10, n.d., 2.

80. *Managing Turmoil*, 149. The PRT in Kandahar focused on three major areas: good governance, security sector reform (including providing training and equipment to Afghan police), and reconstruction and development. The specific PRT tasks were to: promote the extension of the Afghan central and provincial government; implement development and reconstruction programs; assist in stabilizing the local security environment; and support security sector reform. The aims of the CF in Kandahar Province were first and foremost "to provide the people of Afghanistan with the hope for a brighter future by establishing the security necessary to promote development and an environment that is conducive to the improvement of Afghan life." In addition, the CF was to conduct operations in support of the ANSF, strengthen and enhance Afghan governance capacity and to help extend the authority of the government of Afghanistan throughout the southern regions of the country. Finally, the CF effort was to support the larger Canadian-integrated whole of government team to facilitate the delivery of programs and projects that support

the economic recovery and rehabilitation of Afghanistan, as well to assist in addressing humanitarian needs of Afghans by supporting Canadian governmental organizations and NGOs whose efforts meet Canada's objectives. Canada. "Canadian Forces Operations in Afghanistan," DND Backgrounder, 15 May 2007. The Canadian efforts were in support of the internationally supported Afghanistan Compact, which was developed in London 31 January to 1 February 2006. The Compact commits international community (more than 60 countries and international organizations) along with the GIRoA and the U.N. to achieve progress in three critical and interrelated areas of activity for the period 2006–11: security; governance, including rule of law, human rights, and tackling corruption; and economic and social development. The Afghan Compact aimed to: triple the Afghan army to 70,000 troops; disband all illegal militias by 2007; reduce by 70 percent the amount of land made unusable by land mines by 2010; reduce the number of people living on less than $1 a day by 3 percent per year and the proportion of those who are hungry by 5 percent per year, create functioning justice institutions in every province by end of 2010 including prisons with separate facilities for women and juveniles; upgrade the country's main ring road, central to government plans to revive Afghanistan's historic role as a land bridge between Central and South Asia; bring electricity to 65 percent of urban homes and 25 percent of rural homes by end of 2010; enrol 60 percent of girls and 75 percent of boys in primary school by 2010.

81.　NATO took control of ISAF in 2003. Since then it expanded to the North in 2004 (Stage I), to the west in 2005 (Stage II), and its plan to move to the south (Stage III) transpired in 2005/2006. This new evolution of the Canadian mission was called Operation Archer.

82.　The 1 PPCLI Battle Group (BG) consisted of 1 PPCLI, a tactical unmanned aerial vehicle (TUAV) troop, an HSS, company, a forward support group (FSG), and the Kandahar Provincial Reconstruction team. Their mission was outlined as follows: "Task Force Orion will assist Afghans in the establishment of good governance, security and stability, and reconstruction in the province of Kandahar during Op Archer Rotation (Roto) 1 in order to help extend the legitimacy and credibility of the Government of Afghanistan throughout the Islamic Republic of Afghanistan and at the same time help to establish conditions necessary for NATO Stage 3 expansion." Hope stated that he chose the name Orion to give everyone a common identifier. "I chose Orion from the constellation — representing the mythical Greek hunter of mountain beasts — that I knew blessed the Afghan skies, so that our soldiers might look up and seeing it, feel part of a larger entity, enduring and meaningful." Ian Hope, "Reflections on Afghanistan: Commanding Task Force Orion," in Bernd Horn, *In Harm's Way: The Buck Stops Here: Senior Officers on Operations* (Kingston: CDA Press, 2007), 212. See also Lieutenant-Colonel Ian Hope, *Dancing with the Dushman: Command Imperatives for the Counter-Insurgency Fight in Afghanistan* (Kingston: CDA Press, 2008); and "1st Battalion Princess Patricia's Canadian Light Infantry Battle Group (Task Force Orion) — Operational Summary," 12 August 2006.

83. See Rashid, *Taliban*; and Coll, *Ghost Wars* for a detailed account of the rise of the Taliban. In short, Carl Forsberg summarized, "This senior Islamic court [clerics in Kandahar] was 'independent of any of the Resistance political parties and had the final authority on all political-military-juridical matters.' These clerics benefited from their close ties to the population and had a 'more widespread basis of legitimacy' than Kandahar's militia commanders. The clerics who formed the Taliban likewise had a concrete connection to the larger sections of the population in Kandahar alienated from their leadership, and the Taliban rose to power as a popularly supported clerical response to these tribal strongmen." He went on to explain, "The Taliban professed limited aims at their inception, promising to wipe out corruption, provide security, and establish a fair judiciary based on sharia (Islamic law). The Taliban's dramatic demonstrations and noble promises convinced many that Omar and his followers were committed to good governance and could provide relief from the oppression and extortion of local strongmen." Carl Forsberg, "The Taliban's Campaign for Kandahar," *Executive Summary, Afghanistan Report 3* (December 2009), 15.

84. One analyst explained, "Taliban field commanders are brought into the operational planning process through a rotation system, which allows them to spend a portion of their year in Quetta. During their time in Quetta, commanders are updated on the Taliban's strategy and tactics and discuss developments in lessons-learned sessions. A lull in combat operations from October to April, which was an annual occurrence until 2008, gave the Taliban an opportunity to formulate a campaign plan for the coming year, which could then be adjusted during the summer months." Forsberg, 22.

85. One Taliban fighter acknowledged, "The American invasion of Iraq was very positive for us. It distracted the United States from Afghanistan." Maulvi Mohammad Haqqani cited in Sami Yousafzai and Ron Moreau, "The Taliban in their Own Words," *Newsweek.com*, 5 October 2009, 39–40.

86. During this time period the Taliban also received visits from Arab and Iraqi mujahedeen, who, according to Taliban fighters, "began transferring the latest IED technology and suicide-bomber tactics they had learned in the Iraqi resistance during combat with U.S. forces." The Taliban experimented with the new tactics and in June 2003, a suicide bomber, in the first attack of this kind in Afghanistan, killed four German ISAF soldiers and an Afghan national, and wounded many others in Kabul, as their bus was headed to the airport to take the troops home after completion of their tour of duty. Despite its success, the Taliban did not yet fully embrace the tactics of suicide bombing and IEDs. They saw no need to. Their traditional methodology of combating government and Coalition forces seemed to be working just fine. See Maulvi Mohammad Haqqani cited in Sami Yousafzai and Ron Moreau, "The Taliban in their Own Words," *Newsweek.com*, 5 October 2009, 39–40. Strategic analyst Carl Forsberg explained the initial discomfort with the new tactics. He noted as the Taliban "consolidated their lines of communication across southern Afghanistan, the Taliban embarked on a new and more sophisticated bombing campaign in Kandahar City in the fall of 2005. The campaign was led by Mullah Dadullah Akhund, who served as the Taliban's overall field commander and had connections to suicide bombing units in the Kabul area. Dadullah's suicide bombing campaign in 2005 polarized the Taliban's senior leadership, which was concerned by Dadullah's reputation for inflicting violence. As a Taliban commander in the 1990s, he was removed from command on multiple occasions for terrorizing local populations and perpetrating mass killings of non-Pashtuns. Mullah Omar and Mullah Osmani had reservations about Dadullah's use of suicide bombers. In the end, Mullah Omar compromised; Pakistani suicide bombers could be employed for suicide bombings, but locals would not be." Forsberg, 55.

87. Bari Khan cited in Sami Yousafzai and Ron Moreau, "The Taliban in their Own Words," *Newsweek.com*, 5 October 2009, 40.

88. The Senlis Council, *Canada in Kandahar: No Peace to Keep: A Case Study of the Military Coalitions in Southern Afghanistan*, London, June 2006, v.

89.   *Ibid.*, 31.

90.   Rashid, *Taliban*, 229.

91.   Christie Blatchford, *Fifteen Days* (Toronto: Doubleday Canada, 2007), 13.

92.   Lieutenant-Colonel Shane Schreiber, Operations Officer MNB HQ, 1 CMBG briefing, 22 January 2007.

93.   *Ibid.* It is also important to note that in January 2006, the Afghanistan Compact was signed, which was a formal statement of commitment by the GIRoA and the international community that shifted responsibility from lead nations to Afghanistan itself. It established three broad pillars of activity for future efforts — security; governance, the rule of law, and human rights; and economic and social development." See Steve Bowman and Catherine Dale, *War in Afghanistan: Strategy, Military Operations, and Issues for Congress* (Washington, D.C.: Congressional Research Service, 8 June 2010). 14.

94.   *Ibid.*

95.   For a detailed account of the battle(s) see Blatchford, *Fifteen Days*; and Hope *Dancing with the Dushman.*

96.   Blatchford, *Fifteen Days*, 250.

97.   Brigadier-General David Fraser, interview with author, 21 October 2006.

98.   This refers to the Maoist model of insurgency: Phase 1 — Strategic Defence: focus on survival and building support. Bases are established, local leaders are recruited, cellular networks and parallel governments created; Phase 2 — Strategic Stalemate: guerrilla warfare ensues. Insurgents focus on separating population from government; Phase 3 — Strategic Offensive: Insurgents feel they have superior strength and move to conventional operations to destroy government capability.

99.   Brigadier-General David Fraser, interview with author, 21 October 2006.

100. *Ibid.*

101. *Ibid.*

102. Blatchford, *Fifteen Days*, 251.

Chapter 8: A Return to Combat Duty

1.   One reporter noted, "NATO is hoping to bring a new strategy to dealing with the Taliban rebellion: establishing bases rather than chasing militants, and is also hoping to win the support of local people by creating secure zones where development can take place. But questions remain

whether they can quell the violence enough to allow aid workers to get to work in a lawless and impoverished region where [Kandahar province] about a quarter of Afghanistan's huge opium crop is grown, and the narcotics trade fuels the insurgency." Fisnik Abrashi, "NATO takes command in Afghanistan," *The Kingston Whig-Standard,* 31 July 2006, 10.

2. Lieutenant-Colonel Shane Schreiber interview with author, 18 October 2006.

3. Brigadier-General David Fraser, interview with author, 21 October 2006.

4. Lieutenant-Colonel Shane Schreiber, interview with author, 18 October 2006. Schreiber noted, "And a very sophisticated C2 node. Somebody actually reinforcing, directing reinforcements to exact positions. Somebody actually controlling the battle."

5. Lieutenant-Colonel Shane Schreiber, ACOS, Multinational Brigade HQ, 1 CMBG briefing, 22 January 2007.

6. An Army report also noted that their gunnery, "particularly with the SPG [73 mm/82 mm recoilless rifle] was very good resulting in the defeat of a LAV 3 and support vehicles during one assault." Memo, Director Army Training to Commander Land Force Development Training System, "Tactical Reconnaissance Report — Training Assessment OP Archer Rotation 3," 21 September 2006, 3. SPG refers to the Soviet designation Stankovyy Protivotankovyy Granatamet, literally translated as "mounted anti-tank grenade launcher." In NATO terminology it refers to a anti-tank recoilless rifle.

7. General Hillier explained in an interview, "The challenge is that marijuana plants absorb energy, heat very readily. It's very difficult to penetrate them with thermal devices ... And as a result you really have to be careful that the Taliban don't dodge in and out of those marijuana forests. We tried burning them with white phosphorous — it didn't work. We tried burning them with diesel — it didn't work. The plants are so full of water right now ... that we simply couldn't burn them. A couple of brown plants on the edges of some of those [forests] did catch on fire. But a section of soldiers that was downwind from that had some ill effects and decided that was probably not the right course of action." CNN.Com, "Canada troops battle 10-foot Afghan marijuana plants," http://www.cnn. com/2006/WORLD/Americas/10/12/Canada.troops.marijuana.reut/ index.html (accessed 13 October 2006).

8. Memo, Director Army Training to Commander Land Force Development

Training System, "Tactical Reconnaissance Report — Training Assessment OP Archer Rotation 3," 21 September 2006, 3.

9.   Brigadier-General David Fraser, interview with author, 21 October 2006.

10.   Stein, *The Unexpected War*, 219.

11.   Brigadier-General David Fraser, interview with author, 21 October 2006.

12.   Donald McArthur, "Canadian troops pressed ahead on Operation Medusa," Canadia.com 6 September 2006, http://www.canada.com/components/print.aspx?id=5e81f24-dd05-4eb6-88c1-bbd5e09251f8&k=50060 (accessed 10 September 2006). Despite the encouraging rhetoric, the reality on the ground was completely different. It became a largely Canadian fight. "Promises of *in extremis* assistance were a placebo to take the sting away from the constant 'no' that always came following requests to send troops to the south, and meant nothing," stated General Rick Hillier, the CDS at the time. "We were," he angrily recalled, "essentially in it by ourselves." The Americans and British were already engaged in combat elsewhere in Afghanistan and were hard-pressed to assist, although they did what they could. Overall, the Europeans failed their allies and refused to participate. The Dutch declined to assist in the actual combat but did take over FOB Martello, which freed up additional Canadian resources that were fed into the battle. FOB Martello was built on the Tarin Khowt Road on the way to the Dutch AO in the province of Uruzgan by the 1 PPCLI battle group to secure the northern part of Kandahar Province to support NATO's expansion into that province. See Hillier, *A Soldier First*, 475. In the aftermath of Operation Medusa, Hillier told his peers, "Canada feels like we've been abandoned by our allies in the Kandahar province fight." *Ibid.*, 476.

13.   The 1 RCR/1 PPCLI RIP occurred from 24 July to 24 August 2006.

14.   Commander's Entry, TF 3–06 War Diary, 19–31 August 2006.

15.   Colonel Omer Lavoie, "Leadership in Combat and RMC's Role," article for RCR ROIC candidates, 9–10 April 2010, Petawawa. And true to combat throughout the ages, Lavoie noted that "everything that could have possibly gone wrong, seemed to; the enemy was attacking from all directions, serious confusion occurred with regard to identifying friendly Afghan Security Forces in the same battle, ammunition was beginning to run low, there was only one way on to and off of the position, numerous vehicles broke down or got stuck and one LAV III even rolled over."

16.   Warrant Officer Mike Jackson, interview with author, 13 October 2006.

17. Major Wright was later awarded the Medal of Military Valour for his actions on 19 August 2006.

18. For a detailed account of Operation Medusa, see Bernd Horn, *No Lack of Courage: Operation Medusa, Afghanistan* (Toronto: Dundurn, 2010).

19. Lieutenant-Colonel Omer Lavoie, interview with author, 8 October 2006.

20. The concept was that once the enemy had been heavily attrited, through the sustained employment of joint fires, they would be forced to withdraw using their exfiltration routes to the South near Siah Choy, where they would interdicted by SOF elements and completely destroyed. Manoeuvre was actually initiated earlier than had been planned because of the window of availability for key enablers such as the Predator Unmanned Aerial Vehicle (UAV), which were required for Operation Mountain Fury in Regional Command East (RC [E]), which was running concurrently with Operation Medusa. Memo, Director Army Training to Commander Land Force Development Training System, "Tactical Reconnaissance Report — Training Assessment OP Archer Rotation 3," 21 September 2006, 4.

21. "H-Hour" is the designated time given for coordination of movement and fires for all engaged forces for any given operation.

22. Major Greg Ivey, interview with author, 17 October 2006.

23. Major Matthew Sprague, interview with author, 19 November 2007.

24. The school was built in 2004 with funds from the U.S. commander's Emergency Reconstruction Program (CERP).

25. As quoted in Day, "Operation Medusa: The Battle for Panjwai. Part I."

26. Major Matthew Sprague, interview with author, 19 November 2007.

27. Lieutenant-Colonel Shane Schreiber, interview with author, 18 October 2006.

28. *Ibid.*

29. *Ibid.*

30. *Ibid.*

31. Colonel Omer Lavoie, "Leadership in Combat and RMC's Role," article for RCR ROIC candidates, 9–10 April 2010, Petawawa.

32. The change in the original plan created a great deal of dissension within the ranks. Many of the participants could not understand why things were "rushed" and why the additional 48 hours of bombardment were not permitted. Retrospectively, they argued that this would have weakened the enemy physically and psychologically and provided more time to map out the enemy's strength and disposition. "There seemed to be

a rush to get '3' [Charles Coy] across the wadi," commented one soldier, "with no real orders." Another stated, "we were pushed across the wadi but then what? We weren't even sure what the objective was." He asserted, "we were going into the unknown." Private Will Needham offered, "We rolled in, drove right into an ambush site, and it was told to us the night before that this grid was basically an ambush site." One soldier quietly concluded, "The enemy was surrounded, cut off and wildly outgunned. "We held all the cards, and we played their hand." Many of the senior NCOs were equally unimpressed. Master Warrant Officer Keith Olstad summarized their overall dissatisfaction. "There was a plan," he stated emotionlessly, "and you only vary from the plan if the enemy influences events." He assessed, "[the change in plan] was influenced by decisions not by the enemy." Interview with members of 7 Platoon, 14 October 2006; Christie Blatchford, "Did he abandon his troops?" *The Globe and Mail,* 29 December 2006, http://www.theglobeandmail.com/servlet/story/RTGAM.20061229.wxafghan-blatch29B (accessed 30 December 2006); quoted in Adam Day, "Operation Medusa: The Battle For Panjwai, Part 2; Death in a Free Fire Zone," *Legion Magazine,* 1 November 2007, http://www.legionmagazine.com/en/index.php/2007/11/operation-medusa-the-battle-for-panjwai-2/ (accessed 8 July 2008); and Master Warrant Officer Keith Olstad, interview with author, 11 January 2009.

33. Major Matthew Sprague, interview with author, 19 November 2007.

34. The CO remembered, "I was struck that morning by the sheer outward confidence in the plan displayed by the leadership of the BG, despite the fact that for most of them it was their first time experiencing a combat engagement. I am certain many of my officers shared the same misgivings I had. There was certainly huge risk in some areas of the plan, especially if we failed to surprise the enemy." Colonel Omer Lavoie, "Leadership in Combat and RMC's Role," article for RCR ROIC candidates, 9–10 April 2010, Petawawa.

35. Major Greg Ivey, interview with author, 17 October 2006.

36. Major Matthew Sprague, interview with author, 19 November 2007.

37. Christie Blatchford, "Did he abandon his troops?" *The Globe and Mail,* 29 December 2006, http://www.theglobeandmail.com/servlet/story/RTGAM.20061229.wxafghan-blatch29B (accessed 30 December 2006).

38. Lieutenant Jeremy Hiltz, interview with author, 16 October 2006.

39. Major Matthew Sprague, interview with author, 19 November 2007.

40. Lieutenant Jeremy Hiltz, interview with author, 16 October 2006.

41. Adam Day, "Operation Medusa: The Battle For Panjwai, Part 2; Death in a Free Fire Zone," *Legion Magazine*, 1 November 2007, http://www.legion-magazine.com/en/index.php/2007/11/operation-medusa-the-battle-for-panjwai-2/ (accessed 8 July 2008).

42. Mitch Potter, "The Story of C Company," *The Star*, 30 September 2006. http://www.thestar.com/NASApp/cs/contentserver?pagename=thestar (accessed 27 October 2006).

43. Corporal Justin Young, interview with author, 14 October 2006.

44. Lieutenant Jeremy Hiltz, interview with author, 16 October 2006.

45. Potter, "The Story of C Company."

46. Master-Corporal J. O'Neil, interview with author, 18 October 2006.

47. Corporal Sean Teal, interview with author, 14 October 2006.

48. Potter, "The Story of C Company."

49. Day, "Death in a Free Fire Zone."

50. Private Mike O'Rourke, interview with author, 14 October 2006.

51. Corporal Gary Reid, interview with author, 14 October 2006.

52. Niefer was later awarded the Military Medal of Valour.

53. Lieutenant Jeremy Hiltz, interview with author, 16 October 2006.

54. Sergeant Donovan Crawford, interview with author, 14 October 2006.

55. Lieutenant Ray Corby, interview with author, 14 October 2006.

56. Lieutenant Jeremy Hiltz, interview with author, 16 October 2006.

57. Day, "Death in a Free Fire Zone."

58. Private Mike O'Rourke, interview with author, 14 October 2006.

59. Potter, "The Story of C Company."

60. To this date there is no explanation. Two theories exist. One — it was a dud. Two — once the bomb went off its GPS (global positioning system) track its arming device shut off. Sprague opined, "we had lots of bad luck that day, but we also had lots of good luck as well." The aircraft has also been both described as a French Mirage and an American aircraft of unknown type.

61. Lieutenant Jeremy Hiltz, interview with author, 16 October 2006.

62. Lieutenant J. Bules, interview with author, 20 October 2006.

63. Confidential Interview, 8 July 2008.

64. *Ibid.*

65. Major Matthew Sprague, interview with author, 19 November 2007.

66. Captain Rob Carey, interview with author, 16 October 2006.

67. *Ibid.*

68. Sergeant Jamie Walsh, interview with author, 14 October 2006.
69. Confidential Interview, 8 July 2008.
70. Sergeant Jamie Walsh, interview with author, 14 October 2006.
71. Lieutenant Jeremy Hiltz, interview with author, 16 October 2006.
72. Lieutenant J. Bules, interview with author, 20 October 2006.
73. *Ibid.*
74. Major Greg Ivey, interview with author, 17 October 2006. Ivey praised, "and kudos to them because they did an outstanding job. They were able to pull back. They leaguered up on the Arghandab River to consolidate and do their casualty evacuation. So it was quite a day."
75. Master-Corporal J. O'Neil, interview with author, 18 October 2006.
76. Major Matthew Sprague, interview with author, 19 November 2007.
77. As quoted in Blatchford, 256.
78. Potter, "The Story of C Company."
79. Fawcett, Funnel, Niefer, O'Rourke, J.J.L. Ruffolo, and C.J. Orr won Medals of Military Valour and Teal earned a Star of Military Valour.
80. Major Greg Ivey, interview with author, 17 October 2006.
81. Lieutenant-Colonel Shane Schreiber, interview with author, 18 October 2006.
82. Lieutenant Jeremy Hiltz, interview with author, 16 October 2006.
83. *Ibid.*
84. Although the pilot acknowledged immediately that he fired erroneously, the American investigation cast blame on the Canadians. The report noted "that the U.S. pilot, a flight leader and veteran of 60 combat missions, had mistakenly opened up with his 30-milimetre cannon on a garbage fire lit by dusty, exhausted soldiers was never in dispute." However, they cast blame on the Canadians because: "the Canadian soldiers did not have proper identification markers; the Canadian air controller was tired and had been in continuous action for 72 hours with only four hours sleep; and the Canadians had only one soldier to co-ordinate both aircraft and artillery fire." See "U.S. blames Canada for friendly fire; City man died in '06 incident" *The Hamilton Spectator,* 4 September 2009, A1.
85. Brigadier-General David Fraser, presentation — Canadian Infantry Association Annual General Meeting, 25 May 2007.
86. The ISAF commander was not enamoured with the revised slow Canadian approach. However, Fraser simply stated that they could not risk taking many more casualties because of the national political ramifications.

Richards refused to accept this rationale and called Fraser's national command. However, in the end, the ISAF commander was forced to relent.

87. Quoted in Day, "Operation Medusa: The Battle For Panjwai, Part 3." Major Ivey noted, "Scattered on the ground were the leaflets dropped there by NATO, warning the locals that an operation was coming through. The locals had also been warned over the radio and all the local Afghan troops knew the plan as well. This operation was no surprise attack." Major Greg Ivey, interview with author, 17 October 2006.

88. Lieutenant-Colonel Omer Lavoie, interview with author, 8 October 2006.

89. Brigadier-General David Fraser, interview with author, 21 October 2006.

90. Major Greg Ivey, interview with author, 17 October 2006.

91. Captain C. Purdy, interview with author, 17 October 2006.

92. Once they had captured the ground, it became fully apparent the scale of the enemy preparation. "They had extensive fortifications," remembered Captain Pappin, "bunkers, loopholes in thick walls and buildings, and some bunkers were built in the courtyards of mosques." Lieutenant Hiltz explained, "I was able to get a good look at the actual position itself. He described one of the positions "as a bunker system with approximately four feet of earth over top of it, a steel I-beam reinforced roof and the actual interior of it was almost done similar to the crack filling on a wall in a house." He added, "It was done smooth and it could have held anywhere from 15 to 25 personnel. They were able to move into that bunker with pretty much impunity through a ditch system, essentially an irrigation system that was actually ringed with trees, which would have concealed them." He elaborated, "And again, they were low enough that it would have given them cover, so they would have been able to pull back into the bunker unmolested." Hiltz concluded, "In essence, there was quite a significant amount of trench system and bunker systems that they had built." Captain Piers Pappin, interview with author, 14 July 2008; and Lieutenant J. Hiltz, interview with author, 16 October 2006.

93. Major Marty Lipcsey, interview with author, 20 October 2006.

94. Lavoie was awarded the Meritorious Service Medal. The commendation read in part, "LCol Lavoie through his personal courage and example led his Battle Group in a deliberate attack against a well entrenched enemy. Demonstrating a rare high level of professional competence and courage, LCol Lavoie created a detailed attack plan utilising coordinated fires in order to defeat the enemy and secure the objectives in the Panjwayi

region." Commendation Meritorious Service Medal, Lieutenant-Colonel Omer Lavoie, 25 October 2006.

95. Brigadier-General David Fraser, interview with author, 21 October 2006.

96. Paul Koring and Graeme Smith, "The Afghan Mission — Canadian deaths underscore PM's plea to NATO," *The Globe and Mail,* 28 November 2006, A1.

97. Podcast — "Audio Report by Mark Laity, NATO's civilian spokesman in Afghanistan," NATO Speeches, 22 November 06 — NATO Library on-Line, http://www.nato.int/docu/speech/2006/s060922b.htm (accessed 26 November 2006).

98. NATO — Allied Command Operations — SHAPE News, "ISAF concludes Operation Medusa in Southern Afghanistan," 17 September 2006, http://www.nato.int/shape/news/206/09/060917a.htm (accessed 24 November 2006).

99. "Operation Medusa Foiled Taliban Plans, NATO Commander Says," 20 September 2006, http://london.usembassy.gov/afghn187.html (accessed 24 November 2006).

100. NATO — "ISAF concludes Operation Medusa in Southern Afghanistan."

101. "Aid arriving in Panjwayi following Taliban Defeat," *ISAF News,* Issue No. 116, 1.

102. House of Commons Defence Committee, *U.K. Operations in Afghanistan: Thirteenth Report of Session 2006–07* (London: The Stationary Office Ltd, 18 July 2007), 16.

103. David McKeeby, "NATO's Operation Medusa Pushing Taliban from Southern Kandahar," 18 September 2006. http://usinfo.state.gov/xar-chives/display.html?p=washfile-english&y=2006&m=September&cx=20 06091816051idybeckcm0.9616358 (accessed 24 November 2006).

104. CTV news staff, "Operation Medusa a 'significant' success: NATO," 17 September 2006, http://wwwctv.ca/serviet/ArticleNews/story/CTVNews/20060917/suicid bomb 060917?sname=&noads=24Nov06 (accessed 24 November 2006).

105. Graeme Smith, "Taliban 'Eliminated' from Pivotal District," *The Globe and Mail,* 18 September 2006, A14.

106. Richard Foot, "Afghanistan sliding into Chaos," *Montreal Gazette,* 6 January 2007, A3.

107. Paul Koring, "The Afghan Mission — A thin Canadian line holds in Kandahar," *The Globe and Mail,* 6 December 2006, A26.

108. Hillier, *A Soldier First*, 435.

109. Brigadier-General Dave Fraser, interview with author, 21 October 2006.

110. Quoted in Stein, *The Unexpected War*, 219.

111. CTV news staff, "Operation Medusa a 'significant' success: NATO," 17 September 2006, http://www.ctv.ca/serviet/ArticleNews/story/CTVNews/20060917/suicid bomb 060917?sname=&noads=24Nov06 (accessed 24 November 2006).

112. Lieutenant-Colonel Shane Schreiber, ACOS, Multinational Brigade HQ, 1 CMBG briefing, 22 January 2007. General James Jones stated number of killed about 1,000 "but if you said 1,500 it wouldn't surprise me." "Operation Medusa Foiled Taliban Plans, NATO Commander Says," 20 September 2006, http://usinfo.state.gov/xarchives/display.html?p=washfile-english&y=2006&m=September&cx=20060920172756 adtbbed0.444072 (accessed 24 November 2006).

113. Brigadier-General Dave Fraser, interview with author, 21 October 2006.

114. Carl Forsberg, "The Taliban's Campaign for Afghanistan," Institute for the Study of War, *Afghanistan Report*, December 2009, 27.

115. Canada, Chief Reserve Services Evaluation of Land Force Readiness and Training (Ottawa: DND, August 2010), 18. The report also noted, "Since discarding the former Canadian Field Force Equipment Tables (CFFET) for each field unit and formation, the land forces have relied on ad hoc deployment organizations and on the spot reorganizations of personnel, and unit vehicles and equipment. While solving an immediate problem, an institutional problem has been created. Each ROT for Afghanistan has seen a changing CFTPO Task Force organization of both personnel and their vehicles. Field force unit stability has become difficult." *Ibid.*, 19.

116. *Ibid.*

117. *Ibid.*, 25.

118. *Ibid.*, 26.

Chapter 9: The Difficult War

1. "Bloody Monday bomber blows up a crowd of children," *ISAF newspaper*, Issue No. 116, 4.

2. Graeme Smith, "Taliban Vow to Retake Panjwai Redoubt," *The Globe and Mail*, 18 September 2006, A1. Another Taliban insurgent named Ashoor laughed, "You cannot stop us. We've been using these tactics for hundreds

of years and they have always worked." He explained, "After an attack fighters can easily stash their weapons among villagers sympathetic to their cause [and] they can then melt in with the local population and move on to another village, where there are more caches of weapons available to them for mounting another attack." Adnan R. Khan, "Prepare to bury your dead," *Maclean's*, 20 March 2006. http://www.macleans.ca/topstories/world/article.jsp?content=20060320_123593_123593 (accessed 24 November 2006).

3. "Kinetically we had great effect," professed Lieutenant-Colonel Peter Williams, "in stark terms, the number of casualties we inflicted on the enemy was significant. We disrupted their leadership to the point where they realized from a conventional point of view they would not be able to take us on and achieve any sort of success." However, he conceded, "we found that they tended to reverse their tactics … so after Medusa there has been an increase in the number of IEDs and suicide bombers and so on." Interview with Lieutenant-Colonel Peter Williams, joint effects coordination officer, 22 October 2006.

4. One soldier revealed, "The Taliban are going to snipe at us, literally and figuratively. They are going to try to increase the cost of doing business. They can do that at their will, because they can hit us anywhere they want, when they choose. We might be able to hit back hard, but they still control the pace of what goes on, not us. So they really hold the upper hand." Peter Goodspeed, "Battle for Kandahar: Success or failure of Obama's troops to surge lies in Kandahar City," *National Post*, 27 May 2010, http://www.nationalpost.com/news/world/story.html?id=3084975 (accessed 4 June 2010).

5. The "long war" refers to the counterinsurgency conflict. In a more global sense, the Americans also use the phrase to refer to the global counterinsurgency, in which they believe themselves to be against ideologically and religiously motivated adversaries who are intent on fighting them, other Western nations, and their supporters, in a global jihad. Prominent in this enemy grouping is al Qaeda. The "long war" has also come to replace the term *GWOT* (global war on terrorism).

6. Lieutenant-Colonel Shane Schreiber interview with author, 18 October 2006. An IED is defined as a device placed or fabricated in an improvised manner incorporating destructive, lethal, noxious, pyrotechnic or incendiary chemicals that is designed to destroy or incapacitate, harass, or

distract. It may incorporate military stores but is normally devised from non-military components. NATO, *Joint Operational Guideline for Counter Improvised Explosive Devices Activities,* Version 3.0, August 2008, 5.

7. Captain Tim Button, interview with author, 9 January 2009.

8. Lieutenant-Colonel Omer Lavoie, interview with author, 8 October 2006.

9. It is not difficult to understand the sentiments of one local Afghan who captured the sentiments of many. "We are in the middle, we aren't with the Taliban and we aren't with the government," he confessed quite frankly. "If you help us we will be with you. And if not...." Adam Day, "The Battle for the People," *Legion Magazine,* January/February 2007, 24.

10. Elizabeth Rubin, "Taking the Fight to the Taliban," New York Times Online, 29 October 2006, http://www.nytimes.com/2006/10/29taliban. html?ei=5088&en=d739d5ea5377f2aa&ex=1319774400&partner=rs snyt&emc=rss&adxnnlx=1162393246–50VwsPmpRzkq2Jcpu3cVCg (accessed 29 October 2006).

11. Montgomery Mcfate and Andrea V. Jackson, "The Object Beyond War: Counterinsurgency and the Four Tools of Political Competition," *Unrestricted Warfare Symposium 2006 Proceedings,* 150.

12. Lieutenant-Colonel Omer Lavoie, interview with author, 15 October 2006.

13. Mitch Potter, "The Story of C Company," *The Star,* 30 September 2006. http://www.thestar.com/NASApp/cs/contentserver?pagename=thestar (accessed 27 October 2006).

14. Lieutenant-Colonel Omer Lavoie, interview with author, 15 October 2006.

15. Quoted in Declan Walsh, Richard Norton-Taylor, and Julian Borger, "From soft hats to hard facts in battle to beat Taliban," *The Guardian,* 18 November 2006, 5.

16. Quoted in Walsh, et al, 5. A British special operations force officer with vast experience in the new environment asserted, "The sheer velocity of the insurgents' determination to kill us had to be gripped quickly. There was no room for error." He added, "it was kill or be killed." He explained, "It is warfare where the enemy is prepared to die to achieve his objectives. That is hard to counter and the insurgent approach has forced us to think not just out of the box, but around the corner." Michael Smith, "Secret war of the SAS," Mick Smith's Defence Blog, 18 January 2008.

17. Lieutenant-Colonel Omer Lavoie, interview with author, 15 October 2006. Work began on Route Summit on 29 September 2006; paving commenced 18 January 2007 and the project was completed 22 January 2007. Its name

derived from one of the battalion's officers. The operations officer, Captain Chris French, wondered "what do we call the route?" He lived on Summit Trail in Petawawa, Ontario, so the new road quickly became Route Summit.

18. "Route Summit serves two purposes," stated Brigadier-General Tim Grant, "it's a project the local people had asked for because it will allow commerce to flow freely in this particular area." Brian Hutchinson, "Toll for Afghan Road paid in soldiers' lives," *The Star Phoenix,* 12 December 2006, D7.

19. Lieutenant-Colonel Omer Lavoie, interview with author, 8 October 2006.

20. *Ibid.,* 15 October 2006.

21. In the battle group's first two months in theatre, it had suffered 15 killed and 85 wounded. With regard to the HLTA, the section leave plan was adopted from the previous tour, where under the circumstances at the time it was found to be less disruptive and more efficient. The whole question of leave was a difficult one. No one wanted to leave their comrades short in such dangerous conditions, but equally, the long demanding tour made the rest very important.

22. Some ANSF were available but in inadequate numbers. Moreover, their ability, as well as their loyalties quite often, were suspect. The primary concern with the ANA was the fact that they had not yet arrived and their numbers were small. TF 3–06 was partnered with a Kandak from a different province and their companies numbered between 60–80 strong. Lavoie also noted there was confusion over terms when dealing with ANA. ANA troops were actually "under operational control" Lavoie clarified, "but still, once ANA commanders are told what to do they must clear it with their Brigade commander. For example, the order to 'dig in on the road' was delayed for 1.5 days until approved by their chain of command. However, Lavoie note that the ANA "compared to the ANP these guys are Spetznaz (wear a uniform and usually don't shoot at you)." He noted that there are a number of ANP checkpoints in the battle group AOR designed to support security through observation and physical security. But, their value is of question as Lavoie and others have walked in on checkpoints where all members have been sleeping with weapons totally accessible. According to Lavoie, most of the ANP received two weeks of training and were about 17 years old. When the ANP battalion commander arrived, Lavoie found out he was illiterate and was unable to read a map. "I had to take him out to tell/show him where to place his troops at TCPs," related

Lavoie. Moreover, he explained, "ANP don't wear uniforms because they are 'uncomfortable' so there are ANP in civvies carrying AK-47 assault rifles in pick-up trucks. Its hard to tell good guys from bad. For that reason there were some fratricides early on in the operation." Lieutenant-Colonel Omer Lavoie, interview with author, 13 October 2006.

23. *Ibid.*, 15 October 2006.

24. *Ibid.*, 13 October 2006.

25. *Ibid.*, 15 October 2006.

26. Les Perreaux, "19 Day Visit to Hell," Canadian Press, TF 3–06 BG Notable News, http://veritas.mil.ca/showfile.asp?Lang=E&URL=/Clips/National/061023/f00860DN.htm (accessed 23 October 2006).

27. Larochelle was later awarded the Military Star of Valour for his actions.

28. Quoted in Kenneth Finlayson, "Operation Baaz Tsuka, Task Force 31 Returns to the Panjwayi," *Veritas,* Vol. 4, No. 1, 2008, 15.

29. "Hillier: NATO offensive's aim to 'take out' Taliban leaders," CBC News, 15 December 2006, http://www.cbc.ca/world /story/2006/12/15/nato-offensive.html (accessed 29 October 2007).

30. The operation was broken into four phases. The first phase was designed to shape the environment. This phase set the coordination of *shuras* to generate momentum toward a local security arrangement. Phase 2 was designed to interdict and dislocate the enemy. Phase 2a was designed to interdict insurgent reinforcements and exfiltration along Taliban lines of communication. Phase 2b in turn would disrupt the enemy by clearing and securing targeted population centres. Phase 2c was designed to secure designated areas, while Phase 2d would envelop Taliban elements in the respective zones. Phase 3 was designed to consolidate the combination of security, development, and information operations to contain the threat until the local population were able to assume a greater responsibility for their own security, thus allowing a reduction of military forces.

31. Doug Beazley, "Turning up the heat Canadians preparing for major role," *The Toronto Sun,* 17 December 2006, 8.

32. Brian Hutchinson, "Troops Mass to Crush Taliban," *The Ottawa Citizen,* 16 December 2006, A1.

33. *Ibid.*

34. Brian Hutchinson, "Troops Rallied for Falcon Summit," *National Post,* 18 December 2006, http://www.canada.com/globaltv/national/story.html?id=7c3b5ffa-3b92–4f19-a075-a6076a3be794 (accessed 29 October 2007).

35. An important part of the NATO operation, particularly so, because it followed the turmoil emanating from the failure of Operation Medusa to gal-
vanize European allies to fight, was the messaging that stressed, "unity of
effort." The latest operation stressed that "ANSF, supported by ISAF and CF
are successfully accomplishing the decisive phase of the biggest ever combined operation in Southern Afghanistan." NATO themes also underlined
the minimal amount of collateral damage created during the offensive.

36. This, however, was nothing new. "There is no single piece of land in this
country which has not been occupied by a Soviet soldier," observed Sergei
Akhromeév, the Soviet deputy minister of defence in November 1986,
"Nevertheless, the majority of the territory remains in the hands of the rebels ... There is no single military problem that has arisen and that has not
been solved, and yet there is still no result." He noted, "The whole problem
is in the fact that military results are not followed up by political." Quoted
in John Ferris, "Invading Afghanistan, 1836–2006: Politics and Pacification,"
Calgary Papers in Military and Strategic Studies, Vol. 1, Canada in Kandahar
(Calgary: Centre for Military Strategic Studies, 2007), 19.

37. Anthony H. Cordesman, "Winning in Afghanistan: How to face the
Rising Threat," Report for the Center for Strategic and International
Studies, 12 December 2006.

38. ABC News/BBC World Service Poll, "Afghanistan: Where Things Stand,"
7 December 2006.

39. "Afghan Public Opinion Amidst Rising Violence," A World Public
Opinion.Org Poll, 14 December 2006. A survey conducted in Afghanistan
in May 2007 reported that 70 percent of Afghan males believed that the
Taliban will prevail in the conflict. CTV Nightly News, 25 May 2007.

40. Paul Koring, "The Afghan Mission — A thin Canadian line holds in
Kandahar," *The Globe and Mail*, 6 December 2006, A26.

41. Lieutenant-Colonel Shane Schreiber, ACOS, Multinational Brigade HQ, 1
CMBG briefing, 22 January 2007.

42. Brooks Tigner, "Taliban evolves to counter ISAF," *Jane's International
Defence Review*, January 2008, 4.

43. Interview with a SOF commander, Kandahar, Afghanistan, 15 March 2007.

44. Bill Graveland, "NATO says attack on Taliban command post a message
to rebels," *The Guardian*, 15 December 2006, B8.

45. Brigadier-General David Fraser, presentation — Canadian Infantry
Association Annual General Meeting, 25 May 2007.

46. Elizabeth Rubin, "Taking the Fight to the Taliban," New York Times Online, 29 October 2006, http://www.nytimes.com/2006/10/29taliban. html?ei=5088&en=d739d5ea5377f2aa&ex=1319774400&partner=rs snyt&emc=rss&adxnnlx=1162393246–50VwsPmpRzkq2Jcpu3cVCg (accessed 29 October 2006).

47. Jeffrey Simpson, "NATO's very survival hinges on the Afghan mission," *The Globe and Mail,* 29 November 2006, A29. Of note, there were only 46 suicide attacks in Afghanistan up to 22 July 2006. See also "Afghanistan's Taliban — War without End," *The Economist,* 25 October 2007, http://www.economist.com/world/asia/displaystory.cfm?story_id=10026465 (accessed 14 November 2007).

48. Maulvi Mohammad Haqqani cited in Sami Yousafzai and Ron Moreau, "The Taliban in their Own Words," *Newsweek.com,* 5 October 2009, 39–40.

49. Cordesman, "Winning in Afghanistan," 12 December 2006.

50. Brigadier-General David Fraser, interview with author, 21 October 2006.

51. Mitch Potter, "General frets about home front," Middle East Bureau, 1 October 2006.

52. *Ibid.*

53. Brigadier-General David Fraser, presentation — Canadian Infantry Association Annual General Meeting, 25 May 2007.

54. CTV Nightly News, 28 September 2006.

55. Forsberg, 29. Forsberg assessed the Taliban's IED campaign was aimed at limiting Canadian freedom of movement and forcing the Canadians to devote their attention to force protection. He believed the key objectives of the Taliban's campaign were the lines of communication that connected Canadian positions in Zhari and Panjwayi to KAF. Forsberg assessed, "The IED campaign in Zhari and Panjwai had the net effect of taking the initiative away from the Canadians, whose military resources were increasingly focused on force protection and targeting of IED cells, rather than on separating the Taliban from the local population through counterinsurgency operations."

56. Lieutenant-Colonel Rob Walker, interview with author, 5 October 2008.

57. *Ibid.*

58. Captain Marc Côté, interview with author, 17 September 2009. He noted, "The weather was good — not super hot. We could operate for long durations without much support."

59. Quoted in Windsor, et al, *Kandahar Tour,* 91.

60. Lieutenant-Colonel Rob Walker, interview with author, 5 October 2008.

61. *Ibid.* Walker noted, "A key challenge was to bridge the gap between PRT projects and link them to the local *shura* leadership to ensure projects would actually help break Tier 2 fighters away from the Taliban." In the spring of 2007, Michael Callan who became director of CIDA's Kandahar project provided funds for large irrigation canals and a reservoir construction, as well as hiring local, unemployed men as part of the cash-for work program.

62. *Ibid.*

63. "Afghan Public Opinion Amidst Rising Violence," A World Public Opinion.Org Poll, 14 December 2006. However, it also revealed that 70 percent of Afghan males believed that the Taliban will prevail in the conflict. CTV Nightly News, 25 May 2007.

64. Lieutenant-Colonel Rob Walker, interview with author, 5 October 2008. Walker based this number on ISAF intelligence and ANP reports.

65. *Ibid.*

66. *Ibid.* Walker also conceded that, "There were areas that were pro-Taliban. We knew where they were. There was no way would be able to change that."

67. *Ibid.*

68. *Ibid.*

69. *Ibid.*

70. Murray Brewster, "Torch Changes Hands: Turnover in Afghanistan," *Montreal Gazette,* 5 February 2007, A1.

71. Stewart Bell, "Targeting Taliban Bombs," *National Post,* 6 June 2009, A4. It would reach 400 by 2009. This figure was taken from Miles Amoore in Kabul, "Inside the Mind of a Taliban Bomb Master," Timesonline, 30 May 2010, http://timesoline.co.uk/tol/news/world/afghanistan/article7140135.ece (accessed 5 June 2010).

72. "3rd Battalion, The Royal Canadian Regiment," *Pro Patria 2008 — 125th Anniversary Edition,* 38.

73. Major Jason Guiney, interview with author, 10 January 2010.

74. "3rd Battalion, The Royal Canadian Regiment," *Pro Patria 2008 — 125th Anniversary Edition,* 39. McBride also noted, "I think the insurgents were surprised to see such a powerful response from our presence on the ground."

75. Major Marc St-Yves, interview with author, 10 January 2009.

76. *Ibid.*

77.   "CO's Mission Information Line Update for 229 Nov 2008," 3 RCR BG CO's Diary, Vol. 4.

78.   "3rd Battalion, The Royal Canadian Regiment," *Pro Patria 2008 — 125th Anniversary Edition,* 42.

79.   "One BG CO's Perspective — 3 RCR BG," PPT presentation, 27 March 09, 3 RCR BG CO's Diary, Vol. 4. He noted most Afghans were "fence sitters, trying to survive in a difficult and deadly balance of power."

80.   Quoted in "3rd Battalion, The Royal Canadian Regiment," *Pro Patria 2008 — 125th Anniversary Edition,* 43.

81.   "One BG CO's Perspective — 3 RCR BG," PPT presentation, 27 March 09, 3 RCR BG CO's Diary, Vol. 4; and "3rd Battalion, The Royal Canadian Regiment," *Pro Patria 2008 — 125th Anniversary Edition,* 42. It is also worthwhile to note that on 7 March 2009, "N" Coy, 3 RCR commanded by Major Rob McBride conducted the first all Canadian combat airmobile operation in Canadian military history when Canadian CH-47 Chinook helicopters lifted 180 Royals deep into Taliban territory in Zhari District in Southern Afghanistan.

Conclusion

1.   Major-General T.F. de Faye, "The Colonel of the Regiment," *Pro Patria* 2005, 3.

Glossary of Acronyms
and Abbreviations

ACE	Allied Command Europe
ADZ	Afghan Development Zone
AH	Attack Helicopters
ALCANUS	Alaska/Canada/United States
AMF(L)	Allied Command Europe (ACE) Mobile Force (Land)
ANA	Afghan National Army
ANP	Afghan National Police
ANSF	Afghan National Security Forces
APC	Armoured Personnel Carriers
AO	Area of Operations
AOR	Area of Responsibility
AQ	al-Qaeda (AQ)
ARRC	ACE Rapid Reaction Corps
ATA	Afghan Transitional Authority
ATGM	Anti-Tank Guided Missile
ATO	Afghan Theatre of Operations
ATOC	Army Training Operational Cycle
AUSCIVPOL	Australian Civil Police
AVGP	Armoured Vehicle General Purpose
BAOR	British Army of the Rhine
BBC	Blue Beret Camp

BG	Brigade Group or Battle Group (depending on context)
BGen	Brigadier-General
BiH	Bosnia-Herzegovina
BiP	Blow in Place
BSP	Basic Security Plan
BTDF	Bosnian Territorial Defence Force
C2	Command and Control
CANBAT	Canadian Battalion
CANUS	Canada/United States
CAP	Combat Air Patrol
Capt	Captain
CAS	Close Air Support
CAST	Canadian Air/Sea Transportable
CATGME	Canadian Air Task Group Middle East
CBG	Combat Brigade Group
Cbt Gp	Combat Group
CCP	Casualty Collection Point
CD 1	Canada Dry 1
CD 2	Canada Dry 2
CDA	Conference of Defence Associates
Cdn	Canadian
Cdn AB Regt	Canadian Airborne Regiment
Cdn Gds	Canadian Guards
Cdn SAS Coy	Canadian Special Air Service Company
CDS	Chief of the Defence Staff
CENTAG	Central Army Group
CFB	Canadian Forces Base
CFE	Canadian Forces Europe
CFOO	Canadian Forces Organizational Order
CIB	Canadian Infantry Brigade
CIBG	Canadian Infantry Brigade Group
CGS	Chief of the General Staff
CIDA	Canadian International Development Agency
CIMIC	Civil-Military Co-operation
CJATC	Canadian Joint Air Training Centre
CJTF-H	Combined Joint Task Force Haiti

CLN	Comité de libération nationale
CMBG	Canadian Mechanized Brigade Group
CMTC	Combat Manoeuvre Training Centre
CNR	Canadian National Railway
CO	Commanding Officer
Coy	Company
CP	Command Post
Cpl	Corporal
CPX	Command Post Exercise
C/S	Call Sign
CSU	Canadian Support Unit Qatar
CTC	Combat Training Centre
CYC	Company of Young Canadians
DCDS	Deputy Chief of the Defence Staff
DCF	Defence of Canada Force
DCO	Defence of Canada Operations (or Deputy Commanding Officer)
DEU	Distinctive Environmental Uniform
DFAIT	Department of Foreign Affairs and International Trade
DHH	Directorate of History and Heritage
DM	Deputy Minister
DND	Department of National Defence
DPRE	Displaced Persons, Refugees, and Evacuees
DSM	Drill Sergeant Major
DSR	Defence Structure Review
DZ	Drop Zone
EC	European Community
ECMMY	EC Monitoring Mission, Yugoslavia (ECMMY)
EMT	Embedded Mentor Teams
EOD	Explosive Ordnance Disposal
EOKA	National Organization of Cypriot Fighters
EW	Electronic Warfare
Ex	Exercise
FAC	Forward Air Controller

FIBUA	Fighting In Built Up Areas
FLQ	Front de libération du Québec
FMC	Force Mobile Command
FN	Fabrique Nationale
FOB	Forward Operating Base
FOLA	Follow on Force Attack
FOO	Forward Observation Officer
FTX	Field Training Exercise
"G" Wagon	*Gelaendenwagon*
GFAP	General Framework Agreement for Peace
GIRoA	Government of the Islamic Republic of Afghanistan
GPMG	General Purpose Machine Gun
GOC	General Officer Commanding
HiG	Hebz-i-Islami Gulbuddin
HNP	Haitian National Police
HQ	Headquarters
HRH	His (Her) Royal Highness
HRS	Humanitarian Relief Sector
HVO	Croat Home Defence
ICBM	Inter-Continental Ballistic Missile (ICBM)
ICOM	Intercept Communications
IEBL	Inter-Entity Boundary Line
IED	Improvised Explosive Device
IFOR	Implementation Force
IMP	Individual Meal Pack
ISAF	International Security Assistance Force
ISR	Intelligence, Surveillance, Reconnaissance
JNA	Yugoslav People's Army
KAF	Kandahar Airfield
KCP	Kabul City Police
KIA	Killed in Action
KFOR	Kosovo Force

KMNB	Kabul Multinational Brigade
LAC	Library and Archives Canada
LAV III	Light Armoured Vehicle III
LAW	Light Anti-Tank Weapon
LCol	Lieutenant-Colonel
LEA	Law Enforcement Agency
LFCHQ	Land Forces Command Headquarters
LGen	Lieutenant-General
LIB	Light Infantry Battalion
LMG	Light Machine Gun
LSVW	Light Support Vehicle Wheeled
LUVW	Light Utility Vehicle Wheeled
LZ	Landing Zone
MAGTF 8	Marine Air Ground Task Force 8
MAIS	Mobile Automated Information Systems
Maj	Major
MBT	Main Battle Tank
MEDEVAC	Medical Evacuation
MGen	Major-General
MIF	National Interim Force
MINUSTAH	U.N. Stability Mission in Haiti
MMC	Minister's Monitoring Committee
MNB	Multinational Brigade
MND	Minister of National Defence
MND-SW	Multinational Division — Southwest
MRTF	Managed Readiness Training Fleet
MSF	Mobile Striking Force
MTA	Military Technical Agreement
NA	Northern Alliance
NATO	North Atlantic Treaty Organization
NBCD	Nuclear, Biological, Chemical Defence
NBCW	Nuclear, Biological, Chemical Warfare
NCO	Non-Commissioned Officer
NDA	National Defence Act

NDHQ	National Defence Headquarters
NDS	National Directorate of Security
NGO	Non-Governmental Organization
NORAD	North American Aerospace Defence Command
NORTHAG	Northern Army Group
NVG	Night Vision Goggles
OC	Officer Commanding
OEF	Operation Enduring Freedom
OMLT	Operational Mentor Liaison Teams
OP	Operation (or Observation Post depending on context)
OPP	Ontario Provincial Police
Para	Parachute
PBW	Patrol Base Wilson
PMQ	Private Military Quarters
PoW	Prisoner of War
PPCLI	Princess Patricia's Canadian Light Infantry
PRT	Provincial Reconstruction Team
PT	Physical Training
QIP	Quick Impact Project
QRF	Quick Reaction Force
R22R	Royal 22nd Regiment
RC (S)	Regional Command (South)
RCD	Royal Canadian Dragoons
RCE	Royal Canadian Engineers
RCMP	Royal Canadian Mounted Police
RCR	Royal Canadian Regiment
REC	Regimental Executive Committee
Recce	Reconnaissance
REFORGER	Return of Forces to Germany
RHC	Royal Highlanders of Canada
RIN	Rassemblement pour l'indépendance nationale
RIP	Relief in Place
RMA	Requisitioned Manoeuvre Area

RoE	Rules of Engagement
Roto	Rotation
RPG	Rocket-Propelled Grenade
RSM	Regimental Sergeant Major
RTHR	Road to High Readiness
RV	Rendezvous
SACEUR	Supreme Allied Commander Europe
SALY	Same as Last Year
SBA	Sovereign Base Area
SDS	Serbian Democratic Party
SFOR	Stabilization Force
SHAPE	Supreme Headquarters Allied Powers Europe
SHARP	Standard for Harassment and Racism Prevention
SHIRBRIG	Stand-By High Readiness Brigade
SITREP	Situation Report
SOF	Special Operations Forces
SOPs	Standard Operating Procedures
SOVOPs	Sovereignty Exercises
Spetsnaz	Soviet Special Purpose Forces
SQ	Sûreté du Québec
Sr NCO	Senior Non-Commissioned Officer
SSF	Special Service Force
SWAT	Special Weapons and Tactics
TF	Task Force
TFEA	Task Force East Africa
TFK	Task Force Kandahar
TIC	Troops in Contact
TOCA	Transfer of Command Authority
TOW	Tube Launched, Optically Tracked, Wire Guided
TSZ	Temporary Security Zone
TTP	Tactics, Techniques, and Procedures
U.K.	United Kingdom
U.N.	United Nations
UNFICYP	U.N. Force in Cyprus

UNHCR	U.N. High Commission for Refugees
UNMEE	U.N. Mission in Ethiopia and Eritrea
UNPA	U.N. Protected Area
UNPROFOR	U.N. Protection Force
UNSC	U.N. Security Council
UNSCR	U.N. Security Council Resolution
U.S.A.	United States of America
U.S.S.R.	Union of Soviet Socialist Republics
UXO	Unexploded Ordnance
VHF	Very High Frequency
VIP	Very Important Person
VP	Vital Point
WE	War Establishment
WP	Warsaw Pact
2IC	Second-in-Command
3 Cdo	3 Commando
3 Mech Cdo	3 Mechanized Commando
9/11	11 September 2001

Selected Bibliography

Baumann, Robert F., George W. Gawrych and Walter E. Kretchik, *Armed Peacekeepers in Bosnia*. Fort Leavenworth, Kansas: Combat Studies Institute Press, 2004.

Bell, Ken and C.P. Stacey. *100 Years: The Royal Canadian Regiment 1883–1983*. Don Mills, ON: Collier Macmillan, 1983.

Bercuson, D.J. *True Patriot: The Life of Brooke Claxton, 1898-1960*. Toronto: University of Toronto Press, 1993.

Bland, Douglas. *Canada's National Defence, Vol. 1: Defence Policy*. Kingston: Queen's School of Policy Studies, 1997.

____ *The Administration of Defence Policy in Canada 1947–1985*. Kingston: Ronald P. Frye and Company, Publishers, 1987.

Blatchford, Christie. *Fifteen Days*. Toronto: Doubleday Canada, 2007.

Commission of Inquiry into the Deployment of Canadian Forces to Somalia. In *Information Legacy: A Compendium of Source Material* [CD-ROM]. Ottawa: Canadian Government Publishing, 1997.

Conrad, Lieutenant-Colonel John. *What the Thunder Said: Reflections of a Canadian Officer in Kandahar*. Toronto: Dundurn Press, 2009.

Cowley, Robert, ed. *The Cold War: A Military History*. New York: Random House, 2005.

Davis, Sergeant James. *The Sharp End: A Canadian Soldier's Story.* Toronto: Douglas & McIntyre, 1997.

Day, Adam. *Witness to War: Reporting on Afghanistan 2004–2009.* Kingston: CDA Press, 2010.

Eayrs, James. *In Defence of Canada, Volume Four: Growing Up Allied.* Toronto: University of Toronto Press, 1985.

___. *In Defence of Canada, Volume Three: Peacemaking and Deterrence.* Toronto: University of Toronto Press, 1972.

Gaddis, John Lewis. *The Cold War: A New History.* London: Penguin Books, 2005.

Granatstein, J.L. *Canada's Army: Waging War and Keeping the Peace.* Toronto: University of Toronto Press, 2002.

Goodspeed, D.J., ed. *The Armed Forces of Canada, 1867–1967: A Century of Achievement.* Ottawa, Canadian Forces Headquarters, 1967.

Grant, Kurt. *All Tigers, No Donkeys.* St. Catharines, ON: Vanwell, 2004.

Hillier, General Rick. *A Soldier First: Bullets, Bureaucrats and the Politics of War.* Toronto: Harper Collins, 2009.

Hope, Lieutenant-Colonel Ian. *Dancing with the Dushman: Command Imperatives for the Counter-Insurgency Fight in Afghanistan.* Kingston: CDA Press, 2008.

Horn, Bernd. *No Lack of Courage: Operation Medusa, Afghanistan.* Toronto: Dundurn, 2010.

___, ed. *Fortune Favours the Brave: Tales of Tenacity and Courage in Canadian Military History.* Toronto: Dundurn, 2009.

___, *Establishing A Legacy: The History of The Royal Canadian Regiment 1883–1953.* Toronto: Dundurn Press, 2008.

___, ed. *Show No Fear: Daring Actions in Canadian Military History.* Toronto: Dundurn, 2008.

___, ed. *In Harm's Way: The Buck Stops Here: Senior Commanders on Operations Command.* Kingston: Canadian Defence Academy Press, 2007.

___, ed. *In Harm's Way: On the Front Lines of Leadership: Sub-Unit Command.* Kingston: Canadian Defence Academy Press, 2006.

___, ed. *The Canadian Way of War: Serving the National Interest.* Toronto: Dundurn Press, 2006.

___, ed. *Forging a Nation: Perspectives on the Canadian Military Experience.* St. Catharines: Vanwell Publishers, 2002.

___, *Bastard Sons: The Canadian Airborne Experience, 1942–1995.* St. Catharines, ON: Vanwell Publishers, 2001.

___, ed. *Contemporary Issues in Officership: A Canadian Perspective.* Toronto: Canadian Institute of Strategic Studies, 2000.

Jeffery, Michael K. *Inside Canadian Forces Transformation.* Kingston: CDA Press, 2009.

Kitching, George. *Mud and Green Fields: The Memoirs of Major-General George Kitching.* St. Catharines, ON: Vanwell, 1992.

Loomis, Dan G. *Not Much Glory.* Toronto: Deneau, 1984.

___. *The Somalia Affair: Reflections on Peacemaking and Peacekeeping.* Ottawa: DGL Publications, 1996.

MacKenzie, Lewis. *Peacekeeper: The Road to Sarajevo.* Vancouver: Douglas & MacIntyre, 1993.

Maloney, Sean M. *Canada and UN Peacekeeping: Cold War by Other Means 1945–1970.* St. Catharines, ON: Vanwell, 2002.

___, *War Without Battles: Canada's NATO Brigade In Germany 1951–1993.* Whitby, ON: McGraw-Hill Ryerson Limited, 1997.

Middlemiss, D.W. and Sokolsky, J.J. *Canadian Defence: Decisions and Determinants.* Toronto: HBJ, 1989.

Morton, Desmond. *A Military History of Canada.* Toronto: McClelland & Stewart Inc., 1992.

Off, Carol. *The Ghosts of Medak Pocket: The Story of Canada's Secret War.* Toronto: Random House Canada, 2004.

Rashid, Ahmed. *Taliban: Militant Islam, Oil and Fundamentalism in Central Asia.* New Haven: Yale University Press, 2001.

Stein, Janice Gross and Eugene Lange, *The Unexpected War: Canada in Kandahar.* Toronto: Viking Canada, 2007.

Stevens, G.R. *The Royal Canadian Regiment: Volume Two, 1933–1966.* London, ON: London Printing Co., 1967.

Taylor, Scott and Brian Nolan. *Tested Mettle: Canada's Peacekeepers at War.*

Ottawa: Esprit de Corps, 1998.

Winegard, Timothy C. *Oka: A Convergence of Cultures and the Canadian Forces.* Kingston: CDA Press, 2008.

Whitaker, Reg and Gary Marcuse. *Cold War Canada: The Making of a National Insecurity State, 1945–1957.* Toronto: University of Toronto Press, 1996.

Windsor, Lee, David Charters and Brent Wilson. *Kandahar Tour: The Turning Point in Canada's Afghan Mission.* Mississauga, Toronto: John Wiley & Sons, 2008.

Wood, John Wood, ed. *The Chance of War: Canadian Soldiers in the Balkans, 1992–1995.* Toronto: Breakout Educational Network in association with Dundurn Press, 2003.

About the Author

COLONEL BERND HORN, OMM, MSM, CD, Ph.D., attended the University of Waterloo where he obtained an Honours Bachelor of Arts degree in political science. He entered the Canadian Forces by joining the militia in 1981, enrolling in the Highland Fusiliers of Canada. Upon graduation from university in 1983, he transferred to the regular force and received his regimental affiliation with The Royal Canadian Regiment.

Colonel Horn was assigned to 1 RCR from 1983 to 1987 and he held various positions including platoon commander, officer commanding reconnaissance platoon, and executive assistant to the deputy chief of staff, United Nations Force in Cyprus. He attended the Continuous French Language School in Victoria, B.C., in 1987 and was subsequently posted to the Canadian Forces Officer Candidate School in Chilliwack, B.C., in 1988, where he held the positions of platoon commander/instructor and school adjutant.

Colonel Horn attended the Canadian Land Forces Command and Staff College in 1991 and returned to 1 RCR as the second-in-command of Administration Company upon completion. In the summer of 1992, he was appointed officer commanding Bravo Company and in September took his sub-unit to the former Yugoslavia on the first deployment of Operation Cavalier as part of the 2 RCR Battle Group.

In July 1993, Colonel Horn was posted to the Canadian Airborne Regiment as the officer commanding 3 Commando. Following attendance at the Canadian Forces Command and Staff College in Toronto from 1995–96, he became the staff officer to the director general strategic planning in National Defence Headquarters (NDHQ).

Colonel Horn received his master's degree in war studies in June 1997. He was also awarded the Governor General's Gold Medal for academic achievement for his work. That summer he was posted to the Royal Military College (RMC) in Kingston and commenced his Ph.D. program in war studies. He graduated in May 2000 and earned the Barry D. Hunt Memorial Award, which is given to the graduate student of highest academic standing in the departments of history and war studies.

In June 1999, before completing his Ph.D. studies, Colonel Horn was selected as the chief of staff to Lieutenant-General R.A. Dallaire and the OPD 2020 Officership Project in NDHQ. The following summer, he was posted back to RMC as an assistant professor of history, as well as the special assistant to the principal.

From June 2001 until March 2003, Colonel Horn was the commanding officer of the 1st Battalion, The Royal Canadian Regiment in Petawawa, Ontario. During this time, in May 2002, he was inducted by the Governor General of Canada as an Officer of the Order of Military Merit. Following command, he completed a one year tour as the deputy director of the Army's Directorate of Land Strategic Concepts in Kingston, before promotion in June 2004. He was subsequently appointed the director of the Canadian Forces Leadership Institute.

In April 2007, Colonel Horn became the deputy commander of the Canadian Special Operations Forces Command, a position he held until August 2009, when he was appointed chief of staff of the Land Force Doctrine and Training System. That year, the Governor General of Canada also awarded Colonel Horn the Meritorious Service Medal for his contribution to the professional development of Canadian Forces personnel. On 1 March 2010, Colonel Horn was appointed to his present position, the newly created chief of staff, strategic training and education programs, at the Canadian Defence Academy in Kingston, Ontario.

Dr. Horn is also currently an adjunct professor of history at RMC and has authored, co-authored, edited, or co-edited 32 books and more than 100 chapters in books and articles on military history and military affairs.

Index

Index